Islandica

A Series in Icelandic and Norse Studies

Cornell University Library

PATRICK J. STEVENS, MANAGING EDITOR

VOLUME LIII

"Speak Useful Words
or Say Nothing"

Old Norse Studies by Joseph Harris

EDITED BY SUSAN E. DESKIS AND THOMAS D. HILL

"*Speak Useful Words or Say Nothing*"

Old Norse Studies by Joseph Harris

EDITED BY

SUSAN E. DESKIS AND THOMAS D. HILL

ISLANDICA LIII

CORNELL UNIVERSITY LIBRARY
ITHACA, NEW YORK
2008

First published 2008 by Cornell University Library

Printed in the United States of America
Book design and composition: Jack Donner, BookType

CONTENTS

ACKNOWLEDGMENTS

The editors would like to thank the original publishers of these twelve articles for permission to reprint them in this volume.

"Christian Form and Christian Meaning in *Halldórs þáttr I*," *Harvard English Studies* 5 (1974), 249–64.

"*Ǫgmundar þáttr dytts ok Gunnars helmings*: Unity and Literary Relations," *Arkiv för nordisk filologi* 90 (1975), 156–82.

"The Masterbuilder Tale in Snorri's *Edda* and Two Sagas," *Arkiv för nordisk filologi* 91 (1976), 66–101.

"Theme and Genre in Some *Íslendinga þættir*," *Scandinavian Studies* 48 (1976), 1–28.

"*Guðrúnarbrögð* and the Saxon Lay of Grimhild's Perfidy," *Medieval Scandinavia* 9 (1976), 173–80.

"The King in disguise: An International Popular Tale in Two Old Icelandic Adaptations," *Arkiv för nordisk filologi* 94 (1979), 57–81.

"Satire and the Heroic Life: Two Studies (*Helgadviða Hundingsbana I*, 18 and Bjorn Hítdœlakappi's *Grámagaflím*)," in *Oral Traditional Literature: A Festschrift for Albert Bates Lord*, ed. by John Miles Foley (Columbus, OH: Slavica Publishers, 1981), pp. 322–40.

"Eddic Poetry as Oral Poetry: The Evidence of Parallel Passages in the Helgi Poems for Questions of Composition and Performance," in *Edda: A Collection of Essays*, ed. by Robert J. Glendinning and Haraldur Bessason, University of Manitoba Icelandic Studies, No. 4 (Winnipeg: University of Manitoba Press, 1983), pp. 210–42.

"Saga as Historical Novel," in *Structure and Meaning in Old Norse Literature: New Approaches to Textual Analysis and Literary Criticism*, ed. by John Lindow, Lars Lönnroth, and Gerd Wolfgang Weber, The Viking Collection, vol. 3 (Odense: Odense University Press, 1986), pp. 187–219.

"Gender and Genre: Short and Long Forms in the Saga Literature," in *The Making of the Couple: The Social Function of Short-Form Medieval Narrative; A Symposium*, ed. by Flemming G. Andersen and Morten Nøjgaard, Proceedings of the Fifteenth International Symposium organized by the Centre for the Study of Vernacular Literature in the Middle Ages held at Odense University on 19–20 November, 1990 (Odense: Odense University Press, 1991), pp. 43–66.

"Love and Death in the *Männerbund*: An Essay with Special Reference to the *Bjarkamál* and *The Battle of Maldon*," in *Heroic Poetry in the Anglo-Saxon Period: Studies in Honor of Jess B. Bessinger, Jr.*, ed. by Helen Damico and John Leyerle, Studies in Medieval Culture, 32 (Kalamazoo, MI: Medieval Institute Publications, 1993), pp. 77–114.

"Romancing the Rune: Aspects of Literacy in Early Scandinavian Orality," in *Atti* [of the] Accademia Peloritana dei Pericolanti, classe di lettere filosofia e belle arti, Vol. 70. Anno accademico CCLXV: 1994 (Messina: Accademia Peloritana dei Pericolanti, 1996), pp. 109–40.

TABULA GRATULATORIA

Abteilung für Nordische
 Philologie, Deutsches
 Seminar, Universität Zurich
Abteilung für Nordische
 Philologie, Universität Basel
Paul Acker
Frederic Amory and
 Elaine G. Tennant
Flemming G. Andersen
Anders Andrén
Ármann Jakobsson
The Arnamagnæan Institute and
 Dictionary, Copenhagen
Ásdís Egilsdóttir
Sverre Bagge
Heinrich Beck
Larry D. Benson
Maths Bertell
Fred Biggs
Robert E. Bjork
Stefan Brink
George Hardin Brown
Jesse Byock
Centre for Scandinavian Studies,
 University of Aberdeen
Margaret Clunies Ross
Committee on Degrees in
 Folklore and Mythology,
 Harvard University
Patrick W. Connor

Margaret Cormack
Craig R. Davis
Department of English,
 Harvard University
Daniel Donoghue
M. J. Driscoll
Thomas A. DuBois
Einar G. Pétursson
Jonathan D. Evans
Oren Falk
Anthony Faulkes
Fiske Icelandic Collection,
 Cornell University Library
Alison Finlay
John Miles Foley
Peter Foote
Sherry Forste-Grupp
Roberta Frank and
 Walter Goffart
R. D. Fulk
Kari Ellen Gade
Andrew Galloway
Gísli Sigurðsson
Jürg Glauser
Margot Goldsmith
Guðrún Nordal
Guðrún Þórhallsdóttir
Terry Gunnell
Karl S. Guthke
J. R. Hall

Thomas N. Hall
Sarah Harlan-Haughey
Richard L. Harris
Odd Einar Haugen
Wilhelm Heizmann
John Hines
The Icelandic Collection, University of Manitoba Libraries
Institüt für Skandinavistik, Goethe-Universität Frankfurt, Frankfurt am Main
Tatjana N. Jackson
Stephanie Jamison and Calvert Watkins
Jay H. Jasanoff
Kristina Jennbert
Jenny Jochens
Kristen Jóhannesson
Karl G. Johansson
Vera Johanterwage
David F. Johnson
Jón Hnefill Aðalsteinsson
Marianne Kalinke
Merrill Kaplan
James E. Knirk
Susanne Kramarz-Bein
Beatrice La Farge
Carolyne Larrington
William Layher
Bruce Lincoln
John Lindow
Íris and Lars Lönnroth
Emily Lyle
Mats Malm
Edith Marold
John McKinnell
Rory McTurk
Medieval Studies Program, Cornell University
William Ian Miller
Stephen A. Mitchell
Else Mundal
Marina Mundt
Joseph Falaky Nagy

John D. Niles
Andreas Nordberg
Andy Orchard
R. I. Page
Derek Pearsall
Richard Perkins
Thomas Pettitt
Russell Poole
Neil Price
Judy Quinn
Aaron Ralby
Karl Reichl
Matti Rissanen
Elizabeth Ashman Rowe
Runic Archives, University of Oslo
Geoffrey Russom
William Sayers
Ursula Schaefer
Jens Peter Schjødt
Ute Schwab
Klaus von See
Rudy Simek
Eckehard Simon
Peter Springborg
Stofnun Árna Magnússonar í íslenskum fræðum, Reykjavík
Sverrir Tómasson
Karen Swenson
Paul E. Szarmach
Donald Tuckwiller
Torfi H. Tulinius
Úlfar Bragason
Vésteinn Ólason
Andrew Wawn
Diana Whaley
Gordon Whatley
Jonathan Wilcox
Kendra J. Willson
Charles D. Wright
Samantha Zacher
Julia Zernack
Jan M. Ziolkowski
Þórunn Sigurðardóttir

PREFACE

The Cornell University Library published the first volume of the *Islandica* series, a *Bibliography of the Icelandic Saga and Minor Tales*, compiled by Halldór Hermannsson, in 1908. The series, initially conceived as "an annual relating to Iceland and the Fiske Icelandic Collection," has evolved during its century of existence. Over the years, it has included a number of scholarly monographs while maintaining its tradition of publishing learned bibliographies. Now, *Islandica* no longer appears solely in print. Commencing with volume LIII, a version of each series volume will be available online at http://rmc.library.cornell.edu/islandica/.

It is deeply satisfying to present this volume of Joseph Harris's papers in Old Norse studies, *"Speak Useful Words or Say Nothing,"* in *Islandica's* centennial year. The scholarly writings of Dr. Harris, the Francis Lee Higginson Professor of English Literature and Professor of Folklore at Harvard University, have for more than a generation graced the pages of many of Europe's and America's most important journals dedicated to the study of literature and folklore. Joe Harris himself served as series editor for *Islandica* in the 1980s, seeing into publication two bibliographical studies in 1985.

Professor Susan Deskis of Northern Illinois University and Professor Thomas Hill of Cornell University proposed and edited this volume as a tribute to a great scholar and friend, knowing that many of his papers had been previously published in European journals to which libraries in North America have limited access. The wisdom of the editors' selection from Joe Harris's many contributions reflects warmly their own sensitive scholarship.

The Cornell University Press has been graciously forthcoming in its collaboration on the publication process. This volume, and the new electronic home of the *Islandica* series, would not have been possible without the enthusiasm and wisdom of my library colleague, Teresa Ehling, Director of the Center for Innovative Publishing in the Cornell University Library. I am also pleased to acknowledge Elaine Engst, Director of the Division of Rare and Manuscript Collections, for her counsel regarding the future of our venerable series.

Patrick J. Stevens
Curator, the Fiske Icelandic Collection
and Managing Editor, *Islandica*

ABBREVIATIONS

AM	*Edda Snorra Sturlusonar*, Arnamagnaean Commission (Hafniae, 1848–87)
ANF	*Arkiv för Nordisk Filologi*
AnM	*Annuale Mediaevale*
APS	*Acta Philologica Scandinavica*
AUS	*Annales Universitatis Saraviensis*
Beitr	*Beiträge zur Geschichte der Deutschen Sprache und Literatur*
BGDSL	*Beiträge zur Geschichte der Deutschen Sprache und Literatur*
CCIMÆ	Corpus Codicum Islandicorum Medii Ævi
Dan.	Danish
DgF	*Danmarks gamle Folkeviser*, ed. Sven Grundtvig (Copenhagen, 1853–1904)
DI	*Diplomatarium Islandicum*
Eb	*Eyrbyggja saga*
EETS	Early English Text Society
ESA	*English Studies in Africa*
FFC	*Folklore Fellows' Communications*
FJ	*Edda Snorra Sturlusonar*, ed. Finnur Jónsson (Copenhagen, 1931)
Flat. II	*Flateyjarbók II*
FMAS	*Frühmittelalterliche Studien*
Fms	*Fornmanna sögur*
FS	*Fornar smásögur úr noregskonunga sögum*, ed. Edwin Gardiner (Reykjavík, 1949)
Fsk	*Fagrskinna*, ed. P. A. Munch and C. R. Unger (Christiania, 1847)
Ftb	*Flateyjarbók*
GRM	*Germanisch-Romanische Monatsschrift*
HES	*Harvard English Studies*
HH	*Helgakviða Hundingsbana I*
HHII	*Helgakviða Hundingsbana II*
HHv	*Helgakviða Hjo_rrvarðssonar*
HS	*Hervarar saga*
HSCP	*Harvard Studies in Classical Philology*

Hv	*Heiðar-víga saga*
IE	Indo-European
ÍF	Íslenzk fornrit
ÍS	*Íslendinga sögur,* ed. Guðni Jónsson (Reykjavík, 1947)
ÍÞ	*Íslendinga þættir,* ed. Guðni Jónsson (Reykjavík, 1945)
JAF	*Journal of American Folklore*
JEGP	*Journal of English and Germanic Philology*
JFI	*Journal of the Folklore Institute*
KHL	*Kulturhistorisk leksikon for nordisk middelalder fra vikingetid til reformationstid,* ed. Johannes Brøndsted, et al. (Copenhagen, 1956–)
MÆ	*Medium Ævum*
Maldon	*Battle of Maldon*
MDu	Middle Dutch
MGH	Monumenta Germaniae Historica
MGS	*Michigan Germanic Studies*
MHG	Middle High German
MLR	*The Modern Language Review*
MM	*Maal og Minne*
MP	*Modern Philology*
Ms.	Manuscript
MScan	*Mediaeval Scandinavia*: Title changed to *Viking and Medieval Scandinavia*
Msk	*Morkinskinna*
MSS	Manuscripts
N&Q	*Notes and Queries*
Neophil	*Neophilologus*
NgL	*Norges gamle love indtil 1387,* ed. R. Keyser and P. A. Munch (Christiania, 1846–1895)
NL	*Nibelungenlied*
NM	*Neuphilologische Mitteilungen*
OE	Old English
OHG	Old High German
ON	Old Norse
OS	Old Saxon
PBA	*Proceedings of the British Academy*
PMLA	*PMLA: Publications of the Modern Language Association of America*
PQ	*Philological Quarterly*
SBVS	*Saga Book of the Viking Society*
SN	*Studia Neophilologica*
SS	*Scandinavian Studies*
sts	stanzas
TAPA	*Transactions of the American Philological Association*
VS	*Völsunga saga*
ZDA	*Zeitschrift für Deutsches Altertum und Deutsche Literatur*
ZDP	*Zeitschrift für Deutsche Philologie*
6SP	*Sex Sögu-þættir,* ed. Jón Þorkelsson (Reykjavík, 1855)

INTRODUCTION

A full and detailed review of the work of Joseph Harris, the Francis Lee Higginson Professor of English Literature and Professor of Folklore at Harvard University, would be a scholarly and critical project well worth undertaking, but it is not one we propose here. In this volume we have chosen to limit our own words in order to make more room for the work of Joseph Harris. We are confident that the scholarly community will approve our decision, although the choice of which of Joe's articles to reprint will inevitably be more controversial. In making that difficult choice, we debated between ourselves and with wise counselors over two models for a collection honoring the work of a distinguished scholar such as Joseph Harris. We could either choose a representative sample that would reflect the breadth of his work in Old-Norse Icelandic, or gather articles situated within a topical range. After a good deal of debate and considerable consulting, we opted for a representative sample in order to make a range of Joe's work more readily available to students and scholars who do not have easy access to a research library with extensive holdings in the field of Old Norse-Icelandic literature. To some degree we have attempted to choose less accessible papers rather than those which are more widely accessible, but we have also attempted to put together a coherent collection of Joseph Harris's work.

In his years of work at Harvard, Stanford, Cornell, and then Harvard again, Joseph Harris has established himself as one of the most important contemporary scholars in the fields of Old English and Old Norse–Icelandic. His work is characterized by deep learning, openness to the best of both new and old scholarship and criticism, and a kind of judicious balance in dealing with complex problems.

There is a long tradition of scholarly inquiry concerning oral literature and oral tradition at Harvard, extending back to Francis James Child's work on the English and Scottish popular ballad, and continuing with Parry's and Lord's work on South Slavic traditional poetry, B. J. Whiting's work on medieval English proverbs, and Francis P. Magoun's elaboration of the oral formulaic hypothesis to explicate some of the more puzzling features of Old English poetry. Although Joseph Harris's work is certainly in this tradition, he has always articulated a moderated and nuanced version of oral theory as this line of research is currently defined. Whereas Magoun was concerned with setting Old English poetry completely apart from later developments in English literature and in effect reducing the various poets to being simply voices of tradition, Joe has always been sensitive to the differences of individual talent and to the literary quality of the texts he was studying. The result has been a mode of criticism that reflects the importance and fascination of oral traditional literature and is simultaneously sensitive to individual poetic achievement. There is no question that certain genres of medieval (and post-medieval) literature reflect the influence of pre-existing oral literary forms. Genres such as the traditional English and Scottish ballads, the Icelandic sagas (and *þættir*) and the Old English elegies are either oral literature directly (as are the ballads) or draw upon traditional oral forms that must have existed but have not been explicitly preserved. Criticism of these genres has sometimes oscillated between simply ignoring the oral antecedents of the texts we have and romantically invoking "orality" as a concept that somehow explains the survival of these oral traditions in very diverse literary forms.

The work of Joseph Harris mediates between these extremes. Joe is characteristically a critic who "reads" tradition and genre; he will situate a work in the context of its tradition and genre and illuminate it brilliantly and unexpectedly in that context. One of the central problems of medieval literary scholarship for the last two genera-tions is the issue of the aesthetics of traditional and oral literature, and how and whether one can meaningfully talk about the literary history of an oral genre. Joe's studies of such topics as the Old Norse short narrative (the *þáttr*) or of the Masterbuilder tale in Old Norse literature focus precisely on such problems and offer brilliant readings of specific texts as well as models of literary historical discourse. Again, while there has been a certain ideological dissonance between the study of the Latin and Christian sources of these literatures and the understanding of native, vernacular traditions, Joseph Harris has been ready to bridge that divide since his earliest publications. In this collection, his paper on "Christian Form and Meaning in *Halldór's þáttr I*" illustrates Joe's respect for both approaches.

Perhaps the most important, and indeed the most characteristic, feature of Joseph Harris's scholarship is how hard it is to summarize. His papers run the gamut from critical readings of canonical texts to straightforward philological elucidation of Old Norse or Old English literary works to discussions of larger theoretical issues such as oral theory. What is common to this body of work is the combination of good judgment, critical sensitivity, and deep learning that makes it a model for younger scholars to emulate and a hopeful reminder that there are still some contemporary scholars who can return to quite traditional problems with the judicious authority of such masters as Frederick Klaeber, Kemp Malone, or Sigurður Nordal.

We have gathered this collection of papers to honor a mentor and a friend (and a man who combines both roles effortlessly), and to make the work of Joseph Harris more readily available. "Gleawe men sceolon gieddum wrixlan," as the poet who composed the *Exeter Book* maxims remarked, and if we have made the *gieddas* of Joseph Harris more readily accessible, have made his *spraec* more widely audible, we will have done good work.

The reader will find that we have not tried to impose an abso-lute uniformity on these reprinted articles, so forms of citation, for example, may vary among them. We have silently corrected such typographical errors as we found in the originals and have updated bibliographic references when necessary. We are immensely grateful to Patrick J. Stevens, Curator of the Fiske Icelandic Collection at Cornell University, for embracing this volume as part of the Islandica series, and for helping us see it through to completion. Finally, in keeping with the admonition from *Hávamál* that provides the title for this volume, we will now be silent and let the useful words of Joseph Harris speak for themselves.

Susan E. Deskis   Thomas D. Hill

Christian Form and Christian Meaning in *Halldórs þáttr I*

Old Icelandic sources preserve two independent short stories or þættir about Halldórr Snorrason in addition to the numerous passages concerning him in *Haralds saga harðráða* and other texts. The better known of the þættir, *Halldórs þáttr II*, telling of a series of quarrels between Halldórr and King Haraldr and of Halldórr's old age, sketches an early and amusing portrait of this salty Icelander; the less well-known *Halldórs þáttr I* is almost certainly much younger, apparently exhibits a knowledge of Halldórr's character and times based partly on the earlier þáttr, and is of no historical value, being simply a fiction, a novella with historical setting.[1] From the purely literary point of view, however, *Halldórs þáttr I* is one of the most interesting and instructive of the þættir, despite its probable late date, and an analysis of the artistry with which theme here harmonizes with structure and invests it with significance—more exactly, the way *Christian meaning creates Christian form*—may be suggestive for criticism of the saga literature more generally. But we begin with structure.

For Bartlett Jere Whiting on his seventieth birthday: "opt er gott, þat er gamlir kveða" *(Hávamál)*.

1. See Einar Ólafur Sveinsson, ed. *Íslensk fornrit* 5 (Reykjavík, 1934), where *Halldórs þáttr II* is also found; sources for Halldórr's biography are given, pp. lxxxv–xc. Sveinsson's introduction (pp. lxxxii–lxxxv) gives reasons for the dating and literary relations alluded to here and anticipates *in nuce* many of my remarks in this essay, but I believe he underestimates the literary value of the þáttr (p. lxxxii) and perhaps overestimates its historicity (pp. lxxxiv–lxxxv).

The story opens when an Icelander named Eilífr arrives in Norway and offends King Haraldr; Halldórr attempts to intercede for him and, failing to win the king over, leaves the royal court in anger. Halldórr and Eilífr remove to the estate of the powerful Norwegian nobleman Einarr þambarskelfir; there Halldórr incurs the jealousy of a disagreeable young kinsman of Einarr's named Kali, who defames and lampoons the older man. When Halldórr then kills Kali, he comes in mortal danger from Einarr, but on the advice of Einarr's wife Bergljót Halldórr surrenders to Einarr's judgment. Einarr calls an assembly but before announcing his verdict recounts an anecdote from his youth that explains his decision in the case (a separate narrative about King Óláfr Tryggvason, summarized below). Einarr's judgment is that he himself shall pay compensation for Kali's death and that he will hold the peace with Halldórr. Then Halldórr succeeds in making peace for Eilífr and himself with King Haraldr, sends Eilífr home to Iceland, and remains long afterward with the king.

A first glance suffices to show that the þáttr comprises at least two complete narratives, one within the other like Chinese boxes: Halldórr's adventures and Einarr's narration at the assembly. But when examined in the context of the six-part narrative pattern which is characteristic of a large group of þættir, *Halldórs þáttr I* appears to be composed of four narrative structures, three with the Alienation/Reconciliation pattern common to the group and the fourth the tale told by Einarr.[2] The outermost structure concerns Eilífr and King Haraldr, the second Halldórr and Haraldr, the third Halldórr and Einarr, and the inmost Einarr's recollections of King Óláfr Tryggvason, and these strands are related in a manner similar to that of syntactic "nesting structures." The relationship between Halldórr and Einarr replicates closely that between Eilífr and Haraldr, both having not only the common Alienation/Reconciliation structure but, in addition to the two essential role positions or "slots," also a third that is often found in þættir of this type, the intercessor (Halldórr as intercessor for Eilífr, and Bergljót for

---

2. I have discussed the pattern, in which "alienation" and "reconciliation" form the central structural segments, in "Genre and Narrative Structure in Some *Íslendinga þættir*," *Scandinavian Studies*, 44 (1972), 1–27, and "The King and the Icelander: A Study in the Short Narrative Forms of Old Icelandic Prose," Ph.D. diss., Harvard University, 1969.

Halldórr). The relationship between Halldórr and Haraldr is quite similar, but no third person functions as intercessor.[3]

This analysis seems confirmed by the elegant and economical ending of the þáttr where the last three sentences knit up the three outer narrative strands. The opening of the þáttr had presented the Alienations in the order Eilífr/Haraldr, Halldórr/ Haraldr, and Halldórr/Einarr (1, 2, 3); in the closing passage the inmost of these feuds is settled first (3); in the second sentence both the Halldórr/Haraldr and Eilífr/Haraldr feuds are composed, not in the expected order 2, 1, the mirror image of their introduction, but in the order 1, 2. Then the third and last sentence, which concerns only Eilífr and Haraldr, arrives to establish the pattern 1, 2, 3:3, (1), 2, 1, an instance of the aesthetic formula of establishing a strong presumption of a pattern, first violating it, and finally fulfilling it. The þáttr's last sentence, so untypical of saga conclusions,[4] is also remarkable for giving essential information that was withheld at the beginning of the story: we learn only in the last sentence that Eilífr's offense had been killing a courtier of King Haraldr's. This belated information, dropping into place like the keystone of an arch, has the effect of drastically underlining the parallelism between Eilífr's story and Halldórr's. Authorial control of the reader and suspense of a sort extend literally to the last sentence, and by dramatically emphasizing the equivalence of two of the story's personal ratios (Eilífr : Haraldr :: Halldórr : Einarr), it "lays bare the device" (in the famous Russian Formalist phrase) and stimulates the reader's mind to seek the thematic relevance of the story's form.

Framed within the Alienation/Reconciliation structures, a story within the stories, we find Einarr's retrospective narrative: Bjǫrn, an old man, Kolbeinn, who was in middle life, and Einarr, aged eighteen, shipmates aboard the famous Long Serpent, were captured by Danes in the general defeat at the Battle of Svǫldr after King Óláfr Tryggvason had "disap-

---

3. Typical *dramatis personae* of these stories are discussed in "King and Icelander," pp. 151–167. In *Flateyjarbók* (Reykjavík, 1944) I, 562, the story is headed "Einarr hjálpaði Halldóri," as if the copyist were completing the analogies among the three pairs of antagonists.

4. Usual endings of such þættir are discussed in "King and Icelander," pp. 76–80 and p. 260, n.13. The three principal texts of the þáttr (F, S, and B) are, I think, similar enough to warrant this detailed commentary, though, of course, the punctuation of the last three sentences is editorial; on F$_2$ see Sveinsson, pp. lxxxii–lxxxiii, n.1.

peared in the light that shined over him"; they were kept bound in a wood to be sold as slaves. At the slave market a man in a blue cloak like a monk's and masked bargained with the slave master for the three and finally purchased them. As he led them away on a forest path, Einarr asked his name, but the stranger refused to tell. Then he predicted their lives: Bjǫrn had not long to live and should make disposition of his property for his soul's sake; Kolbeinn would be highly esteemed at home; but Einarr would be the greatest. And from Einarr the hooded man required repayment for buying and freeing them: Einarr was laid under obligation to free a man who had offended against him, even though his enemy should stand fully in his power. The stranger lifted his mask as he distracted the three by pointing, and when they looked back, he had disappeared. But they recognized him as Óláfr Tryggvason.

This reminiscence is introduced into the þáttr as an "entertainment" offered at the assembly:

> Ok þenna sama dag stefnir Einarr fjǫlmennt þing. Hann stóð upp á þinginu ok talaði svá: "Ek vil nú skemmta yðr ok segja frá því ..." (P. 255)

> That same day Einarr called an assembly that was heavily attended. He stood up in the meeting and spoke as follows: "I mean to entertain you now by telling about ..."

But its real integrative principle is explained in Einarr's closing words:

> "Nú em ek skyldr til," segir Einarr, "at gera þat, er Óláfr konungr bað mik. Sýnisk mér nú eigi annat líkara, Halldórr, en hann hafi fyrir þér beðit, því at þú ert nú á mínu valdi." (P. 260)

> "Now I am obligated," said Einarr, "to do what King Óláfr asked of me. Nothing seems more likely to me now, Halldórr, than that he was asking it for your sake since you are now in my power."

Mere entertainment is unmasked as the motivating principle of the remainder of the þáttr.[5]

---

5. Cf. the ostensible and real motivation for the tale-within-a-tale in *Morkinskinna*'s story about Úlfr inn auðgi (ed. C. R. Unger [Christiania, 1867], pp. 66–69): at a feast King Haraldr proposed to enliven the occasion with a story *(rœða)* and at the end made the application to his own immediate situation, motivating his ensuing actions.

It should be clear by now that our author's aesthetic sense is strongly symmetrical. The triple Alienation/Reconciliation structures and the retrospective speech are neatly "self-embedded"; the causal principle operates from outer to inner structures and out again from inner to outer: Eilífr's offense causes Halldórr's separation from the king, which leads to his presence at Einarr's and the resulting feud, the assembly, and the "entertainment"; that tale motivates Einarr's reconciliation with Halldórr, which (I shall argue below) leads to Halldórr's reunion with the king, in turn a necessary condition for Eilífr's reconciliation to Haraldr. The triple arrangement of the Alienation/Reconciliation structures suggests that the same action is being replicated at different social levels. Thus the sequence—king vs. otherwise unknown Icelander (Eilífr), king vs. famous Icelander from a great family (Halldórr),[6] great nobleman vs. famous Icelander from a great family—seems to be arranged in descending order of social distance between the antagonists. More obvious is the triple arrangement and gradation of the comrades in Einarr's tale: Bjǫrn is old, Kolbeinn evidently middle-aged, Einarr young; their prices as slaves are graded from Bjǫrn through Kolbeinn to Einarr (respectively one, two, and three marks); and in the prophecy Bjǫrn is told to make his peace with God in preparation for imminent death, while Einarr is to live to a ripe and powerful old age (Kolbeinn being somewhere between).

The most important structural feature (also manifesting a kind of symmetry) of the central "entertainment" leads from discussion of form to theme. Einarr's reminiscence has a symbolic dimension and is, more specifically, a figural or typological narrative. There should be nothing surprising in this since Óláfr Tryggvason was in popular conception very nearly a saint, and every saint's life is to some extent a typological recapitulation of Christ's, an *imitatio Christi;* what is remarkable is to find typology so well integrated into typical themes and structures of the saga literature. But first the details of the typology must be examined.

Svǫldr is Óláfr's last, great *agon,* and like Christ his "death" here is ambiguous; like Enoch and Elijah, Óláfr is taken mysteriously while yet alive, and those prophets were interpreted as types of Christ in the manner

---

6. Cf. *Halldórs þáttr II* on Halldórr's pride of family *(ÍF 5, 269 and 273).*

of their passing.[7] After three days Christ rose from the dead and came to his disciples, just as Óláfr comes to Einarr and his companions (members of Óláfr's crew, his "disciples") after some time; the interval between the battle and Óláfr's "epiphany" cannot be calculated exactly, but there can be no doubt that the author wished to make the parallel clear since he contrives to mention the number three in connection with this time period:

"ok Danir, menn Sveins konungs, tóku oss ok fœrðu konungi, en hann flutti oss til Jótlands, ok váru vér þar upp leiddir ok settir á eina lág ok þar fjǫtraðir ... *ok í þeim skógi sátu vér þrjár nœtr.*" (P. 256)

"And the Danes, the men of King Sveinn, captured us and led us to their king, and he brought us to Jutland, and there we were led ashore, seated on a log, and fettered.... And we sat three nights in that forest."[8]

The effect of Christ's victory over death was the *redemption* or "buying back" of mankind, and imagery of commerce, of slavery, and of bondage is commonplace in this connection; thus Óláfr returned from "death" to purchase his men literally out of thralldom and to release them literally from bondage.[9] Christ was not recognized by his disciples when he appeared to them after the resurrection; so the disguised Óláfr is not recognized at first by his men.

---

7. Gen. 5:24; 2 Kings 2:1–12 (cf. also Romulus, Ovid, *Met.* IV.816ff.). The translations of Enoch and Elijah were usually viewed as figuring Christ's Ascension (e.g., J. P. Migne, ed., *Patrologia Latina* CIX, col. 222–223), which does not fit the action schema of Óláfr's story perfectly, but the eclecticism of my typological interpretation has precedent in medieval methods of composition and interpretation.

8. See W. Baetke, "Das Svoldr-Problem," *Berichte über die Verhandlungen der sächsischen Akademie der Wissenschaften zu Leipzig.* Philological-historical class, vol. 98 (1951), pt. 6, pp. 59–135; if our author thought the battle site near Jutland, he may have meant the interval to be exactly three days, but general Icelandic tradition favored the coast of Pomerania, while the other major tradition, locating it in the Öresund, was Danish. A third location at the Schlei in Schleswig-Holstein would place it near Jutland, but it seems quite impossible that our author belongs to this questionable tradition (Baetke, pp. 59–60) in spite of the fact that he does not name the place "Svǫldr" in the Icelandic manner; Jutland is probably chosen simply as a forbidding place deep in enemy country. With the image of captives fettered and sitting along a log; cf. the Jómsvíkings (ÍF 26, 284). The word *lág* seems to be old; it is used here by Snorri, glossed twice in his *Edda,* and used once in *Egils saga;* cf. n.10 below.

9. The Harrowing of Hell, a mythic elaboration of the idea of redemption, has only general relevance here; but cf. Jesus' words (from Isaiah): "He has sent me to proclaim release to the captives ... to set at liberty those who are oppressed ..." (Luke 4:18).

These parallels will be sufficient for the moment to establish a figural relation between aspects of the death and resurrection of Christ and Óláfr's role in our þáttr, though a few qualifications are in order. Óláfr's disappearance into a cloud of light and some other features of Einarr's tale are traditional, not invented by our author, and other stories do attribute supernatural powers to Óláfr Tryggvason;[10] nevertheless, most of the elements of the story and their constellation as a narrative whole must be credited to him, and in view of the Christian parallels offered so far, both the general and the specific, I think it would "outrage probability" to consider this pattern accidental (R. E. Kaske's criterion). The þáttr's style is "saga realism," and in accord with that peculiar brand of realism the author clothes his figural narrative in the possible if unlikely theory that Óláfr Tryggvason escaped from the battle and lived on as a monk in a distant land; and the stage business at the slave market, the mask and hood, and the sheer weight of mundane detail in these scenes lend further plausibility. But Óláfr's role in the story is supernatural—Sveinsson commented that if the king had survived the battle he would have had better things to do than hang about in his enemy's country—and scarcely to be understood from a purely realistic point of view, without its figural schema and function in the semantic configurations of the þáttr. In short, the author of *Halldórs þáttr I* was not interested in presenting a version of either of the realistic theories of Óláfr's end for its own sake but instead in the king as instrument and spokesman for God and as *deus ex machina* in the realistic human drama of enmity and reconciliation that he laid in Norway.[11]

---

10. Sveinsson places the þáttr in the general tradition of the Óláfr sagas of Oddr and Gunnlaugr (p. lxxxiii). In Oddr (ed. Finnur Jónsson [Copenhagen, 1932]) the author could have found the light, the names of Einarr, Kolbeinn, and Bjǫrn in close proximity as three of the first four named as survivors (identities of Kolbeinn or Kolbjǫrn and Bjǫrn discussed by Sveinsson, pp. 255–256, n.3), the fact that the survivors jumped overboard and were captured, that Óláfr lived on, became a monk, and was seen by certain witnesses. But he may have had recourse to Snorri's version for the information that Einarr was eighteen (*ÍF 26*, 346) and about the legal ages of the crew (p. 344; Sveinsson, p. 256, n.2); cf. n.8 above.

11. Tradition, represented by Oddr, actually reports *three* versions of Óláfr's end: disappearance in light, normal death of wounds or drowning but in unspecified circumstances, escape by swimming to a Wendish ship; the latter two are not only realistic but related, while the first is quite separate. See Lars Lönnroth, "Studier i Olaf Tryggvasons saga," *Samlaren*, 84 (1963), 54–94, for discussion of the sources of the realistic escape legend.

On this basis we may look for some more questionable parallels of detail. In the gospels Christ appears unrecognized three times, in Luke 24, John 20:14–16, and John 21:4; of these the epiphany on the road to Emmaus is most similar, and the parallels are extensive: the epiphany occurs out of doors, on a path, to only a small number (two) of disciples; Christ instructs them before he disappears; they recognize him just as he vanishes from their sight; after Christ has disappeared the men talk about the epiphany ("Did not our hearts burn within us while he talked to us on the road…"); then they return to Jerusalem. Similarly Óláfr leads his three men, a small portion of his crew,[12] down a forest path, instructs them about their future life, and is recognized fully by all only in the moment of his vanishing; afterward the men discuss the event and return to Norway.

One curious feature of the þáttr is possibly to be explained as a confused or, better, imaginatively altered imitation of the passage from Luke: The hooded man and the companions reach a clearing, and they catch a glimpse under his hood: "kippði upp lítt at hettinum" (p. 258) ("he pulled up a little on the hood"). After his prophecy they get a closer look: "Ok at svá tǫluðu lypti kuflmaðrinn grímu frá andliti sér" (p. 259) ("And this said, the cowled man raised the mask from his face"). At the same time he distracted them, and:

"er vér litum aptr, var grímumaðr horfinn, ok síðan sám vér hann aldri. En þenna man kenndu vér allir fullgǫrla, at þetta var Óláfr konungr Tryggvason, því at þegar fyrra sinn, at hann lypti kuflshettinum, kennda ek hann fyrir víst; en síðan hann lypti upp grímunni ok sýndi oss sína ásjónu, kenndu vér hann allir." (P. 259)

"When we looked back, the masked man had disappeared, and we never saw him again. But we all recognized the man quite clearly: it was King Óláfr Tryggvason. For as soon as he pushed back his hood the first time, I was certain I recognized him; but after he raised up his mask and showed us his face, we all recognized him."

---

12. The þáttr says nine survived from the Long Serpent; Oddr says eight but gives only seven names; conceivably Oddr's "eight" derives from the seven named crewmen plus Óláfr and the þáttr's "nine" in the same way from Oddr's "eight."

It is strange that, having recognized Óláfr "for sure" the first time he gave a glimpse of himself, Einarr did not call him by name, give the Good News to his comrades, and "lay hands on him" as the three afterward agreed they should have done (pp. 259–260); instead Einarr waited for the final revelation with his two companions and only tells us after it is all over that he had known from that first glimpse. This is perhaps to be related to the fact that, while Luke states clearly that Jesus appeared to two disciples on the way to Emmaus, he also mentions an earlier epiphany to a single disciple: "And they [the two from Emmaus] rose that same hour and returned to Jerusalem; and they found the eleven gathered together and those who were with them, who said, 'The Lord has risen indeed, and has appeared to Simon!' Then they [the two from Emmaus] told what had happened on the road ..." (24:33–35). Thus the Emmaus passage as a whole mentions three individual disciples (Cleophas, one unnamed, and Simon) as witnesses of Christ's return and seems to make the epiphany to Simon prior to that to the two on the road to Emmaus; in *Halldórs þáttr I* we have Óláfr's appearance to three followers but to one a little before the other two.

Perhaps this explanation is not necessary, but in addition to the questions posed above about the logicality of Einarr's actions judged from purely a realistic perspective, we must explain why, after the first glimpse when he knew with certainty that the stranger was Óláfr Tryggvason, Einarr nevertheless claimed not to know him: "Ek svaraða, at óhœgra væri at launa, ef ek vissa eigi, hverjum at gjalda var" (p. 259) ("I answered that it was very difficult to repay a man if I didn't know who was to be repaid"). It is possible, of course, that Einarr was boasting untruthfully when he said he had recognized the king before the other two or that the author imagined Einarr as having some unexpressed reasons for not making known his discovery immediately and for saying he did not know whom to reward—possible, but as it seems certain that the author had the Luke text in mind, it is at least a likely hypothesis that the illogicality or at least lack of realistic motivation in Einarr's actions here is caused by the imitation or, with Frye, "displacement."

This argument is not damaged by a series of striking if unsystematic agreements with John 21 where the risen Christ, at first not recognized, reveals himself to eight disciples beside the Sea of

Tiberias and breakfasts with them (21:1–14). He then makes a speech (15–19) with strongly marked tripartite form ("Simon, son of John ... Simon, son of John ... Simon, sonof John"; cf. "En þú, Bjǫrn ... En þú Kolbeinn ... En þú, Einarr ..."); the climactic third part is longest and most developed (as with Óláfr's speech). The speech is given before the group but addresses an individual (as Óláfr addresses each of his men individually, and especially Einarr) and treats a commandment (thrice repeated) as an obligation ("do you love me? ... Feed my sheep"; cf. Óláfr's injunction of forgiveness as the obligatory requital for freedom given). Besides the commandment the speech includes prophecy of Peter's old age and death (Óláfr prophesies Bjǫrn's death and Einarr's prosperous old age), and Jesus' words about Peter's life oppose youth and old age, suggesting the contrast between Einarr and Bjǫrn. Finally, an arresting detail: Peter is evidently singled out for the commandment and prophecy here *because* he stands out above the other disciples ("Simon, son of John, do you love me *more than these?* ... Feed my lambs"; cf. Peter's individual actions in 21:7–8 and 11), while Óláfr sets Einarr apart in prophecy and selects him alone for his commandment because Einarr excels the others.[13] If, then, it seems reasonable to say that Einarr's role reflects to some extent Simon Peter's position in John 21, the probability of the same influence from the epiphany to "Simon" in Luke 24:34 seems to gain support.

Figural narrative can be considered a structural device in that a pattern of events is made or seen to conform to that of a part of

---

13. Pp. 257–258, esp. 259: "'En þú, Einarr ... munt verða yðvar mestr maðr ... af þér einum mun ek laun hafa ... því at þér einum hygg ek at mest þykki vert, ef þú ert eigi þræll'" ("'But you, Einarr ... will become the greatest man of the three ... from you alone I must have repayment ... because I think you place the most value on not being a slave'"). An ambiguity in the Vulgate's "diligis me *plus his?*" is reflected in the English translation; the interpretation here is the most natural in context. The John 21 passage includes also "Follow me" (19 and 22; cf. the þáttr, p. 258 and below). Other texts that may have contributed: John 21:12: "Jesus said to them, 'Come and have breakfast.' Now none of the disciples dared ask him, 'Who are you?' They knew it was the Lord" (cf. p. 258: "gekk þá brott ... ok bað fylgja sér ... spurða ek hann at nafni. Hann svarar: 'Ekki varðar þik at vita nafn mitt ...'"); John 20:17: "Jesus said to her, 'Do not hold me, for I have not yet ascended to the Father,'" and other passages about touching the risen Christ, John 20:27 and Luke 24:39 (cf. pp. 259–260: "tǫluðum vár í milli, at oss hefði mjǫk óvitrliga til tekizk er vér hǫfðum eigi hendr á honum ..."); with Óláfr's directives to his "disciples," esp. Einarr, cf. Matthew 28:18–20 (the risen Christ's charge to the apostles); Luke 4:29–30 may perhaps be compared with the final disappearance.

sacred history,[14] but an examination of the *effects* of typology takes us out of formal analysis and into the realm of theme, the semantics of a narrative; in *Halldórs þáttr I* the typology associates Óláfr with Christ, lending his words a deeper resonance which perhaps only grows on the reader as he gradually realizes that Óláfr here is a type of Christ. Most obviously, of course, the dialogue dealing with purchase and sale takes on symbolic force, but perhaps also the harsh slave master *(meistari)* suggests the death to which mankind had been subject before Christ's redeeming victory. (Note that, like the hooded stranger in this scene, the meistari is identified only by his words and actions, an anonymity which increases his symbolic potential.) The universal ring of some of Óláfr's words and an irony (beyond that occasioned by the motif of the king in disguise) in his bargaining become explicable against the figural pattern (are men worthy of redemption?), and the syntactic and lexical balance between the expressions of the meistari's relation to the prisoners and Óláfr's, which cannot be accidental, takes on significance:

"En sá, er oss varðveitti, *vildi selja* oss í þrældóm; hann hét oss afarkostum ok limaláti, *ef vér vildim eigi þjásk."* (P. 256)
"'eru menn takmiklir, *ef þeir vilja mennask; sýnisk mér því ráð* at *kaupa þá alla.'"* (P. 258)

"The one who was guarding us meant to sell us into slavery; he threatened us with rough treatment and mutilation if we would not submit to being slaves."
"'they will be strong if they are willing to act like men [or even: men will be strong ...]; so it seems to me a good idea to buy them all.'"

The conventional symbolism of "forest" and "night" in Christian thought may go some way toward creating the reverberations of "í þeim skógi sátu vér þrjár nætr" and to explaining why in a *merely* realistic fiction (in fiction an author has control of what he says and does

---

14. This is not intended as a definition of typology, and no general treatment will be attempted here; see Erich Auerbach, "Figura," in *Scenes from the Drama of European Literature* (New York: Meridian Books, 1959), Jean Danielou, *From Shadows to Reality: Studies in the Biblical Typology of the Fathers*, trans. W. Hibberd (London: Burns' Dates, 1960), and Charles Donahue, "Patristic Exegesis: Summation," in *Critical Approaches to Medieval Literature*, ed. Dorothy Bethurum (New York: Columbia University Press, 1960), pp. 62–66 and passim.

not say) an assembly or market is called in an unnamed forest vaguely
located in Jutland. Christian-symbolic ideas associated with "path" may
also lend overtones that go beyond geography when Óláfr leads his men
away from the slave market and, showing them the "path" to safety,
immediately adds directives for the future lives of his freedmen.

Finally, of course, comes Óláfr's injunction to Einarr:

> "'því skaltu launa: ef nokkurr maðr gerir svá mjǫk í móti þér, at fyrir
> hvatvetna vilir þú hafa hans líf, ok hafir þú vald yfir honum, þá skaltu eigi
> minna frelsi gefa honum en ek gef nú þér.'" (P. 259)

> "'Here is the way you must repay me: if some man offends you so much
> that you want to take his life and you have him in your power, you must
> give him no less freedom than I have now given you.'"

In this way Einarr (and mankind) must repay the "gift of life and
freedom" ("laun ... fyrir lífgjǫfina ok frelsit," p. 259); Óláfr is not only
enjoining upon Einarr the practice of forgiving an enemy but imag-
ining a situation similar to Einarr's own predicament as a slave, thus
an exemplification of the golden rule in a saga-specific form: if Einarr
should one day find himself with power over an enemy, he shall act in
imitation of the redeemer Óláfr/Christ and not identify himself with
the forces of the meistari/death. More precisely, the imagined situation
explicitly predicts the relationship between Halldórr and Einarr and
by extension that between the other feuding pairs, giving the "correct
solution" to any Alienation/Reconciliation story.

With this injunction we have arrived at the structural and moral heart
of *Halldórs þáttr I*. This teaching of Óláfr's is now applied to Einarr's
grievance against Halldórr and in turn to the feuds between the Icelanders
and King Haraldr. The text, of course, simply juxtaposes Einarr's final
words, quoted above, and his exemplary action with the reconciliation
to King Haraldr and leaves the reader to imagine how it came about.
As so often the saga literature presents us with the "half-sung song,"
but how *did* Halldórr reconcile himself and Eilífr with the king? Must
we not imagine that he recounted Einarr's story, which applies to the
situation of Eilífr almost as well as that of Halldórr, or at least that in
some unspecified way Óláfr's teaching is extended to King Haraldr?
(If Einarr can forbear revenge for his relative, cannot Haraldr do the

same for his unnamed courtier?) This not very bold assumption allows further details to be integrated as thematically functional: Halldórr's first attempt to intercede in Eilífr's behalf is impetuous and demanding and results in an extension of the royal disfavor to himself and indirectly in his feud with Einarr; however, after hearing Óláfr's precept and profiting by Einarr's example, Halldórr succeeds in making peace with Haraldr; Bergljót's initial advice that Halldórr throw himself on Einarr's mercy led ultimately to the settlement, but she appears at the assembly with an armed force ready to fight against her own husband for her protégé Halldórr—just as Einarr is rendering his generous and peaceful decision. The story as a whole, of course, recommends conciliatory attitudes, but with the details of these attempts at intercession the author seems to be making a further statement: human mediation is not necessarily effective; if attempted in the wrong spirit it may cause further trouble (Halldórr's first attempt) or appear absurd in the face of Christian charity (Bergljót with her armed men); to have any effect at all peacemakers must proceed in humility and moderation (Bergljót's advice),[15] but to be finally blessed with success they must also be imbued with Christian intent, a reflex of divine directive (Einarr's exemplum and its effects).

The texture of the narrative in *Halldórs þáttr I* is denser in the center, in Einarr's tale, and thinner, less circumstantial, as we move outward: much is told about Halldórr's conflict with Einarr but very little about that of King Haraldr and the Icelanders. This stylistic gradation seems associated with the fact that the theme of the þáttr is expressed most explicitly in Einarr's tale, and triplication of the Alienation/Reconciliation structure could be seen simply as a kind of "redundancy" that insures communication.[16] But the meaning of even didactic literature is not the same as "information," and a better

---

15. Bergljót's advice is here simplified for the legitimate purpose of bringing out the chiastic pattern; the point to be emphasized is that her advice is sensible (in contrast to Halldórr's worse-than-useless attempt to mediate for Eilífr) but not religiously motivated and so incomplete without Einarr's story of Óláfr.

16. Richard F. Allen, *Fire and Iron: Critical Approaches to Njáls saga* (Pittsburgh: University of Pittsburgh Press, 1971), pp. 47–48, also connects stylistic density with didactic intent, though I disagree about what is taught. (Didactic aims are likely to be ethical, religious, and social, but hardly tactical or strategic.) For two interesting comments on structural replication in myth see Claude Lévi-Strauss, "The Structural Study of Myth," in *Structural Anthropology*, trans. Claire Jacobson and Brooke G. Schoepf (New York: Basic Books, 1963), p. 229 (Formalist view), and Edmund R. Leach, *Genesis as Myth and Other Essays* (London: Cape, 1969), pp. 7–9 (information theory).

view is that the teaching of forgiveness and reconciliation takes effect in concentric circles, widening out from Óláfr's precept and passing through the story's three degrees of social relations; thus the thematic function of triplication may not be mere redundancy but a way of saying that reconciliation is a value that should be carried through these three, hence all social relations. Similarly the three comrades, Bjǫrn the old man, Kolbeinn the middle-aged man, and Einarr the youth, suggest three ages of man in general and make Óláfr's words apply to everyman, including the medieval audience.

Other aspects of the art of this þáttr might be mentioned. Item: the didactic note struck when Einarr stifles his first instincts for revenge, foreshadowing the peaceful outcome and crystalizing the ethical-religious dilemma of reconciliation or revenge, and, like the final settlement, supported by a near saintly royal precept (p. 254). Item: the three examples of *sagnaskemtan* or "saga-telling for amusement" that grade off from good to evil: Einarr's implicitly religious "entertainment"; Halldórr's worldly heroic tales; and Kali's malicious satire "in prose and verse," especially his parody of Halldórr's Byzantine adventures. (Is it oversubtle to add as a fourth Óláfr's divinely sanctioned "sermon" and to compare the narrative structures of the þáttr as a whole?) Item: the choice of setting and persons, Haraldr, Einarr, and Halldórr, for the tale (compare their historical relationships and characters); conceivably even the numbers in the story and the naming of the presumably invented character Eilífr. But perhaps enough has already been said to make my point about Christian form and Christian meaning: *Halldórs þáttr I* embodies the theme of reconciliation in rather simple but skillfully articulated narrative structures that function intimately in the meaning of the story.

No ringing declarations will be risked here on the basis of one possibly isolated short story; however, few works of art are entirely *sui generis*. *Halldórs þáttr I* shows how intricately a "standard" generic form may be varied and related to theme and suggests semantic functions for structural replications and for the familiar saga aesthetic of symmetry. Formal typology is not to be expected as a widespread saga convention, of course, and I know of no exactly comparable case; however, this þáttr does suggest that some aspects of the allegorical sensibility in general and some of its techniques as found elsewhere in medieval literature may not be totally alien to the authors of ostensibly secular sagas. Like this story, most þættir and family sagas are built on conflicts manifested in violent actions and proud passions, but most end in reconciliation and restoration of social balance. However, the question posed for the family sagas by such a story as *Halldórs þáttr I* is rather how far the conciliatory values of the sagas are to be seen in specifically religious light and how a putative religious ethic is there artistically integrated with material partly transmitted by a secular tradition. Finally, the clarity of the didactic intention in the art of *Halldórs þáttr I* may partly be due to the *projective force* immanent in Christian typology, which views history as unfinished but divinely patterned, but it poses the question whether more sagnaskemtan than only that of Einarr þambarskelfir may not reveal itself in the fullness of time as directly relevant to Christian conduct. The Christian interpretation of the saga literature, despite brave hopes of a decade ago, seems now bogged down, and I suggest that if we are to realize the full consequences of the literary nature of our subject—to reap where Nordal sowed—the pot will have to be set boiling again.

Ǫgmundar þáttr dytts ok Gunnars helmings:
Unity and Literary Relations

The story preserved in chapters 275–78 of *Óláfs saga Tryggvasonar in mesta* in *Flateyjarbók* is a single þáttr, "novella" or "short story," about two heroes whose names form the traditional title: *Ǫgmundar þáttr dytts ok Gunnars helmings,* or in short title: *Ǫgmundar þáttr.*[1]

The story opens in Iceland with the family relations of the hero of the story's first half, a handsome young man named Ǫgmundr Hrafnsson. Ǫgmundr bought a ship and sailed to Norway with an inexperienced crew of Icelanders; against the advice of the Norwegian pilots, Ǫgmundr refused to lay by and insisted on continuing his approach to shore, though night had fallen, with the result that they struck and sank a longship belonging to Hallvarðr, a powerful favorite of Jarl Hákon, then ruler of Norway. After negotiations for compensation failed, Hallvarðr took personal revenge in the form of a severe blow with the blunt side of his axe. Ǫgmundr, slowly recovering through the winter, acquired the mocking nickname *dyttr* ("dint"). His kinsman Vigfúss Víga-Glúmsson, a retainer of Jarl Hákon's, had tried to persuade Ǫgmundr to pay compensation; but now he eggs Ǫgmundr to violent revenge, but without success, and Vigfúss himself tries in vain to assault Hallvarðr.

---

1. *Flateyjarbók* …, ed. G. Vigfússon and C. R. Unger (Christiania, 1860–68), I, 332–39. The þáttr is cited in the edition of Jónas Kristjánsson (below).

Ǫgmundr sails home next summer and consistently acts like a man whose voyage has enhanced his reputation though his relative Glúmr is increasingly angered at the dishonor Ǫgmundr has brought on the family and at last dismisses the young man from his home. Two years later, in the reign of Óláfr Tryggvason, Ǫgmundr voyages again to Norway, and this time he kills Hallvarðr, having first exchanged cloaks with a man named Gunnarr helmingr. When Ǫgmundr escapes and returns to Iceland, suspicion of the killing falls on Gunnarr who flees to Sweden where he obtains asylum at a temple of Freyr though it is the priestess, Freyr's "wife," and not the god-idol itself who finds Gunnarr pleasing. Tension rises between Freyr and Gunnarr, but when the time of the winter processions arrives, the Norwegian accompanies the god and his entourage. Gunnarr and Freyr finally come to blows, and with the help of thoughts of the True Faith and of King Óláfr, Gunnarr banishes the demon that had dwelt in the wooden idol. Gunnarr now dons Freyr's clothing and plays his role hoodwinking the heathen Swedes.

When news of this newly vigorous "Freyr" comes to King Óláfr Tryggvason, he suspects that Gunnarr may be involved and sends Gunnarr's brother Sigurðr to fetch him home with a promise of reconciliation. The brothers and the priestess escape with a large treasure and are welcomed home to Óláfr's court where the woman is received into the Christian Church, and they kept the Faith ever after.

Ǫgmundar þáttr is in some ways one of the most interesting of the þættir but is little known except as a document for the reconstruction of pagan Germanic religion. The typical treatment of the þáttr ignores Ǫgmundr and all events except Gunnarr's dealings with Freyr and Freyr's "wife" and uses the story to verify and flesh out the famous allusions of Tacitus and Adam of Bremen or other fragments of the reconstructed mosaic of Vanir worship.[2] Occasionally the point of view has been more specifically an attempt to show through Gunnarr's

---

2. Some examples among many: G. Turville-Petre, *Myth and Religion of the North: the Religion of Ancient Scandinavia* (New York, 1964), pp. 169, 170, 247; Jan de Vries, *Altgermanische Religionsgeschichte,* 2nd rev. ed. (Berlin, 1956–57), II, 473; Nils Lid, "Gudar og gudedyrking," in *Religionshistorie,* ed. N. Lid, Nordisk kultur 24 (Oslo, 1942), p. 112; Peter Gelling and Hilda R. Ellis Davidson, *The Chariot of the Sun and other Rites and Symbols of the Northern Bronze Age* (New York and London, 1969), p. 162; Hilda R. Ellis Davidson, *Scandinavian Mythology* (New York and London, 1969), p. 83.

impersonation of Freyr that priests played the role of the peripatetic vegetation deities in Scandinavia or to support the hypothesis of a cult drama of sacred marriage.[3]

Mainly the property, then, of folklorists and historians of Germanic religion, Ǫgmundar þáttr has been noticed by literary historians and critics only in the context of literary relations, and such notices have consistently treated the þáttr as deeply divided, in fact as two separable stories. However, there are some notable differences of nuance among these uniformly patronizing judgments. Finnur Jónsson treated "Ǫgmundar þáttr" and "Gunnars þáttr" as two independent tales, the first dating from before Snorri's time, while "to it is joined in *Flateyjarbók* the legendary, but amusing tale about ... Gunnarr ... which is certainly a later invention," and Eugen Mogk roundly declared: "der Gunnars þáttr helmings, den die Ftb. an ihn [i.e. to "Ǫgmundr þáttr"] anknüpt, hat nichts mit ihm zu thun."[4] Björn M. Ólsen agrees that "Gunnars þáttr" has been joined to "Ǫgmundr þáttr" with a "thin thread," the incident of the exchange of cloaks, but doubts that the juncture occurred late. Because the story of Ǫgmundr would "cut too short" *(snubbóttur)* if that of Gunnarr did not follow, Ólsen concludes: "Doubtless ancient oral tradition lies at the base here, and there appears to be nothing to oppose the idea that the oral tradition put these two stories together from the beginning."[5] Jónas Kristjánsson regards

---

3. For example: Krappe (cited below); de Vries, *Religionsgeschichte*, II, 192 (with references); Lid, pp. 101–02; Karl Helm, "Die Entwicklung der germanischen Religion," in *Germanische Wiedererstehung*, ed. Hermann Nollau (Heidelberg, 1926), p. 369 (repeated by Danckert, cited below, p. 164). Perhaps this is the place to remark that not only has the literary character of Ǫgmundar þáttr been obscured by such partial treatments, but as a document of Germanic religion the story has been much mishandled through partial and erroneous summaries (notable in Lid, Krappe, Helm, and Danckert) and a tendency to mix analyses and hypotheses with the objective account of the text.

4. *Den oldnorske og oldislandske litteraturs historie*, 2nd ed., II (Copenhagen, 1923), 543; *Geschichte der norwegisch-isländischen Literatur*, 2nd ed. (Strassburg, 1904), p. 217. Guðni Jónsson, *Íslendinga sögur* 8 (Reykjavík, 1947), p. viii agrees; similarly Jan de Vries, *Altnordische Literaturgeschichte*, 2nd rev. ed., II (Berlin, 1967), 430: "Der zweite Teil des þáttr ist eine selbständige Geschichte ... Die Verbindung der beiden Teile ist sehr schwach ... Man muss wohl annehmen, dass erst der Verfasser des þáttr diese beiden Geschichten miteinander verbunden hat." Partial translations of the þáttr have also contributed to the impression of disunity (e.g. *Scandinavian Folk-Lore*, selected and transl. William A. Craigie [London, 1896], pp. 26–32; Régis Boyer, *Trois sagas islandaises du XIIIᵉ siècle et un "tháttr"* [Paris, 1964], pp. 145–48).

5. "Um Íslendingasögur," *Safn til sögu Íslands og íslenzkra bókmennta að fornu og nýju*, VI: 5 (Reykjavík, 1937–39), 413–14.

the þáttr as "in fact two stories" loosely linked together, "Gunnars þáttr" having been added to "Ǫgmundr þáttr" in the original *written* version, the work of the "author"; and he agrees with Ólsen's critical analysis without agreeing with his conclusions about oral tradition: "On the edges of the *þœttir* [i.e. the two parts of the story] the material is weakest, and it is unlikely that such a weak thread will have been sustained long in oral preservation."[6]

Ólsen's position contains the contradiction that while the two parts are recognized as distinct stories, they are supposed to have belonged together in oral tradition "from the beginning," and Jónas Kristjánsson's formulation is to be preferred, though speculations about what kind of story (or combination of stories) can persevere in oral tradition is unsupported. I think there can be no doubt that in *Ǫgmundar þáttr* we are dealing with two *originally*—in a strict sense—separate bodies of story material. Just to point out the obvious: if the materials can be considered to have a historical base, it is clear that no genealogical or other personal links are supplied or can easily be imagined to account for the fusion. However, the fictional element clearly dominates whatever traces of history may be present, and the materials of the two parts stem from different realms of fiction, the first half being composed of motifs and characters drawn from Icelandic life and, as will emerge from a discussion of the story's literary relations, of typically Icelandic themes. No single source for the first half is known though it appears to have derived information from at least one extant saga.

The second part has a very different kind of source which has been studied by Helga Reuschel in an article containing a number of valid insights into the basic nature of the story but mainly intended as a caveat against naive faith in the story of Gunnarr helmingr as a document of Germanic religion.[7] The core of Reuschel's article is her argument that Gunnarr's story is an analogue and ultimately a derivative of an international tale, the earliest extant version of which is told in antiquity of the circumstances leading to the birth of Alexander the Great—a story which remained popular in various forms through the Middle Ages and which Reuschel calls the "Trug des

---

6. *Eyfirðinga sögur,* Íslenzk fornrit 9 (Reykjavík, 1956), pp. LV–LVI.
7. "Der Göttertrug im Gunnarsþáttr helmings," *ZDA* 71 (1934), 155–56.

Nektanebos." This dependence on international narrative material, it is asserted, partially invalidates the þáttr as a source of knowledge about Germanic religion.

It is well known that there is no accepted way to quantify "analogousness," and where one man sees an analogy demanding genetic connections, another sees polygenesis. In fact, A. H. Krappe had previously drawn the conclusion from similar comparative material that both certain ancient Mediterranean stories and the Scandinavian tale were "myths" based on similar fertility rites.[8] Jónas Kristjánsson points out apropos of Reuschel's analogues that "in one respect all those ancient stories ... are distinct from 'Gunnars þáttr': there the woman herself is taken in; she thinks that she is having intercourse with the god and will bear him a child."[9] This is a very basic difference, and in some ways the classical parallels cited by Krappe are closer than Reuschel's. However, none of these parallels compels the assumption of a genetic connection, and Krappe's explanation from a common ritual ought not to be entirely ruled out though I finally must agree again with Jónas Kristjánsson's formulation of the literary-historical implications of Reuschel's parallels: none of these tales could have been the pattern for Gunnarr's adventures, but that pattern must have developed out of some now irretrievably lost southern tale similar to the "Trug des Nektanebos."

Reuschel rightly qualifies the reliability of Gunnarr's story as a religious document by showing that its Christian spirit places it among the typical conversion tales that clustered around the figure of Óláfr Tryggvason and that some of its motifs are very common. However, she also insists that the ironic and satirical *tone* of the story sets it off from other saga material, that the attitude manifested toward pagan religion is "sagafremd." These pronouncements on the tone form an introduction to and support for the derivation of Gunnarr's tale ultimately from southern tales of the "Nektanebos" type, and the implication is that the tone was borrowed along with the story material. Reuschel's characterization of the satirical tone of the tale and her comparison to Enlightenment attitudes toward established

---

8. La Legende de Gunnar Half," *APS* 3 (1928–29), 226–33. Reuschel unaccountably ignores Krappe's contribution.

9. *ÍF* 9: LXIII.

religion (a comparison also made by Krappe) are apt, but she is in error in seeing this þáttr as unique or "un-Scandinavian" in this respect.[10] *Vǫlsa þáttr,* for example, is a masterpiece of Christian satire, like Gunnarr's tale late and shot through with irony yet preserving genuine vestiges of pre-Christian cult; and at a lower literary level we find a somewhat similar attitude toward the gods in *Rǫgnvalds þáttr ok Rauðs, Sveins þáttr ok Finns,* and *Friðþjófs saga.*[11] Nor is a similar ironic and comic sense missing from *Gylfaginning, Ynglinga saga,* and Saxo, and wherever the Christian euhemeristic-demonistic attitude to pagan gods is found in secure possession of the field such a tone is to be expected—compare the treatment of the Moslem "gods" in the *chansons de geste.* It is true, as Reuschel asserts, that *Ǫgmundar þáttr* is light in tone relative to saga-length works and therefore comparable to fabliaux and other short European genres in their relation to romances, chronicles, and so on, but this is true of þættir in general and cannot be used to set *Ǫgmundar þáttr* apart.[12] Finally, literary history shows, I believe, that tone is a very mutable factor in borrowing, that form—in this case a story-pattern—is much more readily preserved in borrowing than spirit.

Unity

Thus the sources and tones of the two parts of *Ǫgmundar þáttr* are obviously disparate. And while such heterogeneity is common in the saga literature—*Víga-Glúms saga* is a case in point—it is easy to see why scholars have, in the case of *Ǫgmundar þáttr,* spoken of two stories loosely joined rather than of a single saga or *þáttr* with inter-polations. An important fact has been overlooked, however, in the persistent search for genesis of materials and discussion of the mode of earliest development: whatever the ultimate origins of its constituent materials and whenever the artistic combination of materials was made (and in whatever mode: oral, literary, or some mediating condi-tion), the modern reader is presented with the fact of an artistically successful, coherent novella, indeed one of the most interesting of its

---

10. Esp. pp. 158–63.

11. *Flateyjarbók,* II, 331–36; I, 288–99; I, 387–93; *Die Friðþjófssaga ...,* ed. G. Wenz (Halle, 1914).

12. Cf. Anthony Faulkes, ed., *Two Icelandic Stories* (London, n.d. [1969]), pp. 3–4.

kind. At some point an "author" of skill and discernment composed the work as it has come down to us, and a literary critic is obliged to reconsider the þáttr in terms of "unity" and to counteract the divisive emphasis of a received opinion formulated by historians whose point of view was so firmly diachronic that they failed to notice the synchronic fact of the integral work of art before them.

Unity is a slippery concept, and in a recent article Arthur K. Moore has attacked as unrigorous many of the unity studies that litter the landscape of medieval studies.[13] Medieval works often seem to lack classical unity; consequently where literary quality is intuitively experienced as high, critics have attempted to discover underlying non-Aristotelian principles of unity. The search has, I believe, widened our knowledge even if "unity" has sometimes come to mean almost any literary excellence; some modes of unity in medieval works, for example, have been shown to depend more upon typological correspondences and other kinds of significant juxtapositions than on the primitive biographical patterns a modern reader may expect of "early" literature.

In the case of Ǫgmundar þáttr, I will try to demonstrate a unity at the level of plot, structure, and theme even though in some sense the story's bipartite nature remains obvious—a trait it shares with diverse medieval works including most notably *Beowulf* and certain sagas to be discussed. Moore cites two principles for demonstrations of unity that should be mentioned here: the mode of existence of a work (orally composed, written for oral delivery, for silent reading, etc.) is relevant to standards of unity; and interpretations of the unity of a work draw strength from relevant parallels in literature and other cultural products. The former, while undoubtedly true, is difficult or impossible to apply to Ǫgmundar þáttr in the face of so much uncertainty about the production and performance of the saga literature; however, I shall attempt to apply the latter principle in support of my reading of the þáttr.

It will be clear from the summary above that Ǫgmundar þáttr is plotted as a continuous causal sequence, each incident in the chain of events being derivable from those that precede even though the line of action does not follow a single man. The heroes of the two parts

---

13. "Medieval English Literature and the Question of Unity," *MP* 65 (1968), 285–300.

actually meet, however, and in the brilliant scene of the exchange of cloaks the "mantle of hero" is literally passed from Ǫgmundr to Gunnarr. Ǫgmundr is never formally declared "out of the saga," and the action takes place in a temporal continuum though the author suspends narrative time as he finishes his account of the events of the first part, then turns back to the point of suspension, emphasizing the continuity of the main thread of action:

> ... en Ǫgmundr hjó hann þegar banahǫgg ... kómu aptr til Íslands ok tóku Eyjafjǫrð ... Var Ǫgmundr þá með Glúmi um vetrinn í góðu yfirlæti. En nú er þar til at taka, at þá er mǫnnum Hallvarðar þótti seinkask innkváma hans, gengu þeir út ok fundu hann liggja dauðan í blóði sínu (p. 111).

Björn M. Ólsen stated that "nowhere else [other than the exchange of cloaks] do they [the two parts of the story or the two stories] extend over into each other, but rather the one tale begins where the other ends."[14] I must object that not only does the "second tale" begin before the first is ended (with the exchange of cloaks) or the first extend well into the second, but the author is at pains to resume the main action exactly where it was left. In fact no clear division between the parts can be drawn because of the artistic success of the joining, the perfectly fashioned narrative continuity.

Moreover, the author brings in Ǫgmundr again at the end of the þáttr in a reference which is so closely woven into the fabric of the narrative that it must be treated as "original" in an artistic sense:

> [King Óláfr sends Sigurðr with a pardon for Gunnarr:] "... vil ek gefa honum upp reiði mína, ef hann vill auðveldliga koma á minn fund, því at ek veit nú, at gmundr dyttr hefir drepit Hallvarð, en eigi Gunnarr" (p. 115).

Thus the hero of the first half is mentioned in a passage deeply organic to the narrative at the end of the story; similarly the king of the second half is invoked at the beginning of the whole þáttr: "Í þenna tíma váru margir menn ok gǫfgir á Íslandi, þeir er í frændsemistǫlu váru við Óláf

---

14. Pp. 413–14.

konung Tryggvason. Einn af þeim var Víga-Glúmr ..." (p. 101). This opening, informal because adapted to its context in *Óláfs saga,* orients the þáttr to the spokesman for the ethically correct in the second part even though the story begins three years before he became king. Its significance is not as an anachronism but as an authorial device to unify the novella; in addition the opening reference to kinship with King Óláfr invests Glúmr with some of the king's authority.

Structural unity is more difficult to demonstrate briefly; by this term I mean that there is a single canonical, genre-determined structural pattern underlying the plot of *Ǫgmundar þáttr.* I have argued elsewhere that this simple pattern, comprising six parts (Introduction, Journey In, Alienation, Reconciliation, Journey Out, Conclusion), can be distinguished more or less convincingly as a generic common denominator of some thirty other þættir.[15] A typical story of this type tells how an Icelander voyages to Norway, experiences some kind of estrangement from the king and is reconciled with him, often through the aid of mediators; his voyage home and a conclusion follow. In one subgroup, the generic structural pattern persists in spite of a shift in the persons who fill the "slots," a shift of dramatis personae, and *Ǫgmundar þáttr* belongs to this subgroup. This can perhaps be visualized most compactly by comparing the outlines of three þættir:

	Þorsteins þáttr forvitna	Þorgríms þáttr Hallasonar	Ǫgmundar þáttr	
Introduction:	Þorsteinn	Þorgrímr (also Kolgrímr and others)	Ǫgmundr	
Journey In:	to Norway	to Norway	to Norway	
				PART
Alienation:	Haraldr harðráði/ Þorsteinn	Kálfr Árnason/ Þorgrímr	Jarl Hákon/ Ǫgmundr (mediator: Vigfúss)	I
Reconciliation:	Haraldr harðráði/ Þorsteinn	King Magnús/ Kolgrímr	King Óláfr/ Gunnarr (mediator: Sigurðr)	PART II
Journey Out:	to Iceland	to Iceland	[missing]	
Conclusion:	prosperity and fate	prosperity and fate	wedding and future	

15. "Genre and Narrative Structure in Some Íslendinga þættir," *SS* 44 (1972), 1–27.

The structural variant found in Ǫgmundar þáttr is quite similar to that of Þorgríms þáttr; there the titular hero dies and is replaced as protagonist midway through the tale, and the hero is estranged from Kálfr Árnason, the usurping substitute king, but reconciled with the true king Magnús Óláfsson. The comparative outlines make it clear that the author of Ǫgmundar þáttr has managed to impose the generic structure on heterogeneous materials, or to take a more organic view, has selected constituent materials that were compatible with an overall schema that is genre-bound: the inherent logic of the bipartite Alienation/Reconciliation structure answered nicely to the original natural divisions of the *Stoff,* but these dichotomies have been subsumed in the larger unity. In addition the two parts of the plot bear some obvious similarities. In both a young man offends a Norwegian ruler and suffers for this in spite of the efforts of a kinsman: Ǫgmundr/Hákon/Vigfúss—Gunnarr/Óláfr/Sigurðr. Thus both parts have a cast of characters comparable to the generic pattern but have been integrated as one Alienation/Reconciliation structure.

The third and most significant level of unity, the thematic, will have emerged at least partially from my summary. Both heroes begin by violating ideals of right action; in both parts the older or more responsible relative acts as spokesman for a conventional ethic which is represented definitively in the person of the ruler.

Ǫgmundr begins to demonstrate his self-will from the time he decides to go abroad with the lukewarm support of Glúmr, and his rashness and blind arrogance are confirmed in the succeeding episodes. First he overrides experienced advice in sailing in to the coast by night; and when some of his men blame him for the resulting accident, Ǫgmundr returns the callous reply "that everyone must look out for himself."[16] Jarl Hákon recognizes that only *snápar* ("bumpkins") would have sailed so recklessly, but Vigfúss, who contrary to Ǫgmundr's dictum will consistently try to guard the interests of his kinsman, raises the possibility of compensation. The Jarl agrees but implies that such fools will not be willing to meet the high penalty he will set for the insult, and as predicted Ǫgmundr returns an arrogant "no" to Vigfúss' good advice that he settle with the Jarl.

---

16. P. 103: "Ǫgmundr svaraði, at hvárir urðu sín at geyma." Variant: "Ǫgmundr segir, at þar yrði hvárir at gæta sín, er komnir væri."

Hallvarðr himself now comes to Ǫgmundr and offers a second chance at peaceful settlement, but Ǫgmundr's self-satisfied replies elicit the hammer blow, and there follow the long recovery, the disgrace, and the mocking nickname of *dyttr* "blow, dint."

The relationship between Vigfúss and Ǫgmundr is now shifted to a new key. Vigfúss had spoken for a respectable and peaceful settlement of what was, after all, an accident, while Ǫgmundr's proud overbearing showed how little he valued another's honor and how intoxicated was his estimation of his own strength; but after Hallvarðr's dishonor-dealing blow, Vigfúss whets Ǫgmundr to revenge, to wipe clean the blotched escutcheon of their family, and charges him with cowardice. Ǫgmundr now returns what appear to be temporizing and sophistical answers claiming his shame is no greater than Hallvarðr's and refusing to take action. Again Vigfúss has spoken for the prevailing ethic, and Ǫgmundr has again, though in a different way, demonstrated his false conception of honor. In addition there has been an ironic and apparently craven reversal of Ǫgmundr's dictum that everyone should look out for himself: the chief reason for forgoing revenge, he says in speeches to Vigfúss and Glúmr, is the danger to his kinsman Vigfúss.

Having returned to Iceland, Ǫgmundr retains his self-important personality, acting as if he had garnered honor and not dishonor by his voyage; Glúmr is increasingly dissatisfied with him and at last censures him directly for the disgrace he has brought on their house. With his second voyage and revenge, however, Ǫgmundr earns Glúmr's approval, and the long delay and even the temporizing speech to Vigfúss now appear in a new light.

Gunnarr also begins as an apparently frivolous character though his personality is sketched more briefly. As the result of the exchange of cloaks, he becomes deeply implicated in the slaying of Hallvarðr, first through the loan of his garment and then through his refusal to expose Ǫgmundr. His words clearly imply his support of Ǫgmundr,[17] and his refusal to divulge what he knows about the slaying, his outlawry and flight to the wilderness proceed from his gratitude to the Icelander—and all for a particolored cloak! King Óláfr's surprise

---

17. P. 110: "'Gef þú manna heilstr,' segir Gunnarr, 'ok vilda ek geta launat þér þessa gjǫf; en heklu þessa skaltu fyrst hafa; má vera, at þér verði at henni gagn.'"

upon hearing of the slaying evidently implies that the king did not think Gunnarr had such a deed in him: "Konungr svarar: 'Hann mynda ek eigi í heldra lagi til kjósa ...'" (p. 111); and his suspicion that Gunnarr is behind the vigorous Swedish "Freyr" bespeaks the king's estimate of the lightness of his character: he would trust such a *Schwank* to Gunnarr but not a hard-minded killing.

Other characteristics shared by the two heroes are their nicknames and their taste in clothing. The þáttr had clearly explained Ǫgmundr's nickname (p. 106), and when the heroes meet their nicknames are carefully juxtaposed to help create an association between the two:

Heklumaðrinn gekk ofan á bryggjurnar ok spurði, hverr fyrir bátinum réði. Ǫgmundr sagði til sín. Bœjarmaðrinn mælti: "Ert þú Ǫgmundr dyttr?" "Kalla svá sumir menn," segir hann, "eða hvat heitir þú?" Hann svarar: "Ek heiti Gunnarr helmingr; en ek em því svá kallaðr, at mér þykkir gaman at hafa hálflit klæði" (p. 109).

There is more than accidental affinity between these two men whose nicknames apparently convey a sense of their low esteem by society at large, for nicknames bear a considerable burden of characterization in the saga literature, and the names here as so frequently are *sannnǫfn* or "true names."[18]

Both parts of the story, then, may be said to deal with the theme of identity and to portray developing characters whose allegiance to ethical norms is vindicated in the end. Ǫgmundr's divided ancestry includes his father Hrafn, a former slave of Glúmr's family, and a free-

---

18. The nickname *dyttr* is found elsewhere and clearly means "blow" (OE *dynt*, NE *dint*). E. H. Lind, *Norsk-isländska personbinamn från medeltiden* (Uppsala, 1921), s.v. *dyntr* connects it also with New Norwegian *dynt* "conceited, lazy, affected person" and suggests it may have some of these overtones; *helmingr* is attested only here as a nickname. But E. H. Lind, *Norsk-isländska dopnamn ock fingerade namn från medeltiden* (Uppsala, 1905–15), s.v. *Helmingr* instances it once as an Icelandic proper name (in one attestation perhaps taken for a nickname: "Thorstanus helming"). The derogatory sense of *helmingr* is obviously less secure than that of *dyttr*, depending on the parallel with *dyttr*, the whole context as here interpreted, the generally unflattering associations of the idea "half," and especially the fact that very many nicknames are derogatory (e.g. *hrúga*); but see further *tvískiptingr*, etc. in n. 21 below. Nicknames are one of the most common characterizing devices in the saga literature and in this, of course, reflected real life; cf. Finnur Jónsson, *Tilnavne i den islandske oldlitteratur* (Copenhagen, 1908) or in *Aarbøger for nordisk oldkyndighed og historie*, 1907, pp. 162–369. Some passages which parallel the quoted exchange of Ǫgmundr and Gunnarr are:

born mother related to Glúmr; thus the identity crisis in Ǫgmundr's case is formulated as the question whether he belongs to the noble or the ignoble line. Glúmr, whose judgments reflect the conservative ethos of the first part of the þáttr, cautions Ǫgmundr before his first voyage to seek honor above wealth:

"... nú þœtti mér miklu skipta, at þú fengir heldr af fǫrinni sœmð ok mannvirðing en mikit fé, ef eigi er hvárstveggja kostr" (p. 102).

But the result of the voyage is Ǫgmundr's *dis*honor with *in*crease of wealth ("he had made great profits on this trip"), and this mean ability to make money links Ǫgmundr to his freedman father, a "rich man" (p. 101). When Glúmr finally banishes Ǫgmundr from his sight,

---

... Grettir gekk fyrir konunginn ok kvaddi hann vel. Konungr leit við honum ok mælti: "Ertu Grettir inn sterki?" Hann svarar: "Kallaðr hefi ek svá verit ..." *(Grettis saga,* ch. 39; ÍF 7: 132).

Konungr svaraði: "Ertu kallaðr Gjafa-Refr?" Hann svaraði: "Þegit hefi ek gjafir at mǫnnum ok þó enn gefit stundum" *(Gautreks saga,* ch. 10; ed. Wilhelm Ranisch, Palaestra XI [Berlin, 1900]).

Especially interesting is *Hróa þáttr (Flat.* II, 73–80) where the hero's changing fortunes are mirrored in his nicknames (spelling altered):

"Hverr ertu?" "Hrói heitir ek," segir hann. Konungr spurði, "Ertu ófara-Hrói?" Hann svarar, "Annars væri mér meir þǫrf af yðr at þiggja en slík skjótyrði" ... Var hann þá kallaðr Hrói hinn auðgi eðr Hrói hinn prúði ... "Hverr ertu?" "Ek heiti Hrói," segir hann. "Ertu Hrói hinn heimski?" segir hon. Hann svarar, "Ek ætla þat nú vera œrit mikit sann-nefni, en átt hefi ek œðri nǫfn fyrr; eðr hvert er þitt nafn?" ... ok var hann nú kallaðr Hrói hinn spaki.

In this connection note that *dyttr* and *helmingr* also have a possible *in bono* interpretation: a "dint" is received but later also given; "half" is unflattering, but in poetry the word can mean "a host, an army." Hallvarðr also has a nickname, and the þáttr characterizes him as a formidable opponent partly by explaining it:

"Hann er nú kallaðr Hallvarðr háls, því at hann var í Jómsvíkingabardaga í fyrra vetr með Hákoni jarli ok fekk þar sár mikit á hálsinn fyrir aptan eyrat, ok berr hann síðan hallt hǫfuðit" (p. 111).

(A closely comparable nickname is attached to the historical Erlingr Kyrpinga-Ormsson in *Orkneyinga saga [ÍF* 34: 225]:

Erlingr fekk þar sár mikit á hálsinn við herðarnar, er hann hljóp upp í drómundinn. Þat greri svá illa, at hann bar jafnan hallt hofuðit síðan; var hann skakkr kallaðr.

Erlingr skakkr had a brother *Ǫgmundr drengr,* and there are narrative similarities with the motifs of the feud in *Orkneyinga saga,* ch. 61 involving Hávarðr, Brynjólfr, and *Hallvarðr.* Presumably accident and a shared stylistic grammar account for these similarities.)

the young man moves in with his father—an action with obvious symbolic significance.[19]

In his reproaches to Ǫgmundr, Vigfúss clearly articulates the dangerous ambiguity of Ǫgmundr's heritage:

"... ætla ek þér heldr ganga til þess hugleysi en varhygð, ok er illt at fylgja þeim manni, er hera hjarta hefir í brjósti; er þat ok líkast, at þér bregði meir í þræla ættina en Þveræinga" (p. 107).[20]

Later Glúmr echoes Vigfúss' speech almost point for point, and his peroration, resembling that of Vigfúss and similarly reinforced with a proverb, sets out clearly the ambiguity and therewith Ǫgmundr's choice:

"Nú er þat annathvárt, at þú ert frá því þróttigr ok þolinn sem flestir menn aðrir, ok muntu sýna af þér karlmennsku, þó at síðar sé, því at í annan stað værir þú eigi svá bleyðimannligr í bragði; ella ert þú með ǫllu ónýtr, ok verðr þat þá ríkara, sem verr gegnir, at opt verðr ódrjúg til drengskaparins in ófrjálsa ættin; en ekki vil ek þik lengr hafa með mér" (p. 108).

This speech, however, contains a new possibility beyond what Vigfúss had recognized: that Ǫgmundr is biding his time and that though

---

19. Relatively little social value was placed on a freedman, and in the literature they tend to have the unaristocratic traits of wealth through money saved (rather than inherited) and lack of courage; freedmen were often presented as trying to marry into the established families, and if they were successful the woman was said to be *gipt til penninga* "married for money" like Ǫgmundr's mother in the *Vatnshyrna* text. For example, in *Valla-Ljóts saga,* ch. 1 (*ÍF* 9: 234–36), Torfi, a rich man of undistinguished family asks for the hand of a widowed aristocrat, promising to make up for the social difference with money. Two of her sons agree, but the third objects: "... mjǫk horfir til lítillar mannvirðingar; slík maðr er ósýnn til fullræðis. Vil ek ekki samþykki þar til gefa at gefa móður mína gǫfga lausingjanum eptir gǫfugt gjaforð." The affair ends in the death of the social climber. On the other hand, the freedman Skíði in *Svarfdœla saga* (*ÍF* 9) successfully marries nobly and proves himself respectable by avenging an old injury—a development anticipated from the time we learn near the beginning of Skíði's story that "Skíði bar þræls nafn; eigi bar hann þat nafn af því, at hann hefði til þess ætt eðr eðli; hann var manna mestr ok fríðastr" (p. 163).

20. The theme of being true or untrue to one's family is often found expressed in similar words; cf. *Þorgils saga ok Hafliða,* ed. Ursula Brown (Oxford, 1952), p. 5 (l. 12): "ór sini ætt," p. 9 (l. 14): "segjask ór sini ætt," and notes pp. 58 and 63; *Laxdæla saga,* ch. 65 (*ÍF* 5: 193–94): "kváðu hann meir hafa sagzk í ætt Þorbjarnar skrjúps en Mýrkjartans Írakonungs"; *Odds þáttr Ófeigssonar* (*ÍF* 7: 372, with n. 3): "segisk í ætt"; *Víga-Glúms saga* (*ÍF* 9: 19): "vilda ek þess at bíða, er þú fœrðir þik með skǫrungsskap í þína ætt"; "ok þœtti mér þú nú eiga at vera brjóst fyrir oss ok segjask svá í góða ætt" (p. 21).

tardy he will prove to be a Þveræingr after all—something we may have suspected already from Ǫgmundr's unshaken self-confidence in the face of disgrace.

Ǫgmundr's revenge is as circumspect as his patience has led us to expect it would be. He carefully arranges his escape and even endures the jeers of his crew in order to carry out his mission perfectly; though not executed with heroic abandon, his revenge reclaims his honor and Glúmr's respect and shows Ǫgmundr's true colors:

> Fór Ǫgmundr á fund Víga-Glúms ok sagði honum sína ferð, kvað þá hefndina komna fram, þó at frestin væri lǫng. Glúmr lét þá vel yfir, kallaði þat ok verit hafa sitt hugboð, at hann myndi verða nýtr maðr um síðir. Var Ǫgmundr þá með Glúmi um vetrinn í góðu yfirlæti (p. 111).

The þáttr expends less detail on a thematically similar problem in the second half. Gunnarr is established as a rash and impulsive character, apparently a fop, and his unflattering nickname "half," along with the symbolism of his two-toned clothing, suggests a potential ambiguity of character.[21] As the story draws to a close the question of identity is clarified in terms of Christianity: Is Gunnarr an irresponsible rascal

---

21. That clothing frequently serves as a signal to the saga reader is commonplace; for example, the social implications of red or green clothing (especially proud and aristocratic persons who have traveled) or the more usual blue cloak (leaders dressed for a special occasion such as a journey or a killing) are well known. Many examples are collected in Valtýr Guðmundsson, "Litklæði," *ANF* 9 (1893), 171–98. Also see Karl Weinhold, *Altnordisches Leben* (Berlin, 1856), pp. 161–62 and G. I. Hughes, "A Possible Saga Convention," *ESA* 12 (1969), 167–73. Instances of less conventional and more subtly symbolic dress occur in *Hreiðars þáttr heimska (ÍF* 10: 248–60), where Hreiðarr's rough and common Icelandic clothing objectifies aspects of the hero's integrity and shy simplicity, and in *Svarfdœla saga (ÍF* 9: 131–32), where the ex-coalbiter and strongman Þorsteinn Þorgnýsson refuses an elaborate mantle of scarlet cloth and fur and a sword (the weapon of a cavalier) for a plain *loðkápa* and *bolǫx;* Grímr in *Gull-Þóris saga* (ed. Kr. Kålund [Copenhagen, 1898], p. 21) is a similar character in similar clothing, and Gunnlaugr ormstunga's appearance before the Norwegian king in homespun is an "objective correlative" of his obstinate provincial pride (*ÍF* 3: 68). Two-toned clothing is mentioned fairly often; see the general treatment and references in Weinhold, p. 162, Guðmundsson, pp. 173–74, Hjalmar Falk, *Altwestnordische Kleider-kunde* (Kristiania, 1919), pp. 81–83 and 155, and Cleasby-Vigfússon, s.v. *tví-* and *hálfskiptr, tví-* and *hálflitr (litaðr).* In general particolored clothing seems to be presented as distinctive, often grand, and the symbolic implications in *Ǫgmundar þáttr* are not as conventional as the opposition between Icelandic homespun and royal purple. But cf. the derogatory meanings of *hálfr* and its many compounds, the meanings and especially extended meanings of *tví-* (e.g., *tvídrœgr* "ambiguous," *tvírœði* "ambiguity," *tvískipta*

and a renegade Christian? King Óláfr's main concern, having solved
the killing of Hallvarðr, is the state of Gunnarr's soul:

> "Nú vil ek senda þik [Sigurð] austr þangat eptir honum, því at þat er
> herfiligt at vita, ef kristins manns sála skal svá sárliga fyrirfarask" (p. 115).

Like Qgmundr, Gunnarr returned home with gold; but as with
Glúmr's heroic code in the first part, allegiance to the Christian ethic
of Óláfr is far more important, and the þáttr's last sentence puts
Gunnarr's adventures in the proper perspective: "Tók hann Gunnar
aptr í sætt við sik, en lét skíra konu hans, ok heldu þau síðan rétta
trú" (p. 115).

The central episodes of Gunnarr's part of the þáttr, his dealings
with Freyr and the Freyr worshipers, also deal with the question of
identity, but I do not believe with Helga Reuschel that, in the context
of the story as a whole, it is a question of who is Freyr?[22] Rather it is
Gunnarr's ambiguous relation to Christianity (especially in the person
of Óláfr) and paganism that is at issue—a question of who is Gunnarr?

"to divide into two parts, to waver," *tvískiptiligr, tvískiptr* "divided, uncertain," *tvíslœgr*
"ambiguous," *tvísýni* "uncertainty, doubt") and *tvískiptingr* "a changeling, idiot," used
at least once as a nickname. External evidence to support the interpretation in *Qgmundar
þáttr* may be seen in the Icelandic episcopal bans of the years 1269 and 1345 against
priests wearing particolored clothing ("prestar skulu eigi bera rauð klæði, gul eða grøn
eða hálfskipt eða rend útan í vási," *DI*, II, 25.31; Falk, p. 82) and in the fact that among
the forbidden garments are "klæði *helmingaskipt*, klæði í *helmingum*" *(DI*, II, 25.31; Falk,
p.81; my italics); cf. the similar Norwegian prohibitions of 1299 and 1319 addressed to the
general public *(NgL*, III, 110 and 116; Falk, p. 82) and to the clergy *(NgL, III*, 303; Falk, p.
82) and the Danish statute of 1283: "statutum est, ut nullus portet vestes in minutas partes
incisas, sed integras *vel saltem bipartitas* (in the ODan translation "eller tweskifftæ"; Falk,
p. 82). Cf. further the symbolism of particolored women's clothing as explained by Werner
Danckert, *Unehrliche Leute: Die verfemten Berufe* (Bern and Munich, 1963), pp. 159–61
and on the whole subject Vincent Lunin, *Kleid und Verkleidung*, Studiorum Romanicorum
Collectio Turicensis, VII (Bern, 1954).

22. Contrary to Reuschel's analysis, Gunnarr's adventures (still less the þáttr as a whole)
are not concerned with the question "Ist der Teufel Freyr? Wer ist der Gott? Oder, auf die
kürzeste Formel gebracht: Wer ist Wer?" Reuschel puzzles over the fact that this question
is not answered by the story: "Auf die Frage, die hier gestellt wird, gibt allerdings die ...
Geschichte keine innerlich notwendige, wirklich lösende Antwort ... Die Lösung ist also
ganz anders, als man von der Frage her erwarten konnte" (p. 161). But it is clear from the
Christian demonistic-euhemeristic point of view that real evil powers are behind the pagan
gods; there was never any question of denying the existence of the gods, and Freyr, like Vǫlsi,
is absurd but real. Thus the question of identity is not asked in the form Reuschel puts it,
and the lack of an answer in the þáttr comes as no surprise.

The strongly marked peripeteia comes when Gunnarr, almost beaten by the devil-animated idol and at his nadir, thinks on Christianity and King Óláfr:

> "... hugsar hann þá fyrir sér, ef hann getr yfirkomit þenna fjánda ok verði honum auðit at koma aptr til Nóregs, at hann skal hverfa aptr til réttrar trúar ok sættask við Óláf konung, ef hann vill við honum taka. Ok þegar eptir þessa hugsan tekr Freyr at hrata fyrir honum... (pp. 113–14).

Gunnarr is not conceived of as a pagan, as Krappe has it,[23] but as an insecure or even lapsed Christian; in this moment he begins the defeat and ridicule of paganism that ends with his complete return to the fold, proven a loyal Christian and true subject of Óláfr.

The sharply realized scenes of the exchange of cloaks on the deserted docks of Niðarholm and the early morning killing and escape seem invested with a superliteral quality, and far from being the "weak thread" of the story these scenes are its strong central knot. The author brings together in an adventitious meeting two men in particolored cloaks; after that meeting and exchange, Ǫgmundr kills Hallvarðr and, as he is escaping, weights the borrowed hood with a stone and sinks it in the bay. Hasty readers may experience this as a blind motif like the ruse of the overturned boat in *Fóstbrœðra saga* or *Arons saga Hjǫrleifssonar,* but its realistic purpose is to make more plausible the killer's escape by disposing of the incriminating disguise. However, in context it seems also to be a symbolic action. Ǫgmundr has just attained his revenge and thus proven himself a true kinsman of Glúmr; his casting off the particolored cloak suggests a determination to have done with his earlier ambivalent status and put on the new man—a burying of the past comparable to the killing of Freyfaxi in *Hrafnkels saga.*

In the case of Gunnarr, particolored clothing helps to establish his personality and association with Ǫgmundr at the beginning of the second section. But the imagery of disguise continues to cling to Gunnarr; he travels to Sweden "allt hulðu hǫfði" or incognito. He hides his true identity at Freyr's shrine by claiming to be "a lone wayfarer, of low station

---

23. Krappe, p. 226.

and a foreigner," though the priestess partially sees through this pose: "... þú ert maðr félauss, ok kann þó vera, at þú sér góðra manna ..." (p. 112). Later he dons the idol's attire, beginning his masquerade as the god, and here the þáttr consistently speaks of Gunnarr as "Freyr"; his mumming enjoys great success: the crops flourish, offerings of gold and silver to the god (i.e. to Gunnarr) increase, the priestess becomes pregnant, even the weather improves. No symbolic casting off of Freyr's attire comparable to Ǫgmundr's disposal of the hooded capelet is made explicit, but Gunnarr and his party escape secretly by night to King Óláfr and the True Faith, presumably not still clothed as Freyr. Clothes do not make the man, but with Teufelsdröckhian logic they both reveal and conceal character.

Literary Relations

Despite the judgment of an earlier editor that the influence of *Víga-Glúms saga* on later writing cannot be demonstrated,[24] it is Jónas Kristjánsson's opinion that such influence is present in *Ǫgmundar þáttr* (as well as in *Þorvalds þáttr tasalda*) though he instances as borrowings only "the names of Glúmr's relatives at the þáttr's opening."[25] A more detailed comparison between the saga and the þáttr will support Jónas Kristjánsson's general contention. The author of *Ǫgmundar þáttr* places the otherwise unattested characters of the first part of his tale, Ǫgmundr and his father Hrafn, against the background of the well-known family of Glúmr, mentioning Eyjólfr hrúga and Ástríðr, father and mother of Glúmr, Vigfúss hersir, the Norwegian nobleman who was Glúmr's maternal grandfather, and Vigfúss Glúmsson—a genealogy that was widely known and need not have come from a written *Víga-Glúms saga*.[26] However, the main text of the þáttr also gives some non-functional information about other relatives of Glúmr:

> Helga hét systir Víga-Glúms; hon var gipt Steingrími í Sigluvík. Þorvaldr hét sonr þeira, er kallaðr var tasaldi (p. 101).

---

24. G. Turville-Petre, ed., *Víga-Glúms saga,* 2nd ed. (Oxford, 1960), pp. XIX–XX.
25. P. LVI.
26. However, cf. *ÍF* 9: 8, n. 2 on the distribution of the nickname *hrúga* with its clear reference to events told in *Glúma*.

These extraneous facts—whether original or interpolated—can most plausibly be explained as derived from *Víga-Glúms saga* where Helga, Steingrímr, and Þorvaldr are introduced to the saga twice in very similar words.[27]

Most of the placenames associated with the historical characters were well known; but *Þverbrekka,* Glúmr's home in old age, is not mentioned in *Landnámabók,* and again it seems likely that the þáttr drew this information from the saga. The residence of Hrafn, Ǫgmundr's father, in *Skagafjǫrðr* (variant: *vestr í Heraði)* seems to be fictional or to depend on traditions not recorded elsewhere, and the þáttr plausibly has him married to an unnamed woman of the *Guðdœlaœtt,* a well-known family of early settlers named for a district in upper Skagafjǫrðr. All this information is without foundation in *Glúma* or elsewhere, and Glúmr's relationship to the Guðdœlaætt seems to be an invention of the author of the þáttr.

The þáttr opens with a reference to Glúmr's kinship with Óláfr Tryggvason—information which might have been drawn from *Glúma* (p. 13) but which is also in *Landnámabók* and elsewhere, including the *Óláfs saga* in which *Ǫgmundar þáttr* is preserved. The story is set carefully in the period just before and after Óláfr came to the throne and fits well into the time scheme of Glúmr's life after his removal to Þverbrekka about 989. The association of Vigfúss Glúmsson with Jarl Hákon, not mentioned in *Landnámabók,* is brought into the saga[28] but was also available in *Óláfs* saga; Vigfúss' role and character in the þáttr answer very well to this information and to the general picture of him in the saga. The genealogical evidence, then, is not conclusive but does include items of information that could only derive from *Glúma* or some similar lost oral or written tradition. I believe that a further consideration of the literary relationship between *Ǫgmundar þáttr* and *Glúma* will support the idea of direct influence though it can never be proven conclusively.

The early parts of *Glúma,* like those of the þáttr, concern initiation and family pride. The parallel adventures of Eyjólfr and Glúmr in

27. "Glúmr hét inn yngsti sonr þeira, en Helga dóttir. Hon var gipt Steingrími í Sigluvík. Þeira sonr var Þorvaldr tasaldi ..." (p. 14); "Helga, systir Glúms, er átt hafði Steingrímr í Sigluvík ... Hon var móðir Þorvalds tasalda ..." (p. 72).

28. P. 57, *Vatnshyrna* text: "Nú gerisk Vigfúss farmaðr ok var hirðmaðr Hákonar jarls ok Eiríks, sonar hans, ok inn kærsti vinr"; *Möðruvallabók* text: "En Vigfúss var farmaðr mikill."

Norway are rites of passage into manhood; and Eyjólfr's nickname *hrúga* ("heap" or "lump") is initially given, like Qgmundr's sobriquet and probably Gunnarr's, in scorn. Eyjólfr and Glúmr, and at last also Qgmundr, prove themselves through deeds in Norway; and Eyjólfr, Glúmr, and in the end also Qgmundr return from their Norwegian adventures with both honor and wealth (cf. Glúmr's warning quoted above to get honor above wealth—if not both). Both Eyjólfr and Glúmr are distinguished for their patience, but this parallel between Glúmr and Qgmundr is especially close since both of them delayed revenge so long that they incurred the reproach of a relative—a reproach that reflects on the hero's relation to his family (with some distant verbal parallels in notes 19–20 above). Like Qgmundr, Glúmr—another "slow developer"—has to prove he is worthy of his family, and in both cases the more immediately noble family link is traced through the mother: Vigfúss hersir, the maternal grandfather, witholds approval, then accepts Glúmr; Glúmr the patriarch, a relative on the mother's side, disapproves, then accepts Qgmundr. *Glúma* itself arranges these events in a slightly jarring way since Glúmr's return to Iceland with honor and familial approval from Norway only leads to another period of lassitude until at last the tardy hero asserts himself a second time, and of course the parallel with *Qgmundar þáttr* is not a minute one.

A number of specific motifs in *Qgmundar þáttr* might have been inspired by *Glúma*. Vigfúss hersir gives the young Glúmr a sword, a spear, and a cloak, and these become psychological symbols, the outward signs of his *gæfa* or "luck." The cloaks in *Qgmundar þáttr* also seem to have a symbolic dimension though here the signification is, roughly speaking, reversed. Glúmr's cloak is prominent in his first killing in Iceland (p. 28) where Glúmr disguises his motives with a request that his mantle be mended, and Vigfúss Glúmsson comes disguised in a *skinnkufl* (hooded leather cape) to Glúmr's aid in chapter 23. In chapter 16, Víga-Skúta makes his appearance in a "vesl ... tvískipt, svart ok hvítt" (two-toned cloak of black and white), and he uses this cloak reversed as a disguise when Glúmr comes searching for him with reinforcements. This cloak seems to correspond to Skúta's tricky nature and thus resembles both sartorially and symbolically Qgmundr's "feld ... vel litan er tvískiptr er" (mantle with good coloring since it is two-toned) and the "hálflit klæði" (particolored clothing) beloved of Gunnarr. Again in the

"Víga-Skútu þáttr," Glúmr made his escape in part by throwing his cape into a river; if this incident gave a hint for the connection of Ǫgmundr's escape with his sinking the borrowed cape, it has undergone a complete seachange.[29]

Finally, *Glúma* portrays two slayings in which blame first falls upon innocent men but which at last are revealed as the work of Glúmr. The slaying of Þorvaldr krókr is foisted off upon the young Guðbrandr Þorvarðsson, and after he is declared an outlaw, Glúmr helps him flee the country (ch. 23). And in chapter 14, Ingólfr flees with Glúmr's aid bearing the blame for the killing of Hlǫðu-Kálfr; however, Glúmr admits the truth, and Ingólfr returns from exile to marry his Icelandic sweetheart (ch. 15). Both of these episodes of displaced responsibility and ultimate revelation resemble the events of the second part of *Ǫgmundar þáttr,* though the parallels with the Ingólfr incident are the more extensive (secret slaying—shifted responsibility—flight into exile—revelation of the truth—return from exile—wedding).[30]

Thus the "hard" evidence of the genealogies and the Þveræingr background of *Ǫgmundar þáttr* suggests (if it does not prove) that the author knew *Víga-Glúms saga,* and a consideration of parts of the respective plots and of certain motifs and literary devices deepens the impression of the saga's influence on the þáttr. If we step back and view the overall contours of the two works, another kind of similarity, not manifested in details, appears. The events of Víga-Glúmr's saga generally fall into two parts associated with the hero's youth and rise to power and his maturity, fall from power, and old age. Moreover, both parts seem to be marked by a peripeteia which is psychological

---

29. The events of ch. 16, the "Víga-Skútu þáttr," are also present in ch. 26 of *Reykdœla saga* (ÍF 10: 231–36). Both Skúta and Ǫgmundr employ a *tvískiptr* cloak as a disguise, but a peculiarity of the passage in "Skútu þáttr" is that *tvískiptr* seems to mean "having two different colors, one inside and one out" rather than "divided into two differently colored parts," that is reversible instead of particolored (cf. ÍF 10: 233, n. 1). Skúta's ploy resembles more closely the device whereby Þormóðr Kolbrúnarskáld escapes after a killing in ch. 23 of *Fóstbrœðra saga* (ÍF 6: 231–34): wearing a *feld tvílóðinn* (not a cloak of doubly thick fur, as Cleasby-Vigfússon have it, but a reversible fur cloak) with the black side out, he approached and killed Þorgrímr, then made his escape by reversing it to the white side and pretending to be searching for the killer.

30. However, the motif of transferred blame is found together with a cloak-reversal trick in *Fóstbrœðra saga* (where Fífl-Egill temporarily diverts suspicion from Þormóðr; cf. n. 29 above); cf. also *Gísla saga* (the death of Þórðr inn huglausi).

though chiefly reflected in external events: the early part concerning a crisis of long-delayed revenge and family pride has already been discussed; the latter part seems to have as its underlying plot another "conversion," a conversion from Freyr worship to the aristocratic, "atheistic" Óðinn cult and the resulting loss of the hero's land.[31]

Anne Holtsmark's theory that the historical Glúmr became an Óðinn worshiper (though this is only imperfectly communicated by the extant saga) seems likely enough, but the saga-writer himself may rather have viewed the religious conflict in the light of that frequent saga figure, the atheistic "might and main man." Already in middle life Glúmr lists his three *fulltrúar* (things in which one trusts) as his purse, his axe, and his blockhouse, and his "conversion" is perhaps as aptly compared with that of Hrafnkell Freysgoði, who ceased to believe in gods, as with that of Egill Skalla-Grímsson, who evidently became an Óðinn worshiper. The godlessmen are connected both with Odinism and with the virtuous pagan or proto-Christian and were often converted to Christianity in literary sources; in the end, of course, Glúmr became a Christian and died in white.[32] In any case, the second half of *Qgmundar þáttr* also (and much more explicitly) features a religious conflict in which the hero turns against Freyr and cynically makes a mockery of an aspect of Freyr worship, as Glúmr apparently does with his equivocal oath. Gunnarr's situation was, of course, very different from Glúmr's, but both works portray Freyr as personally inimical to the hero *(ÍF* 9: 88 and 112–13). In *Glúma* the underlying religious conflict is thought to be between the Freyr worship of Glúmr's *father's* family and the cynical Odinism of his *mother's* side; perhaps it is worth repeating that the first part of *Qgmundar þáttr* contrasts the father's with the mother's family (though in ethical, not religious terms) and that the hero decides for the maternal tradition.

Glúma, then, seems to be a direct source of the þáttr though the qualities that have led literary historians to comment on the duality rather than the unity of *Qgmundar þáttr* distinguish it clearly from the

---

31. Turville-Petre, *Víga-Glúms saga,* pp. xii–xv, cf. p. xxxi; "The Cult of Freyr in the Evening of Paganism," *Proceedings of the Leeds Philosophical and Literary Society,* Lit. & Hist. Sect., III: 6 (1935), 330–33; Anne Holtsmark, "Vitazgjafi," *MM,* 1933, pp. 111–33; Magnus Olsen, "Þundarbenda," *MM,* 1934, pp. 92–97.

32. G. Turville-Petre, *Myth and Religion,* pp. 263–68 and references at p. 328. Lars Lönnroth, "The Noble Heathen: A Theme in the Sagas," *SS* 41 (1969), 16–17 remarks on similarities between the pagan atheist and the proto-Christian in the sagas.

simpler biographical pattern of *Glúma*. However, significant literary relations need not all be genetic, and from the point of view of its "bipartite unity" *Ǫgmundar þáttr* resembles more closely two other þættir and a saga. *Svaða þáttr ok Arnórs kerlinganefs* is a single short story composed of two distinct episodes which are held together by a thematic unity and ordered by the rhetoric of parallelism and contrast.[33] In the first episode, Svaði, a heathen, reacts to the great famine of 975 by forcing a group of paupers to dig their own grave; he fully intends to kill them off but is thwarted by Þorvarðr the Christian, who frees the beggars, and by an act of God: Svaði is killed in a fall from his horse and buried in the grave he had meant for the beggars. (Cf. Eccl. 10: 8: He who digs a pit will fall into it.) In the second episode, Arnórr kerlinganef reacts to the hard times by bravely opposing a decision of his district council to expose and refuse to feed the old and the lame during the famine. Arnórr, though a heathen, has intuitions of the coming Christianity, and his sermon to the farmers' assembly persuades them to reverse their inhuman decision. The þáttr as a whole is a balanced contrast of a "bad" and a "good" heathen, Svaði and Arnórr, showing their contrasting reactions in similar situations and leaving no doubt of the ethical superiority of the latter. In addition, within both episodes Christian or proto-Christian conduct is contrasted with that of unreconstructed heathens, and in both the heathens' action (Svaði's and the farmers') is corrected by a Christian or proto-Christian (Þorvarðr and Arnórr). The first episode shows, further, the reward that an arch-heathen like Svaði can expect, and in the second is implicit the Christian mirror image of this reward.

Svaða þáttr ok Arnórs kerlinganefs is thus a unified short story though its titular heroes are related only by contrast and are never expressly compared. In addition the story has a certain unity of place and time, and one character, Þorvarðr the Christian, appears in both episodes. More important though is the unity the þáttr draws from the treatment of one theme in a bipartite narrative structured by parallelism and contrast.

Þórhalls þáttr knapps is organized in the same fashion.[34] In the first part, Þórhallr, who suffers from leprosy and is a heathen of good

---

33. *Flat.*, I, 435–39.
34. *Flat.*, I, 439–41.

will, has a dream vision in which a bright rider (Óláfr Tryggvason) appears to instruct him to demolish the local heathen temple, build a church with its wood, and accept the new faith when it is preached in Iceland. In the second part, Þórhildr, a heathen woman versed in black arts, has a dream in which she learns of Þórhallr's plan to tear down the temple. When she awakens, she commands her men to bring in all the livestock since any living thing in the fields will be killed by the enraged gods as they leave the district to seek a new home.

Þórhalls þáttr possesses more natural unity than *Svaða þáttr* since Þórhildr is a close neighbor of Þórhallr and is placed in direct connection with his dream and his actions; and the þáttr closes with a short account of how Þórhallr did, in fact, become a good Christian. Nevertheless, the similarity of organization between *Þórhalls þáttr* and *Svaða þáttr* is clear; both comprise two parallel episodes in which proto-Christian conduct is contrasted with heathen conduct; in both the good are rewarded (Þórhallr is healed and prospers) and the evil punished (Þórhildr loses a horse in the exodus of the gods); in both stories the events of the Christian part are the mirror image of those in the heathen part (Svaði wants to exterminate paupers while Arnórr wants to preserve the old and the weak; Þórhallr dreams of the advent of Christ, Þórhildr of the departure of the gods). The organization of *Þórhalls þáttr* is not purely thematic, but the treatment of its didactic theme in terms of parallels and contrasts makes it structurally very similar to *Svaða þáttr*.

Though it may seem an unlikely leap from these humble þættir to *Njáls saga*, we find there a similar kind of symmetry; and as with *Ǫgmundar þáttr*, the early scholarship tended to insist upon the discrete origins and early independent existence of a "Gunnars saga" and a "Njáls saga." It is no longer necessary to argue the unity of *Njála*; but it is worth repeating that when outlined according to its narrative structure, the saga clearly emerges as a bipartite construction, two feud sagas in sequence.[35] Moreover, the narrative connections between parts are, *mutatis mutandis* and given the

---

35. T. M. Andersson, *The Icelandic Family Saga: An Analytic Reading* (Cambridge, Mass., 1967), pp. 291–307. See also Richard F. Allen, *Fire and Iron: Critical Approaches to Njáls Saga* (Pittsburgh, 1971), pp. 26, 76–77, 116–17, 120, etc.; it should be clear that I agree on many points with Allen's admirable interpretation of *Njála*.

different scale of the works, hardly greater than bind the parts of the three þættir.

These four works of different magnitude share a kind of unity that depends in part on theme or the structure of ideas, and it is noticeable that all these bipartite works contrast the pagan or "heroic" ethic with the Christian. *Svaða þáttr* and *Þórhalls þáttr* present the contrast in sharp chiaroscuro though the sheer symmetry of their conception is likely to satisfy esthetically in spite of their lack of subtlety. But *Ǫgmundar þáttr* resembles *Njála* more closely in its more complex and sympathetic portrayal of the pre-Christian ethic. Ǫgmundr's story, set in preconversion times and partly in the realm of the last great pagan ruler of Norway, seems at first sight an ideal fable of a shame-honor (or "heroic") society dominated by family pride and the revenge ethic. Gunnarr helmingr's adventures, though taking place only three years after the beginning of the þáttr, seem to move through another world. Kinship, shame, and honor are here reinterpreted in a Christian sense; King Óláfr and Christianity come to constitute the absolute good which the hero must prove worthy of, and salvation replaces reputation as the supreme value. The first part shows the testing, apparent failure, and final success of a young man in pre-Christian "heroic" times, the second part, in the post-conversion period; yet the work as a whole, coming from the thirteenth century, must reflect its view of the values of the "heroic" and early Christian periods.

A similar pattern manifests itself in *Njála*. Gunnarr's life, set in pre-Christian times, is worked out in terms of a heroic ethic: Gunnarr is a martial man of honor who, through fate, the envy of lesser men, and a certain strain of hubris, loses his life fighting against odds. To some extent the structure of Njáll's story is a replication of that of Gunnarr (as, to some extent, the second part of *Ǫgmundar þáttr* replicates the first), but Njáll's fall takes place in Christian times with the attendant deeper meaning of action. Not fate but providence and not the comforts of earthly honor but a larger hope attend on the martyrdom at Bergþórshváll. Adopting Northrop Frye's simple and satisfying definitions, we may contrast the saga and the þáttr in terms of tragedy and comedy: as Ǫgmundr's and Gunnarr helmingr's stories confirm the heroic and the Christian codes through comedy, the integration of the hero into society, so

Njála ratifies them through tragedy, the isolation of the hero in death.[36]

J. R. R. Tolkien's brilliant judgment of the structure of *Beowulf* was that "it is essentially a balance, an opposition of ends and beginnings. In its simplest terms it is a contrasted description of two moments in a great life, rising and setting; an elaboration of the ancient and intensely moving contrast between youth and age, first achievement and final death."[37] This conception of narrative structure, mirroring a Coleridgean "balance or reconciliation of opposite or discordant qualities," is admirably suggestive but perhaps overly static for the dynamic work it is intended to describe. In the case of *Qgmundar þáttr* and *Njála* the two parts seem to stand in a dialectical relationship, with the Christian comedy of *Qgmundar þáttr* and the Christian tragedy of *Njála* not contradicting or invalidating but superseding the non-Christian parts by virtue of their position in Christian history and the greater burden of meaning attached to their actions.

Unity Again

Of the three aspects of unity I have discussed in *Qgmundar þáttr*—the unity of narrative continuity, the unity of generic structure, and thematic unity—the second is relatively unexplored and perhaps will prove controversial.[38] The first, the "persuasion of continuity, the power that keeps us turning the pages of a novel and that holds us in our seats at the theatre," is a relatively fragile experience; in "Myth, Fiction, and Displacement," Frye observes:

> In our direct experience of fiction we feel how central is the importance of the steady progression of events that holds and guides our

---

36. *Anatomy of Criticism: Four Essays* (Princeton, 1957; rpt. New York, 1970), p. 35.

37. J. R. R. Tolkien, "*Beowulf*: The Monsters and the Critics," *PBA* 22 (1936), 245–95; cited from *An Anthology of Beowulf Criticism*, ed. L. Nicholson (Notre Dame, Ind., 1963), p. 81.

38. Lars Lönnroth's paper "The Concept of Genre in the Saga Literature," read before the Society for the Advancement of Scandinavian Studies at Minneapolis, May 4, 1973 was an answer to some points in my article cited above. But see Børge Hansen, Folkeeventyr: Struktur og Genre (Copenhagen, 1971).

attention. Yet afterwards, when we try to remember or think about
what we have seen, this sense of continuity is one of the most difficult things to recapture. What stands out in our minds is a vivid
characterization, a great speech or striking image, a detached scene,
bits and pieces of unusually convincing realism ... in the direct
experience of fiction, continuity is the center of our attention; our
later memory, or what I call the possession of it, tends to become
discontinuous.[39]

In applying this thought to Ǫgmundar þáttr it is necessary again to
concede the heterogeneous origins of the constituents while affirming
again the narrative unity of the finished work.

Frye continues the passage quoted:

Our attention shifts from the sequence of incidents to another focus:
a sense of what the work of fiction was all about, or what criticism
usually calls its theme.

(This is a leap that has only recently been made in saga criticism.)
Theme or dianoia is the "mythos or plot as a simultaneous unity,
when the entire shape is clear in our minds":

The theme, so considered, differs appreciably from the moving plot: it
is the same in substance, but we are now concerned with the details in
relation to a unity, not in relation to suspense and linear progression.
The unifying factors assume a new and increased importance, and the
smaller details of imagery, which may escape conscious notice in direct
experience, take on their proper significance.

As Frye observes, a good reader of literature continually, if uncon-
sciously, attempts to construct a "larger pattern of simultaneous
significance" as he reads, but it is on rereading, especially, that we
consciously relate the parts to a thematic whole.

The thematic structure of Ǫgmundar þáttr emerges clearly, I think,
from such a second reading though good critics might differ over the

---

39. In Fables of Identity: Studies in Poetic Mythology (New York, 1963); the relevant
pages, from which all the quotations are drawn, are 21–26.

integration of details. For example, opinions could differ over what I view as symbolic clothing or over the thematic function, if any, of other details (such as Ǫgmundr's casting off the particolored cape). For me, those details are natural manifestations of what Frye calls *anagnorisis* or recognition, an important aspect of fiction generally and surely of Ǫgmundar *þáttr:*

> Recognition, and the unity of theme which it manifests, is often symbolized by some kind of emblematic object ... fans, rings, chains.... In any case, the point of recognition seems to be also a point of identification, where a hidden truth about something or somebody emerges into view.

Thus Ǫgmundr and Gunnarr helmingr are at last "recognized," their identities established, and the *anagnoriseis* are, I believe, bound up with the "emblematic object," symbolic clothing.

However, Frye's description and our usual literary expectations imply a single major recognition, and the dual recognitions of Ǫgmundar *þáttr* pose an interesting final problem for a theory of unity, a problem that can perhaps be freshly approached by appeal to the linguistic notion of equivalence classes. In Ǫgmundar *þáttr* the two recognitions belong together by both the criteria used by linguists in establishing equivalence classes: they show structural equivalence because they occur in similar narrative sequences and semantic equivalence by dissecting the "thought-mass" in a similar way, in other words by belonging to a single semantic class. (The class can be regarded as considerably smaller than the class of all recognitions as I hope my discussion of theme has shown.) Thus Ǫgmundr's recognition and Gunnarr helmingr's are equivalents (not identical but "equi–valent," sharing some of the same valences), probably of separate origins but now joined in a single artistic structure because of their potential equivalence. This seems to be a structural parallel to the kind of linking of equivalence classes or "coupling" that S. R. Levin has analyzed at the level of style and which he argues is the source of the heightened unity of poetic language in general and a little recognized source of unity in particular poems.[40] At the thematic level *Ǫgmundar þáttr* may be seen as a "coupling" of equivalent themes, and so it will not seem purely intuitive, I hope, to speak of *the* theme of the story or to argue (on the analogy of Levin's work) that this "coupling" lends a form of literary unity.

---

40. *Linguistic Structures in Poetry,* Janua Linguarum 23 (The Hague, 1962). My usage extends Levin's theory from "poetry" to "literature," but such an extension is obviously warrented since coupling and the special unity it brings are characteristic of what Roman Jacobson calls "the poetic function," more or less present in all literature ("Closing Statement: Linguistics and Poetics," in *Style in Language,* ed. T. Sebeok [Cambridge, Mass., 1960], pp. 350–77), rather than of "verse" as metered language (cf. Frye, *Anatomy,* p. 71); extension of the concepts of equivalence class and coupling from style to a higher level of literary organization (anticipated by Levin, p. 51) is further justified by the analogy between syntagmatic or paradigmatic aspects of language at the sentence level and at the level of narrative, and in general cf. Jacobson's article elaborating his famous thesis that "The poetic function projects the principle of equivalence from the axis of selection into the axis of combination" (p. 358).

The Masterbuilder Tale in Snorri's
Edda and Two Sagas*

"Masterbuilder Tale" designates a widespread story type in which
a human or humans bargain with a supernatural being or beings
for the construction of outstanding works of man (cyclopean
walls, cathedrals, castles) or natural features that seem deliberately
constructed (oddly shaped or placed boulders, landspits), the payment
to be something of great importance to the human if the construction is successfully completed. A deadline is a frequent feature of
the story, and the otherworldly builder is usually cheated of his hire.
The tale is found all over Europe in many versions and variants
and is usually regarded as a migratory legend or *Wandersage*[1] with
etiological function, but the existence of an Old Norse myth telling
a story of the same type and attested at least four centuries before
the earliest folktale versions poses a special problem for historical
study and is further complicated by the fact that the only certain
attestation of the myth is in the late, sophisticated handbook of
Snorri Sturluson and shows strong traces of his creative hand. Various
geographical-historical explanations of the patterns of distribution

*I am grateful to Roberta Frank and John Lindow for careful readings and significant
suggestions at various stages in the development of this article and to the Society for the
Humanities, Cornell University, where most of the work was done. A synopsis of this
paper was read in Section 61, Ninth Conference on Medieval Studies of the Medieval
Institute of Western Michigan University, Kalamazoo, Michigan, 9 May 1974.
    1. Reidar Th. Christiansen, *The Migratory Legends: A Proposed Catalogue and List
of Variants*, FFC 175 (1958), No. 7065.

and the development of the story itself are possible, but no satisfactory solution to the question posed by the parallel existence of the mythic and secular folktale modes in the same type of tale has ever been offered. To quote Jan de Vries: "As to the transition between myth and folk-tale, we grope in the dark."[2] The present paper will attempt to solve this problem by the introduction of a new analogue and the reconstruction of its history and relation to the myth. Let it be conceded in advance that a certain circularity inheres in the method, as in every attempt at deriving literary-historical conclusions from reconstruction, but justification lies in the explanatory power of the resulting genetic account.

I. Folktale or myth?

Since the Masterbuilder Tale has received a good deal of attention from folklorists and several able surveys are available, I shall sketch only briefly the main types of the tale in their geographic distribution.[3] In southern Europe the builder or builders are usually fairies.[4] In Germany, the Low Countries, and Central Europe the devil is the builder, and the reward he demands is a human soul, typically that of the contractor or his child. For example, a legend from Lower Saxony tells how a farmer was in need of an especially large barn. The devil promised to build it for him "in a single night, before cock-crow, if

---

2. *The Problem of Loki*, FFC 110 (1933), p. 76.
3. To the survey of folktale scholarship given by Inger M. Boberg, "Baumeister-sagen," *FFC* 151 (1955), 1–24 add the studies by Krohn, Egardt, and Liungman cited below and Sigfrid Svensson's review of Boberg, "Baumeistersagen," in *Rig* 39 (1956), 30–31; "Sägnerna om den första kyrkplatsen. Finnsägnen," discussants: Dag Strömbäck, Sigfrid Svensson, Olav Bö, Waldemar Liungman, and others, in *Norden och kontinenten: föredrag och diskussioner vid Trettonde nordiska folklivs- och folkminnesforskarmötet i Lund, 1957*, Skrifter från Folklivsarkivet i Lund, Nr 3 (Lund, 1958), pp. 161–90; Christiansen, *Legends*; Niels Lukman, "Finn og St. Laurentius i Lund og i Canterbury," *ANF* 75 (1960), 194–237; Martin Puhvel, "The Legend of the Church-Building Troll in Northern Europe," *Folklore* 72 (1961), 567–83; Lütz Röhrich, "German Devil Tales and Devil Legends," *JFI* 7 (1970), 28–29; see also Hennig K. Sehmsdorf, "Two Legends about St. Olaf, the Masterbuilder. A Clue to the Dramatic Structure of Henrik Ibsen's *Bygmester Solness*" *Edda* 67 (1967), 263–71. Another tale, unmentioned in the surveys, that seems to show influence of the Masterbuilder type is perhaps to be added: "Gobborn Seer" in *A Dictionary of British Folk-Tales*, ed. Katherine M. Briggs, Part A (London, 1970), pp. 277–79 and references there.
4. See Boberg, "Baumeistersagen," pp. 3–4 and notes for full references.

after twelve years the farmer would surrender to him that which was now hidden in his house." The farmer agreed, but his mother divined that the farmer's wife must be with child and that it was the child the devil was after. The devil and his helpers began building the barn the next night. The mother stayed awake; and when the barn was almost finished, she scared up the chickens so that the cock crowed before the usual time. With the cock-crow, the construction ceased, and daylight showed that one wall was still lacking; the blame was laid on a helper who had been too slow with a load of stones, and the devil took revenge on him. The barn with its peculiarities can still be seen.[5] This example is typical of Germany except for the closing, where the cause impeding the building is diverted inconsistently from the direct effect of the cock-crow onto a delayed helper. Most folklorists assume that in these stories the devil has replaced an earlier supernatural creature (such as a giant) and thus that this type of story is very old.

Denmark forms a transitional zone between the Continental versions and the very strongly attested and well-articulated Scandinavian versions where the masterbuilder is a troll or giant, the task normally the construction of a church (also frequent in the south), the most famous being localized at Trondheim, where St. Olaf is the contractor and the troll Skalle the masterbuilder, and at Lund, where Finn is the builder and St. Lawrence the contractor. The most important Scandinavian feature, however, is the addition of a clause to the contract: the troll shall earn the sun and the moon or St. Olaf's life (St. Lawrence's eyes, etc.) unless he fails to finish within the period set *or*—the new feature—unless the contractor can guess his name before the end of the set period. Folklorists have not arrived at a consensus on the origin of this feature (e.g., von Sydow derived it from Type 500 Tom-Tit-Tot, Boberg suggests wider possible sources)[6] or on the origin and spread of the Finn/Skalle type, though it is clear that the naming motif is an addition to the simpler Continental type.

In addition to these two major types, the Continental Devil-as-builder and the Scandinavian Finn/Skalle tale, there are important

---

5. Georg Schambach and Wilhelm Müller, edd., *Niedersächsische Sagen und Märchen* (Göttingen, 1855), p. 152.

6. C. W. von Sydow, "Studier i Finnsägnen och besläktade byggmästarsägner," *Fataburen* (1907), pp. 65–78, 199–218; (1908), pp. 19–27, specifically (1908), pp. 22–23.

related stories from the marginal Celtic and Baltic areas. One Celtic tale (in three variants) concerns a saint who erects a church with the help of an animal (an ox, a horse, or a reindeer); however, in one variant the building motif is overshadowed by the motif of the animal that can be eaten over and over again (e.g., Thor's goat).[7] The fuller of the other two variants tells how St. Mogue (Aidan) began work on his church one evening. There were helpers, and the walls rose rapidly; a gray horse was bringing the last load of stones, and the sun was within a foot of rising when the devil bewitched a red-haired woman into putting her head out her window and crying "Oh, musha, St. Mogue, asthore! Is that all you done the whole night?" The saint was so astounded that he and all the workmen stopped work, and the horse let the load fall. The cathedral was never finished, and the stones can be seen on the hillside nearby. This baffling, probably confused story, already compared by Kennedy to the Finn/Skalle tales,[8] seems to stand closer to the Devil-as-builder type, with the motif of female interference and the false dawn (the meaning of the red hair?). The fact that the saint has switched roles with the devil obviates the contract motif, and the Scandinavian naming motif is missing (or just possibly vestigial).

A second Celtic tale, extant in a single text localized at Stirling, is exactly like the Finn/Skalle type except that the ending (the sidhe-man Thomas flies out through the wall of the castle in a flame, leaving a hole that can be stopped by nothing except horse dung) resembles the Continental tales.[9] Finally, von Sydow and Fossenius cited as parallels several Celtic tales in which a giant enters the service of the hero Fionn and requires an extraordinary reward.[10] Though there is some resemblance to the Scandinavian tales in isolated motifs, the Fionn stories as a whole are not convincing analogues.

In the Baltic area related tales have two giants as builders in compe-

---

7. For references and summaries see C. W. von Sydow, "Tors färd till Utgard," *Danske studier* (1910), pp. 96–97; there are four variants here if von Sydow's Irl. 6 is close enough to count.

8. Patrick Kennedy, ed., *Legendary Fictions of the Irish Celts* (London, 1866), pp. 340–42.

9. James MacDougall, *Folk Tales and Fairy Lore*, ed. G. Calder (Edinburgh, 1910), pp. 168–73; first cited in this connection by Mai Fossenius, "Sägnerna om trollen Finn och Skalle som byggmästare," *Folkkultur* 3 (1943), 82–86.

10. C. W. von Sydow, "Iriskt inflytande på nordisk guda- och hjältesaga," *Vetenskaps-societeten i Lund: årsbok* (1920), pp. 26–27; Fossenius, pp. 74–78.

tition, and in a few St. Olaf does the work himself but falls like Skalle at the last minute. Some variants of this form give Olaf a satanic helper, and others have a motif of female interference.[11]

Finally, we find the Masterbuilder legends sparsely attested in Iceland. In addition to the story of the building of the church at Reyni, obviously a late derivative from the mainland Scandinavian Finn-type which can be ignored here,[12] Iceland has offered only one example of these legends: the famous myth of the building of Asgard. In chapter 42 of *Gylfaginning* Snorri tells how a craftsman came to the gods and offered to build, in a year and a half, a great fortress in which the gods would be safe from attacks of the giants, but he required as his price that he should have Freyja as his wife and also the sun and the moon. The gods retired to take counsel and made a plan. They agreed but set terms that they thought would make it impossible for the workman to keep his end of the bargain, for the work was to be done in one winter and with no aid, but they allowed the craftsman the use of his stallion Svaðilfari. The craftsman and his horse worked chiefly at night, hauling great boulders for the walls, and three days before the end of winter the task was almost finished. The gods, however, hit upon a plan to thwart the completion of the work: Loki took on the form of a mare, luring the stallion away for one night and halting the building. The craftsman, when he saw that the work would not be finished on time, fell into a "giant-rage." The gods then called in Thor, who immediately killed the giant, breaking all oaths.[13]

Gerhard Schoening (1762) was probably the first to compare this myth to the Masterbuilder Tale which he knew in the form connected with Trondheim Cathedral (Skalle's reward to be the sun and moon or St. Olaf himself),[14] and almost all commentators since have agreed that

---

11. For discussion and references see Boberg, "Baumeistersagen," pp. 11–12 and notes.

12. Jón Árnason, ed., *Íslenzkar þjóðsögur og ævintýri* (Leipzig, 1862–64), I, 58, discussed by Einar Ólafur Sveinsson, "Islandske Folkesagn," *Nordisk kultur* 9 (Copenhagen, 1931), 188–89 and *Um íslenzkar þjóðsögur* (Reykjavík, 1940), pp. 47–49.

13. Snorri Sturluson, *Edda: Gylfaginning og prosafortellingene av Skáldskaparmál*, ed. Anne Holtsmark and Jón Helgason, 2nd ed. (Copenhagen, 1968), pp. 45–47; as far as possible quotations are from this edition (abbreviated *Edda*); otherwise from *Edda Snorra Sturlusonar*, ed. Arnamagnaean Commission, 3 vols. (Hafniae, 1848–87) (abbreviated AM) or *Edda Snorra Sturlusonar*, ed. Finnur Jónsson (Copenhagen, 1931) (abbreviated FJ).

14. *Beskrivelse over den vidt berömte Domkirke i Trondhjem*; cited by Fossenius, p. 73.

the similarity between this myth and the folktales is too great to be accidental. The search for a genetic explanation of the similarity offers the familiar three choices of comparative studies, but most commentators have excluded polygenesis because the similarities are both systematic and detailed and do not seem to be rooted in some common social reality such as a widespread type of ritual. Of the remaining explanations, descent from a common original form and derivation of the folktale from the myth or the myth from the folktale, the first has been the most popular though diffusion in both directions has also been proposed, as the following review of opinions will show.

The mythologically oriented folklorists of the nineteenth century were in agreement that the *Sagen* were all descended from the myth, survivals in folk memory of a Germanic myth that Christianity had been able to modify but not suppress, though they did not agree on the exact meaning of the nature symbolism they saw in the myth.[15] More important is the remarkably forward-looking explanation of Sophus Bugge (1881–89), for whom the myth was to be understood within his radical thesis that a great number of Scandinavian heroic legends and myths "reflect or at least developed under the influence of tales, poems, legends, religious or superstitious concepts which the heathen or half-heathen Scandinavians in the British Isles during the Viking period heard from Christians, especially monks and persons educated in monastery schools"—that is, that much of Old Norse narrative is traceable to Judeo-Christian and Classical culture.[16] Bugge rejected the prevalent notion among the older researchers that the folktale was the detritus of the myth, pointing out that the folktale is distributed far beyond the Germanic areas, that the folktale appeared in too many variant forms to be derivable from a single myth, and that there is no trace of the divine personages of the myth, especially Loki, in the folktale. Instead he proposed that a folktale closely related to the ones still current "formed the main basis for the Eddic myth, with which several other elements, quite

---

15. Jacob Grimm, *Deutsche Mythologie*, 2nd ed. (Göttingen, 1844), pp. 514–16; Karl Simrock, *Deutsche Mythologie*, 6th ed. (Bonn, 1887), pp. 55–57; Otto Henne-Am Rhyn, *Die deutsche Volkssage*, 2nd ed. (Leipzig, 1879), pp. 384–92. Sveinsson, *Þjóðsögur*, pp. 47–49 apparently still holds with descent.

16. Sophus Bugge, *Studier over de nordiske Gude- og Heltesagns Oprindelse*, 1. række (Christiania, 1881–89), I, 8–9.

unlike in origin, have fused."[17] After indicating the points at which the myth had diverged from the folktale, Bugge introduced the Laomedon legend (the building of the walls of Troy) as the source of the deviant elements, and he proposed a specific version of the Troy legend, that of the First Vatican Mythographer, as the source; the nexus to Norse myth will have been made in Ireland where the version of the First Vatican Mythographer was known and used in a Troy-book. Bugge shows how individual features of the Troy story were taken out of context and worked into the folktale to give the version known in Old Norse myth. For example, the famous crux *Vǫluspá* 25: "hverr hefði lopt allt / lævi blandit,"[18] is explained as reflecting Apollo's actions after he had been cheated of his reward: "Unde indignatus Apollo pestilentiam eis inmisit." Snorri himself, according to Bugge, did not fully understand and so paraphrased *Vǫluspá* as "hverr því hefði ráðit at spilla loptinu ok himninum svá at taka þaðan sól ok tungl ok gefa jǫtnum." The phrase "the sun and the moon" is explained as drawn from the current folktale—a secondary influence of the tale.

It will not be necessary to mention all the features supposedly drawn from the Laomedon story to show the faults of Bugge's admittedly brilliant theory. His assumption that a *living myth* was drawn from a folktale is unproven and as unjustified as the opposite notion found among Grimm and the older mythographers: that a genuine common Scandinavian myth should have been generated in the narrow and partly bookish way Bugge's theory requires is very unlikely. Nor is the extraction of motifs out of context a plausible process. Why should it have become an article of North Germanic faith—presumably the significance of a "myth"—that Loki poisoned the air because in a different context and in a text with very questionable connections with the North Apollo, whose role in the story corresponds to the builder, not to Loki, "sent them a pestilence?" (The myth-forming process might better have hit upon the revenge taken by the other builder in

---

17. Ibid., p. 259 and generally pp. 257–65. Another early denial that the Christian legends could be descended from a Germanic myth was that of Henrik Schück, *Studier i nordisk litteratur- och religionshistoria*, I (Stockholm, 1904), 21.

18. Thus the text cited in the *Prose Edda;* an important variant, *hverir* for *hverr,* is found in the Codex Regius of the *Elder Edda* (cited throughout from *Edda ...*, ed. G. Neckel, I. Text, 4th ed. rev., Hans Kuhn [Heidelberg, 1962]).

the Latin mythography since "Neptune sent a great whale!") Finally, Bugge's attitude toward Snorri and the *Vǫluspá* is not sufficiently critical; though he recognizes some disagreements between them, he basically accepts both as presenting a living Germanic mythology.

A turning point in the study of the prose *Edda* came with the later work of Eugen Mogk (1920s and 30s);[19] though he did not write specifically on the Asgard story, the scholarly movement started by him is very important, I believe, for finding a satisfactory solution to the Asgard problem. Mogk argued that most of the sources of Scandinavian mythology known to Snorri are also known to us; much has survived in the *Poetic Edda*, skaldic poetry, and verse cited by Snorri himself; and after all Snorri was writing two and a quarter centuries after the conversion in Iceland. It becomes necessary, then, to view critically Snorri's use of his sources, and the possibility arises that some of the stories not attested in verse are fabricated by the author himself. In fact, Mogk went so far as to argue that Snorri had a kind of school of mythological romancers at Reykjaholt; and while most scholars have thought Mogk's case overstated and believed with Anne Holtsmark[20] and Jan de Vries[21] that Snorri did have access to more information about Old Norse paganism than we do, Mogk's *Quellenkritik* is now recognized as a vital principle for dealing with Snorri's *Edda*.

That is, it is recognized among traditional, philologically oriented scholars, not, however, by Georges Dumézil in his important study of Loki (1948). There Dumézil wittily and sometimes personally attacks Mogk and is able to damage some specific analyses of Mogk's.[22] Dumezil's attempt to vindicate the Asgard story as myth is, however,

---

19. Eugen Mogk, *Novellistische Darstellung mythologischer Stoffe Snorris und seiner Schule*, FFC 51 (1923) and "Zur Bewertung der Snorra-Edda als religionsgeschichtliche und mythologische Quelle des nordgermanischen Heidentums," *Berichte über die Verhandlungen der sächsischen Akademie der Wissenschaften zu Leipzig*, Philol.-hist. Kl. 84 (1932), 1–18. The critical spirit is felt before Mogk in Sigurður Nordal's brief discussion of the Asgard story in *Snorri Sturluson* (Reykjavík, 1920), pp. 124–25: Nordal is cautious about taking *Gylfaginning* as a source of pagan religion but believes that the Masterbuilder story is an example of Snorri's being better placed to interpret *Vǫluspá* than we are; yet Nordal points out that Snorri tells the myth as the *first* building of Asgard while a consecutive interpretation of the poem requires that it be a *rebuilding* after the war with the Vanir.

20. Anne Holtsmark, *Studier i Snorres mytologi*, Skrifter utgitt av Det Norske Videnskaps-Akademi i Oslo, II. Hist.-Filos. Kl., N.S. 4 (Oslo, 1964), p. 5.

21. De Vries, *Problem*, p. 288.

22. Georges Dumézil, *Loki* (Paris, 1948), pp. 81–109.

turned against Jan de Vries who had treated the story to an exemplary piece of *Quellenkritik* in his book *The Problem of Loki* (1933).[23] The main accomplishment of this section of de Vries' book is to have proven that the Asgard story is wrongly imposed on stanzas 25–26 of *Vǫluspá*, which seem to refer to quite another situation. This is the main point and the one on which Dumézil attacks him, to my mind without effect. The remainder of de Vries' discussion is less satisfactory. He sees the logic of the assumption Mogk would have made, that Snorri composed the myth himself, though he is unwilling on principle to accept this. He believes that Snorri knew the story as a "myth from oral tradition" (p. 76), and yet his reconstruction of the original form of this myth does require a number of innovations by Snorri: the connection between the building story and the birth of Sleipnir is "an arbitrary combination of Snorri or one of his predecessors" (p. 77); the role of Thor at the end of the story is an accommodation to lines from *Vǫluspá* 26 ("Þórr einn þar vá / þrunginn móði, / hann sialdan sitr / er hann slíkt of fregn") since in the original de Vries imagines Loki as acting singly on behalf of the gods. On the largest issue at stake, "the transition between myth and folk-tale," de Vries can offer no help (p. 76).

The most recent discussion of the Asgard myth, by Anna Birgitta Rooth (1961), is inconclusive from our point of view; this is perhaps due to the exclusive focus of her book on finding the unique and therefore original elements in the figure of Loki.[24] Rooth does, however, accept de Vries' demonstration of the independence of *Vǫluspá* 25–26 from Snorri's myth and seems to approve also of Bugge's general approach.

One of the most comprehensive early discussions of the Asgard story was that of the folklorist C. W. von Sydow (1908).[25] Though he recognized some innovations on Snorri's part, von Sydow does not dwell on the question of the relation of Snorri's prose to *Vǫluspá* but accepts the story as presented in Snorri's *Edda* as a reflection,

---

23. De Vries, *Problem*, pp. 65–82; Dumézil, pp. 124–29.

24. Anna Birgitta Rooth, *Loki in Scandinavian Mythology*, Skrifter utgivna av Kungl. Humanistiska Vetenskapssamfundet i Lund, 61 (Lund, 1961), pp. 35–41. See the review by Anne Holtsmark, "Loki—en omstridt skikkelse i nordisk mytologi," *MM* (1962), pp. 81–89.

25. *Fataburen* (1908), pp. 24–27.

if distorted, of a heathen myth or legend. He solves the problem of the myth's relation to the Finn/Skalle tale in very broad strokes by tracing them as narrative patterns to a single ancestor (hypothetical but resembling *Alvíssmál)* and then accounting for divergent developments such as the introduction of the naming motif in the folktale from the Titeliture märchen (Type 500) and the role of Loki in the myth as an extrapolation from other stories about Loki. De Vries has criticized some details in von Sydow's interpretation (pp. 67–68), but more important is the fact that von Sydow sheds no light on the relation of Snorri to his sources or on the genuineness of the myth, and as to the relation between myth and folktale we still "grope in the dark."

In later work (1920) von Sydow sought to derive the original of both the myth and the Scandinavian Finn/Skalle tale from an Irish source.[26] This explanation was adopted and more fully set forth by Mai Fossenius (1943), who argued as follows:[27] motifs from the Irish Saint-as-builder story combined with motifs from the stories in which a giant serves Fionn MacCumal. The payment of the sun and the moon was due to a misunderstanding of the common Irish oath meaning "I swear by the sun and the moon." Original Norse material was blended in, formed on the pattern of other episodes in the mythology: Freyja, always desired by the giants, was to be the reward; Loki, often rescuer of the gods and sometimes found in the form of a woman, combines those two roles with his role as troublemaker; Thor, perpetual enemy of giants, puts a period to the story; and the purpose of it all is to explain how Loki gave birth to Sleipnir. Fossenius thinks the Finn/Skalle tale had a parallel development to that of the myth (taking on the naming motif, etc.). Most readers will not find this a very satisfactory explanation of the formation of a myth or of its relation to folktale analogues. The derivation of the sun and moon as reward from a misunderstood oath (which is not even shown to occur in any extant variant of any analogue) can be safely rejected;[28] and the parallels from the Fionn-cycle are too general to carry weight. A point by point criticism is unnecessary, but the result of a close examination of Fossenius' and von Sydow's Irish arguments will be the recognition that a Celtic origin is unproven and

---

26. Von Sydow, "Iriskt inflytande," pp. 26–27.
27. Fossenius, pp. 73–86.
28. With Boberg, "Baumeistersagen," p. 7.

in any case would not meet the fundamental objections already raised to von Sydow's earlier work as an explanation of the relationship of the myth to the tales.

Another folklorist, Friedrich von der Leyen, listed briefly the correspondences between various myths and various folktales or folktale motifs, including the Asgard story, in his monograph *Das Märchen in den Göttersagen der Edda* (1899).[29] Von der Leyen and the folkloristic approach in general are brilliantly criticized by Dumézil, in a chapter entitled "Les Abus de la 'science des contes'," chiefly for the atomistic attention to scattered motifs to the neglect of the whole; besides, nothing is "explained" by the accumulation of parallel motifs, except insofar as it is implied that all this material, mythic and folkloristic, somehow constitutes a single corpus. Dumézil's critique of von der Leyen is well-founded; thus it is all the more striking that he is forced to note that the parallels to the Asgard story are not "des motifs de contes pris de droite et de gauche et artificiellement associés, mais exactement *un type de conte* fidèlement suivi" (p. 117).

Kaarle Krohn touched on our subject in his lectures on Old Norse mythology (1922) and in his survey of research on fairy-tales (1931).[30] He is in agreement with von Sydow on the ultimate origin of this kind of story in the amazement of the folk at great works of man or nature but, in accord with his radical attempt to trace most of Scandinavian mythology directly to Christian legends, assumes a simpler form of migration from the south, with additions from other story types, to explain both the Finn/Skalle tale and the myth of Asgard. This is generally convincing for the legend, but Krohn's explanation for the myth is not adequate: "Der Asgardmythus bei Snorri braucht jedoch nicht älter als die kirchenbausage zu sein, aus der er hergeleitet werden kann. Auch ist es nicht nötig, eine andere übergangsform für die sage vom kirchenbau des riesen anzunehmen als die angeführte von der nächtlichen arbeit eines wichtes, um ein gewöhnliches bauwerk aufzuführen. Die entwicklung ist in folgender

---

29. Friedrich von der Leyen, *Das Märchen in den Göttersagen der Edda* (Berlin, 1899), pp. 38–39; see also his "Kleine Anmerkungen zu den Göttergeschichten der Edda," in *Edda-Skalden-Saga: Festschrift zum 70. Geburtstag von Felix Genzmer*, ed. H. Schneider (Heidelberg, 1952), pp. 87–91.

30. Kaarle Krohn, *Übersicht über einige Resultate der Märchenforschung*, FFC 96 (1931), 114–22; slightly altered from his *Skandinavisk mytologi: Olaus-Petri-föreläsningar* (Helsingfors, 1922), pp. 195–202.

richtung vor sich gegangen: eine sage von einem bauern und einem
wichte, eine legende von einem heiligen und einem riesen, ein mythus
von göttern und einem riesen" (pp. 121–22). This is simple and intelli-
gible, but it brings the North Germanic mythopoeic age down almost
to the conversion period (the oldest recorded story that bears a
moderately close resemblance to the Masterbuilder Tales seems to
be one from the ninth century).[31] Of course, all the supporting
evidence deriving Old Norse mythology from Christian legends is
equally questionable, and finally there is no attempt here to come
to terms with the peculiar nature of the sources, especially with the
discrepancies between Snorri and the *Vǫluspá.*

Krohn added a new twist to the discussion by relating the myth
also to a different group of stories that feature a marvelous horse.
Here a man captures a gray horse and performs amazing feats of
labor—sometimes of construction—with it. At the end of the day the
strange horse is freed and leaps into the sea, proving to be a kelpie
(Icel. *nykur,* Sw. *bäckahäst, vattenhäst,* etc.). A variant of this story
is attested in *Landnámabók,* and in a modern Icelandic variant the
kelpie, who had been used to build a church wall, gives it a kick with
his hoof in parting; the resulting hole cannot be stopped.[32] Dumézil
succinctly criticized this "parallel" to the Asgard story: "Même là,
nous sommes loin de la seconde partie du 'mythe' scandinave: Loki
se métamorphosant en jument, détournant de son service le cheval du
géant et mettant bas, lui-même, quelques mois plus tard, le cheval à
huit pieds, le coursier d'Odhinn, Sleipnir" (pp. 118–19).

Nevertheless, the idea that stories about the Kelpie-as-workhorse
were the basis of the Asgard myth was taken up and developed by
Brita Egardt (1944).[33] Egardt compares the Irish story of St. Mogue,
the Asgard myth, and two stories, one Irish, one Icelandic, from the
international stock of Kelpie-as-workhorse tales and finds that they
have three factors in common: (1) the horse has amazing strength; (2)
it is used as a workhorse on a building project; and (3) in two of these

---

31. Boberg, "Baumeistersagen," p. 4 and note.

32. References in Sveinsson, N F 9, pp. 197–98, n. 41 and Egardt, cited below, pp.
162–64.

33. Brita Egardt, "De svenska vattenhästsägnerna och deras ursprung," *Folkkultur*
4 (1944), 119–66, esp. 159–64. The honor of first connecting Svaðilfari with the kelpie
probably belongs to A. Kuhn and W. Schwartz, edd., *Norddeutsche Sagen, Märchen, und
Gebräuche* ... (Leipzig, 1848), p. 476, note; this story is quoted by Egardt.

four stories the horse is gray, while in the Asgard story the descendent Sleipnir is gray. Egardt herself observes that it is a property of supernatural horses to be gray. Moreover, horses *are* used for riding and hauling; and unless we wish to call all supernatural horses kelpies, it seems necessary to reject this overgeneral approach.[34] It goes without saying that Svaðilfari is not an ordinary horse, any more than the builder is an ordinary man, and Egardt's conclusion seems to be based on very thin evidence: "... Asgårdssägnen består av en kontamination av åtminstone två olika sägner, varav den ena utgöres av den om vattenhästen som arbetshäst vid bygge" (p. 164).

Waldemar Liungman (1958–59) apparently took up Egardt's suggestion when he came to give a definite answer to our question as he poses it: "Men varifrån kommer då myten om Asgårds uppbyggande?"[35] He rejects the connection with the Finn/Skalle-*Sage* because the myth lacks what he calls the most important points of the *Sage*: the name guessing, the cradle song, the setting up of the tower or insertion of the last stone (p. 332). But this is far too limited a conception of the most important points of the folktale and ignores the Continental and Irish analogues without the naming motif and its dependent, the cradle song. Liungman's solution is that the Kelpie-as-workhorse, in a form in which the horse is owned by a giant, is the basis of the myth. In criticism it should be observed that the connection Liungman draws is based on a single *dramatis persona,* the supernatural horse or other animal; but secure parallels of this kind should be based on the network of relations among a number of *dramatis personae,* in short upon the structure of a story, supported if possible by details of content. Liungman's conjectural stage with a giant as owner of the horse is plausible enough in a version of the Masterbuilder legend (indeed it is found in the myth), but it would be out of place in the kelpie stories where the kelpie is almost by nature a masterless creature. It is unnecessary to point out other obvious differences between the Masterbuilder

---

34. As Fossenius, p. 77, rejected von Sydow's comparison with "The Pursuit of Gilla Dacker and his Horse," obviously a novelistic adaptation of a Kelpie-as-riding-horse legend.

35. Waldemar Liungman, ed., *Sveriges sägner i ord och bild,* III (Copenhagen, 1959), 331 and generally 67–82, 275–338, II (1958), 39–50, 356–57; and cf. III, 83–94, 338–42.

Tales, including the Asgard myth, and the kelpie stories;[36] they share nothing beyond the supernatural horse with his marvelous strength.

Since Rooth's work the problem of Asgard has not been treated directly,[37] but it is important for our proposed solution to point out that recent scholarship on Snorri's *Edda* has been more in the spirit of Mogk than of Dumézil, and it now seems most significant to scholars to explicate the attitude of Snorri and his time toward his subject. This line of scholarship has culminated in recent years in Walter Baetke's brilliant *Die Götterlehre der Snorra-Edda,*[38] Anne Holtsmark's *Studier i Snorres mytologi,* and Byrge Breiteig's "Snorre Sturlason og æsene."[39] In these works attention has been focused on Snorri's euhemerism, or rather the mixed euhemerism and demonism that Snorri adopted from the medieval church as his way of coming to an understanding of his pagan ancestors' religion; and in spite of some dissenting voices,[40] the *Edda*'s Prologue or "Formáli," which sets out in detail a learned interpretation

---

36. One point of difference which may not be obvious can be mentioned: apparently the kelpie is mainly useful during the *day*; in *Landnámabók*, Auðun stoti captured an applegray kelpie in the usual way, and: "Hestrinn var góðr meðfarar um miðdegit; en er á leið, steig hann í vǫllinn til hófskeggia; en eptir sólarfall sleit hann allan reiðing ok hlióp til vatsins" *(Sturlubók,* ch. 83; *Fortællinger fra Landnámabók,* ed. Jón Helgason [Copenhagen, 1963], p. 67). An exception is the story in Kuhn and Schwartz, p. 476. In contrast, the Masterbuilder's work normally goes on at night.

37. The remarkable essay of Wolfgang Laur, "Die Heldensage vom Finnsburgkampf," *ZDA* 85 (1954–55), 107–37, should also be mentioned in this survey. Laur's aim is to show that the story of the fight at Finnsburg (reconstructed from the OE *Finnsburg Fragment,* the Finnsburg Episode in *Beowulf,* and allusions in *Widsith)* is derived from a myth like that of the building of Asgard. Laur relies heavily on von Sydow and throws no independent light on any matters of concern to the present article; but his view, if acceptable, would support the traditional views of the Asgard story as genuine myth. However, his procedure is so arbitrary that I cannot accept it even on its own terms; for further strictures see Klaus von See, *Germanische Heldensagen* (Frankfurt, 1971), pp. 50–51.

38. *Berichte über die Verhandlungen der sächsischen Akademie der Wissenschaften zu Leipzig,* Philol.-hist. Kl., Bd. 97, Heft 3 (Berlin, 1950).

39. *ANF* 79 (1964), 117–53; and in a similar vein, A. H. Krappe, "Die Blendwerke der Æsir," *ZDP* 62 (1937), 113-24.

40. Lars Lönnroth, "Tesen om de två kulturerna: Kritiska studier i den isländska sagaskrivningens sociala förutsättningar," *Scripta Islandica* 15 (1964), 79–83; Anker Teilgard Laugesen, "Snorres opfattelse af Aserne," *ANF* 56 (1942), 301–15, esp. 309–13; Andreas Heusler, *Die gelehrte Urgeschichte im altisländischen Schrifttum* (Berlin, 1908); see the full review in Breiteig.

of Germanic paganism and prehistory, can now be regarded as Snorri's work and integral to the *Edda* as a whole.[41]

II. A New Analogue

The previous scholarship, then, yields few firm conclusions for the question posed above: myth or folktale? However, a new Icelandic analogue may offer a way around the impasse: the story of the berserk builders in *Heiðarvíga saga* (chapters 3–4) and *Eyrbyggja saga* (chapters 25 and 28) tells how Víga-Styrr acquired two berserk followers. For a time they were content taking part in his feuds; but soon one of the berserks fell in love with Ásdís, Styrr's daughter, and asked her hand in marriage. Styrr consulted Snorri goði and formed a plan to rid himself of the threat of the uncouth berserks. He agreed to give Ásdís to the berserk on the condition that the latter perform certain Herculean building tasks—clear a path across the lavafield to Vermundr's farm, erect a wall at the boundary of Styrr's land, and construct a sheepfold. While both berserks were engaged on this work, Styrr himself built a bathhouse; and when the berserks had finished their work, he enticed them inside where they were scalded and finally killed as they attempted to escape. They were buried in the lavafield near the site of their great works.[42]

In spite of its realism the story of Víga-Styrr and the berserks is easily recognizable as legendary material. The etiological element, though not explicit in either saga, is unmistakable and probably survives from a presumptive oral stage: the modern name of the lavafield and adjoining farm is Berserkjahraun, and the path is called Berserkjagata.[43] But beyond these

---

41. The unity of the *Prose Edda* is effectively argued by Baetke, Holtsmark, Breiteig, and Elias Wessén, ed., *Codex Regius of the Younger Edda* ..., Corpus codicum Islandicorum medii aevi, 14 (Copenhagen, 1940), pp. 11–28.

42. *Heiðarvíga saga* (abbreviated *Hv*) is cited from *Borgfirðinga sögur*, Íslenzk fornrit 3 (Reykjavík, 1938), ed. Sigurður Nordal and Guðni Jónsson; *Eyrbyggja saga* (abbreviated *Eb*) from Íslenzk fornrit 4 (Reykjavík, 1935), ed. Einar Ólafur Sveinsson and Matthías Þórðarson.

43. So Kr. Kålund, *Bidrag til en historisk-topografisk beskrivelse af Island*, I (Copenhagen, 1877), 432–34; but cf. n. 67a below.

general features of oral legend, the tale of the berserks exhibits too many systematic structural similarities to the folktales of the Masterbuilder type to be entirely independent of them. It is, however, very plain that the story in the sagas agrees still more closely with Snorri's myth, where the actors, the relationships among them, and the overt actions form close parallels: Styrr/the gods promise Freyja/Ásdís to an uncouth suitor, the giant/the leading berserk, as payment for a miraculous building feat; the giant/berserk asks for and is allowed the aid of a single helper, his horse/his brother *(Hv* only). The work goes on especially at night *(Hv* only?), involves the hauling of great boulders, and is a wonder to ordinary gods/men. When the work is nearly finished, the contractor, the gods/Styrr, sends a female, Loki as mare/Ásdís, out to approach the workers (only in *Hv* is Ásdís explicitly *sent*). In some way she disturbs the work in progress; and directly afterwards the giant/berserks are slain by Thor/Styrr. Naturally the stories do not coincide in every detail; but the structural similarity and correspondence in details is more than enough to assign the story of the berserk builders to the general type of Masterbuilder Tale. A detailed study of the saga tale in relation to the myth and folktales is in order.

(1) Comparison between the conference of Styrr and Snorri goði and the first or second council of the gods suggests itself as a further similarity of detail, and many of the folktales have a similar feature that might be called "outside advice"; but neither of these councils of the gods coincides exactly in position to the conference in the saga. This discrepancy points to the chief difference in structure between the story in the sagas and the folktale: in the folktale forms the *initial moment* is usually the human contractor's need to raise a building, while in *Eyrbyggja saga* the initial moment is clearly the desire of the leading berserk for Ásdís, and the building tasks follow as a condition of the bargain. This sequence of events suggested to Dehmer that the story in *Eyrbyggja* was fundamentally a wooing tale related to fairy tales in which tasks are imposed on a wooer-hero; he pointed to fairy tales in which "dem unliebsamen armen Freier drei Taten auferlegt werden, wobei man natürlich im stillen hofft, ihn loszuwerden, da man nicht glaubt, dass der Freier die Werke werde vollbringen können. Hausbau und

Ähnliches kommt dabei oft genug als Aufgabe vor. Alles wird mit Unterstützung eines dämonischen Helfers oder dankbarer Tiere zum glücklichen Ende geführt, woran hier die Hilfe des Bruders erinnern könnte."[44] Dehmer cites in support first Type 461 ("Three Hairs from the Devil's Beard"; Grimm No. 29)[45] and then, somewhat more plausibly, Type 513A or B ("Six Go through the Whole World"; Grimm Nos. 134 and 224; "The Land and Water Ship"; Grimm No. 71). In stories of Type 513 the hero has to accomplish tasks or pass tests before receiving in marriage a princess who had been offered to any man who could accomplish the tasks. It seems that Dehmer's discussion is the basis of the saga editors' only comment on the matter; Einar Ólafur Sveinsson observes in a note: "Það er títt í ýkjusögum, að menn verða að vinna þrautir nokkurar til að ná dýrum ráðahag. Þess háttar frásagnir hefur söguritarinn í huga."[46] Later Reidar Christiansen also briefly related the incident in *Eyrbyggja saga* to the imposition of tasks on a wooer-hero in the context of a discussion of Type 313 (Tasks and Magic Flight) and related märchen,[47] and Inger Boberg's motif-index lists the story of Víga-Styrr and the berserks in *Eyrbyggja* as H359.2 Suitor test: clearing land.[48]

Clearly there is a good deal of similarity between Styrr's action in assigning the building tasks and the situation in some of these fairy tales. However, the motifs in question (H335, H336, H338, H359) are in the fairy tales usually bound up with T68 (Princess offered as prize) and F601.2 (Extraordinary companions help hero in suitor tests),

---

44. Heinz Dehmer, *Primitives Erzählungsgut in den Íslendinga-Sögur* (Leipzig, 1927), pp. 86–91, ref. to p. 90.

45. The comparison is very far-fetched as the following outline based on that of A. Aarne and S. Thompson, *Types of the Folktale*, FFC 184 (1964) will show: (I) The prophecy that a certain poor youth ("fortune's favored") will wed the princess comes true despite the king's efforts to kill the boy; then (II) the king assigns him a quest for the devil's three golden hairs; on his way (III) he is posed three questions which he promises to answer on his return from Hell; in Hell (IV) he obtains the hairs and the answers with the help of the Devil's wife or grandmother, and returns giving the answers to each question as he goes (V). The cruel king is punished when he attempts to repeat the boy's journey (VI).

46. *Eb*, p. 72, n. 3; cf. Sveinsson, *Þjóðsögur*, p. 221, n. 1 and pp. 218–21.

47. Reidar Th. Christiansen, *Studies in Irish and Scandinavian Folktales* (Copenhagen, 1959), p. 97 and pp. 81–108.

48. Inger M. Boberg, *Motif-Index of Early Icelandic Literature*, Bibliotheca Arnamagnaeana, 27 (Copenhagen, 1966).

H335.0.1 (Bride helps suitor perform his tasks), or G530.2 (Help from ogre's daughter or son); and in general the task motif is mounted in the sagas in a context quite unlike that of the relevant tale-types (313, 502, 513, 518, 570, 577).[49] Ásdís's part is certainly not to help the berserks, rather it appears that she originally hindered them; and she is not offered as a prize, as is usual in the fairy tales. Halli and Leiknir are by no means fairy-tale heroes; they have, as berserks, much in common with ogres and giants but little beyond their relative poverty in common with the "fortune's favored" märchen hero, and of course the outcome of the story is the reverse of that of the fairy tales. On the other hand, in both saga texts Styrr's ostensible objection to the marriage is the difference in wealth between Ásdís and the berserk, and Styrr's striking reference in the *Eyrbyggja* text to the customs of the ancients may well allude to the fairy-tale situation: "Nú mun ek gera sem fornir menn, at ek mun láta þik vinna til ráðahags þessa þrautir nokkurar" (p. 72). At most, however, these words can refer to the immediate incident, the imposition of tasks on an unwanted wooer, and not to a type of märchen. In the context of the story as a whole such an allusion would be highly ironical, exchanging the roles of protagonist and antagonist; and despite Styrr's allusion the story of the berserks seems to be more closely linked with the *Sagen* and with the myth of Asgard than with märchen of the "giant's daughter" family.

However, it is not entirely clear from the Icelandic texts that wooing was the original initial moment; *Hv* is actually ambiguous on the question: the action is set in motion by the wooing, but Styrr explains that he has long been planning the building project: "Hér er hraun hjá bœ mínum, illt yfirreiðar; hefi ek opt hugsat, at ek vilda láta gera veg þar um ok ryðja þat, en mik hefir skort mannstyrk; nú vilda ek, þú gerðir þat" (p. 222). And in the *Edda* there is a similar ambiguity: "Þat var sima í ǫndverða bygð goðanna, þá er goðin hǫfðu sett Miðgarð ok gert Valhǫll, þá kom þar smiðr nǫkkvorr ok bauð at gera þeim borg á þrim misserum ... En hann mælti sér þat til kaups at hann skyldi eignaz Freyiu, ok hafa vildi hann sól ok mána" (p.

---

49. Another group of motifs which offer similarities with the stories told by Snorri and the sagas is found only in the Baltic area: H335.0.3 Devil as suitor assigned tasks; H1131.2 Devil as suitor assigned to build bridge or dam. Cf. also Baltic references given by Liungman, *Sägner*, III, 332–33; I have not been able to consult these Baltic tales.

45). Presumably the giant builder came to the gods because he desired Freyja; yet the whole situation of the gods implies their need to build a stronghold. Von Sydow (who, of course, was not concerned with the story of the berserks) wished to reconstruct the original form of the myth/folktale by comparison with *Alvíssmál,* where a dwarf suing for the daughter of Thor in marriage is kept talking until the morning sunrise petrifies him. (Some of the Masterbuilder folktales end with somewhat similar petrifications.)[50] The original form would, then, have the builder's wooing as first element, but it is doubtful that von Sydow's rather farfetched comparison can be used in this way. We cannot say with certainty from the sagas and *Edda* whether an Icelandic "oikotype" began with wooing; if it did, then the early Icelandic forms (with some weakening in *Hv* and *Edda*) agree against the usual form elsewhere. It is also possible that the ambiguity of *Hv* and *Edda* is closer to an Icelandic "oikotype" and that the *Eb* author has sharpened the focus on the wooing—something the self-conscious literary reference in "Nú mun ek gera sem fornir menn" might lead us to expect.[51]

(2) The saga incident has *two builders* or a builder and a helper; this agrees especially with the myth, but also with scattered variants of the folktale. Tales with two giants or trolls seem clustered on the eastern side of the Scandinavian area and in the Baltic.[52] In the west one builder aided by an animal is found, sparsely attested, in the Irish area and once in Norway.[53] Thus the Icelandic forms contrast, but not dramatically, with the general form of the folktale where the builder is alone, though many of the Continental versions give the Devil helpers too.

---

50. *Fataburen* (1908), pp. 25–26.

51. In some of the Continental Masterbuilder legends the payment is to be the son or daughter of the mortal (some references at Boberg, "Baumeistersagen," p. 18 and note); in at least one Baltic tale two builders compete for a single sweetheart; and finally, the mortal's daughter in marriage is to be the prize of the otherworld creature in some related tales discussed by Boberg ("Baumeistersagen," pp. 11, 14–18, 20 and notes). All this suggests that the story is naturally unstable at the point under discussion and similar variants could arise independently.

52. For references, Boberg, "Baumeistersagen," pp. 10–12 and n. 49 above.

53. The Norwegian Skalle-variant with a horse (Andreas Faye, ed., *Norske Folke-sagn* [Christiania, 1844], pp. 14–15) is probably of little significance for the history of this family of legends since it seems to be a local innovation stimulated by a peculiar rock formation; de Vries, *Problem,* p. 76 extends this objection to the Irish story of St. Mogue.

(3) In the myth and normally in the folktales the work goes on *at night*:

> Hann [the giant] tók til hinn fyrsta vetrardag at gera borgina, en of nætr dró hann til grjót á hestinum. [...] Ok it sama kveld er smiðrinn ók út eptir griótinu með hestinn Svaðilfœra ... En þessi hross hlaupa alla nótt ok dvelzt smíðin þá nótt. Ok eptir um daginn varð ekki svá smíðat sem fyrr hafði orðit (*Edda*, p. 46).

Heiðarvíga saga is in explicit agreement:

> Taka nú berserkirnir at ryðja hraunit at kveldi dags, ok at þeiri sýslan eru þeir um nóttina ... Um morgininn hǫfðu þeir því lokit ... Skulu þeir nú gera eitt gerði ok hafa því lokit at dagmálum *(Hv, p. 222)*.

However, *Eyrbyggja* makes no reference to the time of day until the berserks have finished their work: "Berserkirnir gengu heim um kveldit ok váru móðir mjǫk ..." (p. 74). The implication here would seem to be that the work was done during the day; which saga is to be preferred at this point is a problem that depends on our interpretation of further temporal indications in *Eb* (below, n. 54) and our general view of the relations of the two sagas (discussed below). I tentatively posit night-time work in the original of *Hv* and in the local legend on which it is based; here, then, the Icelandic versions do not contrast with the general folktale form, but the unrealistic night-time labor reinforces the folktale affinities of the saga analogues.

(4) In both the myth and the saga the builders move *great boulders*: "En þat þótti ásunum mikit undr hversu *stór bjǫrg* sá hestr dró ..." *(Edda, p. 46)*; "... vega þeir *stór bjǫrg* upp, þar þess þurfti, ok fœra út fyrir brautina, en sums staðar koma þeir *stórum steinum* í gryfjurnar, en gera slétt yfir, sem enn má sjá ..." *(Hv, p. 222)*. The stones are missing in the condensed account of *Eyrbyggja*: "Eptir þetta tóku þeir at ryðja gǫtuna, ok er þat it mesta mannvirki. Þeir lǫgðu ok garðinn, sem enn sér merki" *(Eb, p. 72)*. This detail of the Icelandic versions is found in scattered folktales and, of course, does not belong to the significant structural features of the tale.

(5) Both the myth and the sagas make explicit the *wonder* of ordinary persons at the mighty construction: "En þat þótti ásunum

mikit undr ..." *(Edda,* p. 46); "... var þá á þeim inn mesti berserksgangr ... er þat eitt it mesta stórvirki, er menn vita, ok mun sá vegr æ
haldask með þeim um merkjum, sem á eru, meðan landit stendr" *(Hv,*
p. 222). Again less explicit is the spare *Eyrbyggja* version: "... ok er
þat it mesta mannvirki ... sem enn sér merki" (p. 72). This detail, too,
is implicit in the folktale and surfaces in many individual variants.

These details (1–5) have the general effect of supporting the identity
of the berserk story as a Masterbuilder Tale and of emphasizing the
closeness of the two early Icelandic versions, the myth and the saga
tale, against the international folktale background. Four further
details in the form of minor incongruities in the saga narrative
confirm these results since they can best be explained by positing an
original form (a local legend) of the saga tale still closer to the folktale
and especially to the myth.

(1) Snorri's myth speaks of a bargain with two conditions: the
giant builder must accomplish his task under a *limitation on aid,* only
his horse Svaðilfari helping, and within a set period of time. The saga
tale offers parallels to both these conditions, though the limitation on
aid is explicit only in *Heiðarvíga saga:* "Leiknir segir, þat þykki sér
eigi mikit fyrir, ef hann njóti liðs Halla, bróður síns. Styrr sagði, hann
mætti þat við hann eiga" (p. 222). Compare Snorri: "... ok var þat
kaup gert við smiðinn at hann skyldi eignaz þat er hann mælti til ...
skildi hann af øngum manni lið þiggia til verksins. Ok er þeir sǫgðu
honum þessa kosti, þá beiddiz hann at þeir skyldu lofa <at hann>
hefði lið af hesti sínum er Svaðilfœri hét. En því réð Loki er þat var
til lagt við hann" (p. 45).

(2) The second condition, the *deadline,* is one of the most characteristic elements of the Masterbuilder Tale in the folktale and mythic
forms; it is the essence of the story that the work be interrupted at
the "last minute" before the building will have been finished and the
contract fulfilled. The notion of a time clause seems to survive vestigially in the saga version also. In *Hv* the work is apparently carried out
in a single night—the text is not very explicit here—but the sentence
"Skulu þeir nú gera eitt gerði ok hafa því lokit at dagmálum" is best
interpreted as a vague survival of the deadline motif: they were to
have the sheep pen finished by midmorning (cf. *Hv,* p. 222, n. 2). *Eb*
also seems to allude to a deadline: "Ok er lokit var mjǫk hvárutveggja
verkinu [both the works of the berserks and the bath being built by

Styrr], var þat *inn síðasta dag* er þeir váru at byrginu ..." (p. 73). In the immediate context the phrase "the last day" lacks meaning and gives the impression of being a vestigial survival of a deadline; however, the analysis of *inn síðasta dag* here is a little more complex.

The author of *Eyrbyggja* (in contrast to *Hv*) has his leading berserk give Styrr a deadline for returning an answer to his proposal of marriage:

> Halli mælti: "Þetta mál skaltu tala við þá menn, er þér líkar, *innan þriggja nátta*; vil ek eigi þessi svǫr láta draga fyrir mér lengr, því at ek vil eigi vera vánbiðill þessa ráðs" (p. 71).

The three days are then accounted for: "Um morguninn eptir reið Styrr inn til Helgafells ... gengu þeir á fjallit upp ok sátu þar á tali allt til kvelds ... Síðan reið Styrr heim" (pp. 71–72); "Um morguninn eptir gengu þeir Halli á tal ... Eptir þetta tóku þeir at ryðja gǫtuna ..." (p. 72); "Ok er lokit var mjǫk hvárutveggja verkinu, var þat inn síðasta dag ..." (p. 73). The use of this deadline is, however, not very logical; Halli wanted an *answer* within three days; assuming the phrase *inn síðasta dag* does refer to Halli's stipulated sequence of three days, it is illogically applied to the *completion of the work* after an answer has already been given. A possible explanation for this incongruity is that a local legend, the source of *Heiðarvíga saga* and indirectly of *Eyrbyggja*, had a survival of the work deadline; this was vaguely alluded to in *Hv* but clarified and altered to a deadline for the answer in *Eb*—a displacement consonant with *Eb*'s emphasis on the wooing but logically inconsistent. The original deadline in the oral legend of the berserks may have been one night (*Hv* and many folktales) or three days or nights in view of the three nights of *Eb* and the three separate tasks; Snorri's giant's initial offer mentions building the fortress "á þrim misserum" (p. 45), and the myth actually focuses on the last three days of the contract period.[54]

(3) The deadline survives formally in the myth, but its function is much weakened as compared with the folktales. In the developed

---

54. These temporal indications in *Eb* may also point to original *night work*, the labor beginning about midday on the second day of the period given Styrr (p. 72), continuing by implication through the night between the second and third days and ending at evening of the third day (p. 73).

Devil-as-builder type, the demonic builder is prevented at the eleventh hour from finishing through a trick or delay of some kind; here the deadline is still fully functional in the story. In the Finn/Skalle type the naming motif has replaced the simpler Continental ending, and the function of the deadline has changed. In Snorri's myth the giant is not killed by being delayed until the rising sun should petrify him (as in *Alvíssmál*) or put him to flight (as sometimes told of the Devil-as-builder) or by having his name spoken out, rather the myth employs the normal method of killing giants in the mythology: he is struck down directly by Thor. The deadline is not altogether without a function here since it is the giant's realization that he cannot meet the deadline that leads to his *jǫtunmóðr,* which in turn exposes him as a giant and leads to Thor's return and his death; however, the connection between the deadline and the resolution of the story in the killing does seem tenuous by comparison to the Continental folktales.

The story of the berserks shares this loss of connection between the bargain with its deadline and the resolution of the story where Styrr takes direct action comparable to Thor's, and in this respect the early Icelandic versions agree against all others. However, as in the myth, the loss of direct function for the deadline may have been off-set in the original of the saga story by an indirect function: the deadline may originally have caused the berserks to labor in a berserk-fury rendering them weak enough for Styrr to kill; if such was the original form, it is easy to see how the addition of the motifs of the bathhouse[55] and fresh hide[56] eliminated even that function for the deadline, which then survived only vestigially. Such detailed reconstruction is of course very speculative, but there is a striking similarity between the essence and function in the stories of Snorri's *jǫtunmóðr* and the *berserksgangr* of the sagas, together with the panic effected by the bathhouse scalding. And this is coupled with a kind of "over-determined" ending offering

---

55. Dehmer connected the death of the berserks in or near the bathhouse with a fairy-tale motif which he instances from Grimm Nos. 11 and 13 (in an Estonian variant); cf. (Thompson) motif S113.2.2 and Boberg, *Motif-Index*, S113.2.2. Dehmer also compares the bathhouse death to the motif of the Iron House as it occurs in Grimm No. 71; the Iron House is a well-known murderous device, and it is not impossible that the killing of the berserks distantly reflects it. However, the presence of the Iron House motif in Grimm No. 71, which Dehmer claims with little reason as an analogue of the whole story of the berserks, is an accident without significance.

56. References at *Eb*, p. 74, n. 2 and p. xxvi.

what appear to be three different motifs that explain Styrr's victory: fatigue after the *berserksgangr,* panic in the scalding bathhouse, and slipping on the fresh hide. The evolutionary hypothesis accounts for all these features: the original folktale-like deadline was weakened when a violent ending was substituted (evidence of this stage is preserved in the *Edda*); then the motifs of the bathhouse and, finally, the fresh hide were added totally depriving the deadline of any function but leaving a hollow vestige; *Hv* dealt with this situation by alluding vaguely to a deadline, while the author of *Eb* tried to improve the story by shifting place and function of the deadline.

(4) Finally, there is the narrative cul-de-sac that occurs when Ásdís appears before the laboring berserks. In *Eb* Ásdís simply walks out near the berserks dressed in her best clothing and answers nothing when Halli calls to her; then each of the berserks composes a stanza stating the bare situation described in the prose. In *Hv* Styrr is responsible for having his daughter dress in her best clothes and sending her out near the berserks as they work; he forbade her to warn them of his plan,[57] and she does not answer when her wooer calls; a single poem follows. It is possible that this appearance of Ásdís is inserted merely to justify the verses; but as all agree that the verses are not genuine, we might have expected Ásdís's sally to have led to some narrative consequences.[58] In the present form of the story this is a blind motif, but it is explainable as a vestige of a motif of *female interference* as found in Loki's role as mare and in some of the folktales.[59] Again *Hv* bears the greater resemblance to the story of Asgard in which the gods (like Styrr) send out their female saboteur, Loki dressed in his most attractive mare form.

These four incongruous features of the saga narrative, the limitation on aid, the deadline, the peculiar lack of function of the deadline, and the blind motif of female interference, are explainable as displacements from an oral legendary tale localized at Berserkjahraun and originally considerably closer in details to the myth and folktale forms.

---

57. Nordal comments on this warning as unlikely in a genuine saga text and probably an addition by Jón Ólafsson *(Hv,* p. cxiv, n. 2), whose work is discussed below.

58. The verses (including Styrr's) are generally agreed to be later than the tenth century and therefore not genuine *(Eb,* pp. ix–x; *Hv,* p. cxl); Einar Ólafur Sveinsson, "Eyrbyggja sagas kilder," *Scripta Islandica* 19 (1968), 3–38, here 4–6.

59. For references, Boberg, "Baumeistersagen," pp. 4–6, 10–12, 18 and notes.

III. Eyrbyggja and Heiðarviga saga

So far I have ignored the complex textual relations of *Hv* and *Eb*. The story of the sole manuscript of *Hv* is well known: Árni Magnússon set the Icelandic amanuensis-antiquarian Jón Ólafsson frá Grunnavík to copy the parchment about New Year of 1727–28; the great fire of Copenhagen destroyed both parchment and copies in October 1728; over a year later Jón wrote down everything he could remember; that retelling is the only surviving text of the first part of the saga, and the *Hv* version of the story of Víga-Styrr and the berserks exists only in the part retold by Jón.[60] Jón made it clear in a note that he had consulted *Eb* for the version he gives of the berserk's poem *(Hv,* p. 223, n. 1), and of course he must have been generally familiar with *Eb*. Furthermore, *Eb* itself cites *Hv* as one of its sources *(Eb,* p. 180). Whether we interpret *Eb's* dependence on *Hv* as written or oral, there is a sense in which *neither* of our surviving texts of the berserk story can be said to be a totally independent witness; and doubt of the value of *Hv* and *Eb* can be raised also in terms of the reliability of Jón's memory, as well as in terms of the possible dependence of *Eb* on the original *Hv* and of the surviving *Hv* retelling on *Eb*—an unpromising situation which would make a confident reconstruction of the exact words of the original *Hv* impossible.

However, the different texts are not valueless as versions of a story whose main lines and tendencies we are after. For one thing, Jón Ólafsson's memory of the main actions of the saga was obviously excellent;[61] the fact that he several times appended a note showing that he was in doubt about the name of a minor character and that a few errors of his with regard to placenames have been exposed simply makes more convincing his overall faithfulness to the original. Moreover, the story of the berserks in particular is a coherent, easily remembered segment, a unified story on its own; and the fact that many details of the story survive only in Jón's retelling argues for according it a certain limited independent value; in other words, since we know he reconsulted *Eb*, if

---

60. The best accounts of the textual relations of *Hv* and *Eb* are in the introductions to the editions cited.

61. For a full assessment of the value of Jón's retelling see Nordal's introduction to *Hv*, pp. cvi–cxv, esp. pp. cvii–cviii; also Jón Helgason, *Jón Ólafsson frá Grunnavík* (Copenhagen, 1925), pp. 42–44.

his retelling nevertheless diverged from *Eb*, he must have remembered the story as somewhat different in *Hv*.

Similar reasons salvage, at least partly, the value of *Eb*.[62] In *Eb* the story is one strand in the tapestry-like narrative of the saga, and it can be accounted a digression insofar as *Eb* is a saga about Snorri goði. The author retained this digression, however, even though it was his habit generally not to retell material that had already achieved written form.[63] The retention may be due to the striking character of the story itself, but another incentive seems to have been the author's ability to add some facts and corrections to *Hv* and to integrate the "digression" to some extent by weighting it to emphasize the role of *Eb*'s hero Snorri goði. Unlike the author of *Hv*, the author of *Eb* lived in the area of Helgafell and was able to add certain details to the account of the burial site and correct a few details about the bathhouse killing. This, then, accounts for the peculiar nature of the *Eb* text in comparison to *Hv*: the *Eb* author condensed where he had nothing to add or modify and narrated more fully where he wanted to improve the story (e.g., the deadline and reference to *fornir menn*), to correct it (e.g., details of the burial and bathhouse), or to adjust the perspective (especially in the role of Snorri).

In *Hv* the tale has noticeable anti-Styrr coloring as compared with the *Eb* version. *Hv* seems to have a two-part structure, the first half of which is the "Víga-Styrs saga"; the earlier parts of the "Víga-Styrs saga" consist of unrequited killings by Styrr. Though continuity is mainly supplied by Styrr's personality as *ójafnaðarmaðr*, the killings show the escalation of Styrr's arrogance until he is killed by the son of one of his victims. Thus Styrr, though the main character of the first half of the saga is in a sense not a "hero," and in *Hv* the legend of Berserkjahraun reflects this critical point of view and belongs to the main action of the saga (is not a digression as in *Eb*). In the episode of the killing of the berserks, Styrr acts underhandedly but manfully; and consistent with its focus on this main character, *Hv* is explicit in having Styrr responsible for Ásdís's promenade past the laboring berserks, a motivation lost in *Eb*. In *Hv* Styrr sacrifices two oxen (called *blótnaut* in other sagas) following the killing—an unflattering

---

62. This argument is supported by Sveinsson, *Eb*, pp. xxxviii–xxxix.
63. *Eb*, pp. xxxviii–xxxix, with references.

allusion to an old pagan usage designed to block revenge, apparently by declaring a killing ex post facto a duel.[64] And finally, in Jón Ólafsson's retelling the episode ends with an anonymous community evaluation of the killing that mirrors the saga's whole attitude toward Styrr: "Spurðisk þetta víða, ok rœddu menn misjafnt of víg þessi" (p. 224).

The author of *Eyrbyggja,* now assigned to the second quarter of the thirteenth century,[65] wove the borrowed story into the complex structure of his book in a very different way and with a different point of view. In *Eb* the visit to Snorri for advice is told more fully than in Jón Ólafsson's text and with a significant reference to the fact that "þau ráð hafa sízt at engu orðit, er þar [on the Helgafell] hafa ráðin verit" (p. 72); this, together with another daylong conference with Snorri after the killing and burial (a conference not mentioned at all by *Hv*), frames the main events. The marriage of Snorri to Ásdís, which was the subject of this second talk, is mentioned only briefly in *Hv* but more fully in *Eb*. Finally, the story in *Eb* closes with a direct comparison of Snorri with Styrr: "var Snorri goði ráðagørðarmaðr meiri ok vitrari, en Styrr atgøngumeiri; báðir váru þeir frændmargir ok fjǫlmennir innan heraðs" (p. 75). Generally, then, *Eb* increases the role of Snorri while remaining neutral or favorable toward Styrr who is presented as acting as the instrument of Snorri.

The story in *Eyrbyggja* is a little more compact than in Jón Ólafsson's retelling, and in any case it is more successful from a literary point of view despite its omissions. The author of *Eb* was writing with a self-conscious literary intention as Styrr's reference to the custom of *fornir menn* shows. This sentence would be out of place in an oral legend, and since so striking a phrase is missing in Jón's text, it may be assumed to be the addition of the author of *Eyrbyggja,* an addition that serves the double purpose of alerting the reader to the traditional nature of the story as a whole and the fairy-tale quality of the motif immediately referred to and of again underlining the role of Snorri goði whom the *Eb* author imagined as setting out his plan for

---

64. *Hv*, p. 224, n. 2.

65. *Eb*, pp. xlv–lii; this dating is supported by Hallvard Lie, "Tanker omkring en 'uekte' replikk in Eyrbyggjasaga," *ANF* 65 (1950), 160–77; cf. Jean-Pierre Mabire, *La composition de la Eyrbyggja saga* (Caen, 1971).

Styrr in terms of an old story. This kind of attention to antiquarian detail and the subtle and allusive mode of expression agree with all we know about the psychology of the author of *Eb*.[66]

If, then, we are justified in assuming that the source of the tale told by the sagas was a migratory legend of the Masterbuilder type localized at Berserkjahraun and if the lack of exact agreement between *Hv* and *Eb* can be interpreted as I have suggested, we may try to reconstruct the development from oral legend to the saga form. A migratory legend related to the later Continental Devil-as-builder tales and to an early stage of the Scandinavia Finn/Skalle tales before the addition of the naming motif came to Iceland where its features included: two builders or a builder and a helper; a bargain with time clause, the work going on at night; the builder's reward was to be a woman related to the contractor. Possibly the feature of information or outside advice (deduced from Styrr's consultations with Snorri and the councils of the gods and found in scattered variants of the legends) was included, and certainly the story turned on female interference, perhaps in the form of some kind of flirtatious behavior by the girl, delaying the work and preventing completion until the deadline was past. This legend became localized to at least one Icelandic site, Berserkjahraun, where it attached itself to certain landmarks; possibly there was no historical basis at all, but it seems more likely that actual events (of around 984) attracted the folktale and that several kinds of assimilations among the folktale pattern, other traditional motifs, and historical facts followed. The bathhouse ruse itself may be a traditional motif, and the fresh hide certainly is. This leaves as historical core little more than the fact that Styrr killed two foreign berserks.[67] One nexus, then, between the migratory legend and the facts may have been the otherworldly characteristics

---

66. See esp. Lie, pp. 166–77, and Sveinsson, "Kilder," esp. pp. 9–15.

67. Hans Kuhn, "Kappar og berserkir," *Skírnir* 123 (1949), 108 considers Halli and Leiknir to be probably the only historical instances of berserks who came out to Iceland. The path could perhaps date from Christian times as a well-known type of "good work" (see esp. Dag Strömbäck, *The Epiphany in Runic Art: the Dynna and Sika Stones*, Dorothea Coke Memorial Lecture, 1969 [London, 1970], pp. 6–8 and references), and according to Kålund, p. 433, this path is not unique ("just ikke så meget forskellig fra en af de almindelige hraunstier"); however, there is no concrete reason to doubt the sagas on the age of the works, and the *dys* does not sort particularly well with an origin in the Christian period.

of berserks who, in legend and literature, stand outside the human pale and, like giants, go about demanding women; Snorri's "Formáli," for example, couples berserks together with giants as victims of Trór or Thor (AM, p. 22; FJ, p. 4). *Eb* adds that they were Swedes, often thought of as an uncanny race—Glámr was a Swede—and both texts comment on the strange phenomenon of the *berserksgangr*.

This notion of an actual incident assimilated to a traditional pattern perhaps gains some support from the character of the site and the duality of the etiological explanation it requires. Berserkjagata is still easily passable on foot or on horse, and the stone fence that originally separated Styrr's land from Vermundr's is still plainly visible. However, the sheep pen seems to have been destroyed by modern roadwork.[67a] Close beside the path in a low spot between two deep pits in the lava stands *Berserkjadys*, which is a rectangular, tomb-like heap of stones. All four features were man-made, but they would seem to call for two different types of explanation, one concerning construction (the path, wall, and pen), the other death and burial (the *dys*, itself a formidable construction). The historical events may have culminated in the *dys*,[67b] while the contiguous path, the wall, and the pen attracted an international folktale of wondrous building. The resulting assimilation may explain the fact that it is in the final section of the story, the killing, that the legend of Berserkjahraun most conspicuously differs from other exemplars of the Masterbuilder type, with the exception of the myth. Some Finn/Skalle tales, supporting a similar dual etiology (the church is the work of the troll, the nearby stone, pit, etc. all that remains of the troll himself), show how easily such an adaptation can occur in oral tradition. The whole process of assimilation outlined here conforms to what is known of the way memories of actual events (*memorates, Erinnerungssagen*) pass to fictional legends (*fabulates,*

67a. Thanks to the hospitality of Jón Bjarnason of Bjarnarhöfn I was able to make a tour of the whole site in July 1975. Kålund's description from 1877 is still accurate except for the missing pen, which he says was called *Krossrétt*, and the modern name of Styrr's farm: Hraun, as in the sagas, rather than Kålund's Berserkjahraun.

67b. Kålund reports that at the beginning of the nineteenth century the *dys* was opened and bones of two men found, not especially big but heavy; however, he prefaces this potential support for a historical core by "det påstås, at..." (p. 433); Ebenezer Henderson's detailed account *(Iceland; or the Journal of a Residence in that Island ... 1814 and 1815 ...,* II [Edinburgh, 1818], 59–64) does not mention a disinterment.

Sagen) in folk tradition, and the passage from fully formed local legend to the artistic and realistic saga conforms to what we expect of the relation of the literary sagas to local *Sagen*.[68] However, no final decision can be reached about many details: neither or both of the two essential motifs, building and killing, could have a historical basis; the bathhouse may have been adapted to local circumstances out of the repertoire of traditional motifs or may have been historical; the fresh hide may have been added at an oral or a written stage. The vestigial survival of the deadline would further suggest that the original local oral form had a killing in which Styrr took advantage of the exhaustion that follows the *berserksgangr* (cf. *Hervarar saga*, ch. 3); if the bathhouse motif were then redundantly imposed on this form of the story, it would deprive the deadline of function—the situation we find in the reconstructed original of the local legend.

IV. The New Analogue and the *Edda*

If there was a Masterbuilder legend of the international type localized at Berserkjahraun and variously reflected in the surviving *Eb* and *Hv* texts, what was its relation to the myth narrated in Snorri's *Edda*? The addition of the berserk story as a new analogue of the Eddic myth does not significantly change the overall picture of the worldwide,[69] but especially European, Masterbuilder Tale as given in the survey articles. However, the introduction of a new analogue, which stands much closer to the myth than to any other version of the Masterbuilder Tale and which is attested from approximately the same time and place, presents a local Icelandic question in literary history along with a new avenue to solution of the initial problem: myth or folktale?

The question as applied to Iceland presents the same possibilities as we considered above: a common source going back to very ancient pre-Christian times or recent diffusion in either direction. The difficulties with an ancient heathen source are, first, that the myth is totally

---

68. Cf., e.g., Helga Reuschel, "Melkorka," *ZDA* 75 (1938), 297–304, and Sveinsson, "Kilder", pp. 7–9.

69. Rooth, pp. 37–39; de Vries, *Problem*, pp. 69–70.

unsupported by independent evidence in kennings, Eddic (once we accept de Vries' analysis of *Vǫluspá*) and skaldic poetry and, second, that the saga tale and the myth are too close to be accounted for by divergence from some common source in the *Urzeit*. This, of course, is a matter of opinion, and a hypothesis of contamination between the myth and the legend on Icelandic soil could salvage the theory of common origin; however, if the legend of Berserkjahraun and the Asgard myth go back to a common source, with or without subsequent contamination, we are no closer to an explanation of what de Vries referred to as "the transition between myth and folktale." Similar objections may be raised against the tale of Berserkjahraun being a relatively recent derivation from the myth. The myth is unattested elsewhere as myth, but the story is widely known as a folktale; it seems simplest to derive the story of Berserkjahraun directly from European migratory legends of the same type. And, again, deriving the local legend from the myth would not solve the question of the relation of the myth to the folktales generally or be easy to explain in literary-historical terms. The remaining possibility would derive the myth from the folktale, either generally or from the specific form attested at Berserkjahraun; of course, a genuine, ancient Germanic myth could not be so derived, and I will argue that Snorri created the myth out of materials he had at hand, including the tale of Berserkjahraun.

Others have found all or parts of Snorri's "novelistic" myth of Asgard suspicious; it is too logical and coherent, and its exact coincidence with a certain type of folktale is properly viewed not as a guarantee of its genuineness but as a very questionable circumstance since no other ancient Germanic myth coincides so completely with a folktale, the "folktale element" usually being limited to scattered motifs. The roles of Loki as evil counselor and as shapeshifter who bears off-spring, of Thor as giant-slayer, and of Freyja as the coveted bride of giants are common in Norse mythology and may be interpreted as borrowed from genuine myths. The only unique detail and the only point for which there is external corroboration is the fact that Loki gave birth to Sleipnir by Svaðilfari. The general form of the Masterbuilder Tale does not lead easily to this conclusion, which has no parallel among the folktales, and the combination of the building story with the birth of Sleipnir is almost certainly due to Snorri himself. Above all the absence of other references to the Masterbuilder myth makes it suspicious.

As an antiquarian Snorri will have been interested in legends, and as a widely traveled man he may have known the Masterbuilder Tale in more than one form, perhaps in the form later found at Trondheim Cathedral. But there is definite reason to suppose that he also knew the Icelandic form localized at Berserkjahraun. Snorri Sturluson was the namesake and descendant of Snorri goði, who figures so prominently in the story of Berserkjahraun, especially in the *Eb* version, and we know from the notes at the end of *Eb* that Snorri Sturluson's mother Guðný Bǫðvarsdóttir was present at the exhumation of Snorri goði. Moreover, Guðný kept house for her son Þórðr at Staðr or at Eyrr about 1218, just before she came to stay with Snorri at Reykjaholt where she died in 1221; Staðr is on the south coast of Snæfellsnes not far from Berserkjahraun, while (Ǫndurð)-Eyrr is on the north coast and even closer. Snorri Sturluson's brother Þórðr lived at Eyrr which passed from him to Snorri's nephew Sturla Þórðarson, the historian and lawman; and Einar Ólafur Sveinsson observes, in the context of the possible authorship of *Eb*, that Þórðr had plenty of occasion to travel around the peninsula. Any anecdote involving Snorri goði is very likely to have been known to Snorri Sturluson.[70]

A second reason for believing that Snorri Sturluson was influenced by the legend of Berserkjahraun is the way the closeness of the saga tale and the myth mounts even to verbal agreements: "hann mælti sér þat til kaups" (*Edda*): "Styrr kvað þá þessu kaupa mundu" (*Eb*); "Ok it sama kveld ..." (*Edda*): "Taka ... at ryðja hraunit at kveld dags" (*Hv*); "of nætr dró hann ..." (*Edda*): "at þeiri sýslan eru þeir um nóttina" (*Hv*); "Ok eptir um daginn ..." (*Edda*): "... at dagmálum" (*Hv*); "stór bjǫrg sá hestr dró" (*Edda*); "vega þeir stór bjǫrg upp ... koma þeir stórum steinum" (*Hv*); "En þá er .iii. dagar vóro til sumars, þá var komit mjǫk at borghliði" (*Edda*): "Ok er lokit var mjǫk hvárutveggja verkinu, var þat inn síðasta dag, er þeir váru at byrginu" (*Eb*). Given the simplicity of the language of Old Icelandic prose, none of these verbal agreements seem particularly significant, and of course I have already argued from the congruence of ideas that the saga tale and the myth had to be closely related. One verbal

---

70. Major references for the many certain and possible connections between Snorri Sturluson and the region of Berserkjahraun will be found in Einar Ólafur Sveinsson's introduction (*Eb*, pp. xliii—lvii) and *Eb*, pp. 180–86 (cf. *ættaskrár*).

agreement of this kind, however, seems to me to go beyond what we would expect of the "same" story told independently in the same traditional style but without recent direct contact:

Leiknir segir, þat þykki sér eigi mikit fyrir *ef hann njóti liðs Halla, bróður síns. Styrr sagði, hann mætti þat við hann eiga. (Hv)*

skildi hann af ǫngum manni lið þiggia til verksins. Ok er þeir sǫgðu honum þessa kosti, þá beiddiz hann *at þeir skyldu lofa <at hann> hefði lið af hesti sínum er Svaðilfœri hét. En því réð Loki er þat var til lagt við hann. (Edda)*

There are no canons for judging in such matters, but here the agreement of ideas, the "motif" of the two stories, seems to me significantly minute and the syntactic and lexical agreements beyond the range of accident. A plausible explanation is that Snorri remembered some actual passages of the legend.

A less plausible explanation, but one that must be mentioned, is that Jón Ólafsson was influenced in his retelling by his memory of the story in the *Snorra Edda,* for the most impressive agreements with the *Edda* are found in *Hv,* not in *Eb.* However, Jón managed to retell the incident from memory without echoing *Eb* significantly (except for the verse) though we know he had recently consulted that saga. Since he (unlike Snorri, I will argue below) had no reason to think of the tale of the berserk builders in connection with the myth, any influence from Snorri on Jón's memory would have to be explained as taking place at some deep subconscious level. This distant possibility must qualify our further conclusions, but on balance such a psychological explanation seems to me more cumbersome than the assumptions made above: that the retelling here fairly reflects the original *Hv* and that the original *Hv* was somewhat closer to the oral legend than the more sophisticated *Eb* which condensed and adjusted the narrative.

V. Snorri's Motivation

If Snorri changed a legend into a myth, what could have been his motives? In writing *Gylfaginning* he was attempting to systematize and concatenate the myths and mythic allusions he found in his sources. Where we can compare Snorri's sources directly with his own work it is perfectly clear that most of the sources take place *in illo tempore,* in that time out of time so well known from Eliade's work, while Snorri himself is continually fashioning causal connections and anticipating "future" events; a good example of this is the paraphrase of *Skírnismál* which seems to make the whole myth an explanation of why Freyr has no sword at Ragnarǫk.

However, Snorri's major source, the *Vǫluspá,* did have a strong sense of chronological sequence, and in the part of *Gylfaginning* with which we are concerned Snorri was following this poem and trying to interpret stanzas 25–26. These stanzas seem to allude to oaths made and broken and a goddess delivered into the power of giants. De Vries argued that this sequence of motifs in the stanzas suggested to Snorri a *myth* which he knew from (prose) oral tradition and that Snorri applied the *myth* none too successfully to the task of illuminating these problematic stanzas. I propose to substitute *folktale* for *myth* in de Vries' hypothesis. De Vries' oral myth is uncertain: there *may* have been genuine pagan myths told in prose and current in what we suppose to be the thoroughly Christian Iceland of about 1220, but if so, so appealing a tale should have left other traces.[70a] On the other hand we know that a closely analogous folktale, the legend of Berserkjahraun, even showing some verbal agreements was current there at that time and have every reason to believe that Snorri had been exposed to it. So one motive for Snorri's creation of a myth from a folktale may have been desperation in the face of those stanzas of *Vǫluspá,* but further investigation suggests another, more creditable motive on Snorri's part.

Snorri's "Formáli" or Prologue and *Gylfaginning* agree on what might be called the Trojan theory of Scandinavian paganism. The "Formáli" begins with biblical material but quickly moves to Troy whence Óðinn emigrated to Sweden; there he established a new kingdom on the pattern of Troy. This is called Asgard, the palace to which King Gylfi comes in *Gylfaginning*; in Asgard Gylfi is told

---

70a. Cf. Hans Kuhn, "Das Fortleben des germanischen Heidentums nach der Christianisierung," in *La Conversione al Cristianesimo nell' Europa dell' Alto Medioevo* (Settimane di studio del Centro Italiano di Studi sull' Alto Medioevo, XIV; Spoleto, 1968), pp. 743–57, esp. pp. 752–55.

stories set in "old Asgard", that is Troy.[71] The Swedish Asgard is distinguished from "Ásgarðr inn forni," and of "old Asgard" we are told expressly: "Ásgarðr, þat kǫllum vér Troia."[72] Finnur Jónsson and some others have taken the Troy-clause here for an interpolation in spite of its presence in three of the four major manuscripts,[73] but the description of Asgard-Troy at this point agrees with the Troy of the "Formáli"; and if we are to accept (as Finnur Jónsson also does) the "Formáli" as basically the work of Snorri, it is natural also to accept this clause.[74] Much more controversial is the so-called "Eftirmáli" where the identification between old Asgard and Troy is carried still further; for example: "Sá salr hinn ágæti, er Æsir kallaðu Brímis sal eða bjórsal; þat var höll Priamus konúngs. En þat, er þeir gera lánga frásögn of ragnarökr: þat er Trójomanna orrosta."[75] The authenticity of the "Eftirmáli" (and the neighboring "Bragaræður"), and indeed of the "Formáli" and many suspected interpolations, is among the most difficult questions in Old Norse literary history, and I cannot pretend to offer answers or even to understand fully the implications of the

---

71. AM, I, 8–30; FJ, pp. 3–8; cf. Holtsmark, pp. 55–60. An older general discussion of the Trojan background, with references, is found in Viktor Rydberg's *Teutonic Mythology: Gods and Goddesses of the Northland*, tr. R. B. Anderson, Norrœna Society (New York, 1906), I, 44–98.

72. *Edda*, p. 11 (reading of MS. R[egius]); FJ, p. 16; AM, I, 54; the other readings: "þat kalla menn troia" (MS. T[rajectinus]); "þat kallaz troia" (MS. W[ormianus]). Ernst Wilken, *Untersuchungen zur Snorra Edda: als Einleitung zur "Prosaischen Edda im Auszuge"* (Paderborn, 1878), p. 157, n. 70, gives a cogent reason for preferring the reading of W here: "Vielleicht war aber mit W þat kallaz (heisst gewöhnlich sonst) Trója zu schreiben, denn der den Göttern geläufige Name ist vielmehr Ásgarðr."

73. FJ, p. xliii and p. 16, notes. Finnur Jónsson tolerated only with difficulty the Troy theory as Snorri's work (cf. esp. p. xxv and Snorri Sturluson, *Edda*, ed. Finnur Jónsson [Copenhagen, 1900], p. vii), relying where possible on the strongly abbreviated Uppsala manuscript; nevertheless, it proves impossible to remove the entire Troy apparatus unless one follows the extreme view of Heusler, and perhaps it is worthwhile recalling that even the astringent Ari Þorgilsson referred to "Yngvi Tyrkjakonungr" (*Íslendingabók [and] Landnámabók*, ed. Jakob Benediktsson, Íslenzk fornrit 1, pt. 1 [Reykjavík, 1968], p. 27).

74. Cf. Wilken, p. 157: "Die Anknüpfung an Trója ... findet sich in der ganzen pros. Edda so feststehend, dass es mir unberechtigt erscheint, sie im Gylf. IX (AM I, 54) als spätere Zuthat zu verdächtigen"; cf. Holtsmark, p. 56.

75. AM, I, 226; FJ, p. 87; cf. also the closing words of *Gylfaginning* in the three MSS. RWT: "... sá er Öku-Þórr, ok honum eru kennd þau stórvirki er Ektor gerði í Trójo. En þat hyggja menn, at Tyrkir hafi sagt frá Úlixes, ok hafi þeir hann kallat Loka, þvíat Tyrkir voru hans hinir mestu úvinir" (AM, I, 206 = FJ, p. 77); both these passages are rejected by Finnur Jónsson; cf. Holtsmark, p. 60.

Troy theory.[76] But it certainly appears that in Snorri's theory the city about which myths were told to Gylfi was Troy, and it follows that the story of the building or rebuilding of Troy would be to Snorri a myth cognate with those of Asgard.

We cannot know all the possible forms in which Snorri might have encountered a story of the construction of Troy, but a number of scholars have proposed on grounds totally independent of the present argument that *Trójumanna saga* (c. 1200) has influenced the extant texts of Snorri's *Edda*, especially "Formáli":[77]

Er Troo var eflð annan tima

> Nv er þar til at taka at þa er Lamedon konvngr var drepin ok s(ynir) hans ok dottir hans hertekin en brotin borgin ok rænt fenv var Priamvs ecki nær ok er hann fra þersi tiðindi bra honvm við miok. hann for þa til Iliam með allt sitt goz. hann let þegar til borgar efna myklv sterkari enn fyʀ hafði hon verit enn eigi varð hon fyʀ allger sva sem þeir villdv fyʀ en Neptvnvs ok Apollo solar gvð gerðv hana. þangat vorv veit stor votn með miklvm bro<g>ðvm. þar vorv þa gervir kastalar storir ok tvrnar. eigi vorv ok borgar liðin *aptr læst avðvelldri at sœkia en veɢirnir liðlavsir.[78]

Here we have a construction legend with a human contractor and two otherworldly builders. The situation differs from that of the Norse legend/myth in that the builders are gods, but the point of view is the same: the action is seen from the side of the more human actors, the Trojans and the Æsir.

The surviving version of the Troy tale in *Trójumanna saga* does not make clear the fact that Priamus cheats the builders of their payment,

---

76. Cf. Jan de Vries, *Altnordische Literaturgeschichte*, 2nd ed. rev. (Berlin, 1962), II, 214–33 and references; also Baetke, Holtsmark, and Breiteig.

77. Breiteig, p. 122; Heusler, pp. 36, 62–63 (rejecting the "Formáli"); Fredrik Paasche, *Norges og Islands litteratur inntil utgangen av middelalderen*, 2nd ed. (Oslo, 1957), p. 410: "Snorre *kan* ha kjent den" [i.e. *Trójumanna saga*]; Holtsmark doubts the connection pp. 57–60; admittedly the evidence is circular, being based mostly on suspect parts. Besides by Bugge, the Troy story has been compared to that of Asgard by D. C. Fox, "Labyrinth und Totenreich", *Paideuma* I (1938–40), 387–88; cf. de Vries' justified criticism *(Altgermanische Religionsgeschichte*, II [Berlin, 1957], 257).

78. *Trójumanna saga*, ed. Jonna Louis-Jensen, Editiones Arnamagnaeanae, Ser. A, vol. 8 (Copenhagen, 1963), p. 36; the Hauksbók text is quoted here though MS. O is very close at this point.

but other versions, perhaps versions accessible to Snorri, did (see the discussion of Bugge's theory, above); and *Trójumanna saga* does mention that the cheated builders were among the gods who broke down the walls at the fall of Troy: "oc <er> hann [Aeneas] kemr ad borgarhlídino sier hann ad Neftúnus oc Apollo solar god oc Sif brvtu nídr borgarueggína."[79] Apollo and Poseidon build nearly impregnable walls ("... kastalar storir ok tvrnar. eigi vorv ok borgar liðin *aptr læst avðvelldri at sœkia en veɢirnir liðlavsir," *Hauksbók;* MS O adds after the preceding sentence: "oc sva var firir melt at hon skyldi aldri unnin verda af ofrefli fiolmennis") like the walls of Asgard ("þá kom þar smiðr nǫkkvorr ok bauð at gera þeim borg ... svá góða at trú ok ørugg væri firir bergrisum ok hrímþursum, þótt þeir komi inn um Miðgarð," *Edda,* p. 45). And perhaps one is justified in comparing the *stór biǫrg* brought by Svaðilfari and the *mikit undr* excited by his work with the sentence: "þangat vorv veit stor votn með miklvm bro<g>ðvm."

Snorri, then, probably knew this story from *Trójumanna saga* and may have known other versions of the Troy story, and he probably knew the legend of Berserkjahraun and perhaps other versions of the Masterbuilder Tale. Of the two the folktale must be designated his source, but the Troy myth may have provided a justification for his adaptation of a folktale. Given his general "Troy theory," we may assume that Snorri accorded the Troy story or myth an *interpretatio germana* and "recognized" in the folktale the Germanic cognate of the Troy myth. In fact, his procedure may be imagined as similar to that of the older folklorists in taking a folktale for the detritus of myth and supporting a reconstruction by a foreign parallel considered "cognate." Recent scholarship portrays Snorri as interpreting Germanic mythology through the eyes of a Christian and even, to some extent, a classicist, and the admittedly complex hypothesis offered here for the Asgard myth has the virtue of suggesting the mythographic and psychological conditions required by a real explanation of the relationship between Snorri's myth and the Masterbuilder Tales and is in harmony with the best contemporary interpretations of Snorri's attitude and understanding of his material (i.e. Baetke,

---

79. Ibid., p. 231 (Hauksbók); note also that as Thor is equated with Hector (or with Tros) and Loki with Ulysses (whose hallmark is also a *horse ruse*), Óðinn is connected with Priam (AM, I, 12–13, 20).

Holtsmark, Breiteig, and to a degree de Vries). I do not believe with Eugen Mogk that Snorri meant to establish a school of mythographic romancers at Reykjaholt, and I trust, with Holtsmark and de Vries, that Snorri did have access to more information about Old Norse paganism than we do. Nevertheless, students of the *Prose Edda* now agree, in the spirit if not the letter of Mogk, that Snorri invented, colored, and interpreted more or less continuously. My proposal should be seen in this scholarly context, but it changes the motivation from purely artistic or unspecified (in Mogk) to that of a serious medieval mythographer working, in the dominant theoretical posture of his time, with a theory that combined euhemerism with demonism, took what we would now call a comparative point of view, and did not distinguish closely between evidence and interpretation.

VI. Remaining Problems

At least four problems remain to be discussed. The first three constitute possible objections to the derivation of Snorri's myth from the legend of Berserkjahraun. Though the explanation of Snorri's myth advanced here need not be confined to derivation from the version known at Berserkjahraun (Snorri may have known several versions), this narrower form of the theory is the tidier and the more demanding, and I shall stick to it in discussion of these problems. The fourth is a possible objection to the role I propose for the Troy myth.

(1) The sun and the moon as reward. Snorri's myth agrees with several exemplars of the Finn/Skalle folktale that the builder was to be rewarded with the sun and moon; this constitutes a double threat to our explanation of the myth. First, it may be objected (with de Vries)[80] that the motif of the sun and the moon as reward belongs only in a myth, a story with gods as actors, since mortals do not dispose over the heavenly bodies. This objection overlooks the fact that the motif of sun and moon functions as an *impossible demand* in the folktales, which present this as an (impossible) alternative to the life or soul of the contractor (e.g., either the sun and moon or St. Olaf's heart's blood); the impossible demand tantamount to the life of the contractor in the Finn/Skalle tales is not very far from the devil's simple demand

---

80. De Vries, *Problem*, p. 68; cf. Sveinsson, *Þjóðsögur*, p. 48.

for possession of the contractor or another person in the Continental forms (cf. also motif K194). Moreover, we can easily imagine the transition from the folktale form of impossible demand to the mythic form with *both* the sun and moon *and* the goddess demanded; if Snorri found in his source something like "the sun and moon *or* the farmer's daughter", he had only to make the demand cumulative instead of alternative to give "the sun and moon *and* Freyja." In this change he was very clearly motivated by the desperately difficult lines in *Vǫluspá* 25: "hverr hefði lopt allt / lævi blandit"; and his interpretation has not satisfied many scholars: "Þá settuz guðin á dómstóla sína ok leituðu ráða, ok spurði ... hverr því hefði ráðit at gipta Freyju í Iǫtunheima eða spilla loptinu ok himninum svá at taka þaðan sól ok tungl ok gefa iǫtnum" *(Edda,* p. 46). However, a transition in the other direction, from myth (sun and moon *and* Freyja) to folktale (sun and moon *or* farmer's daughter) would be very difficult to explain and motivate.

Granted, then, that the motif of sun and moon is more original to folktales, a second and more difficult objection is raised to the derivation of Snorri's myth from the legend of Berserkjahraun, which gives no hint of a sun and moon motif. Snorri may have drawn the motif from some other version of the folktale, but it is not impossible that the oral legend localized at Berserkjahraun may have contained the motif. That *Eb* and *Hv* present realistic reworkings of the more folktale-like oral original is clear, and the motif itself as impossible demand is not an unlikely element in the oral milieu of Snæfellsnes. This possibility must be left open.[81]

(2) The horse as helper. Similarly, the fact that the builder's helper in Snorri's myth is a horse, in agreement with scattered versions of the Masterbuilder folktales against the legend of Berserkjahraun, poses another difficulty for the narrow form of our derivation

---

81. Common innovation here seems unlikely (cf. Krohn, *Übersicht*, p. 120), but it is possible that the modern Norwegian folktales have drawn the motif from Snorri's famous text. A. H. Krappe, "Riesen und Göttinnen," *ZDA* 70 (1933), 206–08 asserts that the idea of giants desiring goddesses and that of giants trying to steal the sun or moon are borrowed into the North from Mediterranean culture, specifically certain late Classical texts. This totally unconvincing argument may serve to remind how common the idea of loss of sun or moon is in mythology and folklore; cf. motifs A721.1, A728, A758, and A737.1 and Röhrich, p. 29.

of the myth. However, in contrast to the problem of the sun and moon, I would argue here that the underlying form of the motif is simply that of a builder with helper(s) and that the manifestation of the helper as a horse could be an accidental similarity liable to occur independently. None of the folktales tell much about the horse, and the feature of a horse as helper in scattered localities would seem adequately explained by the circumstances of real life; other draft animals also occur in the tales. It is certain, however, that Snorri had a good reason for letting the helper be manifested as a horse since he wanted not only to explain stanzas 25–26 of *Vǫluspá* but at the same time to account for the origin of Sleipnir. Probably his only information about the parentage of Sleipnir came from a line in *Vǫluspá in skamma*: "[Loki] enn Sleipni gat við Svaðilfara"; and he may simply have drawn the logical conclusion that because Sleipnir was a horse, Svaðilfari must have been one too.[82] In any case, Svaðilfari appears nowhere else, either as a heiti for a horse or in any other equine sense.

From *Eb* and *Hv* we can only assume that the oral legend had one more-or-less giant-like builder and a helper because unlike the possible loss of a sun and moon motif from that legend, it seems unlikely that a simple process of rationalization could derive the berserk helper from an original horse. (But see Conclusion below.) However, Snorri could easily have made the opposite change to accomplish his wish to give a local habitation to the name Svaðilfari, and such a transformation would follow a familiar pattern of shapeshifting. Or Snorri may have been influenced by a specific myth or tale such as the similar story of Gefjun, who came in guise of a "traveling woman" to King Gylfi and "as a reward for her entertainment" got all the land she could plow up in a day and a night with four oxen; she turned her four sons by a giant into oxen and plowed free the island of Zealand *(Gylfaginning,* ch. 1). In fact, with Gefjun in mind it is not impossible to read such a transformation between the lines of Snorri's story, especially in the prohibition "skildi hann af ǫngum *manni* lið þiggia til verksins"

---

82. The context of the line in *Vǫluspá in skamma* seems to show that there is no necessary correspondence between the nature of a monster and its parentage: Angrboða is a giantess, but Loki sired a wolf on her; a *scars* "ogress" (though perhaps referring to the Serpent or Wolf) stems from Loki; another monster comes from the eaten human heart that impregnated Loki.

and the immediate counterrequest "at þeir skyldu lofa <at hann> hefði lið af *hesti* sínum"; it was the shapeshifter Loki who advised that the request be granted. And the text twice uses the plural where we would expect a singular referring to the builder alone: "iǫtnum þótti ekki trygt at vera með ásum griðalaust ..."; "... at taka þaðan sól ok tungl ok gefa iǫtnum" (*Edda,* pp. 45–46). Of course, other explanations of *jǫtnum* here are possible.[83] Loki's role here is clearly dictated by conceptions of him elsewhere in the mythology (evil counselor, shapeshifter, "transsexual," and trickster) and by the information that he gave birth to Sleipnir—he must have been in mare form when Sleipnir was conceived. And even if there was a genuine myth about the building of Asgard, Snorri has obviously tampered with it at this point by introducing Loki as mare in the position where the myth seems to require a motif of female interference. The feature of the helper as horse, then, can be explained on the basis of other demands on Snorri's ingenuity and the narrow form of the folktale-source theory.

(3) The ending of the tale. The two early Icelandic forms of the Masterbuilder Tale agree against the normal form elsewhere in having the contractor strike down the builder(s). Both the saga (legend) form and the myth offer clear reasons for this peculiarity in assimilation of the international story to the external facts of the tomb-like *dys* (cf. n. 67b) and *Vǫluspá* 26 respectively, and both forms are associated with further external facts that can agree with a construction story (Berserkjagata, the wall, and the pen; the destruction of the walls in *Vǫluspá* 24). This is essentially an accidental coincidence, but it poses a threat to the derivation of the myth from the local legend in that both Icelandic forms have a reason for introducing a common innovation independently;[84] that is, both forms could derive independently from

---

83. If plurals, they may refer to the giants in general; but the Arnamagnaean edition, citing Rask's edition, takes them for dative singulars ("quod pro dat. sing. syncopato accipiendum, jǫtninum, quod dedit Raskius," AM, I, 135, n.), and this is Wilken's interpretation also (*Die prosaische Edda im Auszuge nebst Vǫlsunga-saga und Nornagests-þáttr,* ed. E. Wilken, II [Paderborn, 1913], s.v. *jǫtunn*).

84. An example of such an independent assimilation of the Masterbuilder Tale to external facts is the version told by J. G. Hallman, *Beskrifning öfver Köping* (Stockholm, 1728), accessible to me in Harald Falk, "Sankt Olofs minne i Sverige," *Kyrkohistorisk Årsskrift* 3 (1902), 83–86: a scene of St. Olaf with his feet on a dragon-bodied, man-headed creature is explained by a version of the tale in which after casting himself down from the tower, Skalle is struck by the saint's axe, bound, and laid under his footstool; the ending

a normal form of the folktale without a killing at the end, and Snorri could know such a folktale from Iceland or from Norway. However, this would mean acceptance of many other coincidences as accidental: the coexistence of two such similar stories in almost the same time and place, probably both known to the same author; the verbal similarities; the agreement of these two versions against all (?) others in the peculiar form of the female interference (Ásdís' promenade; Loki's romp as mare); and other agreements discussed above (such as the feature of two builders) which are not exclusive to the Icelandic versions. One of these, the "great boulders," seems a fairly minor surface agreement, easily developed independently, until one considers that a really ancient Germanic myth is unlikely to have described construction of a fortress of *stone;* this detail in Snorri's account is at very least to be considered rather late. Certainty is impossible, but I prefer to regard as accidental the first group of coincidences, the very distant agreement of the sequence of motifs in *Vǫluspá* 24–26 (one cannot speak of a story here) with that of the local legend and its site, and to accept the second group (between the local legend and Snorri) as too close for chance, as evidence of contact.

(4) Second building or first? A consecutive interpretation of *Vǫluspá* would require that any construction tale applied to stanzas 25–26 be the *re*building of the fortress after its destruction in the war of the Æsir and Vanir (24,5–8: "brotinn var borðveggr / borgar ása, / knátto vanir vígspá / vǫllo sporna"), but Snorri presents the building tale as the first foundation of Asgard ("Þat var snima í ǫndverða bygð goðanna, þá er goðin hefðu sett Miðgarð ok gert Valhǫll ..."). It is striking that the construction myth about Troy is also a second construction, and, given the coincidence on this point of *Vǫluspá* with the Troy story, we may object to the theory of secondary influence from the Troy story on the grounds that with this double encouragement Snorri should have made his construction myth a rebuilding.[85]

---

is obviously an accommodation to the iconography. (Thus Hallman's version does not lend any *particular* support to the thesis that St. Olaf took over Thor's functions, as argued by Wolfgang Lange, *Studien zur christlichen Dichtung der Nordgermanen, 1000–1200,* Palaestra, 222 [Göttingen, 1958], pp. 136–37, Ludvig Daae, *Norges Helgener* [Christiania, 1879], pp. 106–07, and others.)

85. A presumably accidental verbal similarity might have reinforced Snorri's association of the Troy story with the folktale; cf. *Vǫluspá* 24, 5–6: "brotin var borðveggr / borgar ása" and *Trójumanna saga,* p. 36: "... brotin var borgin oll."

The objection is valid but, I think, not very significant; Snorri's focus from the beginning of chapter 42 is not on the construction itself but on its results in the form of the birth of Sleipnir and on the explanation of the dark stanzas 25–26. And the fact that it is apparently the first building of the fortress of the gods in chapter 42, *despite* the authority of *Vǫluspá* (and *Trójumanna saga?*) lends weight to our assumption that Snorri was adapting a folktale—which, of course, could only have an initial construction, not a rebuilding.

VII. Conclusions and Summary

For modern writers the Masterbuilder Tale has acquired "mythic" value in an important current literary sense of the word. Wagner transformed Snorri's version in *Das Rheingold,* into an integral part of his parable of greed and broken promises, changing the ending and many details to accommodate the moral meaning of the myth in his interpretation and the mechanics of his fusion of the divine and human histories in his sources, but it is a striking comment on the permutations of the Asgard story that the relatively realistic Wagnerian metamorphosis, lacking Svaðilfari and Loki's shape-shifting, re-approaches the saga episode in some features: there are again two superhuman builders, the brothers Fasolt and Fafner, who, like the berserks of the sagas, actually finished their mighty work, and that in a single night. Later the story—this time drawn from some Norwegian folktale—underwent a still more realistic and radical reshaping in Ibsen's *Bygmester Solness.* The Masterbuilder's fall just after Hilde has called out "Hurra for bygmester Solness!" (a dead-naming) suggests a version of the Finn/Skalle tale with female interference,[86] but Ibsen has by no means been dominated by the structure of his chosen "myth." This kind of "myth" in literature stands in no contradictory relationship to the narrower use of the word in the body of the present study, but Wagner and Ibsen here represent more self-conscious examples of types of permutations of traditional story with retention of "mythic" force, not wholly unlike those of medieval Iceland.

The main historical conclusions of the present study can be summarized in the form of the stemma that follows below. But if

---

86. Cf. n. 51; essential evidence and interpretation in Sehmsdorf (cited n. 3).

correct, these results do not merely annex another bit of apparently autochthonous Nordic narrative for "Southern influence" but provide a glimpse into the workings of oral traditions underlying the realistic sagas and (following Baetke, Holtsmark, and Breiteig) some insight into the workshop of a thirteenth-century scholar. Yet general conclusions, especially of the kind Mogk rushed to, would be very premature. I am aware that an investigation of the present kind must be erected on foundations that often raise grave methodological questions; especially tenuous and perhaps personal are the discernment of "similarities" and judgments of them as genetically significant or not. However, I believe we cannot make progress in the study of Nordic narrative by resigned restatement of the obvious but must be willing to venture into the realm of arguable hypothesis. If the explanatory power of the hypothesis serves to clarify previously problematical relationships, then it has at least a temporary value. I have attempted the "narrow" or more demanding form of the argument at two points—the derivation of Snorri's myth (14) from the local tale at Berserkjahraun (7) rather than the folktale in general (6 or 3) and from *Trójumanna saga* (15) rather than some unspecified form of the Troy story—because even if the "narrow" form with links 7–14 and 15–14 fails to convince, most of the arguments advanced can apply to the vaguer alternative.

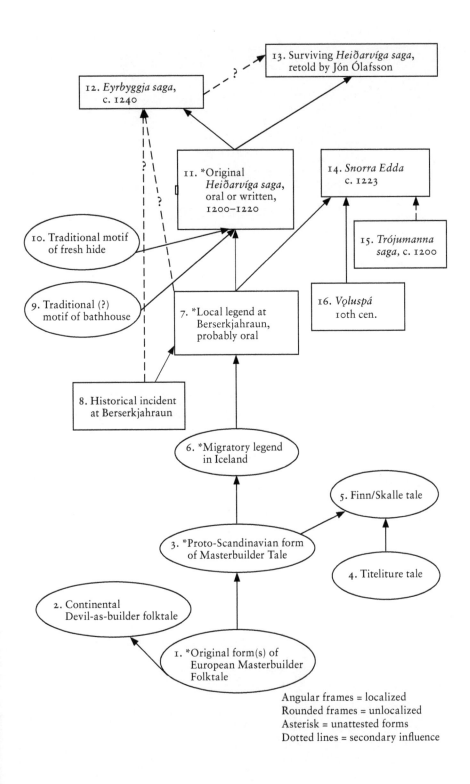

13. Surviving *Heiðarvíga saga*, retold by Jón Ólafsson

12. *Eyrbyggja saga*, c. 1240

11. *Original *Heiðarvíga saga*, oral or written, 1200–1220

14. *Snorra Edda* c. 1223

10. Traditional motif of fresh hide

9. Traditional (?) motif of bathhouse

7. *Local legend at Berserkjahraun, probably oral

15. *Trójumanna saga*, c. 1200

16. *Vǫluspá* 10th cen.

8. Historical incident at Berserkjahraun

6. *Migratory legend in Iceland

5. Finn/Skalle tale

3. *Proto-Scandinavian form of Masterbuilder Tale

4. Titeliture tale

2. Continental Devil-as-builder folktale

1. *Original form(s) of European Masterbuilder Folktale

Angular frames = localized
Rounded frames = unlocalized
Asterisk = unattested forms
Dotted lines = secondary influence

Theme and Genre in Some *Íslendinga Þættir*

The Old Icelandic short stories or novelle conventionally termed þættir[1] seem to be consistently distinguishable from the whole body of relatively long works or sagas only by the criterion of relative length. Except for discussions on a high level of generality, it is less enlightening to speak of *the* saga as a genre inclusive of such widely disparate works as, for example, a contemporary royal biography such as Sturla's *Hákonar saga* and a typical *lygisaga* than to employ smaller categories; similarly it is of limited use to deal critically with the whole heterogeneous body of short narratives as *the* þáttr.[2] Instead we need a division of þættir into their most natural or at least critically revealing groupings based on a sustained attempt to analyse and describe the

---

1. The whole corpus of þættir is estimated at about 100 by Wolfgang Lange, "Einige Bemerkungen zur altnordischen Novelle," *ZDA* 88 (1957), 150–59, and surveyed for content in Herbert S. Joseph, "The Þáttr and the Theory of Saga Origins," *ANF* 87 (1972), 89–96.

2. Anthony Faulkes offers a brief but lucid contrast of þáttr and saga in general, supported by comparison to short and long narrative forms in continental literature, in *Two Icelandic Stories: Hreiðars þáttr [and] Orms þáttr*, Viking Society for Northern Research, Text Series 4 (London, 1968), pp. 1–5; and there are comments on "the" þáttr in Lange and Joseph. However, criteria other than length (and of course there are some "þættir" that are longer than some "sagas"; examples in Lange, p. 153) are difficult to generalize as typical, let alone exclusive, and really seem to characterize only certain groups of þættir. For example, the general features of the whole corpus of þættir (or its best exemplars) mentioned by Andreas Heusler *(Die altgermanische Dichtung,* 2nd ed. rev. [Potsdam, 1941], p. 222), "verdichtete Problemstellung" and concentration on a single point, and by Lange, "inneres Gewicht des Erzählten," describe the group discussed in this paper but not necessarily the entire corpus.

tales according to shared features. In "Genre and Narrative Structure in Some *Íslendinga þættir*"[3] I attempted one aspect of this critical taxonomy by isolating one group of some thirty-one þættir according to Wellek and Warren's prescription for genre study:

> Genre should be conceived, we think, as a grouping of literary works based, theoretically, upon both outer form (specific metre or structure) and also upon inner form (attitude, tone, purpose—more crudely, subject and audience). The ostensible basis may be one or the other ... but the critical problem will then be to find the *other* dimension, to complete the diagram.[4]

The earlier paper dealt with "outer form," especially narrative structure, while my aim here is in the spirit of experimentation to test whether the "diagram" can be completed by finding the "other dimension" in an examination of the "inner form" of the same group of stories.

1. Inner Form as Theme

Wellek and Warren's very general notion of inner form can be interpreted as comprising a work's whole conceptual structure including what Northrop Frye calls theme. In Frye's extended Aristotelian terminology the relevant aspects of narrative are *mythos* (plot) and *dianoia* (thought):

> When a reader of a novel asks, "How is this story going to turn out?" he is asking a question about the plot, specifically about that crucial aspect of the plot which Aristotle calls discovery or *anagnorisis*. But he is equally likely to ask, "What's the *point* of this story?" This question relates to *dianoia* and indicates that themes have their elements of discovery just as plots do.

---

3. SS 44 (1972), 1–27; that article introduces the thirty-one stories, which are cited according to references and abbreviations given there, pp. 2–3, n. 7; no attempt will be made in the present article to cite the literature on all the stories.

4. René Wellek and Austin Warren, *Theory of Literature,* 3rd ed. (New York, 1942), p. 231.

A narrative may emphasize plot, thought, or Frye's third element character and setting, but even the most "objective," plot-dominated work cannot be without its thematic aspect: "There can hardly be a work of literature without some kind of relation, implied or expressed, between its creator and its auditors."[5] In dealing with ancient and anonymous works such as the saga literature there is every reason for caution in drawing conclusions about the relation between the work and its audience, but there is no justification for ignoring the subject altogether. The new view of this material as trustworthy literature rather than history of questionable reliability has opened the way for a criticism that goes beyond the formalism that was the only literary viewpoint until recent decades. Several studies of the methods by which a saga or þáttr communicates meaning have appeared,[6] and the terms "didactic" and "exemplary" have even been used in this connection.[7] The supposed uninterpretability of the sagas has given way to an interest in saga ethics not as historical reflections of the Saga Age but as the literary meaning of predominantly thirteenth century works; however, the conceptual dimension of saga literature has not, as far as I know, been explicitly linked with the problem of genre.[8]

Objections to literary treatment of the thirty-one stories that form the subject of this study could still be raised from the points of view of unity and independence.[9] They are preserved for the most part as episodes in large compilations dealing with the kings of Norway,

---

5. *Anatomy of Criticism* (Princeton, 1957), pp. 52–53; see also the clear discussion by Robert Kellogg and Robert Scholes, *The Nature of Narrative* (New York, 1966), ch. 4.

6. Especially Lars Lönnroth, "Rhetorical Persuasion in the Sagas," *SS* 42 (1970), 157–89; Paul Schach, "Some Forms of Writer Intrusion in the *Íslendingasögur*," *SS* 42 (1970), 128–56; Richard F. Allen, *Fire and Iron: Critical Approaches to Njáls saga* (Pittsburgh, 1971), ch. 5; and Joseph Harris, "Christian Form and Christian Meaning in *Halldórs þáttr I*," *HES* 5 (1974), 249–64. [Reprinted in this volume, Eds.]

7. Especially the work of Hermann Pálsson, but also Lönnroth, "Persuasion" and "Tesen om de två kulturerna: Kritiska studier i den isländska sagaskrivningens sociala förutsättningar," *Scripta Islandica* 15 (1964), 26–28.

8. But cf. T. M. Andersson, "The Displacement of the Heroic Ideal in the Family Sagas," *Speculum* 45 (1970), 575–93, where a connection between common "conceptual interest" in the ten sagas examined and the *Íslendinga sögur* as a genre seems implicit, as is the connection between structure and genre in his *The Icelandic Family Saga: an Analytic Reading* (Cambridge, Mass., 1967).

9. Another type of objection involving the usage of terms like *þáttr* has been raised by Lars Lönnroth, "Tesen," pp. 19–21, and answered by Harris, "Genre and Narrative Structure," pp. 21–27; the debate is continued in *SS* 47 (1975), 419–41.

sometimes headed "þáttr af ..." or "Frá...," sometimes marked off only as separate chapters or occasionally not at all. Nevertheless, virtually all literary historians have offered the opinion that þættir in general were originally independent works; Guðni Jónsson reflects this consensus when he writes:

> Sennilegt er um flesta þættina, að þeir sé upphaflega sjálfstæðar frásag-nir, samdir án þess að til væri beint ætlazt, að þeir væri teknir upp í önnur rit. En vegna efnis þeirra hafa þeir snemma verið felldir inn í sögur þeirra konunga, sem þeir sögðu frá, og hefir það vafalaust orðið til þess að bjarga þeim frá glötun mörgum hverjum.[10]

Jan de Vries explicitly refers to þættir as "kurze selbständige Erzäh-lungen," and this is the implication of most of the critical commentary, translation, and anthologies that have dealt with þættir.[11] The evidence for this view derives from such paleographic facts as the discrepancy between the number of þættir in the existing kings' sagas,[12] the shifting place of some that appear in full or as synopses in several compilations,[13] and linguistic indications that date some

---

10. *ÍF* 7: xcix; cf. *ÍP*, pp. v–vi. Björn Sigfússon has expressed a different view of the relationship of the þættir to the kings' saga (*ÍF* 10: xci): "Þættir eru samdir til fyllingar konunga sögum," but he sees them as "sjálfstæðir." Cf. Sir William Craigie's "Prefa-tory Note" in *Fornar smásögur*, p. iv: "These [full-length sagas], on account of their length, have been preserved as separate works, even although a number of them might be included in one manuscript. On the other hand, each short story would have been written on at most a few leaves of parchment, and so ran a risk of being lost or destroyed in course of time. In this way they would have disappeared if they had not been inserted in, or added to, the longer sagas under the name of þ æ t t i r" (cf. Gardiner, p. x).

11. Jan de Vries, *Altnordische Literaturgeschichte*, 2nd rev. ed. (Berlin, 1964–67), I, 359, II, 326, 337, 427; Finnur Jónsson, *Den oldnorske og oldislandske litteraturs historie*, 2nd ed. (Copenhagen, 1920–23), II, 620 (of *Msk*); *Flateyjarbók*, Corpus Codicum Islandi-corum Medii Ævi, I (Copenhagen, 1930), unpaginated introduction by Finnur Jónsson; *Morkinskinna*, CCIMÆ, VII (Copenhagen, 1934), introduction by Jón Helgason, pp. 13–14; Hans Bekker-Nielsen, Thorkil Damsgaard Olsen, and Ole Widding, *Norrøn fortællekunst* (n.p., 1965), pp. 70, 72; Guðni Jónsson, *Íslendinga þættir* (Reykjavík, 1935), pp. v–vi and *ÍF* 6: cix; W. H. Wolf-Rottkay, *Altnordisch-isländisches Lesebuch* (Munich, 1967), p. 6; this independence is also widely assumed where unstated: Stefán Einarsson, *A History of Icelandic Literature* (Baltimore, 1957), pp. 114, 122, 137; Kurt Schier, *Sagaliteratur* (Stuttgart, 1970), p. 2; Eugen Mogk, *Norwegisch-isländische Lit-eratur*, Grundriss der germanischen Philologie, ed. H. Paul, 2nd ed., II: 1 (Strassburg, 1901–09), 771–79, etc.

12. Especially important is the discrepancy between *Msk* and *Flat*; cf. Jón Helgason, p. 14; de Vries, II, 280.

13. For example, *Sneglu-Halla þáttr* is found abbreviated but in place in the extant

þættir, at least in the case of *Morkinskinna,* earlier than the main history.[14] Internal references in some stories are redundant in the larger context or even contradict that context or other þættir,[15] and reading sequentially through a compilation such as *Morkinskinna* reveals great differences in style.[16]

In addition some þættir exist also in anthology manuscripts independent of any "host" saga. In some cases these independent texts may have been excerpted from the *konunga sögur,* but this would at least be evidence that the anthologists of the later Middle Ages regarded the stories as more or less self-sufficient. These conclusions about the original independence of þættir are best supported by particular text histories. *Stúfs þáttr,* the best example, is extant in an independent version and a version adapted and trimmed to its place in *Morkinskinna,* and B. M. Ólsen has shown conclusively that the independent version, though extant in later manuscripts, represents the original more closely.[17] Somewhat similarly *Gull-Ásu-Þórðar þáttr* is found in an independent form, attested late, and also adapted in the continuum of *Morkinskinna;*[18] and *Þorsteins þáttr sögufróða* probably existed first only independently, though now represented by a kings' saga version and a fuller independent

---

Msk but very much fuller and added as an appendix in *Flat*. Probably the original of *Msk* did not have the þáttr, and the extant *Msk* added it, while severely condensing, from an independent source also known to *Flat* (see *ÍF* 9: cix–cxiv).

14. Finnur Jónsson, ed., *Morkinskinna* (Copenhagen, 1932), pp. viii–xl (for *Hreiðars þáttr* cf. Faulkes, pp. 20–22).

15. Especially brought out by Bjarni Aðalbjarnason, *Om de norske kongers sagaer,* Skrifter utgitt av Det Norske Videnskaps-Akademi i Oslo, II. Hist.-Filos. Klasse, 1936, no. 4 (Oslo, 1937), 154–59, but also mentioned elsewhere. Some evidence, too, may be derived from express comments of contemporaries as in the preface of *Flat* which enumerates the manuscript's contents in such terms as: "Þar næst frá Ólafi konungi Tryggvasyni meðr öllum sínum þáttum. Því næst er saga Ólafs konungs hins helga Haraldssonar meðr öllum sínum þáttum" *(Flateyjarbók,* ed. V. Bjarnar and F. Guðmundsson [Reykjavík, 1944–45], I).

16. Final word on all matters relating to the textual history of the þættir of *Msk* must await publication of the book on that subject in preparation by Heinrich Gimmler. [*Die Thættir der Morkinskinna: ein Beitrag zur Uberlieferungsproblematik und zur Typologie der altnordischen Kurzerzählung,* Johann Wolfgang Goethe-Universität zu Frankfurt am Main, Fachbereich 10—Neuere Philologien, Diss., 1972. Eds.]

17. B. M. Ólsen, *Stúfs saga,* Árbók háskóla Íslands, 1911 (Reykjavík, 1911); cf. *ÍF* 5: xcii–xciv; the kings' saga version is found in *Msk, Hulda, Hrokkinskinna,* and *Flat*; both versions are edited in *ÍF* 5 and *Íslendinga sögur,* ed. Guðni Jónsson (= *ÍS*; Reykjavík, 1953), vol. 4.

18. *ÍF* 11: cxiv–cxvii (Jón Jóhannesson).

version in later manuscripts.[19] Only one of this group of þættir exists *only* in an independent form: *Þorsteins þáttr Austfirðings* is headed "Af Þorsteini Austfirðing" and "Ævintýr af Þorsteini nokkrum aust-firzkum" in its paper manuscripts; it was never adapted for inclusion in a king's saga.[20]

While the arguments behind the assumption of original independence of the þættir in general are impressive and supported by such clear cases as that of *Stúfs þáttr,* it may yet be that not all þættir or even all of the group under study can be regarded as artistically autonomous works. Hence the more cautious formulations of some literary historians are entirely justified, for example: "many such episodes were themselves originally independent stories ... little doubt that many of them were originally independent" (Anthony Faulkes); "der tildeles dem en vis selvstændighed indenfor disse [større saga-værker] og med rette" (Finnur Jónsson).[21] Among the thirty-one þættir some will be more readily accepted as independent than others; *Auðunar þáttr* and *Hreiðars þáttr,* for example, are widely known and appreciated, but *Þorsteins þáttr Síðu-Hallssonar* was omitted from the collected *Íslendinga þættir* and the appropriate *Fornrit* edition and has attracted no critical comment or translation.[22]

From another point of view the question of independence is replaced by that of unity: are these whole and unified works and therefore fit objects of critical scrutiny? The consensus agrees in general that they are; *Sneglu-Halla þáttr, Ísleifs þáttr,* and a few others less tightly composed than most have already been discussed in this connection but seem to exhibit enough common features of the genre to be included, while *Ögmundar þáttr* has, I have argued elsewhere, a

---

19. *ÍF* 11: cxii–cxiv (Jón Jóhannesson).

20. *ÍF* 11: cxi–cxii (Jón Jóhannesson); also *Þorsteins þáttr forvitna* is found only independently though included with other þættir appended to the sagas of Magnús and Haraldr in *Flat.*

21. Faulkes, pp. 1–2; *Litt. hist.,* II, 540; also Sigurður Nordal, "Sagalitteraturen," in *Litteraturhistorie: B. Norge og Island,* Nordisk kultur 8:B (Oslo, 1953), 243–44; B. Kahle, *Kristnisaga ... ,* Altnordische Saga-Bibliothek 11 (Halle, 1905), xvi.

22. *Þorsteins þáttr* is recognized by Finnur Jónsson, *Litt. hist.,* II, 620–21 and *Msk,* p. xix; Bjarni Aðalbjarnarson, pp. 154–56; Einar Ólafur Sveinsson, *ÍF* 8: cxvii–cxviii; but is printed separately only in *ÍS* 10. One factor determining which stories we regard as autonomous seems to be the accidents of scholarly tradition since some þættir were culled out as "pearls" (the insistent metaphor of generations of scholars) of Old Norse narrative art in early translations.

unity all its own.[23] Clearly the modern compositions such as "Sighvats þáttr" cannot be admitted, even though some manuscripts did occasionally divide a story into separated sections.[24] *Sturlu þáttr* forms a case apart; since it seems to be intended as a continuation of *Þorgils saga skarða* and opens with a cross-reference to a passage in that saga, it is probably best not to consider this þáttr as artistically autonomous in the sense that the others of this group apparently are. Nevertheless there are real similarities between the story material, structure and tone of *Sturlu þáttr* and others of the group.[25]

With caution, then, and pending more detailed study in several specific cases, we can assume that the thirty-one þættir are largely independent and more or less unified works of literature and hence that Frye's question "What is the point of this story?" is not misplaced. However, the saga literature offers no terminology to indicate the presence of theoretical thought about literature in terms of outer and inner form or *mythos* and *dianoia*, nothing analogous to Chrétien de Troyes' celebrated triad of *matière, sens,* and *conjointure,* the Chaucerian *fruit* and *chaff,* or the patristic *cortex* and *medulla (integumentum, nux, nucleus,* etc.). Usually saga *sens* is deeply implicit, but among the þættir at least scribes and authors sometimes speak out in one way or another about the meaning of their work, occasionally very clearly.

For example, *Þorsteins þáttr Ausfirðings* tells how a poor Icelander saved the life of a stranger who had been deserted in combat by his comrades and who later proved to be King Magnús Ólafsson; when the Icelander is mocked by the retainers, King Magnús defends him:

"Sá inn sami maðr veitti mér mikit lið, þá er þér váruð hvergi í nánd ok gerði þat við þann, er hann vissi eigi hverr at var, ok mun hann vera góðr drengr, ok er þat vitugra, at gera eigi mikit spott at ókunnum manni, því at leitun mun í vera, at röskvari maðr fáisk ok betr hugaðr, ok svá mun ok sumum sýnask, at þat væri happ, er honum bar til handa." (*ÍÞ*, p. 351)

---

23. Ögmundar þáttr dytts ok Gunnars helmings: Unity and Literary Relations," forthcoming in *ANF.* [Reprinted in this volume, Eds.]

24. "Genre and Narrative Structure," p. 3, n. 7 and p. 15.

25. B. M. Ólsen, *Um Sturlunga,* Safn til sögu Íslands 3 (1902), 495–98; Pétur Sigurðsson, *Um Íslendinga sögu Sturla Þórðarsonar,* SSÍ 6 (1933), 137–38; *Sturlunga saga,* ed. Jón Jóhannesson, Magnús Finnbogason, and Kristján Eldjárn (Reykjavík, 1946), II, xlviii–xlix; *Sturlunga saga,* ed. Guðni Jónsson (Reykjavík, 1954), III, xi.

To this Þorsteinn replies:

"Auðsét var þat, herra, at guð sendi mik yðr til hlífðar, þvi at miklu meira fannsk mér um yðar ásjónu en þú værir alþýðu maðr, ok brá mér þessu í skap, at duga þér." (*ÍP*, p. 351)

Thus the story concerns appearance and reality in human relations, the best attitude toward a stranger, and the potential powerful friend in any stranger; and these themes are given a numinous quality and divine sanction by references to fortune and God's will. This story, a version of the international tale known as "The King in Disguise," has analogues which interpret themselves similarly, and with these parallels there can be no misunderstanding the "point" or "points" of the story of Þorsteinn.[26]

Nevertheless, the meaning of a story was not fixed for all time by the author or first recorder, and sometimes a diachronic factor has to be considered. For example, the most familiar version of *Steins þáttr,* that of *Heimskringla,* tells how the hero fell out with King Ólafr Haraldsson and fled from court and how a partial reconciliation was brought about through the mediation of friends. Steinn owed his life to an earlier good deed through which he gained the lasting friendship of Ragnhildr Erlingsdóttir, and the þáttr introduces this information as a rare authorial retrogression after the story has unrolled to its structural midpoint. The retrogression seems to be an intentional artistic device having the effect of holding the reader's attention and bringing a cause, actually distant in time, into direct juxtaposition with its effect: Steinn sowed kindness and harvested friendship and support. We witness the snowballing effect of support so well known to the sagas, and blame for the initial estrangement between Steinn and Ólafr is equally distributed in this objective treatment. In a later manuscript, however, a scribe, perhaps offended by Steinn's defiance of the king and saint, has "reinterpreted" the story to the Icelander's discredit by adding an epilogue telling how he came to a bad end and explaining: "Gafsk honum svá af ofmetnaði ok óhlýðni við Óláf konung" (*ÍP*, p. 266).

---

26. Full discussion in Joseph Harris, "The King in Disguise: An International Popular Tale in Two Old Icelandic Adaptations" [reprinted in this volume, Eds.].

A similar reinterpretation seems to have occurred in the case of *Ásbjarnar þáttr Selsbana* where the older texts present an impartial story which in the oldest non-fragmentary version carries the following sober authorial or scribal indication to the reader of the significance of the tale: "Af þui likum lutum ma nokcot marka um viðr skipti þæirra Olafs konongs oc ærlings."[27] However, the redactor of the *Flateyjarbók* version is of a slightly different opinion as to the "point" of the story: "koma þó öll [stories about St. Ólafr] í einn stað niðr áðr lúki, þvíat þau hníga ok hallast öll til vegs og virðingar hinum heilaga Ólafi annathvot sakir jarteignagerðar eðr frægðar ok framaverka, einarðar eðr öruggleiks, sem enn mun lýsat í eftirfaranda efni ok æfintýri."[28] This statement clearly represents a more pious reading of the story. It appears that in the course of its evolution the þáttr has acquired the extended episode of Ásbjörn's death, and the correspondence of a simple historical explanation with the short version of the hero's death in the earliest version and a religious "moral" with the expansively told slaying of Ásbjörn in the later version probably constitute two interpretations separated by more than a century.

Such scribal interpretations can be misleading. In the case of *Ívars þáttr,* for example, the story itself suggests an interpretation emphasizing the friendship and the *confidant* relationship between king and Icelander, and King Eysteinn observes that Ívarr should come to him each day to talk about his lost sweetheart: "því at þat verðr stundum, at mönnum verðr harms síns at léttara, er um er rœtt"—a sentiment that suggests unforced the courtly idea that heart's ease is the sharing of heart's sorrow.[29] Yet to this tale of *amour de loin,* its effect, and its resolution in the confidences of a friend, a scribe or redactor has appended an interpretation that narrows the themes of the þáttr to an exposition of the relevant aspects of the king's character: "Í þeima hlut má marka, er nú mun ek segja, hverr dýrðarmaðr Eysteinn konungr

---

27. *Ólafs saga hins helga,* ed. O. A. Johnsen (Kristiania, 1922), p. 47.

28. *Fornar smásögur,* p. 153.

29. *ÍÞ,* p. 154; the sentiment quoted is paralleled in the *Roman de la Rose* (ll. 3099–3110) but also in *Hávamál* (121, 8–10; 124, 1–3) and probably widely elsewhere (e.g., Harley lyrics [ed. G. Brook], No. 9, ll. 41–44); the universal nature of "courtly love" is argued with Scandinavian examples in Peter Dronke, *Medieval Latin and the Rise of European Love-Lyric* (Oxford, 1965), I, 39–42, 243–47; for connections with various sagas and a different interpretation see Hermann Pálsson, *Hrafnkel's Saga and Other Icelandic Stories* (Penguin: Baltimore, 1971), pp. 21–22.

var, eða hvé mjök hann var vinhollr ok hugkvæmr eptir at leita við sína ástmenn, hvat þeim væri at harmi" (*ÍP*, p. 151).

Caution is necessary, then, in treating these stories as literature: basic thematic contents of the stories were subject to reinterpretation by scribe/redactors with consonant changes in the narratives; and it is not established for every exemplar of the group that it was created as an artistically independent, unitary work, though that is a safe generalization. But with the additional caveat that literary meaning is never exactly paraphrasable and always distorted in analysis, we may survey the thirty-one þættir for thematic common denominators and attempt finally to sketch the inner form of the group.

2. Survey of Thematic Content

The theme of friendship, though in forms less sentimental than *Ívars þáttr*, is important in these stories generally. *Gull-Ásu-Þórðar þáttr, Þorsteins þáttr Síðu-Hallssonar,* and *Steins þáttr* (already discussed) embody this theme in a peculiarly effective form since in each the hero's survival depends entirely on the intervention of his friends. All three stories make it clear that even one friend can be a man's salvation in dire circumstances since that friend may lead to another more powerful ally, and all three imply the rather unromantic notion of friendship as a practical reciprocal arrangement.

In fact friendship is not easily dissociated in these stories from another general ethical principle, equally unromantically conceived, that of gift-giving. Gull-Ásu-Þórðr overcomes the disdain of Víðkunnr by the timely presentation of a poem; and when real trouble begins for Þórðr, Víðkunnr backs him, then calls on his own more powerful friend Sigurðr Hranason, who in turn calls in the most powerful friend of all King Eysteinn (both friendships are based on obligations incurred in the past). Similarly Þorsteinn Síðu-Hallsson first establishes his claim on Einarr, who in the end is able to reconcile King Magnús to the Icelander, through a persuasive gift of fine horses; Einarr himself is too old and careful to accept the gift with its obligation, but his son Eindriði welcomes the horses and the Icelander's case. The stories of Auðunn vestfirzkr and Þorvarðr krákunef can be understood as glosses on the proverb "æ sér gjöf til gjafar"; both *Auðunar þáttr* and *Þorvarðs þáttr* concern a hero from the West

Fjords whose regal gift is the occasion for a contrast between the all too human Haraldr harðráði and a rival. Though *Auðunar þáttr* is far too rich and complex to be adequately summed up with the proverb, *Þorvarðs þáttr* gives a good illustration of the reciprocity and obligatory nature of gift-giving in archaic and primitive societies: a gift must not be refused without reason, should not be hoarded, and must be repaid.[30] Thus King Haraldr's initial act in refusing the sail proffered by Þorvarðr is anti-social, and Eysteinn orri, stepping into the king's role, accepts and repays the gift, later relaying it to the king. Though Haraldr acquires the sail in the end, his behavior has been thoroughly discredited.

The closely related theme of generosity and its proper limits is common to *Brands þáttr, Ísleifs þáttr,* and *Þáttr Þormóðar.* In the first of these King Haraldr harðráði becomes annoyed hearing again and again about the far-famed generosity of Brandr and decides to test the Icelander by demanding first his cloak, second his axe, and third the very tunic off his back. Brandr hands over each immediately but cuts one sleeve off the tunic, and Haraldr draws the right conclusion, underscoring the point of the tale: "Þessi maðr er bæði vitr ok stór-lyndr. Auðsét er mér, hví hann hefir erminni af sprett; honum þykkir sem ek eiga eina höndina, ok þá þó at þiggja ávallt en veita aldrigi" (*ÍP*, p. 20). Thus generosity is presented as a praiseworthy quality, but its proper nature also involves mutual obligation and reciprocity. In the first episode of *Ísleifs þáttr* Brandr and Ísleifr stand briefly in the shadow of King Haraldr's displeasure because Brandr had passed on with unseemly swiftness the king's gift mantle; a king's gift might be given away, but the circumstances should be extraordinary (as King Sveinn had pointed out in *Auðunar þáttr).* The tension is resolved when Haraldr sees the good priest Ísleifr wearing the mantle and is so impressed that he pronounces the cloak his own gift to Ísleifr, giving Brandr an equivalent reward and commending himself to Ísleifr's prayers. In this episode, as in that of Ísleifr's marriage, the þáttr emphasizes the godliness that shone through in the young priest's appearance; one glance told the astute king that Brandr's

---

30. The anthropological view of Marcel Mauss, *The Gift: Forms and Functions of Exchange in Archaic Societies,* transl. I. Cunnison (Glencoe, Ill., 1954), throws an interesting light on Germanic gift-giving.

generosity had not been rashly bestowed, and Haraldr's own generosity is doubled.

Þáttr Þormóðar contrasts the treacherous and stingy character of Knútr inn ríki with the divinely colored generosity of Saint Ólafr. The first part of the þáttr tells how Þormóðr reluctantly comes to serve Knútr as court poet and how he has to wring his agreed-upon reward from the close-fisted Dane; in addition Knútr puts Þormóðr's life in danger by prevailing on him much against his will to accept the post of *stafnbúi* with a disreputable viking attached to the Danes. In the second part, by contrast, King Ólafr grants the poet his life in spite of his great offense in having killed the Norwegian *stafnbúi*. Established ethical values—royal generosity, the loyalty it inspires, and a king's regard for the life and wishes of a follower—are here employed for a tendentious historical comparison as in *Þorleifs þáttr, Hreiðars þáttr,* and widely elsewhere.

A number of the stories hold up for admiration the value of wit, the ready answer and facile verse or tale, portraying situations in which the hero's advancement into favor with the king depends on his verbal wit. *Óttars þáttr* is a typical case of headransoming through poetry, but it is interesting that Óttarr's initial offense also derives from his having been too bold with words. In this respect it resembles *Sneglu-Halla þáttr,* a tale which more than any other is predicated on the value of wit; one of Halli's taunts in his flyting with Þjóðólfr is that the rival poet had carried out ashes as a child because he was thought "til einkis annars fœrr fyrir vitsmuna sakir, ok varð þó um at sjá, at eigi væri eldr í, því at hann þurfti allt vit sitt í þann tíma" (*ÍP*, p. 232). *Þorsteins þáttr sögufróða* and *Sturlu þáttr* are both familiar examples of the averting of a king's wrath through saga-telling, though Sturla also presented his poems so well that the king observed he recited better than the Pope. A similar situation in *Stúfs þáttr* is resolved through the hero's feats of memory and poetic composition; here the theme of wit is underscored in the king's final speech: "Satt er þat, at kvæðit er allvel kveðit, ok ek skil nú, hver efni í eru um þitt mál, at þú munt eiga mikit undir þér um vitsmuni ... skal þér ok kostr hirðvistar ok at vera með oss, ef þú vill" (*ÍP*, p. 273). In general the literature shows poets surviving and sometimes imperiled by their wits, and the opportune (e.g. *Gull-Ásu-Þórðar þáttr*) or rash (e.g. *Steins þáttr*) verse has a role in several other stories of our group.

Þorleifs þáttr jarlsskálds shows the dark side of the universal theme of the power of poetry. Þorleifr suffers under the arbitrary violence of Hákon jarl and flees to Denmark, but he returns in disguise in a kind of mock reconciliation scene to blast Hákon with a magical satire; for Þorleifr knew not only to compose praise poetry but had learned the ancient art that made the poet feared: *níð*.[31]

However, the surviving version of *Þorleifs þáttr* emphasizes the ethical-religious situation above all. Hákon's tyrannical behavior is natural to a man who traditionally represented the worst in heathendom, and the þáttr confronts him with a foil in the Christian king of Denmark, Sveinn Forkbeard. The author had a talent not only for the grotesque but for effective contrasts, and the central part of the þáttr is structured as four contrasting scenes. At Sveinn's court Þorleifr asks to present a poem, and the king inquires about his qualifications; the poem is a "fertug drápa," the most honorable and ornate of poems, having a refrain that links Sveinn with divine authority ("gipta öðlings himins röðla"), and is presented by a brilliant young (nineteen) skáld. In the corresponding scene in Norway, Þorleifr appears as an old churl calling himself Níðungr Gjalandason, asks to recite and is questioned on his qualifications; the poem itself is the "verstrbragr," a *níð* that shatters Hákon's reputation instead of enhancing it. Sveinn gave distinguished gifts as a "kvæðislaun," but Hákon received a terrible *kvæði* as *laun* for his greed and overbearing. Upon his return to Denmark Sveinn welcomed Þorleifr and outfitted him with a ship, cargo, and crew, while in the contrasting scene in Norway, the initial meeting of the jarl and the poet, Hákon had threatened Þorleifr, burned his ship, stolen his cargo, and hanged his crew. Finally, as if we might miss this message, the þáttr opens with a long and extreme denunciation of the pagan Hákon in heavy Christian rhetoric, closing on a similar note, and the author's or redactor's Christian indignation stands in amusing juxtaposition to the Odinic role of his hero and the primitive character of his basic *Stoff*.

---

31. *Sneglu-Halla þáttr* probably provides the best gloss on the central implications of Þorleifr's story: King Haraldr said to Einarr fluga: "svá mun fara með ykkr, sem fór með þeim Hákoni Hlaðajarli ok Þorleifi skáldi, ok þat sama gerir Halli ... ok megu vit sjá, at bitit hefir níðit ríkari mann en svá sem þú ert, Einarr, sem var Hákon jarl, ok mun þat munat, meðan Norðrlönd eru byggð, ok er verri einn kviðlingr, um dýran mann kveðinn, ef munaðr er eptir, en lítil fémúta" *(ÍP, p. 239–40).*

Christian views come to dominate in nine further stories. *Gísls þáttr, Halldórs þáttr I,* and *Hrafns þáttr* all establish a situation in which a magistrate has the power to avenge a killing but is moved by religious considerations to forgiveness and reconciliation, and all three stories contrast the oldfashioned retaliatory ethic as practiced by the protagonists with Christian leniency on the part of the rulers. This same formulation also covers the special case of the two-part *Ögmundar þáttr* (perhaps also *Þáttr Þormóðar* though the religious atmosphere is not so strong there), and these four stories are among the richest of the group.

In *Gísls þáttr* the young hero arrives in Norway with a mission of revenge against one of King Magnús Bareleg's retainers, and he carries it out manfully despite great odds. The Icelanders then in Niðarós, under the leadership of Teitr Ísleifsson, band together and resolve to free their countryman; their conduct is honorable but ultimately ineffective, and the causes of the king's relenting are the justice of the hero's grievance, his own courage and rectitude, and especially the supernatural aid mediated by the Icelandic priest Jón Ögmundarson. At Gísl's nadir he is fettered and cast into a dungeon; his execution is ordered, but all this takes place on a Saturday, and before the king's command can be carried out church bells ring to signal the official beginning of the holy day. The author is delightfully evasive about the ringing of the bells: the king attributes it to a conspiracy of ecclesiastics; and though the bishop denies this, Priest Jón says nothing; Gísl himself attributes his rescue by the "noon-bells" to his having twice spared the life of his enemy Gjafvaldr out of pious motives. The author does not take a position between these two opinions, but when we compare the very similar motifs in *Ásbjarnar þáttr,* where Þórarinn Nefjólfsson bribes the bellman to ring in Easter Sunday early in order to save the life of Ásbjörn, it becomes clear that the author has provided us with a real choice between the divine agency imagined by the idealistic Gísl and the rationalistic alternative envisioned by the king. In either case these bells, like those of *Ásbjarnar þáttr* and *Þorsteins þáttr skelks* (perhaps even like the Easter bells of Goethe's *Faust),* mark a peripeteia and a salvation. The shadow of Jón the Priest also falls over the episode of Gjafvaldr's repentance, and the reconciliation completed, the narrative focuses on Jón and how he cured a repentant antagonist who was certain that Jón's words had "bitten" him—again a divine act through the agency of Priest Jón.

Halldórs þáttr I comprises a triple Alienation/Reconciliation structure with motivation for the reconciliations generated by a story-within-the-story, Einarr þambarskelfir's retelling of his youthful experience with King Ólafr Tryggvason. I have argued elsewhere that the story-within-the-story, which so obviously carries exemplary force, is in fact a typological narrative;[32] but whether I have proved my case or not the force of the Christian values of forgiveness and reconciliation are especially clear in this tale.

Hrafns þáttr, like *Gísls þáttr* and *Halldórs þáttr I*, presents a hero who is saved from the king's wrath more by an act of God through his saints than by worldly power and influence.[33] The contrast of effective divine causation with ineffective secular strength is present in all three—Teitr's forces and Bergljót's show of strength do not achieve the reconciliations—but is especially emphasized in Hrafn's story. In parallel scenes Sighvatr, Hrafn's kinsman, approaches the two powerful nobles Einarr inn naumdælski and Einarr þambarskelfir seeking help: "Eða hvat skal ek þar eiga, er þú ert? ... Skal ek nökkut traust eiga, þar er þú ert, Einarr?" (*ÍÞ*, p. 108). When both fail him, Sighvatr makes his third appeal, this time to the true source of help, religion in the form of the sainted Ólafr: "er ok enn eptir fulltrúinn minn, ok skal nú þagat leita traustsins, sem enn hefir aldrei bilat; en þat er inn heilagi Óláfr konungr" (*ÍÞ*, p. 109). Later, after the saint's intervention has succeeded, Sighvatr reveals to all assembled that he had prayed to the saint for help "þá er hann hafði ekki traust af félögum sínum" (*ÍÞ*, p. 112). So *Hrafns þáttr* emphasizes more than its two companion þættir that true *traust* is in God and his saints. Divine intervention, however, begins before Sighvatr's prayer since in view of the ending it is in this light that we must see the two major coincidences of Hrafn's Norwegian outlawry: his chance encounter with King Magnús in the woods and his arrival at the site where Magnús's fleet was anchored awaiting a wind (a wind which seems to stay only for Hrafn and indeed springs up after Sighvatr's prayer).

---

32. Harris, "Christian Form."
33. Cf. Einar Ólafur Sveinsson's introduction, *ÍF* 8: cxvii–cxx.

The prayer brings Saint Ólafr's aid in the form of a dream appearance and admonition to Magnús, and in the battle itself the saint was seen fighting on Magnús's side.

Hrafns þáttr shares a number of other features with *Gísls þáttr* and *Halldórs þáttr I*; all are late and largely fictional, and all show strong traces of the learned style, with alliteration, pairing of words and phrases, and parallel constructions. More strikingly, all end in an assembly or trial scene in which the premises for the story's reconciliations are revealed as one or more retrospective narratives. Hrafn is, like Gísl, a young man more sinned against than sinning; like Gísl he shows heroic virtue and stoic courage at every point, and his revenge—both in the Icelandic feud that forms the Introduction and in the main part of his þáttr—is justified though the lesson of all three stories clearly lies in tempering justice with mercy.

Ögmundar þáttr dytts ok Gunnars helmings is a single þáttr composed of two parallel parts with different sets of characters, but as a whole it fits into the thematic pattern of the three tales just discussed. The first half is set in pagan times during the rule of Hákon jarl and concerns the personal honor, family pride, and revenge of the pre-Christian ethical code, while the second half takes place against a Christian background in the reign of King Ólafr Tryggvason and concerns allegiance to Christianity and the king who embodies it. Since *Ögmundar þáttr* has been discussed in detail elsewhere,[34] I will only add that a kind of typology may be observed here too; the type of the Old Law correlates with the period before the *siðaskipti*, with its story of an eye for an eye, and that of the New Dispensation, with its tale of salvation and reconciliation, with the Christian period in Scandinavia.

Three more stories, *Þorvalds þáttr tasalda, Egils þáttr Síðu-Halls-sonar,* and *Þorsteins þáttr forvitna,* employ the device of a mission whereby the hero wins forgiveness of his sovereign. All are actuated by the kind of divine intervention that we have seen especially in *Hrafns þáttr,* and *Egils þáttr* and *Þorvalds þáttr* also show the blessings of Christian conversion in similar ways. *Þorvalds þáttr*[35] is a relatively uncomplicated tale given a rather schematic treatment and composed of a frame and an episode: the former telling how

---

34. Harris, *"Ögmundar þáttr."*
35. Cf. Jónas Kristjánsson's introduction, *ÍF* 9: lxiv–lxvi.

Þorvaldr was defamed to King Ólafr by one Helgi, a retainer, and how he redeemed himself by bringing in the old heathen Bárðr for baptism; the latter relating Þorvaldr's conflict with Bárðr. The Bárðr episode is romantic and shows numerous similarities with *Þorsteins þáttr uxafóts* and other monster-quelling tales and some remarkable resemblances to Snorri's tale of Útgarðaloki. Of thematic importance, however, is that Þorvaldr's victory is due to the intervention in a dream of the saintly King Ólafr Tryggvason, to an amulet with the names of God, and to the hero's timely prayer (as in *Ögmundar þáttr* and many versions of the Beowulf-Grettir story). Bárðr had always been one of those redeemable heathens who rejected idols and sacrifices but believed in his own might and main; and now that he has found a man who is stronger, through God's help, he is willing to worship that man's God. The story closes with Bárðr's soul-saving conversion, death in white, and the happy disposition of his property and daughter; Þorvaldr shows restraint in dealing with the villain Helgi, who is merely turned out of service.

Like *Þorvalds þáttr*, *Egils þáttr*[36] tells of a young Icelander who is readmitted to the king's (Ólafr Haraldsson's) favor on condition of his bringing in a recalcitrant old heathen for baptism, also having a plot structure composed of a frame and an inset episode (the mission). Throughout both stories the hero is closely accompanied by his faithful Pylades (Sigurðr, Tófi), and these friends take over the land and possessions of the ex-renegade who dies soon after baptism (Tófi succeeds Valgautr as son and heir; Sigurðr marries Bárðr's daughter and inherits his land). In both stories the heroes are captured and stay overnight with their pagan host-captor; in both the hero receives divine aid on his mission, and the king comes out of town to meet the approaching heathen and baptize him there. Despite these similarities, however, *Egils þáttr* is written in a different style

---

36. *Egils þáttr* is treated as independent by Finnur Jónsson, *Litt. hist.*, II, 551 and Mogk, p. 775; its manuscripts are: (1) *Flat,* (2) *Tómasskinna,* (3) *Bergsbók,* (4) Legendary Saga (ed. Johnsen, pp. 48–51); (5) paper manuscripts *(Sex söguþættir,* ed. Jón Þorkelsson [Reykjavík, 1855]); and a summary in *Heimskringla (Ólafs saga helga,* ch. 155) and Snorri's Separate Saga of St. Ólafr. The relationships among the first four are discussed by Sigurður Nordal, *Om Olaf den helliges saga: en kritisk undersøgelse* (Copenhagen, 1914), pp. 65–66, 124–25, but the changes in *Tómasskinna* and other literary relations (for example with *Jóns saga helga)* require more study; the þáttr is discussed here in the *Flat* version *(ÍÞ).*

from that of *Þorvalds þáttr,* more realistic, set in a more modern period, and less openly relying on supernatural agency; and despite a few flaws, *Egils þáttr* is one of the most complex and highly wrought of the group.

Egils þáttr is emphatically a religious story embodying themes of reconciliation and conversion, each especially associated with one part of the plot structure; but as the main plot and the episode (mission) converge at the end, so do the separate themes. The episode (mission to Valgautr) establishes a contrast between the Christian court of Ólafr and that of the heathen jarl, who is so opposed to the king and his faith that he imprisons his guests, including his own son Tófi; but Egill speaks to the jarl of Saint Ólafr with a wondrous, even unearthly eloquence that moves Valgautr to relent so far as to promise to meet with the king. This secures the king's pardon for Egill and Tófi, but the old man still refuses conversion until, suddenly falling sick, he feels the wrath of God.

The main story tells of Egill's offense to the king, how he suffered for it, and how reconciliation was at last achieved. The sickness that falls so heavily on Egill, though naturalistically motivated, is expressive of his estrangement from the holy king; and when Ólafr relents in his anger and touches Egill, his cure begins. Not only is the theme of Christian reconciliation expressed in the main action of the story, but it is underscored by thematic use of words and phrases such as *sáttar-fund* and *koma á fund* throughout. It is only at the end of the story, however, when the action of the episode and that of the main story converge that we realize conversion is also a kind of *sáttarfund* and retrospectively notice the parallelism between events and language of the episode and those of the main tale.

Þorsteins þáttr forvitna does not so much condemn the curiosity of the title as exalt the power of Saint Ólafr who from the first protects and guides Þorsteinn on his quest for a golden bough. Perhaps it is the saint himself who appears as a hermit to end Þorsteinn's wanderings in the woods, to hear a kind of confession from him, to chastize his meddling, and to put him on the "right way" ("en réttan farveg hefir þú enn"). In any case Þorsteinn withstands his penance bravely though he must call on the saint for protection against the dragon. In almost any other medieval language a story such as Þorsteinn's would be said to possess allegorical resonances, but perhaps it is as well to rest content with its obvious religious significance.

Þorsteins þáttr skelks, a delightful anecdote with folktale connections, is neither solemn nor heavily didactic; in form it is a farcical version of the kind of tragic encounter with evil presented by *Þiðranda þáttr ok Þorhalls.* Nevertheless its Christian message and values are serious. Þorsteinn (like Þorsteinn forvitni and Egill Síðu-Hallsson) endures his adventure in consequence of having disobeyed his king (Ólafr Tryggvason); but luckily he has the *sang-froid* to deceive the devil into giving vent to screams, knowing that King Ólafr will awaken and have the church bells rung to put the demon to flight. The Christian powers are more than sufficient to save the hero, but the devil's information about Hell is also edifying: Sigurðr Fafnisbani and Starkaðr inn gamli, the best and the worst of the pre-Christian heroes, suffer accordingly.

Finally there is *Þórarins þáttr I,* a story concerned with liberality and hospitality that indicates a "brother's keeper" is rewarded and protected by God. Þórarinn and Þorsteinn pledge mutual friendship and that they will always lodge together when in the same land. First this is exemplified in Þorsteinn's visit to Iceland; then in Norway Þórarinn uses his old friendship with King Ólafr to obtain lodgings at court for Þorsteinn—a seemingly impossible request on behalf of a Dane and retainer of Ólafr's archenemy King Knútr. Þórarinn is next forced to procure a place in the hall for his nephew Bjarni and to take responsibility for Bjarni's actions. All this creates a situation in which Ólafr is susceptible to suspicion, and the jealousy of two treacherous courtiers, Helgi and Þórir, is excited. A conspiracy and slander result in a false accusation and a trial: in the ordeal the innocence of the three heroes is attested by the judgment of God, and the plotters are eventually punished. *Þórarins þáttr* is one of the richest and best of the group. Like *Halldórs þáttr I, Gísls þáttr,* and *Hrafns þáttr* it climaxes in a trial scene where a story is told that explains the outcome of the trial and thus the main tale, and like them this þáttr shows the heroic code in a sympathetic, if whimsical light but emphasizes religious values and divine power.

To summarize the types of thematic content in the twenty-six stories from the group surveyed thus far: it appears that about seventeen have what we might call humanistic themes and about nine religious, though there is no sharp line between them (e.g. in *Þorleifs þáttr*). The humanistic group could be broken down into those that seem to emphasize the practical value of friendship (*Ívars þáttr, Gull-Ásu-Þórðar þáttr,* and *Þorsteins þáttr Síðu-Hallssonar*), gift-giving and generosity (*Auðunar þáttr, Brands þáttr, Þorvarðar þáttr, Ísleifs þáttr,* and *Þáttr Þormóðar*), and verbal wit (*Óttars þáttr, Sneglu-Halla þáttr, Þorsteins þáttr sögufróða, Sturlu þáttr, Stúfs þáttr,* and *Þorleifs þáttr*). The remaining three tales could perhaps be comprised in a group that also shows the value of friendship but specifically in the context of the properly hospitable or at least courteous treatment of a stranger (*Þorsteins þáttr Austfirðings, Steins þáttr, Ásbjarnar þáttr*). Within the religious group we can recognize themes of forgiveness and reconciliation, of punishment and testing, of Christian responsibility, and of conversion, supernatural intervention being present in all nine, but the stories are difficult to pidgeonhole. *Gísls þáttr, Halldors þáttr I,* and *Hrafns þáttr* are all about forgiveness for a killing, all climaxing with a trial scene. *Þorsteins þáttr forvitna, Þorsteins þáttr skelks,* and *Þórarins þáttr I* portray punishments and testing, the last also Christian responsibility and its reward in a trial scene ending in reconciliation. *Egils þáttr* and *Þorvalds þáttr* show forgiveness and reconciliation (for a falsely alleged wrong in the latter) achieved through a conversion mission, and *Ögmundar þáttr* also has reconciliation and conversion coupled.

3. Inner Form as Ethos

Admittedly analysis of what any story is "about" is debatable. Such thumbnail interpretations as I have indulged in here are necessarily reductive and no doubt subject to the charge of the "Procrustean fallacy" associated with any kind of criticism that goes beyond an individual work to a group. The five stories not yet mentioned (*Hreiðars þáttr, Þorgríms þáttr, Halldórs þáttr II, Odds þáttr,* and *Þórodds þáttr*) for various reasons defy assignment to one of the interpretative categories used above, and the variety of themes in the twenty-six stories discussed does not show as much unity of conceptual interest as, for example, Andersson found in his study of sophrosyne in a group of ten family sagas.[37] Nevertheless it is clear that the þættir of

---

37. Andersson, "Displacement."

this group as a whole tend toward humane and conciliatory values; not all honor specifically Christian values but none conflict severely with medieval Christianity.

However, with an interpretation of "inner form" at a higher level of generality, as Weltanschauung, tone, or ethos, the group exhibits more conceptual unity, and the common denominators of subject matter and structure seem to be concrete reflexes of a spiritual bias common to the optimistic outlook of the stories under study. All chart the relationship between two main characters, a king and a commoner, usually an Icelander; the Icelander is the hero with whom the reader identifies, and his relationship to the king is normally one of relative dependence and powerlessness. In many (not all) ethical authority rests with the king or one of two kings, and the hero's success and failure are measured in terms of royal favor. In several stories the hero is specifically said to be poor;[38] and these þættir often present their heroes as victims of Norwegian prejudice, sometimes in form of suspicion and a diffuse hostility as in *Steins þáttr,* sometimes clearly focused as in the jealous lack of acceptance faced by Gull-Ásu-Þórðr as a poor Icelander making good through his own efforts. The Norwegian nobleman Einarr fluga shows a general dislike of Icelanders in both *Sneglu-Halla þáttr* and *Odds þáttr,* and an undercurrent of court hostility toward the Icelandic hero is important in *Óttars þáttr, Þorsteins þáttr sögufróða,* and *Þorsteins þáttr Austfirðings.* A more specific attitude is shown in a reference to the traditional accusation of indolence in the Icelandic national character in *Gísls þáttr.*[39] In *Þorsteins þáttr skelks* Ólafr Tryggvason comments on Þorsteinn: "sýnir þú þat sem talat er til yðvar Íslendinga, at þér séð mjök einrænir" *(FS,* p. 87), and the traditional insult of calling an Icelander *mörlandi* ("suet-lander," in effect "eater of greasy sausages") occurs several times.[40]

---

38. Cf. Lange, pp. 153, 155; Auðun, Gull-Ásu-Þórðr, Þorsteinn sögufróði, and Þorstein forvitni are explicitly "poor," and four more are implied to be.

39. "Eigi váru þér nú tómlátir, Íslendingar," *ÍÞ,* p. 44.

40. These stories may also reveal something of real thirteenth-century Icelandic attitudes toward Norway and the kingship (as suggested by several scholars including Mohr, cited below, and Marlene Ciklamini, "Medieval Icelanders at the Royal Court as Described in the Þættir," a paper read before the Scandinavian Literature Section of the Northeast Modern Languages Association, Spring, 1972); they are not out of harmony with famous passages often cited in this connection (such as Stefnir's description of the Icelanders in *Stefnis þáttr, ÍÞ,* p. 250). However, a Norwegian document like *Konungs skuggsjá* also offers a great number of parallels to the outlook of the stories,

The function of such attitudes in the stories is the same as that of the poverty of some of the heroes: to dramatise the hero's achievement in moving from rags to riches and from disfavor to reconciliation. Moreover the adverse judgments on Icelanders are carefully controlled by the Icelandic authors and often mixed with grudging admiration (as on the part of Einar fluga). The Icelander is pictured as a breed apart, cleverer and more tough-minded than the Norwegian in spite of his disadvantages as a provincial or even foreigner. If he is eccentric *(einrænn)*, he is also admired for courage ("þér séð ofrhugar miklir, Íslendingar").[41] He may be "stríðmæltr ok harðorðr, en mjök fátalaðr ... þykkjumikill sem aðrir Íslendingar,"[42] but he is often also unbending in the face of superior power ("djarfmæltr við tigna menn").[43] Or he may be a witty literary man like Stúfr ("Ok hér er kominn íslenzkr maðr; þat horfir til gamans").[44] In most cases derogation of Icelanders is placed in the mouths of inferior or disreputable people rather than the king. It is true that King Haraldr harðráði pronounced Icelanders self-willed and unsociable ("Eru þér einráðir, Íslendingar, ok ósiðblandnir"),[45] but the context here and in the other þættir that show his relations with an Icelander tends to support the judgment of the *Flateyjarbók* interpolator that "Haraldr konungr elskaði mjök Íslendinga"[46] and to show him generally well disposed to Icelanders though his own touchy, jealous, and harsh temperament in tradition insures that King Haraldr will never shower affection on anyone.

The ethos of our stories emerges most clearly, perhaps, from a comparison of their characters with those of the family saga. The sagas are in many respects far removed from the heroic world they portray, and the saga authors clearly did not stand for an ideal of pure self-assertion. But as every reader, at least since Ker, has been

---

for example: "You shall also know that many come to court from the country who were considered of little consequence there; and yet, it often happens that the king gives high honors to such men in return for their service, if they perform it well, though they are but slightly honored in their own homes," *The King's Mirror*, transl. L. M. Larson (New York, 1917), p. 169.

41. *Ögmundar þáttr, ÍÞ*, p. 450.
42. *Halldórs þáttr I, ÍÞ*, p. 69.
43. Of Þórarinn Nefjólfsson, *ÍÞ*, p. 289 (also elsewhere).
44. *ÍÞ*, p. 268.
45. *Sneglu-Halla þáttr, ÍÞ*, p. 224.
46. *ÍÞ*, p. 221; this passage is missing in the *Msk* version and appears to be an expansion by *Flat* or a predecessor.

aware, they still reflect a heroic ethos in the choice and portrayal of their main characters and plots. The men of the þættir are not of the same cut. Wolfgang Mohr, putting the opposition þáttr-man: saga-man in strongest contrast, phrased it very simply: the þættir present an image of man that "... nicht altheroisch, sondern mittelalterlich [ist]." Mohr's article, "Wandel des Menschenbildes in der mittelalterlichen Dichtung," touches only briefly on this contrast in Icelandic literature, viewing it in a broad European perspective; and if his contrast of fated man in the sagas with the selfless, Christian image of man in the þættir (Mohr is obviously thinking chiefly of the group of þættir under study) is oversimplified, it at least points to a valid distinction.[47] Revenge and honor continue to be important in the world of the thirty-one stories; but where the family sagas are set in a society of potential equals, in these þættir we identify with the little man in an unequal social situation. The values of these þættir are chiefly survival values.

The difference between the family saga's structure (the feud or conflict structure) and the Alienation/Reconciliation structure of our stories corresponds to the opposition tragedy: comedy in the broadest senses of those words. Frye shows how in tragedy the hero becomes isolated from his society but is incorporated into society in comedy; common forms of isolation in tragedy are death or the fall from high estate; some forms of integration into society in comedy are what Frye calls the "theme of acceptance" and the "theme of salvation" (as in Dante's *Commedia*). Most of the family sagas are tragic in this sense, and most of our group of þættir are comic.

Frye shows further that tragedy and comedy in this sense often correspond to "high mimetic" and "low mimetic" on his scale of modes (the relation of author and audience to the characters or to the hero). In the "high mimetic" mode characters are heroically larger than life; their wills and powers are greater than ours though fully human. In the "low mimetic" mode the characters (or the hero) are people of the same limitations and, metaphorically, of the same stature as we the readers. This

---

47. *Wirkendes Wort*, 1. Sonderheft (1952), pp. 37–48; cited from rpt. in *Wirkendes Wort: Sammelband II* (Düsseldorf, 1963), 127–38; on the same theme see W. H. Vogt, "Wandel im altnordischen Menschentum," *Preussisches Jahrbuch* (Sept., 1923), pp. 315–22 and Hans Naumann, "Die altnordischen Verwandten des Ruodlieb-Romans," in *Edda-Skalden-Saga, Festschrift ... Genzmer*, ed. Hermann Schneider (Heidelberg, 1952), pp. 307–24.

is roughly the "modal" relationship of saga-hero to þáttr-hero too; and even though this is a broad generalization that inevitably does not do justice to every case, a comparison of the life and temper of, say, Egill Skallagrímsson with Egill Síðu-Hallsson or Gunnarr of Hlíðarendi with Gunnarr helmingr (of *Ögmundar þáttr)* reveals their difference in magnitude. Frye found that the resolution of "low mimetic" comedy often involves a social promotion, and this is true for a number of our þættir, while the most typical family sagas are not success stories but stories of failure, the "doomed defense of a narrow place against odds" (to quote Ker again). If the saga in its tragic aspect is the heir of heroic poetry, as many scholars including Andersson have asserted, perhaps we can carry the analogy of the dichotomy we are discussing one step further and wonder whether this kind of short story can be viewed as the heir of the folktale.[48] Certainly many of these stories manifest a folktale glow of wish-fullfillment: a young man of ability but penniless sets out for the court; he overcomes difficulties, proves his worth to the king, makes his fortune and marries—not a princess as these are realistic tales—but perhaps a rich widow. The triumphant underdog of folklore may be the prototype.

In any case we cannot fail to notice the contrast of the *conflict* and *fate* of the heroic literature with the *reconciliation* and *luck* of these þættir and to observe the difference in scale between the doomed tragic hero (Grettir: "sitt er hvárt, gæfa ok gervileikr") and the prospering þáttr hero (Auðunn: "þótti vera hinn mesti gæfumaðr"). Contrasting medieval man with his heroic ancestor, Mohr summarized: "Er hat

---

48. Andersson, *Family Saga,* ch. 3 ("The Heroic Legacy"); unlike others who derive the family sagas from the tradition of heroic poetry, Andersson's main evidence is the correspondence of structural patterns. A similar congruence between the þættir discussed here and folktale as analyzed by Propp is arguable (based on the essential pair of "functions"); but while I believe that homologous structures may indicate literary "relationship," I doubt that they here prove filiation in any simple historical sense, and it seems enough if they help to establish an "order of works." Cf. two recent articles on the "folktale structure" of *Beowulf:* T. A Shippey, "The Fairy-Tale Structure of 'Beowulf,'" *N&Q* 16 (1969), 2–11 and Daniel R. Barnes, "Folktale Morphology and the Structure of *Beowulf,*" *Speculum* 45 (1970), 416–34. Analogies between the þættir and the folktale in rhetoric ("epic laws") hardly exceed those of the saga. On the underdog theme in folklore see Max Lüthi, "Parallel Themes in Folk Narrative in Art and Literature," *JFI* 4 (1967), 3–16 and Richard Dorson, "Esthetic Form in British and American Folk Narrative" in *Medieval Literature and Folklore Studies,* ed. J. Mandel and B. Rosenberg (New Brunswick, N.Y., 1970), 320–21.

kein Schicksal, sondern Geschick und Glück," and he writes of this shift in the literary imagination:

> An die Stelle der heroischen Fabeln treten anekdotische und novel-listische Themen. Jetzt wird es erzählenswert, wie ein Mensch sich im Widereinanderspiel der Gesellschaft durchsetzt, wie er sich geschickt aus der Klemme zieht, oder umgekehrt, wie sich der Ungeschickte blamiert und der Spitzbube entlarvt wird.[49]

This change is common to European literature, and Frye also observes that Western literature has moved steadily down the scale of modes. This contrast, overdrawn for clarity, need not be conceived except very broadly in chronological terms; *Ruodlieb* antedates the *Nibelungenlied,* some of the þættir are earlier than most family sagas, *chansons de geste* are written side by side with *fabliaux,* etc. Nevertheless we do find medieval Icelandic recognition of such differences:

> Haraldr spurði lát tveggja hirðmanna sinna af Íslandi, Bolla ins prúða ok Sneglu-Halla. Hann svaraði svá til Bolla: "Fyrir dörrum mun drengrinn hnigit hafa." En til Halla sagði hann svá: "Á grauti myndi greyit sprungit hafa" *(ÍÞ, p. 248)*.

It is comforting to see such an authority on Icelanders as King Haraldr harðráði also prone to exaggerate this contrast.

There is no better representative of the comic outlook of these stories than *Hreiðars þáttr heimska,* a brilliant character study. Medieval literature, we are told, provides few examples of character development except on the religious pattern of conversion, but folk literature provided another pattern, the coming-of-age or initiation into manhood and a full share in society. Initiatory patterns are common in the family sagas, where they are often set in Norway;[50] and the plot structure of the þættir under study lent itself to such a treatment (especially for Gísl, Hrafn, Ögmundr dyttr, Gunnarr helmingr, and Kolgrímr in *Þorgríms þáttr).*

---

49. Mohr, pp. 129–30.
50. Cf. Mary Danielli, "Initiation Ceremonial from Norse Literature," *Folk-Lore* 56 (1945), 229–48.

Hreiðarr then is shown coming of age in three stages. In the first the "home fool" is brought to Norway and into the sphere of King Magnús; Hreiðarr's brother Þórðr claims that he was motivated to bring his retarded brother out of fairness and the hope that he might gain some luck *(gæfa)* by contact with the king, and this proves to be the case. Magnús sees far more in Hreiðarr than most people, and predicts that he will experience wrath and prove to be a skilled artist; these predictions come true in the second and third stages, but first Hreiðar acquires experience in Magnús's court. Acceptance at court is the start of the hero's "socialization" process, and this is crystallized in a scene in which the Icelander sheds his dirt and old clothes for a new suit. Despite his brother's urging that he dress himself after the courtly fashion, Hreiðarr refuses, maintaining his integrity, but does agree to a new suit of homespun. In the second stage Hreiðarr learns anger at the expense of the life of one of King Haraldr's retainers and incurs the wrath of Magnús's joint king. Finally the prophesy of Hreiðarr's innate talent as a craftsman proves true when he meets with Haraldr again but is not reconciled.

The fourth and last section of the story explicitly recapitulates this development and projects it into the future at a second meeting with King Magnús:

> Nú kveðr Hreiðarr kvæðit ok er þat allundarligt, fyrst kynligast, en því betra er síðar er. Ok er lokit er kvæði, mælti konungr: "Þetta kvæði sýnisk mér undarligt ok þó gott at nestlokum; en kvæðit mun vera með þeim hætti sem ævi þín; hon hefir fyrst verit með kynligu móti ok einrœnligu, en hon mun þó vera því betr er meir líðr á" *(ÍP*, p. 131).

Analogy between poet and poem is used in *Gunnlaugs saga* to characterize Gunnlaugr and Hrafn, but those are static portraits; in *Hreiðars þáttr* we seem to have encountered a character truly in transition, a transition that continues beyond the end of the story, for the narrator reports of Hreiðarr's later life: "ok ferr hans ráð mjök eptir getu Magnúss konungs, at þess betr er, er meir líðr fram hans ævi" *(ÍP*, p. 132). However, the narrator adds "ok hefir hann gört sér at mestum hluta þau kynjalæti, er hann sló á sik inn fyrra hlut ævinnar," and we are left with the recurring riddle whether or not a medieval character development must be viewed as revelation of previously hidden features.

As a character Hreiðarr is related to the folk type of "coalbiter," "Askeladd," or "despised youngest brother." The coalbiter would lie beside the kitchen fire all day getting in everyone's way, but great power, nobility, and kindness had been disguised in his ungainly form, and Askeladd succeeds where others fail. Hreiðarr, however, is even more like Parzival, whose "tôren kleider" in Wolfram's version symbolize the hero's ignorance and country manners and who also has a comical habit of blurting out his thoughts.[51] Probably the similarities are traceable to folktale types; but in the case of Parzival we are left with no doubt that our hero actually changes and matures in the course of his story; with Hreiðarr the question remains.

Hreiðars þáttr makes use of parallels and contrasts for some very subtle effects; for example, in each of the hero's first three stages of growth he asserts himself against opposition to go to a meeting with a king, and Magnús himself points out these parallels. This trick of construction has thematic significance when the brothers are introduced as a contrasting pair, Þórðr popular, sophisticated, and handsome but small in stature, Hreiðarr big, ugly, and considered a fool. Still, as the story progresses, it is Hreiðarr who earns the respect and affection of the king and about whom the story is told. The contrast between the two brothers and the relationship of physical size to qualities of the inner man seem to be isolated for inspection in a curious incident in the story; Hreiðarr has impetuously set out running to the assembly, while Þórðr tries to overtake him but falls further and further behind:

> Ok er Hreiðarr sér, at Þórðr fór seint, þá mælti hann: "Þat er þó satt, at illt er lítill at vera, þá er aflit nær ekki, en þó mætti vera fráleikrinn, en lítit ætla ek þik af honum hafa hlotit, ok væria þér verri vænleikr minni ok kœmisk þú með öðrum mönnum" *(ÍP, p. 116)*.

---

51. David Blamires, *Characterization and Individuality in Wolfram's Parzival* (Cambridge, 1966), pp. 142–45 and 214, calls this aspect of Parzival's personality the *Dümmling* theme. G. B. Woods, *The Unpromising Hero in Folklore* (Harvard Diss., 1910) catalogues types of the Male-Cinderella, several of which show similarities to Hreiðarr and some other þáttr heroes.

The hero's unusual size and strength reflect his superior character, and his brother's smallness corresponds to his relative inferiority in the story, while Hreiðarr's ugliness, the physical reflex of his admirably simple and open nature, contrasts with Þórðr's good looks and the sophistication that goes with them.

This alignment of personality and body forms an interesting contrast to the other outstanding example of the body as mirror of the soul in these þættir, the case of Galti and Kolgrímr in Þorgríms þáttr.[52] Þorgrímr had two retainers: "hét annarr Galti, mikill maðr ok styrkr, annarr Kolgrímr, lítill ok fráligr" *(ÍÞ, p. 311)*. When their master was to stand trial for manslaughter in the prejudiced and actually illegal court of Kálfr Árnason, Galti disobeyed Kálfr's ruling about coming to court unarmed and concealed an axe under his cloak; at that moment in the story Galti is distinguished by his nickname: "Galti inn sterki, fylgðarmaðr Þorgríms, greip upp boløxi" *(ÍÞ, p. 313)*. In the assembly Kálfr pronounced Þorgrímr an outlaw, and the slain man's brother suddenly rushed out of the crowd and struck him his death blow. Kolgrímr turned to Galti and urged him to avenge their master, and at that point the narrator uses Kolgrímr's nickname with an apposition that underscores the parallelism: "Þá mælti Kolgrímr inn litli, fylgðarmaðr Þorgríms: 'Hefn þú hans, Galti, þú hefir øxina'" *(ÍÞ, p. 314)*. Galti is afraid even to give the axe to Kolgrímr, and finally Kolgrímr snatches it away commenting that if Galti is so afraid, he will not dare to hinder him either. Then Kolgrímr gives his master's assailant a fatal wound.

Here the arrangement of *Hreiðars þáttr* is reversed. Galti's size and strength do not mirror greatness, and it is Kolgrímr the Little who possesses the heart to take an honorable revenge. Thus in *Þorgríms þáttr* too the same ethos of the success of an unlikely hero obtains. Þorgrímr's opponents, the Icelanders Bjarni and Þórðr, are shown at every point as bullies who victimize an older man out of spite and as flatterers of the pretender to authority Kálfr Árnason. The ultimate hero is the little man Kolgrímr, at the beginning only one of Þorgrímr's followers but later the leader of the party; the

---

52. Cf. Lars Lönnroth, "Kroppen som själens spegel—ett motiv i de isländska sagorna," *Lychnos*, 1964, pp. 24–61.

final evaluation of Kolgrímr closes the þáttr: "ok þótti inn besti kaupdrengr."

If the generalizations offered about theme and ethos require no qualification in the case of *Þorgríms þáttr,* some modification is in order for a few of the group. *Steins þáttr* and *Ásbjarnar þáttr* have a harsher view of realities, whether or not they originally ended with the hero's death. In *Odds þáttr* Icelanders successfully elude the king's authority; but the usual conciliatory ending is neutralized, and the story does not produce the happy effect typical of the group. *Þórodds þáttr Snorrasonar,* like *Þorsteins þáttr tasalda* and others, employs the Alienation/Reconciliation structure as a frame for the narration of adventures on a mission. The framed tale of adventures is interesting for its construction in three scenes of increasing danger and decreasing realism, and the story is told with humor; but *Þórodds þáttr* appears to be thematically sterile, and even the happy ending seems perfunctory.[53] Finally *Halldórs þáttr II* and *Þorleifs þáttr* both recount in an epilogue (Conclusion) some further dealings between those Icelanders and the respective Norwegian rulers; in Þorleifr's case a trick of Hákon jarl's causes his death, while King Haraldr tries unsuccessfully to take vengeance on Halldórr; nevertheless both stories agree well with the temper of the group.

It appears, then, that the thirty-one þættir all share a common outlook on man and the world and most (perhaps twenty-six) manifest a limited range of generally humane and conciliatory themes. This would constitute a shared "inner form" in the terminology of Wellek and Warren, corresponding to a common "outer form" revealed in narrative structure and common features of characterization and rhetoric. This closes the generic circle, but a number of cautions are in order. The stories of the group are not "all the same." Neither formal analysis nor conceptual analysis is a science; our notions of "inner

---

53. *Þórodds þáttr* first appears in Snorri's work (Separate Saga and *Heimskringla*) and is taken over into *Flat*; however, an allusion in Legendary Saga (ed. Johnsen, p. 80) suggests that its compiler knew the story. De Vries, Finnur Jónsson, and Mogk do not give the þáttr separate treatment, but it is anthologized by 40*ÍÞ*, *ÍÞ*, and *ÍS* 4.

form" are vague; other groupings are possible and other interpretations. And of course "outer" and "inner" forms are *not* independent variables but directly interdependent.

So the value of the experiment proposed at the outset is not scientific; but if the generic approach has a place in literary criticism of the sagas, our understanding of the individual stories must have been enhanced by the discussion of them as a group. Failing the objective tests of a science, that is our only control on criticism.

Guðrúnarbrögð and the Saxon
Lay of Grimhild's Perfidy

In two recent articles T. M. Andersson has attempted to reconstruct the contents of the collateral source of the *Niflunga saga* in *Þiðreks saga* and to distinguish it from Heusler's "Ältere Not."[1] He agrees with Heinrich Hempel that this secondary source was a short Saxon lay and not the chronicle from Soest proposed by Roswitha Wisniewski.[2] Andersson found external evidence for the existence of the lay and independent indication of its contents in Saxo Grammaticus' story of the singer who attempted to warn Knud Lavard of the ambush prepared for him in the year 1131.

Further external evidence for the existence of the Saxon lay is perhaps to be found in *Norna-Gests þáttr* where Gestr entertains Ólafr Tryggvason's court with a poem called *Guðrúnarbrögð*:

Hætta þeir nú sínu tali, tekr Gestr hǫrpu sína ok slær vel ok lengi um
kveldit, svá at ǫllum þykkir unað í á at heyra, ok slær þó Gunnarsslag

---

1. "The Epic Source of Niflunga Saga and the Nibelungenlied," *ANF* 88 (1973), 1–54; the references here are to the second article: "*Niflunga saga* in the Light of German and Danish Materials," *MScan* 7 (1974), 22–30.

2. Hempel, *Nibelungenstudien I. Nibelungenlied, Thidrekssaga und Balladen,* Germanische Bibliothek, Abteilung Untersuchungen und Texte 22 (Heidelberg, 1926); Wisniewski, *Die Darstellung des Niflungenunterganges in der Thidrekssaga. Eine quellenkritische Untersuchung,* Hermaea 9 (Tübingen, 1961); Wisniewski (pp. 302–08) affirms the lost Saxon lay, which she calls "Grimhilds Verrat" after Saxo, but makes it a source of the "Ältere Not" rather than the saga. Cf. also items 7, 13, and 14 in Hempel's *Kleine Schriften,* ed. H. M. Heinrichs (Heidelberg, 1966). I wish to thank Prof. Heinrichs for a helpful critique of this note.

bezt, ok at lyktum slær hann Guðrúnarbrǫgð in fornu, þau hǫfðu menn eigi fyrr heyrt; ok eptir þat sváfu menn af um nóttina.[3]

Guðrúnarbrögð may be a translation of the "title" of the Saxon lay known to Saxo and the compiler of the *Niflunga saga; bragð,* plural *brögð,* has to do with tricks and especially with deceit, and this answers well to Saxo's "cantor" who, "speciosissimi carminis contextu notissimam Grimildæ erga fratres perfidiam de industria memorare adorsus, famosæ fraudis exemplo similium ei metum ingenerare tentabat."[4] Saxo's allusion to the song specifies not merely revenge against the brothers but *perfidia,* and Andersson has argued that this must imply deceit and specifically a treacherous invitation. The *brögð* referred to could be this initial motif of the reconstructed Saxon lay or perhaps equally well the tricks which Grimhild later uses to dispatch her brothers (Andersson's points 4 and 5, p. 29). If *Grimildae perfidia notissima* reflects in some sort the same familiar designation ("title") for the same song as *Guðrúnarbrögð in fornu,* it may be that Saxo has heightened slightly the moral sense in harmony with his general approach to his material. The point is not lost even if *brögð* is not claimed as a close equivalent of Saxo's *perfidia* and his phrase is regarded as only a description, not a "title"; however, in Saxo's usage *perfidia* usually indicates not a mere attitude or potentiality but concrete acts of treachery.[5]

Supporting this interpretation of the passage from *Norna-Gests þáttr* is the striking fact that the audience of Norwegians at Ólafr's court had never before heard the lay even though it is designated "in fornu"; naturally they were familiar with the Scandinavian version (revenge for the brothers), rather than the German version (revenge on the brothers). The fact that *Guðrúnarbrögð in fornu* was not known to the Norwegian audience also argues against the possibility that

---

3. *Die prosaische Edda im Auszuge nebst Vǫlsunga-saga und Nornagests-þáttr, mit ausführlichem Glossar,* ed. Ernst Wilken, 2nd ed. rev., 2 vols., Bibliothek der ältesten deutschen Literatur-Denkmäler, XI-XII (Paderborn, 1912–13), I, 239–40.

4. Saxo Grammaticus, *Gesta Danorum,* ed. C. Knabe and P. Herrmann, rev. J. Olrik and H. Ræder (Copenhagen, 1931), p. 355 (Book XIII, Ch. VI, Par. 7).

5. See Franz Blatt, ed., *Saxonis Gesta Danorum,* II (Copenhagen, 1957), s.v. *perfidia* for a (representative, not complete) collection of occurrences; Blatt's gloss: "facinus vel dictum infidum, fraus, infidelitas."

the *brögð* referred to might be Guðrún's revenge on Atli. The South
Germanic origin of *Guðrúnarbrögð* is further supported by the fact
that Gestr himself is a Dane (from Grœningr) who has spent a great
deal of his supernaturally long life in South Germanic lands, and
the Southern version is obviously more appropriate to this devoted
follower and personal friend of Sigurðr Fáfnisbani who would be
imagined as telling about the revenge for his lord.[6]

What objections may be raised to this interpretation? *Norna-Gests
þáttr* is late (usually dated about 1300), and Finnur Jónsson dismisses
both *Gunnarsslagr* and *Guðrúnarbrögð* as invented names.[7] However,
there is no positive reason for believing these names invented, and
the detail about not having heard *Guðrúnarbrögð* before would be
gratuitous if the author of the þáttr had not had something particular
in mind. Nora Chadwick was certainly mistaken in her translation of
the passage: "What he rendered best was *The Harping of Gunnar*;
and last of all he played the ancient *Wiles of Guthrun, neither of
which* [my italics] they had heard before."[8] The plural in *þau hǫfðu
menn eigi fyrr heyrt* refers only to the *brögð*; and in fact the passage
may be interpreted as opposing pleasure-giving familiar pieces, the
best of which was *Gunnarsslagr (slær vel ok lengi um kveldit, svá
at ǫllum þykkir unað í á at heyra, ok slær þó Gunnarsslag bezt)*, to
the foreign *Guðrúnarbrögð*. There may be an artistic reason for this
arrangement: the central strategy of this "short story" is the gradual
revelation of Gestr's mysterious history. In the second chapter he
demurs when the retainers are admiring the ring Hnituðr; this leads
to a wager that Gestr can produce better gold, which in turn leads
to Gestr's life story and the included heroic legends beginning in
Chapter III. Here at the end of Chapter II the mystery and anticipa-
tion are at their highest; so it is fitting that Gestr's performances
in the last lines of the chapter should end with allusion to a song
unknown to his audience and hinting unsettlingly of Gestr's superior

---

6. Esp. Wilken, pp. 241–42, 250, 253, 259; for the consistency and artistic care my
argument assumes, cf. the þáttr author's comments on the lack of (stone) halls in the
Norway of Ólafr's time (p. 238) and on the political geography of Europe (esp. p. 244).

7. *Den oldnorske og oldislandske litteraturs historie*, 2nd ed., II (Copenhagen, 1923),
839–40.

8. *Stories and Ballads of the Far Past*, tr. with introduction and notes by N. Kershaw
[Chadwick] (Cambridge, 1921), p. 19.

knowledge and experience and his connection with the glamorous South Germanic region.

Mrs Chadwick thought *Guðrúnarbrögð* might possibly be identical with *Guðrúnarkviða II* because another possible interpretation of *brögð* would be "deeds, adventures," which could fit almost any Guðrún poem, and because *Guðrúnarkviða II* is referred to in the *Poetic Edda* ("Frá dauða Sigurðar") as *Guðrúnarkviða in forna.*[9] However, "the ancient" is a designation carried by other poems as well *(e.g. Hamðismál, Bjarkamál)* and may be an honorific (cf. Bragi inn gamli); *brögð* in the plural seems most frequently to carry a sense of deceit or cunning,[10] and in the present context the standard interpretations (without reference to Saxo and the Saxon lay, of course) have carried this sense.[11] Furthermore, *Norna-Gests þáttr* definitely alludes to *Guðrúnarkviða II* further along as *Guðrúnarrœða* in a passage apparently lifted from "Frá dauða Sigurðar";[12] in other words, *Guðrúnarrœða* was the þáttr author's title for the poem that the *Poetic Edda* calls *Guðrúnarkviða in forna,* and there is no reason for him to use two different titles for the same work. In fact, it is just possible that he changed to *Guðrúnarrœða* here in order to avoid confusion with the Guðrún poem he had previously subtitled *in fornu.* In any case it would be pointless to refer to *Guðrúnarkviða II* as a poem that King Ólafr's Norwegian court had never heard before.

---

9. p. 222 (note); cf. Pálmi Pálsson, "Górúnargaldr," ANF 23 (1907), 97–99.

10. Cleasby-Vigfusson, s.v. *bragð,* II, 2 and 3 ("a *trick, scheme, device* ... chiefly in pl. ... but also sing."), ß ("with a notion of deceit, *a trick, crafty scheme* ... In Swed. 'bragder' means *an exploit, action,* whilst the Icel. implies some notion of subtlety or craft; yet cp. phrases as stór brögð, *great exploits* ..."); Fritzner, s.v. *bragd,* 2 ("Gjerning, Foretagende"), 3 ("List, Kneb, kløgtigt Paafund, hvormed man søger at opnaa, udrette noget"), cf. *bragðadrykkr* ("Drik som er beredet i svigefuld Hensigt"). Cf. also Finnur Jónsson, *Ordbog til ... rímur ...* (Copenhagen, 1926–27), s.v. *bragð* ("bedrift ... i pl. heltebedrifter ... slet handling, skarnstreg ... list, underfundighed ..."); M. A. Jacobsen and Chr. Matras, *Føroysk-Donsk orðabók,* 2nd ed. rev. (Tórshavn, 1961), s.v. *bragð/ bragd* ("manddomsstykke, bedrift ... kneb, puds ..."); and *Svabos glossar til færøske visehaandskrifter,* ed. Chr. Matras (Copenhagen, 1943), s.v. *bragd.*

11. Cf. "wiles" in Chadwick's main text (p. 19) and *Volsunga- und Ragnars-Saga nebst der Geschichte von Nornagest,* tr. F. H. von der Hagen, 2nd ed. rev. Anton Edzardi, Altdeutsche und altnordische Heldensagen, III. Bd. (Stuttgart, 1880): "Schwerlich eines der erhaltenen Gudrunlieder, sondern ein Lied, welches Gudrun's Rache für den Tod ihrer Brüder zum Gegenstand hatte. Eigentlich Steht im Text: die alten 'Gudruns-Listen'" (p. 353, n.); Wilken, II, 256: "ein altes uns verlorenes episches Lied (vgl. bragð n. = List, Anschlag)."

12. Wilken, I, 253 text and n. 11; II, 256.

The most serious objection that may be raised against the proposals in this note is that if the *Guðrúnarbrögð* were the Saxon lay of *perfidia* it would have used the Southern name Grimhildr instead of Guðrún; the objection is especially important since the name Grimhildr for Guðrún's mother does not occur in *Norna-Gests þáttr*. Nevertheless, I would argue that the North Germanic name could be used here partly because of the confusion that would be created by allusion to "Grimhildr" in a tradition where that name was applied regularly to Guðrún's mother, as in the textually closely allied *Völsunga saga* and *Poetic Edda*. (Compare the relationship between the names Sigrdrífa and Brynhildr in the *Edda* and in *Völsunga saga*.) However, one other piece of external evidence, though notoriously hard to interpret, may be introduced to counter this onomastic objection. The portion of the Faroese ballad cycle of the Nibelungs that relates the fall of the Burgundians, *Högna táttur*, may also contain allusions to the *Guðrúnarbrögð*; for example:

> Artala kongur í Húnalandi,
> bróti úr bragdartátti;
> festi Guðruna Júkadóttur,
> ið Sjúrður snari átti.[13]

> Artála kongur í Húnalandi
> (sigist í bragda tátti)
> festi frúnna Guðrunu,
> ið Sjúrður frægi átti (H, 18; I, 205).

Hans Christian Lyngbye, Wilhelm Grimm, P. E. Müller, and Max Vogler have taken this *bragdar táttur* or *bragda táttur* to be the name of a lost poem, and Müller and Vogler equated it with the *Guðrúnarbrögð* of *Norna-Gests þáttr*, observing that the *bragdar/bragda táttur*

---

13. *Føroya kvæði: Corpus Carminum Færoensium*, compiled by Sv. Grundtvig and J. Bloch, ed. N. Djurhuus and Chr. Matras, I (Copenhagen, 1951–63), p. 22 (= Sjúrðar kvæði, version A, st. 1); further references give version letter, stanza number, volume and page number; the thirteen occurrences of the phrase in *Högna táttur*'s versions are A, 1, 5 (I, 22), Ba, 1 (I, 50), Bb, 1, 5 (I, 76–77), C, 255, 261 (I, 99), D, 1, 6 (I, 127), E, 25 (I, 153), G, 271, 277 (I, 182–83), H, 18 (I, 205); there are seven occurrences in *Brynhildar táttur*'s versions: A, 4 (I, 8), Ba, 7 (I, 41), Bb, 8 (I, 64), C, 105 (I, 91), D, 8 (I, 114), G, 112 (I, 174), H, 6 (I, 196).

must have treated of a trick and concerned Atli and Guðrún.[14] But in the present context the striking thing about *Högna táttur* is that not only does it allude to a *bragdar/bragda táttur* but also here the Northern name Guðrún is combined with the Southern role of revenge on the brothers accomplished through the deceitful invitation and the later tricks—just as in our conception of *Guðrúnarbrögð.*

The question of the relationship of *Högna táttur* to the Danish ballad of *Grimilds Hævn, Den hvenske Krønike, Þiðreks saga,* and the "Ältere Not" is still open after more than a century and a half, but Heusler, Hempel, and Schneider[15] all agree on the necessity of two sources for *Högna táttur:* (1) a Scandinavian ballad (which is the common source of *Högna táttur, Grimilds Hævn,* and the chronicle), and (2) the *Þiðreks saga* directly. Hempel derives the first, the **Urballade,* from a **sächsisches Lied* which is the second source of *Niflunga saga.* It seems plausible to me to assume that the allusions to a *bragdar/ bragda táttur* are to the **Urballade* or more generally the tradition of the **sächsisches Lied,* while the actual extant *Högna táttur* represents a *remaniement* after the establishment of the influence of *Þiðreks saga.* It is true that de Boor[16] dismissed this phrase as a tag without significance, and one might add two more objections to my proposal: first, the phrase usually occurs in the singular and second, it also appears in *Brynhildar táttur.* But if the phrase were a formula like "Árla um morgunin," it should occur more widely than in these two oldest songs, and the comments of Müller and other students[17]

---

14. *Færöiske Qvæder om Sigurd Fofnersbane og hans Æt. Med et Anhang,* samlede og oversatte af Hans Christian Lyngbye, Sognepræst i Gjesing, med en Indledning af P. E. Müller, Dr. og Prof. i Theol.... (Randers, 1822); Lyngbye's notes and Müller's introduction are available to me only through Vogler's paraphrase in *Sjúrðar kvæði. Die färöischen Lieder von Sigurd ... I. Regin smiður,* ed. Max Vogler (Paderborn, 1877), pp. 24–26; Grimm's opinion appears in his marginal notations in a copy of Lyngbye (reported by Vogler, p. 25).

15. Heusler, "Die deutsche Quelle der Ballade von Kremolds Rache," *Sitzungsberichte der Preussischen Akademie, Berlin* (1921), pp. 445–69; Hempel, esp. pp. 34–37; Hermann Schneider, *Germanische Heldensage,* I (Berlin, 1962), 110–13 (Schneider accepts Hempel's Saxon lay as the second source of *Þiðreks saga,* p. 107, but is unclear about the relation between this lay and the ballad tradition); further references in agreement, Hempel, pp. 35–36.

16. Helmut de Boor, *Die färöischen Lieder des Nibelungenzyklus* (Heidelberg, 1918), p. 179.

17. Vogler, p. 25 (reporting Lyngbye and Müller); cf. *Sigurd the Dragon-Slayer: a Faroese Ballad-Cycle,* tr. E. M. Smith-Dampier (Oxford, 1934), p. 93, st. 18: "In Bragdar tale 'tis told."

indicate that *bragdar/bragda táttur* was not really understood in the modern ballad tradition. The only plausible explanation that has been offered is implicit in Müller's equation of the phrase with the poem mentioned in *Norna-Gests þáttr:* it must be a source citation that became frozen and meaningless in the memorial transmission of *Högna táttur;*[18] its appearance in *Brynhildar táttur* may indicate some early imitation or influence which similarly survived as a petrified phrase. R. C. Boer's study of the ballad, which, however, derives *Högna táttur* entirely from *Þiðreks saga,* gives *bragdar/bragda táttur* full semantic value but equates it with other source allusions (e.g., "sum sögan sigir frá"; H, 200; I, 212) as references to *Þiðreks saga.*[19] However, the theory of two (successive) sources seems superior and neatly accounts for the incompatibility of allusion to a poetic and also a prose source. Possibly, then, we have references to a Saxon lay of the twelfth century *(Grimildae perfidia),* a thirteenth-century North Germanic translation of it *(Guðrúnarbrögð),* and a Scandinavian ballad version of perhaps the thirteenth or fourteenth century *(bragdar/bragda táttur).*[20]

---

18. I refer especially to the work of Prof. Patricia Conroy (a paper read before the Society for the Advancement of Scandinavian Studies, Washington, D.C., May 1974; Ph.D. diss. University of California, Berkeley).

19. R. C. Boer, "Das Högnilied und seine verwandten," *ANF* 20 (1904), 162, 167; cf. B. Döring, "Die Quellen der Niflungasaga in der Darstellung der Thidrekssaga und der von diesen abhängigen Fassungen," *ZDP* 2 (1870), 283 (multiple source allusions and multiple sources), and cf. 269–70.

20. Prof. Andersson points out by letter that *bragð* occurs in the context of the deceitful invitation in *Atlamál* 2, 7–8: "[Atli] af bragði boð sendi,/ at kvæmi brátt mágar" (ed. U. Dronke [Oxford, 1969]); Dronke, H. Gering (*Vollständiges Wörterbuch* ... [Halle, 1903]), and Finnur Jónsson *(Lexicon poeticum* ... [Copenhagen, 1931]) interpret "on the instant," but G. Neckel *(Edda* ..., II Kommentierendes Glossar [Heidelberg, 1927]) gives "aus listiger absicht heraus" (3rd ed. rev. Hans Kuhn [1968] adds question mark). One might speculate (developing a suggestion in Andersson's letter) that *af bragði* is here "with wiliness" and that the phrase in this context reflects the language of the Saxon lay, which is widely believed on independent grounds to have influenced *Atlamál* (Andersson, p. 28; Wisniewski, pp. 302–08; Mohr [cited below], pp. 266–74; cf. Dronke, pp. 100–05), that poem having shifted the *bragð* from Guðrún to Atli. This is an interesting possibility though in prose (see Dronke, pp. 106–07, on the relation of the language of *Atlamál* to prose) and in its other Eddic occurrence *(Grottasöngr* 19) *af bragði* clearly means "instantly"; the collocation of *brátt* and *bragðz/af bragði* in *Atlamál* 2, 7–8 and 37, 5–6 would seem to support "instantly" although F. Detter and R. Heinzel, *Sæmundar Edda* (Leipzig, 1903) cite the collocation with *brátt* in st. 2 as evidence in favor of "listig, verrätherisch" (their interpretation of *bragdz* in st. 37, their 40, is not clear to me). Cf. also *Atlakviða* 15, 6–7: "hvat muntu rikr, vinna / við Húna harmbrǫgðum."

A final difficulty is posed by the relation of harp and poem in the allusion to *Guðrúnarbrögð*. Early references, especially West Germanic, show that some poetry (whether sung, chanted, or recited) was accompanied by the harp or lyre; but Scandinavian sources associating harping with poetry are rare and problematic,[21] and in *Norna-Gests þáttr* the verb *slá* suggests harping alone, not a harped accompaniment to a lay as I have assumed. Opinions differ sharply on the general questions involved here,[22] but even if *Gunnarsslagr* and *Guðrúnarbrögð* were considered tunes only by the fourteenth-century author of the þáttr, they reflect the earlier existence of the poems whose names they bear.[23] It does seem possible that the name *Gunnarsslagr* was from the beginning applied only to the tune Gunnarr was supposed to have played in the snake-pit,[24] and not

---

21. Much evidence is assembled in Finnur Jónsson, "Das Harfenspiel des Nordens in der alten Zeit," *Sammelbände der internationalen Musikgesellschaft 9* (1908), 530–37. Finnur Jónsson's conclusions are based chiefly on the silence of Icelandic sources and would not seem to carry much weight for the Saxon-Danish area.

22. Finnur Jónsson, "Harfenspiel"; Jón Helgason, "Norges og Islands digtning," *Litteraturhistorie. B. Norge og Island*, ed. Sigurður Nordal, Nordisk Kultur 8: B (Stockholm, 1953), pp. 21–22; Andreas Heusler, *Die altgermanische Dichtung*, 2nd ed. rev. (Darmstadt, 1957), pp. 37–40; H. M. and N. K. Chadwick, *The Growth of Literature*, I (Cambridge, 1932), 568–91; Stefán Einarsson, "Harp Song, Heroic Poetry (Chadwicks), Greek and Germanic Alternate Singing," *Budkavlen* 42 (1963), 13–28 (and Stefán Einarsson's other articles cited there); Otto Andersson, "Nordisk musikkultur i äldsta tider," *Musik og musikinstrumenter*, ed. O. Andersson, Nordisk Kultur 25 (Stockholm, 1934), pp. 10–23; Dietrich Hofmann, "Die Frage des musikalischen Vortrags der altgermanischen Stabreimdichtung in philologischer Sicht. Mit 11 Notenbeispiele," *ZDA* 92 (1963), 83–121; Ewald Jammers, "Der Vortrag des altgermanischen Stabreimverses in musikwissenschaftlicher Sicht," *ZDA* 93 (1964), 1–13; Dietrich Hofmann and Ewald Jammers, "Zur Frage des Vortrags der altgermanischer Stabreimdichtung," *ZDA* 94 (1965), 185–95; Lars Lönnroth, "Hjálmar's Death-Song and the Delivery of Eddic Poetry," *Speculum* 46 (1971), 1–20. I agree with the Chadwicks, pp. 577, 588–89 and Eugen Mogk, who interpreted "er singt zu der Harfe den *Gunnarslag* und die *Guðrúnarbrǫgð*" *(Geschichte der norwegisch-isländischen Literatur*, 2nd ed. rev., Strassburg, 1904, p. 822).

23. *Bósa saga* (cited by Finnur Jónsson, "Harfenspiel") presents an example similar to *Gunnarsslagr*: there *Hjarrandahljóð* would seem to reflect a genuine old tradition. The whole problem of tune and text bears comparison with the Breton lay.

24. As it happens there actually is a *Gunnars slagr* printed in the Arnamagnæan edition of the *Sæmundar Edda* (II [Copenhagen, 1818], 1000–10) and in Rask's edition (Stockholm, 1818), pp. 274–77; it seems to be the work of the learned Icelander Séra Gunnar Pálsson, one of the editors of the Copenhagen edition (Rask, p. 274, n.; Sophus Bugge, *Sæmundar Edda* [Christiania, 1867], p. xlix). It is of interest, though hardly strong evidence, that he interpreted the þáttr's reference as to a poem (and cf. Arnamagnæan ed., II, 1000, n.); similarly the Chadwicks guessed that *Gunnarsslagr* might be the same as *Oddrúnargrátr* or one of the Atli poems *(Growth*, I, 576).

to a lament such as King Gelimer of the Vandals wished to sing to the accompaniment of a harp on a similar occasion. But a name like *Guðrúnarbrögð in fornu* could hardly have arisen as the name of a tune without words.

The literary-historical milieu required by these lost poems is a transitional one with a mixture of traditions and forms: South Germanic revenge on the brothers carries the Northern name of the heroine in *Högna táttur* and presumably in *bragdar/bragda táttur* and *Guðrúnarbrögð;* in Danish ballad tradition a *Grimilds Hævn* exists side by side with a *Frœndehævn,* though the latter eventually lost explicit connection with the Burgundians; the collateral source of *Þiðreks saga,* the Saxon lay, did not yet have the subsidiary characters from the epic, Dietrich, Rüdiger, and others.[25] *Guðrúnarbrögð* seems, then, to fit easily into the transitional North German-Danish milieu evoked by Wolfgang Mohr's important work and most recently by E. E. Metzner.[26]

Further external evidence for the currency of the lay and its "title" turned up after the completion of this article: (1) Der Marner (fl. 1230–67), lists part of his repertoire: "Sing ich dien liuten mîniu liet, / sô wil der erste daz / wie Dietrîch von Berne schiet / ... / Der fünfte wen Kriemhilt verriet ..." *(Der Marner, ed. Philipp Strauch [Quellen und Forschungen zur Sprach- und Cultur-geschichte der germanischen Völker, XIV], Strassburg, 1876: XV, 14, 11.261–67);* (2) Hugo von Trimberg (c. 1230–1313) gives a similar list of poems: "Der niunde wil Kriemhilden mort / Der zehende der Nibelunge hort" *(Der Renner, ed. G. Ehrismann [Bibliothek des litterarischen Vereins in Stuttgart, CCXLVIII],* Tübingen, 1909, II, 283). Hugo's reference is not independent evidence because it is an imitation of the Marner's passage, but his nominalization of "wen K. verriet" suggests the kind of title found in *Guðrúnarbrögð* (MHG *mort* = treacherous killing,

---

25. On Dietrich, Hempel, pp. 100–04, 108–09, but cf. Andersson, p. 29; on the Danish ballads, *DgF,* I, 24–55 (nos. 4–5), and cf. *DgF,* IV, 586–600; mixture of names can, of course, arise independently as in the A Ms. of *Þiðreks saga* (ed. H. Bertelsen [Copenhagen, 1905–11]).

26. Mohr, "Entstehungsgeschichte und Heimat der jüngeren Eddalieder südgermanischen Stoffes," *ZDA* 75 (1938), 217–80; Metzner, *Zur frühesten Geschichte der europäischen Balladendichtung. Der Tanz in Kölbigk,* Frankfurter Beiträge zur Germanistik, Bd. 14 (Frankfurt, 1972).

Verrat). The Marner's editor Strauch compares Saxo's *Grimildae perfidia* and shows (a conclusion going back to Grimm) that the Marner must have still known the story of the Nibelungs in separate lays, not as a single epic (pp. 34–36); surprisingly the Marner's allusion has not been mentioned in connection with the Saxon lay by Wisniewski, Hempel, or Heusler. The Marner was a Swabian (and Hugo an East Franconian), but this has no significance here since he travelled widely and was familiar enough with Saxony to be criticized and mourned by a Saxon poet.

The King in Disguise:
An International Popular Tale
in Two Old Icelandic Adaptations*

For Professor Albert Bates Lord on his sixtieth birthday
15 September 1977

One of Professor Lord's continuing concerns and an interest he has instilled in his students is the importance of relations between oral and literary traditions. The problem is controversial in many fields and nowhere more so than in the study of the saga literature where it is not always recognized how intimate are the connections between the oral-literary question and the problem of European influence, the problem of the uniqueness of the saga literature. The following essay is intended as a contribution to the current reassessment of the relationship of Old Icelandic saga literature to the European mainstream and of the ways of literary tradition in dealing with oral sources. Part I discusses the assimilation of a widely known international tale to its place in the saga histories of Norway, while Part II shows how the same tale is adapted in a different genre. In Part III the thematic contents of the story in the two adaptations are compared with each other and with the meanings attached to a similar tale in Old Icelandic, and Part IV briefly draws some conclusions for the comparative study of saga literature.

---

*My thanks to the Society for the Humanities, Cornell University, where this article was first written in 1971. In the meantime, a new survey of the international tale by Elizabeth Walsh (to which the original version of the present article contributed [cf. her n. 30]) has appeared in print: "The King in Disguise," *Folklore* 86 (1975), 3–24; Walsh's survey should be added to the works cited in my notes 6 and 7.

I

Snorri Sturluson's account of the Battle of the Nissa (9 August 1062) follows the actions of the Norwegian earl Hákon Ívarsson more closely than those of Hákon's sovereign Haraldr Sigurðarson.

Battle was joined late in the day and continued all night with Hákon fighting fiercely and directing his ships to whatever part of the fleet was at the moment hard pressed by the superior Danish force. However, when the ship of the Danish king, Sveinn Úlfsson, had been cleared of men so that all were dead or overboard and the rout of the Danish fleet began, Hákon's ships were blocked from the pursuit and had to stay behind. A stranger dressed in a hood came rowing up to Hákon's ship in a small boat and called out to the earl; the stranger identified himself as Vandráðr and asked quarter of the earl. Hákon sent two men to row with Vandráðr in to the coast of Halland and to escort him to Karl, a farmer, who would speed him on his way. The refugee Vandráðr and his companions arrived just as the farmer and his wife were rising for the day. Karl invited them to breakfast, and the wife scolded Vandráðr for drying his hands on the middle of the towel. Karl's son accompanied Vandráðr as his guide in the forest. Later it was learned that King Sveinn had escaped from the battle, and soon a message came to Karl and his wife to come to the Danish court. At court it became clear that Vandráðr was none other than the king himself, and Karl was now rewarded with lands in Zealand and eventually with extensive power. However, King Sveinn sent the old wife back to Halland and married Karl to a nobler woman.[1]

Lest the reader wonder how this little Danish success story was known to Snorri, he assures us, "The story spread far and wide, and news of it reached Norway"; and there were other stories attached to the Nissa encounter: "That autumn, when the army came back from Denmark, there was a tremendous amount of talk and story-telling about the battle, for everyone who had taken part in it felt he had something worth telling about it."[2] However, Snorri's source here is

---

1. *Heimskringla*, III, ed. Bjarni Aðalbjarnarson, Íslenzk fornrit (=*ÍF*)28 (Reykjavík, 1951), esp. ch. 64 and 67, pp. 152–54, 155–56 (*Harald's saga Sigurðarsonar*).

2. Translated passages from Snorri's *Haralds saga Sigurðarsonar* are from *King Harold's Saga*, tr. Magnus Magnusson and Hermann Pálsson (Baltimore, 1966), pp. 115–20; other translations are my own.

not an oral one but the now-fragmentary *Hákonar saga Ívarsson,* the only extant example of a saga about a non-royal Norwegian.[3] The first part of the story of Vandráðr and Karl is lost in the source, but from the summons to court to the end of the tale Snorri remains closely true to *Hákonar saga* while steadily simplifying and condensing; for example, Snorri excised most of the references to the providential nature of Karl's aid and omitted all reference to the conferral of the office of steward *(ármenning),* to the son's reward, and the didactic and proverbial close of the episode in *Hákonar saga.* This last element, in particular, gives the tale in *Hákonar saga* the flavor of fable, and one result of Snorri's alterations is to increase the historical plausibility of the tale.

However, the story of Vandráðr and Karl possesses but a tenuous claim to historicity, for the ultimate source of *Hákonar saga* for this episode is the tale somewhat inaptly called the King in Disguise. Tales of this type tell how a king accidentally comes to benefit from the hospitality of one of his poorer subjects and how the hospitality is later rewarded; the king is unrecognized but not always in disguise. The tale embodies the *Allerweltsmotiv* of an incognito king or god among his people[4] but is itself not merely a common "motif" or "theme" but an articulated narrative that maintains much of its structural identity and many details from one version to another, in short, an international popular tale.[5]

---

3. *Hákonar saga Ívarssonar,* ed. Jón Helgason and Jakob Benediktsson (Copenhagen, 1952), pp. 29–30; all the following quotations and translations from *Hákonar saga* refer to these pages. Cf. Gustav Storm, *Snorri Sturlassøns historieskrivning* (Copenhagen, 1873), pp. 236–59.

4. The motif of major concern in this paper is (Stith Thompson, *Motif-Index of Folk Literature,* rev. ed. [Bloomington, Ind., 1955]) K1812 *King in disguise* or K1812.1 *Incognito king helped by humble man. Gives reward;* the first of the Icelandic versions discussed here has not been noticed, but the second is entered in Inger Boberg, *Motif-Index of Early Icelandic Literature,* Bibliotheca Arnamagnæana 27 (Copenhagen, 1966) as K1812.19 *King in disguise as one of his own men rescued in fighting alone against four.* Also see Thompson, K1816.9, K1812.4, K1812.9, K1812.10, K1811, Q1, Q1.1, and Boberg, P322.2, P324.1, P336.2, and Q45.4.

5. With this term I mean essentially the same as Kenneth H. Jackson, *The International Popular Tale and Early Welsh Tradition* (Cardiff, 1961), esp. ch. 1 and 2. The distinction from "folktale," which is freed to mean not a class of literature but one mode of existence (oral) of the "international popular tale," seems to me particularly useful in dealing with the complex relations between oral tradition and writing one finds in Old Icelandic.

Probably the best known version is preserved in the first part of the Scottish romance *The Taill of Rauf Coilȝear*:

Rauf, a humble collier, gives a night's lodging to Charlemagne, whom he finds straying through a snowstorm in the mountains surrounding Paris. He does not recognize his royal guest, and while showering him with bounteous hospitality treats him with rough-handed familiarity. Charlemagne, who takes all in good part, describes himself as a servant of the queen—"Wymond of the Wardrobe"—and promises his host that if he will bring a load of coals to court, he shall be guaranteed an excellent market for them. The next morning the king is directed on his way; he soon meets Roland, Oliver, Turpin, and many others, who congratulate him on his safe return. Rauf sets about preparing his load of charcoal, despite the forebodings of his wife that Wymond's intentions may not be amicable. In Paris, Rauf gains admission, with some difficulty, to the royal hall, where he learns the identity of his late guest. He is considerably alarmed to recall the violence of his hospitality, but the Emperor forgives him his offenses and rewards his bounty with knighthood.[6]

The second part of the romance, which begins with Rauf's quarrel with Roland on the way to Paris, concerns Rauf's mock heroic exploits as a peasant-knight.

No geographic-historic study of the King in Disguise has been attempted, but enough versions have been reported to show that it was international property in the later Middle Ages. Among analogues of the whole story of Karl and Vandráðr, five medieval versions, four extant in English and one in Latin, are well known; the oldest of these is Giraldus Cambrensis' tale of Henry II and the Cistercian abbot.[7] Older than Giraldus and probably from the late

---

6. Summary adapted from that of H. M. Smyser, "'The Taill of Rauf Coilȝear' and its Sources," *Harvard Studies and Notes* 14 (1932), 137–38. Besides this article (pp. 135–50), still the most complete account of the tale, the King in Disguise is discussed by F. J. Child, *English and Scottish Popular Ballads*, V (Boston, 1894), 67–75; by E. K. Chambers, *English Literature at the Close of the Middle Ages* (Oxford, 1945), pp. 128–29, 223–24; by Max Tonndorf, *Rauf Coilyear ...* (Halle, 1893), and earlier by Percy and Hazlitt.

7. Giraldus Cambrensis, *Speculum Ecclesiæ*, ed. S. Brewer, Opera, IV, Rolls Series (London, 1873), pp. 213–15 (cf. pp. xxxix–xli); "King Edward and the Shepherd" in

eleventh or early twelfth century is the story of King Alfred and
the cakes, which, however, is only a partial analogue in its oldest
forms.[8] Other partial analogues in Western literature date back to

Ancient Metrical Tales, ed. C. H. Hartshorne (London, 1829), pp. 35–80; "John de Reeve,"
in Bishop Percy's Folio Manuscript, ed. J. W. Hales and F. J. Furnival, II (London, 1868),
559–94; "The King and the Hermyt" in Remains of the Early Popular Poetry of England, ed.
W. C. Hazlitt, I (London, 1864), 11–34; and "Rauf Coilȝear" in The Taill ofRauf Coilȝear,
with Fragments of Roland and Vernagu and Otuel, ed. S. J. H. Herrtage, EETS, ES 39
(London, 1882). Among the later relatively close analogues are "The King and the Barker,"
Hazlitt, I, 1–10; "The Kinge and the Miller," Percy Folio MS, II, 147–57; "King Alfred and
the Shepherd," The Roxburghe Ballads, III (Hertford, 1880), ed. W. Chappell, 210–19;
"The History of the King and the Cobbler" ("First Part"), a summary in Descriptive Notices
of Popular English Histories, by J. O. Halliwell Phillips, Percy Society 23 (London, 1848),
48–50, doubled in "Second Part"; "King Edward IV and the Tanner of Tamworth," Child,
V, 67–87; "King James V and the Tinker," a ballad in Andrew Small, Interesting Roman
Antiquities Recently Discovered in Fife ... (Edinburgh, 1823), pp. 283–85 (summary in
Child, V, 73–74); a story of King James V (the Guidman of Ballangeich) and a miller, Small,
pp. 277–80; a story of James V and a shepherd, Small, pp. 280–82 (cf. also the other stories
of the disguisings of James V, Small, pp. 285–91); "The King and the Forrester," Rox-
burghe Ballads, VII (Hertford, 1893), ed. J. W. Ebsworth, 763–64; "Der Köhler und Kaiser
Maximilian II," in Westslawischer Märchenschatz, ed. Joseph Wenzig (Leipzig, 1857), pp.
179–81; "Grand Nez," in Contes populaires de la Haute-Bretagne, ed. Paul Sébillot, II
(Paris, 1881), 149–50 (also told of Henri IV in Guirlandes des Marguerites [Nérac et Bor-
deaux, 1876], a text I have not seen [now cf. Walsh, n. 39]); No. 160 in Danske sagn, ed.
E. T. Kristensen, IV (Aarhus, 1896), 41; "Brot und Salz segnet Gott" (No. 572) in Deutsche
Sagen, by J. and W. Grimm, ed. H. Grimm (Berlin, 1891), p. 190; a story of Charlemagne
and a shoemaker in Die Sagen Belgiens, ed. Maria von Ploennies (Cologne, 1846), pp.
242–45; a story of Charlemagne and a farmer, Sagen Belgiens, pp. 246–47; and esp. a story
of Charlemagne and a farmer, Sagen Belgiens, pp. 249–53 (cf. also pp. 245–46). More
distant analogues of the whole tale are "Christian den Fjerde og bonden" in J. M. Thiele,
Danmarks folkesagn, ed. Per Skar, I (Copenhagen, 1968), 57–58; "Kongen og bonden,"
Thiele, I, 58–59; Fit VII of "The Little Gest of Robin Hood," Child, III, 73–75; and perhaps
the adventures of Haroun-al-Rashid in the 1001 Nights (for references see Victor Chauvin,
Bibliographie des ouvrages arabes ou relatifs aux arabes, VI [Leipzig and Liège, 1902],
44–45); "The Royal Frolic ...," Roxburghe Ballads, VII, 756–57, also 758–60, 761–62;
Nos. 157 and 158 in Danske sagn, IV (cf. Small, p. 287); D. D. Cardonne, Mélanges de
littérature orientale ... (Paris, 1770), I, 104–16. Among the partial analogues, cf. Nos.
556 and 569 in Deutsche Sagen, pp. 176–77, 187 (other versions of No. 556 discussed in
Kinderling, "Nähere Erläuterung über den in der Schmiede zu Ruhla hart geschmiedeten
Landgrafen Ludwig den Eisernen," Odina und Teutona, ed. F. D. Gräter, I [Breslau, 1812],
140–51); Gesta Romanorum, ed. Hermann Oesterley (Berlin, 1872), pp. 315–19 (Cap. 20),
and with a few variations in the early modern German Gesta Romanorum ..., ed. J. G. T.
Grässe (Dresden and Leipzig, 1842), II, 198–206; "La Princesse du palais enchanté" in
Contes populaires de la Basse-Bretagne, ed. Francois Luzel, I (Paris, 1887), 259–88. This
list of analogues is a revised and supplemented version of that given by Smyser; among the
omissions here are all late literary versions, for which see Smyser and Child.
    8. W. H. Stevenson, ed., Asser's Life of Alfred (Oxford, 1904), pp. 41–42, 256–61;
the story makes its appearance in the brief familiar form in the lost Life of St. Neot (probably late 11th or early 12th century) used in the Annals of St. Neot's (early 12th century);

the tenth century,[9] and the widely disseminated folktale of the King and the Soldier (Type 952) is comparable to the two Icelandic tales discussed here.[10] None of the early versions is close enough to those in Old Icelandic to raise the question of a "source," and we must rest content with a discussion of the probable adaptation of the Old Icelandic forms based on a comparison with the analogues.

The opening of the story in *Heimskringla* (in all probability very close to its source in *Hákonar saga)* is fully adapted to the historical setting. In the analogues we find the king is regularly identified,[11] but often the setting is very vague while the story of Vandráðr is linked to a firmly historical battle. Hákon Ívarsson's action is also plausible: he had experienced kindness at the hands of King Sveinn, and his real life-long enemy was King Haraldr. Thus our episode is much better motivated than the analogues, in which, typically, the king becomes separated from his courtiers and lost on a hunt or is brought in contact with the peasant by some even more adventitious device.[12]

As in most of the analogues King Sveinn conceals his identity by his less than regal clothing; however, the disguise is not a vital element in these stories, and Sveinn's "broad cowl" is the conven-

---

the later (12th and 13th century) lives of St. Neot, various medieval chronical versions, and the early English homily on St. Neot derive ultimately from the lost *Life;* much later (17th century) we find a fuller version that is a complete analogue to the Icelandic stories ("King Alfred and the Shepherd," cited above). Walsh, p. 8, probably gives too much credence to the possible early existence of the anecdote; cf. Stevenson's summary: "... we have no evidence of this story of Alfred and the cakes before the Norman Conquest" (p. 261).

9. Liutprand of Cremona, *Antapodosis,* Lib. I, Cap. XI *(MGH* V, Scriptorum III [Hannover, 1839], 277–78); and telling the same story: No. 159, *Danske sagn,* IV, 40; No. 571, *Deutsche Sagen,* pp. 189–90.

10. Stith Thompson and Antti Aarne, *Types of the Folktale,* FFC No. 184 (Helsinki, 1964): Type 952 (=Grimm No. 199; cf. J. Bolte and G. Polívka, *Anmerkungen zu den Kinder- und Hausmärchen der Brüder Grimm,* III [Leipzig, 1918], 450–55); cf. also Types 750A, B, C, 750*, 751, 752A, 753, 768, 791, 951A, C. The tales of the King in Disguise have not usually been considered by folktale taxonomists, though one folklorist (Katherine M. Briggs, *A Dictionary of British Folk-Tales in the English Language,* Part A, vol. 2 [Bloomington, Ind., 1970], 418–23, 433–37, 437–38; also Pt. A, vol. 1, Index of Types) classifies them as "distant variants" of Type 921 The King and the Peasant's Son; this tale type also belongs to the novella group (Types 850–999), but the tales of the King in Disguise normally appear as historical legends. The Type that seems closest to me is 952.

11. E.g., Henry II, Charlemagne, Edward III, Edward IV, Christian IV, but also "a king of France," "a prince," etc.

12. E.g., Maximilian II and Christian IV are out for a walk.

tional, minimal disguise of Old Icelandic literature. The false names used in the analogues tend to the mildly humorous; perhaps the best in this respect is a continental folktale that tells how an emperor met a collier at work in the forest. Asked his name the emperor answered "Maximilian," but the collier did not understand the strange name and assimilated it to a more familiar word, dubbing the emperor "Herr Marzipan."[13] Sveinn's alias is found elsewhere in the saga literature; like "Grímr" ("Masked One") for anyone in disguise, "Vandráðr" ("One in Trouble") for any fugitive gives a more conventional impression than the aliases encountered in the analogues.[14] *Hákonar saga's* garrulous Karl comments at length on the aptness of the name—comments omitted by Snorri: "... you called yourself Vandráðr. And that was aptly invented since at that time you had sufficient 'trouble' *[vandrœði]* to deal with." This accords with the convention of self-conscious use of meaningful names found frequently in the saga literature.[15]

In many of the analogues the king requires shelter for the night,[16] but the story of Karl is given a realistic touch as Vandráðr spends

13. Cf. "Jolly Robin," "Wymonde of the Wardrobe," "Harry Tudor," "Pierce Pay-for-all," "Jack Fletcher," "a gentleman of King Alfred's court."

14. *Víglundar saga*, ed. Jóhannes Halldórsson, ÍF 14 (Reykjavík, 1949), 101: Vandráðr and Torráðr = Víglundr and Trausti (note, however, that Vandráðr and Torráðr are the real names of Guðrún's brothers in *Laxdœla saga*, ÍF 5). Cf., e.g., "Grímr" for the disguised men in Vǫlsa þáttr *(Flateyjarbók: en Samling of norske Konge-Sagaer ...*, eds. C. R. Unger and G. Vigfússon, II [Christiania, 1862], 331–36).

15. Cf., for example, *Gísls þáttr Illugasonar* (ÍF 3:333): "hét ek Vígfúss í morgin, en í kveld væni ek, at ek heita Ófeigr"; *Víga-Glums saga (ÍF 9:54)*: "Ek heiti Margr í Mývatnshverfi, en Fár í Fiskilœkjarhverfi" (of Skúta, punning on *skúti* "cave"); *Fóstrbrœðra saga (ÍF 6:233–41)* Ch. 23: Þormóðr=Ótryggr Tortryggsson, Vígfúss, and Torráðr; Ch. 24: Þormóðr=Ósvífr (cf. the comment: "Svá er hverr sem heitir," p. 249); *Þorleifs þáttr jarlsskalds* (ÍF 9:220–22): Þorleifr = Níðungr Gjallandason; *Kormaks saga* (ÍF 8:247): Steinarr =Glúmr or Skúma (cf. n. 3); and cf. the wordplay on "Stúfr," "Kǫttr," and "Sigurðr syr" in *Stúfs þáttr* (ÍF 5). Many other aliases are apparently without secondary meanings, e.g., *Þorsteins saga hvíta* (ÍF 11:12): Þorsteinn = Sigurðr; and *Víglundar saga* (ÍF 14:103, 115): Helgi Eiríksson = Þórðr í Gautavík; but "Qrn and Hrafn" for Víglundr and Trausti (pp. 103–15) is suggestive. "Þjófr" for Friðþjófr *(Die Friðþjófssaga*, ed. G. Wenz [Halle, 1914], pp. 28–30) and "Óli" for "Óláfr" *(Óláfs saga Tryggvasonar*, ÍF 26:266–68) seem to belong in another tradition; cf. "Tantris" for Tristan. With the explication of "Vandráðr" in *Hákonar saga*, cf. *Víglundar saga* (ÍF 14:101): "... spurði Gunnlaugr inn mikla mann, hví hann nefndist Vandráðr. 'Því nefndumst ek Vandráðr', segir hann, 'at þar eru til nóg vandræði mín, en ek heitir Víglundr ... .'"

16. E.g., "Rauf Coilȝear" and "Grand Nez"; *Morkinskinna* and *Fagrskinna* (cited below) explain that the king went "til kotbeiar nocquers firir þa savcc at Norþmenn ransaucodo of þorpit oc stor beina" *(Msk*, p. 214).

the night in battle and in the escape to arrive at the farm just as Karl and his wife are rising. The givers of hospitality in the analogues are of a low social class, though not all are the poorest of peasants; Karl seems to be a yeoman farmer of modest means (the farm is referred to as a *búkot*). His name, of course, suggests the free peasantry and usually also a man who is no longer young.[17] Like most of the peasants in the analogues, Karl insists on a meal for his guests, but it is with the humorous interchanges between the king and the farmer's wife that the folktale foundation of the story shines through most clearly.

First the woman complains that the noise of the fighting had kept her awake all night; then she observes that "our king," Sveinn, will have fled from battle again:

> "What a wretched king we have," said the woman. "He not only walks with a limp, but he's a coward as well."
> Then Vandrad said, "I don't think the king is a coward; but he hasn't much victory luck."

Similarly some of the kings in the analogues learn unpleasant truths about themselves or their administration from the unsuspecting mouths of the folk, and in some related tales the king's purpose in going about in disguise is to listen to the *vox populi*.[18] Some versions, however, turn the tables and expose instead the easy ways of the peasantry in dealing with the law and especially with the king's venison, and in the best of them this glimpse of peasant life is accorded an enthusiastic development comparable to genre painting.[19]

Next Vandráðr gets a rude lesson in lower class courtesy:

---

17. Cf. esp. the use of "Karl" as representative of the franklin class in "Rígsþula" and the description of Karl's life there.

18. Personal criticism of the ruler in *Deutsche Sagen*, No. 556; oppression and taxes in "King Edward and the Shepherd," "John de Reeve," "Christian den Fjerde og bonden," and *Danske sagn*, No. 157; praise of the king in "The Royal Frolic," and so on. The king wishes to sample public opinion in "The King and the Barker," "Grand Nez," and *Danske sagn*, Nos. 157 and 158; cf. Thompson motifs J21.43 *A country not examined in disguise will always be ruined*, N467 *King in disguise learns secrets of his subjects*, P14.19, and K1812.17.

19. E.g., most of the English versions, "Grand Nez," and "La Princesse."

Vandrad was the last to wash his hands, and afterwards he dried them on the middle part of the towel. The woman of the house snatched the towel away from him and said, "How uncouth you are! It's boorish to wet the towel all over at the same time."

The courtesy lesson is found in a number of the analogues; for example, Rauf the collier clouts Charlemagne soundly to teach him obedience to his host, and a shepherd's wife scolds and threatens King Alfred for letting the cakes burn.[20] Probably to be considered variants of the courtesy lesson are the silly drinking customs taught the king in other analogues, as when Henry II learns "Pril" and "Wril" instead of "Wesheil" and "Drincheil" as toast and response.[21]

Finally, Karl aids the king's journey back to court, and the farmer's son accompanies him. Snorri does not mention the son again, but *Hákonar saga* informs us that King Sveinn later took the boy in at court and made a *hirðmaðr* of him. This is paralleled in at least one extant analogue where the peasant's son has a considerable role.[22]

Back at court, Sveinn sends for Karl and his family. The analogues are divided between the motifs of a royal summons and a pre-arranged trip to court for commercial purposes. The saga version has nothing corresponding to the fears of Rauf s wife[23] and none of the comedy of the spectacle of a boorish peasant at court, and its recognition scene is not quite like that of any other version:

When they arrived at the royal court, the king summoned Karl to his presence, and asked whether he recognized him or thought he had seen him before.

Karl said, "I recognize you now, sire, and I recognized you then, as soon as I saw you. May God be praised that the little help I gave you was of some use to you."

---

20. Also in "John de Reeve," "King and the Miller," "La Princesse," and perhaps in others.

21. Giraldus; cf. "King Edward and the Shepherd" and "King Edward and the Hermyt."

22. "John de Reeve"; cf. the tale cited from *Gesta Romanorum* (Cap. 20) and "La Princesse."

23. Similar fears in "John de Reeve," "The King and the Miller," "King Alfred and the Shepherd," "Grand Nez," and "Christian den Fjerde og bonden."

In some of the analogues this and associated scenes at court are the occasion for a great deal of fun at the peasant's expense, and in some there follows an incongruous application of the rustic courtesy to court life, as when Henry II insists on drinking to "Pril-Wril." King Sveinn now expresses his obligation to Karl and confers on him the lands of his choice in Zealand along with the office of *ármaðr;* similar rewards are found in the analogues.

Most of the differences between the tale of Karl and Vandráðr and its analogues contribute to realism and historical plausibility, and this adaptation involved suppression of most of the comedy of the popular versions. The adaptation entailed no important structural changes except at the beginning of the tale, but the two most striking differences of detail between our story and its analogues may be explained as products of the adaptation to sober "history": Karl, unlike all his confreres, claims to have recognized the king from the beginning, and the old wife is punished for speaking her mind, while Karl is to receive "a much wiser and better woman for a wife."[24]

In *Hákonar saga* the story closes with the author's pointing a moral, partly through proverbs: "It's always important that a man take much care to make friends, for he who has good friends will always have support." This produces a clear end to the tale and an effect close to that of the simplistically didactic oral tale, while Snorri has endeavored to create an apparent continuity with the following chapter by leaving out this epilogue and thus emphasizing the themes of "story" and "talk" in both chapters. Similar proverbial associations are found in some of the analogues;[25] however, the proverbial ending of the episode in *Hákonar saga* will be a reflection not of a particular source-tale or a particular tradition but of the oral folktale style in general.

How historical, then, is the episode of Karl and Vandráðr? Most of the elements of the episode are paralleled not as scattered "motifs" in assorted folklore but as parts of a single, well-attested, independent

---

24. The differential reward and initial recognition or near recognition may, however, be traditional; cf. the Thompson motifs under Q1 *Hospitality rewarded—opposite punished* and pp. 119–121 below.

25. "Le Bûcheron est maître dans sa hutte ... comme le roi dans son palais" ("La Princesse"); cf. "Chascun est roy en sa maison, comme respondit le charbonnier [to a king of France]" *(Commentaires de Blaise de Monluc*, ed. Paul Courteault, III [Paris, 1925], 395) and the discussion in Smyser, pp. 141–43 and references cited, p. 143, n. 2.

international tale. Most of the remainder of the tale can be explained as adaptations to the historical format or to the Scandinavian context. Nevertheless, there may be, in the well-worn phrase, a "historical kernel" in the tale.

Morkinskinna and *Fagrskinna* present the career of Hákon Ívarsson and the events of the first half of the 1060's in a very different way from that of *Heimskringla-Hákonar saga*; and in following chiefly *Hákonar saga* against *Morkinskinna*, Snorri seems to have chosen the more fabulous alternative.[26] Nevertheless, the story we are concerned with is present in *Morkinskinna* and *Fagrskinna* though in a much briefer form. There we are told that King Sveinn and one follower fled to land and arrived at a cotter's farm *(kotbœr)* in the morning. They were met by an old woman *(kerling)* who asked who they were; the follower answered that they were travelers in need of help. The woman comments suspiciously on their appearance.[27] She asks the news and whether a battle between the kings caused the noise that kept her from sleeping during the night, and the dialogue continues almost as in *Heimskringla*. The washing scene and breakfast follow, but the anecdote ends with the king's memorable *réplique*: "'It may yet be', he said, 'if God wills it, that we shall receive so much esteem that we may dry our hands in the middle of the towel'" *(Msk)*.

It would be tempting to regard the incident as presented by the *Morkinskinna-Fagrskinna* tradition as an only slightly embellished attestation of the "historical kernel." In that case the historical incident would have attracted to itself the folktale, which bore a real similarity to the truth in several of its motifs; then a mutual assimilation would have gone on in the oral tradition. Such an escape and encounter and such a sentiment on the part of the king appear not improbable when the incident is considered in isolation. However, at the beginning of Snorri's *Haralds saga* we hear of a very similar escape and a similar quip:

---

26. *Morkinskinna ... (=Msk)*, ed. Finnur Jónsson (Copenhagen, 1932), pp. 214–15; *Fagrskinna: kortfattet norsk Konge-Saga ... (=Fsk)*, eds. P. A. Munch and C. R. Unger (Christiania, 1847), pp. 131–32; Edvard Bull, "Håkon Ivarsons saga," *Edda* 27 (1927), 33–44.

27. *Msk*: "Þit latið ouenliga" or possibly (editor's note) "miceliga"; *Fsk* would support the latter: "Munn þit vera svá miklir menn, sem þit látið ríkliga." Further minor differences among the Icelandic texts will not be noticed here.

The young Haraldr Sigurðarson escaped from the defeat at Stiklastaðir with one man (Rǫgnvaldr Brúsason), who brought him wounded to an unnamed farmer on an isolated farm in a forest. When Haraldr was well again, the *bondi*'s son guided him east over the Kjølen. "The farmer's son had no idea who his companion was; and as they were riding across from one wild forest to another, Harald composed this stanza:

> Now I go creeping from forest
> To forest with little honour;
> Who knows, my name may yet become
> Renowned far and wide in the end (pp. 45–46).

In view of this and similar escapes[28] and in view of the international tales of the King in Disguise, the events as told in *Morkinskinna-Fagrskinna* appear more conventional. Moreover, the differences between the narrative (or at least longer) version in *Heimskringla-Hákonar saga* and the anecdotal (or shorter) version in *Morkinskinna-Fagrskinna* seem easier to account for as the reduction of a full-fledged oral tale to its comic core than as accretion of the legendary narrative to a historical central incident.[29]

Finally, *Morkinskinna-Fagrskinna* openly cautions us that this incident is fabulous: "Þetta er gamans frasaugn oc eigi sauguligt eins-

---

28. Cf. the escapes of Óláfr Tryggvason and Harold, Godwin's son, after their defeats at Svǫldr and Hastings (references and discussion in Lars Lönnroth, "Studier i Olaf Tryggvasons saga," *Samlaren* 84 [1963], 77–83).

29. Admittedly this conjecture is unprovable and contradicts the very tentative speculation of Bjarni Aðalbjarnarson (ÍF 28: XXVI; cf. *Om de norske kongers sagaer* [Oslo, 1937], pp. 153–54) about the relationship between *Hákonar saga* and *Msk*. That brief anecdotes bound to a quip (as in *Msk-Fsk*) do live in tradition unsupported by rounded tales is well known. In the present instance, however, I find it easier to believe that *Msk* is condensing for the following (inconclusive) reasons: (1) the comment about "speki ok óvizka" that concludes the *Msk* anecdote seems to be the reduction of a moral such as we find in the developed tale in *Hákonar saga;* (2) since "speki" is not, in fact, rewarded or "óvizka" punished in the *Msk* anecdote as it stands, a fuller version probably lies behind the text, and the phrase may be an allusion, specifically, to differential rewards for hospitality and inhospitality (cf. n. 24 above); (3) that the *kerling* is hostess and speaks in the plural could be because she is a widow and herself head of the farm, but an equally satisfactory explanation is that her *karl* has been dropped from the anecdote. However, I should point out the counter-example of Alfred and the cakes, which first appears in a very similar anecdotal form and only later is found as a developed tale (see n. 8 above).

costar nema fyr þa sauc at her er lyst grein speci oc ovizco" *(Msk)*. In other words, the "truth" of the incident is of a moral or ethical, not a historical kind. Surely this is a reference to an oral tale *(frásögn)* with historical setting and didactic function—just such a tale as we suspect, on the basis of the comparative evidence, beneath the full story of Karl and Vandráðr in *Heimskringla* and *Hákonar saga*.

II

Our second Icelandic adaptation of the King in Disguise has still less claim to historical truth but is less easily recognizable as a version of the international popular tale. Nevertheless, *Þorsteins þáttr Austfirðings* (or *suðrfara)*, an independent short story found in two paper manuscripts, can tell us still more about the adaptation of international narrative material in Old Icelandic literature:

> Þorsteinn, a young Icelander, met and saved the life of a man who gave his name as "Styrbjǫrn" and claimed to be a retainer of King Magnús Óláfsson. He invited Þorsteinn to court; and after completing his pilgrimage to Rome, Þorsteinn arrives at court. At the door he asks for "Styrbjǫrn" and is mocked by the retainers until the king himself goes to the door, leads Þorsteinn in, and presents him with his own robe. "Styrbjǫrn" is identified as the king. On a bivouac in the north (of Norway), Þorsteinn is mocked by the retainers for his manners, but the king defends him. Later Magnús offers Þorsteinn a wife and position in Norway, but the Icelander knows that he would have to live with the hostility of those who would envy the king's protégé and instead chooses to sail back to Iceland with rich rewards. Back home he settled and was thought a very lucky man.[30]

Even in this bare outline Þorsteinn's story bears a definite family resemblance to that of Karl and the tribe of Rauf the collier. The initial encounter takes place in Denmark, and in a gesture toward historical coloring the author explains that it was the time when King Magnús was having great campaigns there. In a scene set "one day" in "a wood"

---

30. ÍF 11 (Reykjavík, 1950), pp. 330–33; page references to this short work will be unnecessary.

Þorsteinn discovers Magnús, deserted by his men, his back to a tree, being attacked by four of the enemy—a heroic opening that contrasts with the extant non-Scandinavian analogues. During the interview in the forest, Þorsteinn speaks plainly about his sovereign, unaware that he is addressing the king himself; unlike Karl's wife, however, Þorsteinn speaks in purest praise. The motif of the incognito king learning home truths from a commoner is here presented in a polite form.

Some of the disjointed quality of *Þorsteins þáttr* emanates from unskillful strokes associated with Magnús' false name:

> When Þorsteinn returns from Rome and seeks "Styrbjǫrn" at court, he is first refused admission by the porters. Þorsteinn then asks that "Styrbjǫrn" be sent out, and this occasions enormous malicious merriment which the king puts an end to. He then welcomes the Icelander, and Þorsteinn settles down among the retinue. Some time later, the king asked, "Now which of us do you think might be 'Styrbjǫrn?'" And Þorsteinn rightly identified the king as the bearer of that alias.

Many of the analogues depict the peasant as under some difficulty in recognizing his former guest or as slow to understand that his former guest and present host is the king,[31] but the length of time implied and the whole situation involved in this recognition in the þáttr taxes the limits of logic.[32] Some of the analogues portray a good deal of merriment over the alias, but this is because it amuses the courtiers to see the still unenlightened peasant addressing their king as "Jolly Robin," etc. In *Þorsteins þáttr* the laughter is caused by the fact that no one by the name of "Styrbjǫrn" belongs to the court, and anyone who appreciates humor will agree with King Magnús: "This is not very funny...." Finally, the þáttr implies that, as with "Vandráðr," there is a special significance in the name "Styrbjǫrn": "The king took the floor and said: '... men's names can be compared in many ways. And you must no longer mock that name.'" This suggests a pun or other play on the name or that it is a recomposition or anagram of

---

31. Cf., e.g., "King Edward and the Shepherd," "Maximilian II und der Köhler," and the rather different group of recognitions in "Kongen og bonden," "King James and the Tinker," "The King and the Barker," "King Edward IV and the Tanner of Tamworth."

32. A considerable delay before recognition is implicit: "Síðan var hann með hirðinni... Konungr mælti við hann eitt sinn...."

the king's real name; but apparently no such wordplay is present, and the whole incident is to be explained as an imperfect adaptation from a source similar to the tale of Vandráðr.[33]

A further infelicity is found in connection with the þáttr's only verse.

King and retinue journeyed north; one day in camp, they cooked porridge *(grautr),* "and when the (communal) bowl was passed to Þorsteinn, he ate up everything in the bowl." The courtiers laughed at this breach of etiquette and mocked: "You really know what to do with porridge, you hick *(landi)*." The king smiled and extemporized a poem: "This warrior alone quickly felled three men in battle; he excells men. But, good with his hands, he ate porridge prepared on the journey north equal to those three; he excells them." Then the king explained to the company that "this man gave me aid when you were nowhere near" and goes on to praise Þorsteinn.

This speech cannot have been a revelation to the retainers since earlier, before the journey north, the king had told "all the true story and told everything from the beginning when they met in Denmark." While the repetition is not, strictly speaking, inconsistent, it seems that the author has, at least, not managed to dispose the ingredients of his tale in an effective way. The international tale, to judge by the analogues, required the revelation about "Styrbjǫrn" and the encounter in the Danish wood to be made at court, but the verse mentioned a "norðrfǫr" together with the heroic porridge eating. To accommodate the verse the author has created a second revelation scene in connection with Þorsteinn's rustic manners (a motif in agreement with the international tale).

---

33. The verb *saman bera* should mean "agree with, coincide with, be comparable to" and possibly "bring together, recompose." (The textual variant from 6SP [cited below], "megu manna nöfn margra saman bera," is no help.) Perhaps the author had in mind a comparison between Magnús - "brought to bay" alone, his back to a tree, attacked by a "pack" of enemies—and an "Embattled Bear" or, perhaps, "Styr-bjǫrn," "Battle-Bear," as a periphrasis for "warrior." The metaphorical use of "bear" for "man" occurs often (e.g., *Óláfs saga Tryggvasonar,* ÍF 26:278: "Væri yðr meiri veiðr at taka bjǫrninn, er nú er nær kominn á bjarnbásinn"; the bear *fylgjur* of *Njáls saga,* ch. 23, and of *Þorsteins þáttr uxafóts;* and *Helga kviða Hundingsbana II,* 8); for "Styr" in names cf. the change of "Arngrímr" to "(Víga-)Styrr" in *Eyrbyggja saga.*

The verse itself can hardly stem from the time of Magnús the Good (*ÍF* 11: CXI), but it seems safe to assume that it is older than the prose and that the imperfect assimilation of the verse has caused some of the narrative infelicities of the þáttr. If these assumptions hold, the verse originally referred to an unknown situation and had no connection with the international popular tale; rather its incorporation in such a story was an act of "interpretation" by the þáttr's author.

Thus (to elaborate this hypothesis), the author was in possession of a verse supposedly composed by King Magnús; the verse contained two motifs: (1) a fight in which the hero kills three men; and (2) an incident on a "norðrfǫr" in which the hero eats the porridge of three. The author interpreted the verse in terms of a tale that sometimes contains, among others, the following motifs: (1) initial encounter afield between disguised king and poor subject; (2) subject's hospitality to unrecognized king; (3) false name given; (4) king's return to court; (5) subject comes to court as agreed (or is summoned); (6) by-play with the porter; (7) amusement over the name; (8) revelation of the truth; (9) amusement over the rustic's manners at court; (10) the subject rewarded. The author has been able to preserve all these motifs in essence, but the hard fact of the "norðrfǫr" split motif (8) from (9) and caused (8) to be doubled.

Even if this explanation of the composition of *Þorsteins þáttr* is acceptable, it does not reveal the þáttr's literary models or the patterns used in adaptation of the tale. One of these patterns is to be found, I believe, in a particular group of Old Icelandic short stories with distinctive generic features.[34] These stories chart the course of the relationship of an Icelander with a Norwegian king in a story that begins with an Introduction and Journey In from Iceland and ends with a return to Iceland (Journey Out) and concluding remarks (Conclusion). The kernel of these stories can be described as an Alienation section followed by a Reconciliation; an uncomplicated example, *Þorsteins þáttr forvitna,* may be summarized and its structure outlined as follows:[35]

---

34. See the author's "Genre and Narrative Structure in Some *Íslendinga Þættir*," *SS* 44 (1972), 1–27; "Theme and Genre in Some *Íslendinga Þættir*," *SS* 48 (1976), 1–28; and "*Qgmundar þáttr dytts ok Gunnars helmings*: Unity and Literary Relations," *ANF* 90 (1975), 156–82. [The latter two articles are reprinted in this volume, Eds.]

35. *Íslendinga þættir* (=*ÍÞ*), ed. Guðni Jónsson (Reykjavík, 1935), pp. 353–55.

INTRODUCTION. There was a poor but valiant Icelander named
  Þorsteinn.

JOURNEY IN. He sailed in to Norway and joined King Haraldr
  Sigurðarson at court.

ALIENATION. Once when the king was bathing, Þorsteinn rummaged
  in his kit and saw a knife handle of wood that resembled gold. The
  king berated Þorsteinn for his curiosity and was angry with him.
  Later Haraldr offered Þorsteinn one chance to regain his friendship:
  he must bring the king another handle of the same kind. Þorsteinn's
  hard quest led far afield.

RECONCILIATION. But by the help of St. Óláfr and a hermit he came
  to a lake-isle where a dragon guarded a tree with golden wood.
  Þorsteinn narrowly escaped with a piece of wood which he brought
  back to Norway. Haraldr accepted the wood, praised Þorsteinn,
  and rewarded him with trading goods.

JOURNEY OUT. Þorsteinn returned to Iceland.

CONCLUSION. Þorsteinn (later) died in Haraldr's invasion of
  England.

The stories of this group have a limited cast of characters; the protagonists are an Icelander and a king (usually Norwegian), and the few
secondary characters are either friends or enemies of the Icelandic
hero whose function is to cause or heal his estrangement from the
king. Characterization is similar to that of the sagas, except that the
brevity of the stories imposes stricter limitations. The ethos of these
þættir is comic, and a number end in social promotion for the hero.

Viewed against this background, it is clear that the author of
Þorsteins þáttr Austfirðings has adopted a number of features,
including some formal conventions, from this short story genre and
that those conventions further explain his fundamental modifications
of the international popular tale of the King in Disguise. Thus, for
example, the tale is attached to King Magnús, but the hero, instead of
being a Norwegian peasant or *bondi,* becomes an Icelander. However,
though the beginning and ending of the story, the cast of characters,
and many of the relationships among them were amenable to treatment
in terms of the genre, the core of the generic narrative structure, the
Alienation-Reconciliation relationship between king and Icelander,
could not really be adapted to the folktale material even though both

patterns have a first meeting, a separation, and a reunion. Consequently *Þorsteins þáttr Austfirðings* differs from other members of its genre in having a geographical alienation only, followed by reunion and advancement of the Icelander over the hostility of the retinue, which functions here to supply the tension that is lacking between king and Icelander.

The possible influence of specific members of the genre and of other texts on *Þorsteins þáttr Austfirðings* should also be considered here in spite of the unlikelihood of establishing any such specific influence as proven to everyone's satisfaction. We may begin with the main character. Þorsteinn is not said to be a poor man, but he is dealt with as if he were. He encounters hostility at court, and his reasons for declining the king's offer of an establishment in Norway are that he will have earned enemies through his preferment. We might compare *Gull-Ásu-Þórðar þáttr,* a story of social and economic success of an Icelander against general opposition in Norway; but there is little beyond the home and poverty of the hero ("austfirzkr at ætt ok félítill ... gørviligr maðr ok fǫðurbetringr") and the envy he incurs in Norway to link Þorsteinn with Þórðr.[36] The ending of *Þorsteins þáttr* resembles more that of *Hreiðars þáttr* where the king (here also Magnús the Good) prefers to reward the Icelander and send him home rather than settle him in Norway, giving as his reason: "I think I see how King Haraldr would like to dispose of your future if he had the power—as he will have if you stay longer in Norway" (*ÍF* 10:260). Þorsteinn's porridge eating seems pale by comparison to the porridge episode in the story of the irrepressible Sneglu-Halli, otherwise known as Grautar-Halli; and rather than being a borrowing from *Sneglu-Halla þáttr,* the prose of *Þorsteins þáttr* seems at this point to be a timid interpretation of the information in the verse (*ÍF* 9:263–95). Thus, detailed similarities with *Gull-Ásu-Þórðar þáttr, Hreiðars þáttr,* and *Sneglu-Halla þáttr,* similarities that extend beyond what is common to the genre, are very slight; however, a more extensive comparison is possible between *Þorsteins þáttr* and *Auðunar þáttr vestfirzka* (*ÍF* 6:361–68).

Besides the generic formal features of *dramatis personae,* struc-

---

36. *ÍF* 11:339–49; cf. also Þorsteinn sǫgufróði, likewise a poor man from the East Fjords who wins the king's favor (*ÍF* 11:335–36).

ture, and style, both *Auðunar þáttr* and *Þorsteins þáttr* connect the generic structure with a pilgrimage to Rome, and in both the action is located partly in Norway, partly in Denmark. Nothing in Þorsteinn's tale resembles Auðunn's relationship to King Haraldr or the box-within-box effect of that story's doubled plot, but Þorsteinn's dealings with Magnús (involving geographical separation, reunion, and final reluctant parting) resemble Auðunn's with Sveinn more than is the case with any other þáttr. In both þættir the pilgrim is abused by officers of the king (Áki the *ármaðr* of King Sveinn; the *duraverðir* of King Magnús), though Auðunn was travelling to Rome, Þorsteinn returning from Rome when the incident occurred; and both pilgrims are ridiculed by the retinues and defended by the kings. These general parallels seem to warrant a closer, point-by-point comparison:

Auðunar þáttr	*Þorsteins þáttr*
1. Maðr hét Auðunn, vestfirzkr at kyni ok félítill.	Þorsteinn hét maðr, austfirzkr at ætt, ungr at aldri ok fráligr....

This kind of Introduction (often in the order here: name, home, condition in life, personal qualities) is a generic feature and, beyond that, is extremely common in all types of saga literature.[37]

2. Hann fór útan ... fara þeir aptr til Nóregs ... ok ætlar nú at fara suðr til Danmerkr.	Hann fór útan ok ætlaði til Nóregs ok svá til Róms. Hann fór til Danmerkr (a variant text).[38]

The phrases used in the Journey In in most of the stories of the genre and, indeed, throughout the saga literature are largely stereotyped.[39] Further, *Þorsteins þáttr* is much simpler at this point than *Auðunar*

---

37. "Genre and Narrative Structure," pp. 9–10; cf., e.g., *Gull-Ásu-Þórðar þáttr, Þorsteins (Íslendings) þáttr sǫgufróða, Þorvarðar þáttr krákunefs, Hrafns þáttr Hrútfirðings (Guðrúnarsonar)*, and *Þorsteins þáttr forvitna* (ÍF: 11:339; 335; 6:317; ÍP, p. 353).

38. The main text (ÍF 11:329) has "ætlaði til Róms, en fór til Danmerkr." The text cited is from *Sex sögu-þættir* (=6SP), ed. Jón Þorkelsson (Reykjavík, 1855), p. 13, based on a paper manuscript (in private possession at that time, p. VII); this text has little or no authority (cf. the discussion of MSS, ÍF 11: CXI and XII-XIII) but is interesting in the present connection.

39. "Genre and Narrative Structure," p. 10.

þáttr, which tells how Auðunn came into possession of his bear and other details; what seems significant here is not the normal progression from Norway to Denmark (which is also based on a doubtful text) but the general fact that both pilgrim stories are set in the two countries.[40]

At his first meeting with the king (Sveinn/Magnús) the Icelander identifies himself:

3. Konungr ... mælti síðan til   Hann [the king] svarar: "...
   Auðunar: "Hverr ertu?" segir   Eða hvat er ráðs þíns?" Þorsteinn
   hann. Hann svarar: "Ek em   mælti: "Ek em íslenzkr
   íslenzkr maðr...."   maðr...."

The verbal resemblance here is due to a commonplace formula that depends on the situation depicted. Both Icelanders are pilgrims:

4. Hann segir: "Suðr vil ek ganga."   "...ok ætla ek suðr at ganga."

Again, the expression is formulistic; what is, perhaps, significant is the general similarity of the two interviews, both taking place in Denmark.

Both kings are reluctant to see the Icelanders go but understand the value of the pilgrimage:

5. "Braut fýsir mik nú, herra."
      Konungr svarar heldr seint: Styrbjǫrn [King Magnús] mælti:
   "Hvat villtu þá," segir hann,   "Mantu eigi hafa saltat
   "ef þú vill eigi með oss   suðrferðina?" ...
   vera?" Hann segir: "Suðr   Styrbjǫrn mælti:
   vil ek ganga." "Ef þú   "Ek kalla ráðligt, at þú
   vildir eigi svá gott ráð   haldir fram ferðinni, því at
   taka," segir konungr, "þá   hér var nauðsyn til."
   myndi mer fyr þykkja í, er
   þú fýsisk í brott."

---

40. This is a safe inference even though the text in *ÍF* 11 only mentions a *norðrfǫr* without stating explicitly that this occurs in Norway.

The kings invite the Icelanders to visit them at court upon their return from Rome:

6. ... ok skipaði konungr   "En vitja mín, þá er þú kemr
   til um ferð hans, bað hann   aptr, því at ek em jafnan með
   koma til sín, er hann kœmi aptr.   hirð Magnúss konungs."

And the pilgrimage itself is of little interest to either author:

7. Nú fór hann ferðar sinnar,   Síðan skilðu þeir, ok fór
   unz hann kømr suðr í   Þorsteinn til Róms ok kom
   Rómaborg. Ok er hann hefir   sunnan um várit.
   þar dvalizk sem hann tíðir,
   þá ferr hann aptr....

However, in accord with its superior style and complexity, *Auðunar þáttr* adds a few (functional) details about the hero's condition on the journey.

It is a striking coincidence, in view of all the other agreements between the two stories, that both pilgrims return at Easter time:

8. Hann kømr aptr í Danmǫrk   ... ok kom sunnan um várit.
   at páskum, þangat sem   Hann kom þar, sem Magnús
   konungr er þá staddr....   konungr var at veizlu....

Both heroes experience difficulties at this point in the narrative (9) in gaining access to the kings. Auðunn is held back by his own modesty and fear of being ridiculed for his ragged and sickly condition; Þorsteinn is denied admission by the porters. There are no verbal resemblances.

As soon as they learn of the Icelander's presence, both kings hasten personally to welcome them back and bring them in:

10. Ok þegar er konungr veit,   Síðan stóð konungr upp ór
    hverr hann er, tók konungr   sæti sínu ok gengr út ...
    í hǫnd honum Auðuni ok bað   ok mælti: "Vel þú kominn,
    hann vel kominn ...   Íslendingr ...
    leiðir hann eptir sér inn.   ok gakk inn."

At this point in *Auðunar þáttr* the returning pilgrim is ridiculed by the retainers; in *Þorsteins þáttr* the laughter precedes the king's welcome:

11. Ok er hirðin sá hann,   ... með hlátri ... slógu þeir
    hlógu þeir at honum ...   í spott ok mikinn dáruskap, hverr
                       í sínu rúmi....

The cause of the laughter is different in the two þættir; Auðunn is thin, bald, wasted by illness, and dressed as a beggar, while Þorsteinn made the mistake of asking for the fictional "Styrbjǫrn."

The King silences the laughter and defends the pilgrim before the court:

12. ... en konungr sagði: Konungr tók til orða ok mælti:
    "Eigi þurfu þér at honum   "Lítit gaman er þetta ...
    at hlæja, því at betr hefir   ok skulu þér ekki spotta nafn
    hann sét fyrir sinni sál   þetta lengr."
    heldr en ér."

These words of Magnús' do correspond in position in the narrative to Sveinn's defence of Auðunn but are not of the same purport and are tied to the name motif in *Þorsteins þáttr;* a few sentences later Magnús is more direct: "... ok engin skal svá djarfr, at þér geri nǫkkut mein." But *Þorsteins þáttr* repeats the motif of the king's defence a little later, and this time Magnús, like Auðunn's King Sveinn, compares the listening courtiers unfavorably with the Icelander whom they have been mocking:

                     Konungsmenn hlógu enn at þessu ...
                     Konungr brosti at ok kvað þetta:
                     "... Sjá inn sami maðr veitti mér
                     mikit lið, þá er þér váruð hvergi
                     í nánd...."

Now the kings serve the pilgrims with bath and clothing; and the Icelanders join the retine:

13. Þá lét konungr gera honum
laug ok gaf honum síðan
klæði, ok er hann nú með
honum.[41]

"... ok tak yfir þik skikkju þessa
ok gakk inn. Skal þér búa laug,
ok ver vel kominn með hirðinni ... "
Síðan var hann með hirðinni.

At this point the stories both comment on the Icelander's general
conduct at court. The passage in *Auðunar þáttr* is, however, present
only in a minor manuscript, *Hulda* (AM 66 fol.):

14. ... var hann þar um hríð.
Auðun kunni vel at hafa sik
í fjölmenni; var hann maðr
ótyrrinn, orðgætinn ok ekki
margtalaðr.

Síðan var hann með hirðinni.
Hann var einlyndr ok fálátr.
(Text of *6SP*: Hann var
lítillátr ok fálátr.)

In *Hulda* (only) there follows immediately a statement of Auðunn's
general popularity. We infer that Þorsteinn was never popular with
the court (or at least with some persons in Norway), but Magnús's
affection for him is comparable with Sveinn's for Auðunn, though
coming a little later in the narrative:

15. ... líkaði öllum mönnum vel
við hann. Sveinn konungr var
ok hinn blíðasti til hans.[42]

Konungr var vel við hann.[43]

Later both kings offer the Icelanders a chance to settle in the Kingdom
with the royal favor:

---

41. The *Flateyjarbók* text (III, 413) makes it clear that the king gives his *own* robe as
in *Þorsteins þáttr*.

42. *Fornmanna sögur* (=*Fms*) VI (Copenhagen, 1831), 303–04. Some confusion has
been created by the fact that the *Fornrit* editors (*ÍF* 6:365, n. 3) attribute these two passages to *Flateyjarbók* when, in fact, they stem from *Hulda* (AM 66 fol.). *Hulda* is the base
text of the story as printed in *Fms* VI; the conflated text in *Fjörutíu Íslendinga-þættir*,
ed. Þorleifr Jónsson (Reykjavík, 1904) also contains the *Hulda* passage. *Hulda* is much
more discursive at this point than the oldest text, that of *Msk*; *Flateyjarbók* usually offers
fuller texts than *Msk* but here is actually the briefest; thus both major texts agree against
Hulda.

43. Cf. *ÍF* 9:280 (*Sneglu-Halla þáttr*).

16. Þat er nú sagt einhverju
sinni of várit, at konungr
býðr Auðuni at vera með sér
álengðar ok kvezk mundu gera
hann skutilsvein sinn ok
leggja til hans góða virðing.

Ok eitt sinn mælti konungr
við hann: "Hversu er þá við
þik búit, er þér þykkir bezt ok
þér má helzt líka? Viltu hér
staðfestask ok kvángask?"

The Icelanders reply with gratitude but decline, giving their reasons
for now wishing to return to Iceland. The reasons are unlike—Auðunn
must return to care for his aged mother while Þorsteinn fears the
envy his preferment has stirred—and there are no verbal resemblances
except the commonplaces of thanks:

17. Auðun svarar: "Guð þakki
yðr, herra, ágætt boð, ok
alla þá sæmd, sem þér
veiti mér.... *(Hulda)*[44]

Þorsteinn svaraði: "Þat er boðit
ágætliga. En á meðan þér lifið,
mun minn frami hér mestr vera."
(6SP: "Ágætliga er þetta boðit,
herra....")

The kings, though anxious to have the Icelanders stay, must approve
their reason for returning home:

18. Konungr svarar: "Vel er
mælt," segir hann, "ok
mannliga ok muntu verða
giptumaðr; sjá einn var sá
hlutrinn, at mér myndi eigi
mislíka, at þú færir í braut
heðan...."

Konungr mælti: "Vitrliga er
þetta mælt."

Then the kings prepare the Icelanders' journey home:

19. "... ok ver nú með mér, þar
til er skip búask." Hann
gerir svá.

Síðan bjó konungr hann til Íslands
ágætliga vel með miklu fé ...

---

44. *Msk (ÍF* 6:366): "Auðunn segir: 'Guð þakki yðr, herra, sóma þann allan, er þér
vilit til mín leggja...";*Flateyjarbók:* "Hann mællti. þat er vel bodit herra...."

Following this, *Auðunar þáttr* describes Sveinn's magnificent gifts in detail. Journey Out and Conclusion:

20. Auðunn ... fór út þegar um   Síðan bjó konungr hann til Íslands
    sumarit til Íslands ok   ... ok staðfestisk þar síðan ok
    þótti vera inn mesti gæfumaðr.   þótti vera inn mesti gæfumaðr.
    Frá þessum manni, Auðuni, var   Ok lýksk þar frá honum at segja.
    kominn Þorsteinn Gyðuson.

To a large extent common genre accounts for the similarities here, and many þættir offer parallels for the final evaluation of the hero, including some of the formulas used.[45] No doubt there are also many *gæfumenn* in the saga literature, but only in these two stories is the phrase "ok þótti vera inn mesti gæfumaðr" used as the *explicit* of such similar tales.

Such a series of parallels is difficult to evaluate. Some are explainable through the requisites of genre (such as the Introduction and Conclusion); some may be too general to bear much weight or dependent on ordinary customs (such as the kings' inquiry and the Icelanders' answer "I am an Icelander," etc.). The agreement of the motifs associated with the pilgrimage is striking, but we also find some of those motifs paralleled in *Mána þáttr Íslendings* and *Þórarins þáttr stuttfeldar*. Máni came to the court of the Norwegian king Magnús Erlingsson from Rome, like Auðunn a "stafkarl ... ekki féligr ... kollóttr ok magr ok nær klæðlauss"; when the king asked "hverr hann væri, ... [h]ann kvezk heita Máni ok vera Íslenzkr ok þá kominn frá Rómi sunnan" (*ÍÞ*, p. 157).

Þórarins þáttr begins with a scene outside church that reminds somewhat of Auðunn's reunion with the Danish king:

Auðunar þáttr
Ok nú of aptanin, er konungr
gekk til kveldsongs, ætlaði
Auðunn at hitta hann, ok svá
mikit sem honum þótti fyrr

Þórarins þáttr
Svá barsk at eitt sinn, at Sigurðr
konungr [Jórsalafari] gekk frá
skytningi til aptansöngs; váru
menn drukknir mjök ok kátir. Sat

---

45. "Genre and Narrative Structure," pp. 13–14.

fyr, jók nú miklu á, er þeir
váru drukknir hirðmennir.
Ok er þeir gengu inn aptr,
þá þekkði konungr mann ok
þóttisk finna, at eigi hafði
frama til at ganga at hitta
hann. Ok nú er hirðin gekk
inn, þá veik konungr út ok
mælti: "Gangi sá nú fram,
er mik vill finna; mik grunar,
at sá muni vera maðrinn."

konungr ok hirðin úti fyrir kirkju
ok lásu aptansönginn, ok varð
söngrinn eigi greiðligr. Þá mælti
Sigurðr konungr: "Hvat karla er
þat, er ek sé þar hjá kirkjunni í
feldi nökkurum stuttum." ... Karl
gekk fram ok mælti... Konungr
mælti: "Kom til mín á morgin þar
sem ek drekk" (*ÍÞ*, p. 308).

When Þórarinn comes to court next day, a trick is played on him
by one of the retainers who meets him at the door; the scene is a
little reminiscent of Þorsteinn Austfirðingr's entry, and like Þorsteinn,
Þórarinn incurs the enmity of some retainers and must be protected.
Þórarinn then wins the king's friendship with a praise poem:

En er lokit var kvæðinu, spurði konungr, hvat hann vildi ráða sinna.
Hann kvezk hafa ætlat ferð sína til Róms. Þá fekk konungr honum fé
mikit ok bað hann vitja sín, er hann kœmi aptr, ok kvazk þá mundu
gera sóma hans. En hér er eigi greint, hvárt þeir fundusk síðan *(ÍÞ,*
pp. 309–10).

Here we have several more parallels in both motifs and diction. It
is not clear what the relationships among these þættir are, but the
parallels from *Mána þáttr* and *Þórarins þáttr* should restrain us
from seeing too much in the agreements between *Þorsteins þáttr* and
Auðunar þáttr.

Nevertheless, those agreements are not isolated but systematic,
and they must be pursued a bit further. *Auðunar þáttr* can be dated
with some confidence to the years 1190–1220; and the Þorsteinn
Gyðuson mentioned at the end of the story was the father of Gellir,
who married Vigdís, daughter of Hvamm-Sturla, and became the
brother-in-law of Snorri, Sighvatr, and Þórðr. If Snorri Sturluson
wrote the þáttr, an explanation for the resemblances with *Mána
þáttr* is offered: Máni's story is preserved in one manuscript of

Sverris saga, and Snorri knew *Sverris saga.*[46] There is much less external evidence to pin down Þorsteins þáttr; it is extant in paper manuscripts only, and no traceable Icelanders are mentioned in it. The verse attributed to King Magnús cannot be from the eleventh century, but comparison with other tales of the King in Disguise and the internal awkwardness of the narrative make it unlikely that the verse was composed by the author of the þáttr. The editor's (Jón Jóhannesson's) guess of "sometime in the thirteenth century" may be as close as we can come in dating the story; however, the fact that, so far as is known, it existed only in independent form—that is, was never brought into (or taken out of) a king's saga as were the majority of the þættir—suggests not only that the þáttr was little known (as the editor points out [*ÍF* 11: CXI]), but also that it is very late. It may well belong to the fourteenth century, a period that also accords well with the probable time of the greatest popularity of the international tale of the King in Disguise. (Cf. *6SP,* p. VII: Þorsteins þáttr is "ekki yngri en frá 14. öld.") As literary works the two þættir stand at opposite poles, Auðunar þáttr being one of the great short stories in European literature, and Þorsteins þáttr an ill-executed outline. There can be no doubt in which direction the putative influence flowed.[47]

---

46. *ÍF* 6: CV-CVII; cf. Regis Boyer, *Trois sagas islandaises du XIIIe siècle et un "tháttr"* (Paris, 1964), pp. 229–34.

47. The hypothesis of influence from *Auðunar þáttr* could explain the inconsistency that develops when "Styrbjǫrn" asks if Þorsteinn could postpone his pilgrimage and the Icelander answers that he could for the sake of King Magnús or his men. "Styrbjǫrn" then replies illogically: "Ek held ráðligt, at þú haldir fram ferðinni, því at hér var nauðsyn til, en vitja mín, þá er þú kemr aptr...." Nothing in the story prepares for or explains this "necessity" that changes the king's mind so quickly. However, in *Auðunar þáttr* there is a necessity in the journey that grows out of the hero's patient, uncompromising and resourceful character (see *ÍF* 6: CIV-CV for one of many appreciations of Auðunn's character; the dissenting analysis of Stig Wikander, "Från indisk djurfabel till isländsk saga," *Vetenskaps-societeten i Lund: Årsbok,* 1964, pp. 87–114, seems eccentric), and the word *nauðsyn* is used by King Haraldr in connection with the journey south (once in *Msk* [*ÍF* 6:362] and twice in *Hulda* [*Fms* VI, 299, 306]; not in *Flateyjarbók).* Thus a flaw in Þorsteins þáttr is, perhaps, to be explained by the tug of incompatible models: "Styrbjǫrn's" question follows the model of *Auðunar þáttr;* the Icelander's answer and praise of the king derives from the international tale; and "Styrbjǫrn's" reply switches back to the model of *Auðunar þáttr,* producing a logical non-sequitur and motivating it with an unexplained "necessity." Similarly the robe and bath with which the king greets the Icelander, though commonplace, is better motivated in *Auðunar þáttr* since we are never told explicitly that Þorsteinn was poor and ill-clothed like the returning Auðunn.

III

Section II has argued that the constituents of *Þorsteins þáttr* are (1) an international popular tale, adapted to (2) an unrelated poem and cast in (3) a generic mold. Since the mold could be known to an author only through specific þættir, we examined the surviving members of the genre for evidence of direct connections with *Þorsteins þáttr* and found that (4) *Auðunar þáttr* is a possible source of such influence. These are formal and content features, but the story is not an objective report of events, historical or fictional; despite its brevity it possesses distinct themes, the dimension of meaning. The thematic content of *Þorsteins þáttr* is more conspicuous than in most sagas and þættir since the author highlights it by means of what is very nearly a "moral," delivered, however, not in the narrator's words but dramatically by the king and the Icelander:

> [Magnús said:] "This same man gave me important aid when you [the retainers] were nowhere near, and he did that for a man whose identity he did not know, and he is a good warrior. And it is wiser to make no mockery of an unknown man, for it may turn out that he is a more vigorous and more courageous man. And it will also appear to some people as if it were Fate that brought him to me."
>
> Þorsteinn answered: "It is easy to see, my lord, that God sent me to your aid. For I was much more impressed by your appearance than if you had been an ordinary man, and it came into my mind to help you."

In secular terms: do not mock a stranger, he may prove to be a better man than you suppose; and conversely, help a stranger, he may prove a powerful friend. And this simple theme is given a numinous quality by attributing Þorsteinn's arrival to Fortune and a divine sanction through the mysterious way in which Þorsteinn sees more than is apparent in the embattled stranger.

The story of Karl and Vandráðr points its moral in a way quite comparable to *Þorsteins þáttr*, though in *Hákonar saga* no dramatic spokesman for the narrator is employed:

> This now became very famous both in Norway and in Denmark: such was the lot that father and son drew from Earl Hákon. And the saying

proved true that one always gets a good deal from good men. It is always very important that a man take great pains to make friends; for the man who has good friends will always have support.

The two proverbial points here are reduceable to the injunction to make friends for the good one derives from them.[48] Thus *Þorsteins þáttr* and the episode from *Hákonar saga* tell structurally similar versions of the same international popular tale and use the story as the vehicle of similar didactic points, the one being interpreted in terms of the value of friends, the other in terms of the potential friend in every stranger.

The tone of *Þorsteins þáttr* as well as its specific message is in harmony with the tone and thematic content of its genre as a whole.[49] But what is of interest here is the possible source of this theme in the þáttr, and we must consider the possibility that the international tale came to the author of *Þorsteins þáttr* in the form of the story of Karl and Vandráðr, that there is a direct connection between the two. Six points of similarity between the Old Icelandic adaptations contrast with the general tradition represented by the analogues:

1. The king and commoner are brought together as a result of battle.

2. The identity of the king is concealed (though thinly and conventionally) from the reader until it is revealed to the commoner in a scene at court:

Hákonar saga
Enn er þau komu fyri konung
s(pyrr) konungr karll ef
[hann hafdi sied] hann fyrr
eda huort hann kendi hann.

Þorsteins þáttr
Konungr mælti við hann eitt
sinn: "Hverr hyggr þú nú
várr Styrbjǫrn sé?"

3. Karl's story differs from all its analogues in asserting that Karl *did* in fact recognize the king at their first meeting. Something similar

---

48. The moral seems to apply most naturally to Sveinn and Karl or both, and the somewhat strained reference to Jarl Hákon may be due to the author of his saga.
49. "Theme and Genre."

is found in *Þorsteins þáttr,* where Þorsteinn did not recognize "Styr-bjǫrn" as the king but did see something extraordinary in him:

Kenni ek þik nu konungr	Hann svarar: "Yðr sé ek vænstan
s(eiger) kall enda	til at hafa svá kallazk ... miklu
kenda ek ydur fyrr [þá	fannsk mér meira um yðra ásjónu en
er] þier komut til min	þú værir alþýðligr maðr, ok brá
þo at þu nefndizt Wandradr.	mér þessu í skap at duga þér."

4. The commoner's aid is placed against a background of divine providence or Fortune:

[Karl said:] enn þat er	[Magnús said:] "Ok svá mun ok sumum
guð at þacka er ydur kom til	sýnask, at þat væri happ, er honum
gagns sa [litli for] beine	bar til handa." Þorsteinn svaraði:
sem ek gioda ydur kom þar	"Auðsét er þat, herra, at guð sendi
miog til goduilld ydur ok	mik yðr til hlíðar...."
audna.	

5. Both kings emphasize that they owe their lives to the commoner:

Þat er satt ath [seigia	Konungr mælti: "Rétt muntu þetta
seiger] konungr at ek aa þier	kalla, at þú sér lífsgjafi minn,
alla mina lifdaga at launa med	ok skyldi þér þat vel launa."
gudi þa ek lifi hedan fra mun	
... þat vilia er mik sendi	
til þin enn nu mun þier	
litlu launad uerda. bondi	
s(eiger) konungr epter þui	
sem [uerdu] ueri.	

6. The stories bear similar "morals," as set out above.

These parallels between Karl's story and Þorsteinn's are somewhat easier to judge than those that involve *Auðunar þáttr.* There is little here to speak for direct contact, and an adequate hypothesis for explaining their relationship will be the assumption that oral versions of the King in Disguise current in medieval Scandinavia had a martial setting and were equipped with a moral.[50] The six specific points of congruency over against the analogues might have arisen independently in stories that are, after all, analogues of each other or may have inhered in the oral tradition on which both stories drew. Point (5) is the consequence of point (1) and thus may have belonged to the Scandinavian oral redaction (loosely "oicotype"), and the "morals" (point 6) are in the last analysis not exactly identical. Points (2) and (4) might simply be due to common literary fashion. However, point (3) is impressive enough to give pause, and a seventh agreement already discussed should probably be added: wordplay on the alias "Vandráðr" is explicit, while the context in Þorsteins þáttr seems to call for similar wordplay which is apparently lacking. However, these two telling details fail of full agreement, and finally in the absence of striking verbal similarities there does not seem to be enough detailed evidence to warrent the assumption of direct dependence of the þáttr on the version of the King in Disguise recorded in Hákonar saga though its source must have been quite similar.

This negative conclusion is supported by the existence of at least one other anecdote in which an incognito king encounters some of his subjects and at a later meeting reveals himself; the anecdote is also used as an *exemplum* to teach a lesson similar to that of Þorsteins þáttr:

Some men molest an unknown pilgrim, accosting him as "félagi." Next day King Óláfr Haraldsson summons them before him and asks: "huat er nu vm felag vort þat er ek aa hia yckr?" Óláfr is punning on *félagi* as "business partner" and as "fellow" (a familiar term) and is in effect demanding his money back from a non-existant partnership. The men are dismayed, but the king cheers them and gives them no more punishment than a piece of advice: "... enn þat raad vil ek gefa yckr. makit þeim einum haadung er þit vitid huerr er."[51]

---

50. Smyser, p. 145, assumed an original continental folktale with Charlemagne as the king in disguise; cf. Walsh, p. 18. Charlemagne lore was, of course, very popular in Scandinavia as the name of Magnús himself testifies.

51. *Flateyjarbók*, III, 239 (=*Óláfs saga hins helga*, ed. O. A. Johnsen [Kristiania, 1922], pp. 55–56); cf. the humorous use of a proverb of similar import in *Jóns saga helga* (*Byskupa sögur*, ed. Guðni Jónsson, 2nd ed. [Akureyri, 1953], II, 21); also ÍF 9:10 (*Víga-Glúms saga*).

Thus it seems likely that tales of disguise and morals of this kind are so natural a combination that we need seek no source for the combination in Þorsteins þáttr other than the common source of both Karl's tale and Þorsteinn's in the international popular tale.

IV

The relationship of the sagas to the mainstream of European medieval literature has rightly become one of the principal themes in current saga scholarship.[52] However, this interest builds on a considerable amount of earlier comparative work, some of which has recently been accorded an able survey.[53] Reviewing this scholarship, I am left with the impression that its main fault lies in a superficial conception of the goals of this kind of investigation; it is not sufficient to demonstrate a similarity between a European story, motif, or literary device and an Icelandic parallel and to trace their respective histories to discover where coincidence might have occurred. Exact sources are almost never to be found; and while source-hunting is a worthy enterprise, the information derived from a source—or more frequently analogue—study should yield increased understanding of how authors worked, the creative process; of what is distinctively Icelandic, as well as what is foreign; of what interpretation or function different authors saw in the common material; and of the ways of oral tradition.

A pattern worthy of imitation was provided by Dag Strömbäck in his study of *Hróa þáttr*, a story which is easily traceable to French or English and ultimately to oriental sources, probably oral.[54] Strömbäck shows how *Hróa þáttr* is composed from native elements and a foreign source and comments: "... ett främmande stoff växer vanligen fram på ett inhemskt substrat och får sin specifika utgestaltning i den nya

---

52. A good example among the more recent is Robert J. Glendinning, "Grettis Saga and European Literature in the Late Middle Ages," *Mosaic* 4 (1970), 49–61.

53. Mattias Tveitane, "Europeisk påvirkning på den norrøne sagalitteraturen," *Edda* 69 (1969), 73–95.

54. "En orientalisk saga i fornnordisk dräkt," in *Donum Grapeanum: Festskrift ... Anders Grape* (Uppsala, 1945), pp. 408–44; also "Uppsala, Iceland and the Orient," in *Early English and Norse Studies Presented to Hugh Smith*, edd. Arthur Brown and Peter Foote (London, 1963), pp. 178–90; the source of *Hróa þáttr* had been noted previously. Cf. also Dag Strömbäck, "Some Remarks on Learned and Novelistic Elements in the Icelandic Sagas," in *Nordica et Anglica ... Stefán Einarsson* (The Hague: Mouton, 1968), pp. 140–47.

miljön under där rådande förutsättningar" (p. 431). Much of what he wrote about the tale of Hrói applies also to the two Icelandic adaptations of the King in Disguise: *"Hróa þáttr visar som så många andra 'småsagor' Islands öppenhet för vandrande sagomotiv och islänningarnas överlägsna konst att kunna inarbeta internationellt gods i sin historiska sagoskatt"* (p. 425). With *Hróa þáttr* one might go farther than Strömbäck and show the possible influence of the story pattern discussed above, the distinctively Scandinavian concept of *gæfumaðr,* as found especially in these short stories, a literary convention of nicknames used to mark stages in Hrói's career, and so on.

It may seem that *Þorsteins þáttr* and *Hróa þáttr* are frail vessels for this kind of scrutiny, but the complexity of the compositional history of even such simple tales has been underestimated. It has been justly pointed out by a recent writer that it is a circular error to dismiss everything that seems dissonant in a saga as a failure of the author to reconcile divergent sources,[55] but it is equally circular and erroneous to begin with the assumption that every work of art is a perfect work of art. We should continue to seek sources and analogues, including foreign ones, to observe their adaptation in Old Icelandic, and to draw every possible conclusion about the composition of the saga literature, even if we can only go part way down the road to Xanadu.

---

55. Robert G. Cook, "The Character of Gunnlaug Serpent-Tongue," *SS* 43 (1971), 1–21.

Satire and the Heroic Life:
Two Studies

(Helgakviða Hundingsbana I, 18
and Bjǫrn Hítdœlakappi's Grámagaflím)

Scholars like Otto Rank, Lord Raglan, and Jan de Vries have pointed out a remarkably rigid patterning in the lives of many legendary "heroes,"[1] and one of the most interesting recent tendencies in the study of heroic legend pursues such patterns to the influence of myth or ritual or, at least, to tradition in an oral culture.[2] Another route to what might be called "heroic conformity" begins with the elusive background in a heroic ethos, and George Fenwick Jones' *The Ethos of the Song of Roland* can stand as a good representative of this more sociological (and hence less exact) scholarly direction.[3] Strangely the two approaches—the one from traditional narrative structures and the other from the real-life ideological matrix supporting such

---

1. Otto Rank, *The Myth of the Birth of the Hero: a Psychological Interpretation of Mythology*, tr. by F. Robbins and S. E. Jelliffe (New York, 1955); Lord Raglan, *The Hero: a Study in Tradition, Myth, and Drama* (London, 1936); Jan de Vries, *Betrachtungen zum Märchen...*, FFC 150 (Helsinki, 1954) and in more popular form in *Heroic Song and Heroic Legend*, tr. B. J. Timmer (London, 1963), ch. 11.

2. A few examples: Otto Höfler, "Das Opfer im Semnonenhain und die Edda," in *Edda, Skalden, Saga: Festschrift zum 70. Geburtstag von Felix Genzmer*, ed. by Hermann Schneider (Heidelberg, 1952), pp. 1–67; Franz Rolf Schröder, "Mythos und Heldensage," *GRM*, 36(1955), 1–21 and revised in *Zur germanisch-deutschen Heldensage*, ed. by Karl Hauck (Bad Homburg, 1961), pp. 285–317; Jan de Vries, "Das Motiv des Vater-Son-Kampfes im Hildebrandslied," *GRM*, 34(1953), 257–74 and expanded in Hauck, pp. 248–84; Georges Dumézil, *From Myth to Fiction: the Saga of Hadingus*, tr. by D. Coltman (Chicago, 1973).

3. (Baltimore, 1963); another good example: George Clark, "*The Battle of Maldon*: A Heroic Poem," *Speculum* 43(1968), 52–71.

structures—are never combined. As a general assignment the task would be too large for the present small contribution to the honor of Professor Lord; but if I focus here on a single neglected feature common to both approaches, perhaps the results, though minor, will be suggestive.

The connection of satire with the hero-life, its role in a *Heldenleben,* may not appear obvious at first glance. We are accustomed to thinking of our heroes as shining figures, glowing with a generous inner passion for heroic accomplishment; in this we are still seeing through idealistic nineteenth-century eyes, eyes like those of a Carlyle who could make even the treacherous, contradictory, and, arguably, neurotic Odin an object of "hero-worship." But there is evidence that heroic society embodied a strong dash of paranoia, that conformity to social ideals was achieved partly through fear of criticism and, especially, of satire—criticism in comic form. In such a "shame culture," which Jones contrasts with the predominant modern "guilt culture," a Roland's quintessentially "heroic" act, his refusal to blow his horn for help, arises largely in his fear of "male chançun," satirical songs that might be composed to his shame.[4] At the Battle of Maldon in 991 Earl Byrhtnoth's men voiced a number of varied reasons, some as old as Tacitus, for fighting on to the last man; among them was Leofsunu, who promised not to flee but to advance because the "steadfast heroes around Sturmere" were not to be given cause to "criticize [him] with words," alleging that he turned from battle now that his lord lay dead.[5] Leofsunu's *wordum ætwitan* may or may not imply verse satire, but his probable pun on *stedefæste hælæð,* where "steadfast" could mean "unswerving" or "stay-at-home," certainly looks like a satirical preemptive strike.[6] No formal satire has survived in Old English, but in early Old English times the major word for poet, *scop,* must have carried connotations of its origin in "scoffing" and derision. In the closely related Old Frisian, *skof* meant "mockery," and Old High German *scof* embraced both

---

4. Jones, pp. 89, 96–98, and *passim.*

5. *The Battle of Maldon,* ll. 246–53a, esp. 249–50, in *The Anglo-Saxon Poetic Records,* VI, ed. by E. van Kirk Dobbie (New York, 1942).

6. I have not seen this (probable) pun pointed out, but on the topic generally cf. Roberta Frank, "Some Uses of Paronomasia in Old English Scriptural Verse," *Speculum* 47(1972), 207–26.

"poet" and "derision."[7] A favored etymology for Old Norse *skáld* "poet" relates the word to these unromantic concepts, and English *scold* ("to abuse verbally," etc., or "an abusive person, especially a woman") is probably borrowed from Old Norse. The Scandinavian institution of *níð* (roughly: "legally culpable insults") is closely linked with poets and poetry.[8] Many of the heroes of the realistic family sagas are intimately involved with various forms of satire, either as its victims or its perpetrators, and such mudslinging extends more often than one would expect to the heroes of tradition, the "heroes" *par excellence.*

I. *Óneiss sem kattar sonr: Helgakviða Hundingsbana I*, 18

Notable for their satirical components are the first and third Helgi poems in the *Poetic Edda;* called *Helgakviða Hundingsbana I* and *II,* they tell different but overlapping segments of the same heroic biography.[9] The most likely explanation of the historical relationship between the two poems is that both derive chiefly from an "Old Lay of the Vǫlsungs" *(Vǫlsungakviða in forna).*[10] Both poems (along with the more distantly related *Helgakviða Hjǫrvarðzsonar)* contain long *sennur,* formal exchanges of abuse equivalent to the English and Scottish flytings, between the antagonist and Helgi's representative Sinfjǫtli, a certified specialist in billingsgate. Helgi himself intervenes only to put an end to the flyting, but other heroes, including the sterling Beowulf,[11] speak for themselves. Helgi's valkyrie heroine

---

7. Cf. further MDu *schop,* ON *skop, skaup,* Dan. *skuf,* and MHG *schelte,* and see C. T. Onions, *The Oxford Dictionary of English Etymology* (Oxford, 1966), s.v. *scop, scold;* F. Holthausen, *Altenglisches etymologisches Wörterbuch* (Heidelberg, 1963), s.v. *scop;* Jan de Vries, *Altnordisches etymologisches Wörterbuch,* 2nd ed. rev. (Leiden, 1962), s.v. *skald;* and Klaus von See, "Skop und Skald. Zur Auffassung des Dichters bei den Germanen," *GRM,* 14(1964), 1–14.

8. The great study of *níð* is Bo Almqvist, *Norrön niddiktning: traditionshistoriska studier i versmagi,* vol. 1: *Nid mot furstar* (Uppsala, 1965) and vol. 2: *Nid mot missionärer. Senmedeltida nidtraditioner* (Uppsala, 1974) (= Nordiska texter och undersökningar, 21 and 23).

9. Eddic poems are quoted from Gustav Neckel, ed., *Edda: die Lieder des Codex Regius nebst verwandten Denkmälern,* 3rd ed. rev. by Hans Kuhn (Heidelberg, 1962); the major Helgi poems are abbreviated *HH* and *HHII.*

10. The best study nevertheless presents an unclear picture of these relationships: Jan de Vries, "Die Helgilieder," *ANF,* 72(1957), 123–54.

unleashes her sharp tongue in a curse directed at her brother, Helgi's slayer *(HHII, 31–33)*; her first words to Helgi have a sarcastic edge *(HH, 17)*; and in *HHII, 25* she has the poor taste to jeer at Helgi's dying rival. Helgi himself bluntly blames Sigrún for the death of her father and brother *(HHII, 26–29)* and is even presented as jibing unsportingly at his enemy Hundingr when they meet in Valhöll after death *(HHII, 39)*—this last passage has seemed so offensive that many commentators brand it a late interpolation.

The remarks I wish to examine here are of this kind but more cryptically satirical. In *Helgakviða Hundingsbana I* Sigrún, accompanied by other valkyries and dramatic celestial lighting effects, has sought out the victorious young Helgi on a battlefield to complain that she has been betrothed against her will to Hǫðbroddr; it is up to Helgi to save her, and the rest of the poem narrates the preparations for and approach to battle, the insults before battle, and the enemy's preparations; the concluding stanzas describe Helgi's victory in the words of his valkyrie consort.

In the problematical stanza 18, Sigrún protests:

> Hefir minn faðir   meyio sinni
> grimmon heitit   Granmars syni;
> enn ec hefi, Helgi,   Hǫðbrodd qveðinn,
> konung óneisan,   sem kattar son.
> (My father has pledged   his daughter fair
> As bride to Granmar's   son so grim;
> But, Helgi, I   once Hothbrodd called
> As fine a king   as the son of a cat.)[12]

The groundwork for a full understanding of this debated passage has been laid by Anne Holtsmark's definitive establishment of the basic

---

11. Two recent articles study the "Unferth-Intermezzo" as a flyting: Carol Clover (forthcoming) ["The Germanic Context of the Unferth Episode," *Speculum* 55 (1980), 444–68; rpt. in *Beowulf: Basic Readings*, ed. Peter S. Baker (New York: Garland, 1995), pp. 127–54. Eds.] and J. Harris, "The *senna:* From Description to Literary Theory," *MGS*, 5 (1979), 65–74.

12. Unless otherwise noted, translations are those of Henry Adams Bellows, *The Poetic Edda* (New York, 1923); Bellows' stanza numbers often differ from the standard Neckel-Kuhn; this is Bellows' st. 19.

meaning of *óneiss* and her discussion of *kattar sonr*,[13] and Bjarne Fidjestøl has added an interesting further ramification.[14] It remains to offer a clear statement of the primary meaning of the last line and to suggest a number of more problematic refinements.

The difficulty in fully capturing the primary sense of the second helming or half-stanza has apparently been caused by the lack of a close parallel, having the structure: adjective + *sem* + an animal, where the adjective is complimentary and the comparison derogatory. In other words, something like "as fierce as a lion" or "timid as a mouse" is of no use as a parallel since there must be an ironic discrepancy between the adjective and the comparison; the apparent absence of anything like "as fierce as a mouse" elsewhere in Old Norse poetry has made scholars very cautious about accepting the fairly obvious irony here. An analogue that fulfills these conditions and should remove the remaining skepticism about the irony is to be found in Bjǫrn Hitdœlakappi's satire *Grámagaflím*, where Bjǫrn claims that his enemy Þórðr is *jafnsnjallr sem geit* "just as bold as a she-goat."[15] Here there can be no doubt

---

13. "Kattar sonr," *Saga-Book*, 16(1962–65), 144–55. Older references are given in full by Holtsmark; translations and commentaries appearing since her article seem to have taken little note of it: Hans Kuhn, *Edda...*, II. Kurzes Wörterbuch (Heidelberg, 1968): "óneiss: ohne tadel"; Ólafur Briem, ed., *Eddukvæði*, Íslenzk úrvalsrit 5 (Skálholt, 1968), p. 269: "óneis: sem ekki þarf að blygðast sín, frægur, ágætur"; Patricia Terry, tr., *Poems of the Vikings: the Elder Edda* (Indianapolis and New York, 1969), p. 111: "but I, Helgi, have said that Hodbrodd, famed for his courage, is a feeble kitten." Terry seems to have been following F. Detter and R. Heinzel *(Sæmundar Edda mit einem Anhang,* II. *Anmerkungen* [Leipzig, 1903]) who, while not defining *óneiss*, says plausibly enough that it is to be taken as "concessive" here. L. M. Hollander, tr., *The Poetic Edda,* 2nd ed. rev. (Austin, 1962) goes his own way with "callow like a kitten" (p. 183) and equally arbitrary translations at *Atlakviða* 12 ("faithful"), 18 [=19] ("brave and bold"), and *HH* 23 ("mighty"). Not cited by Holtsmark: B. Kummer, ed., *Die Lieder des Codex Regius (Edda) und verwandten Denkmäler.* B. II. *Heldendichtung.* Erster Teil: Die Dichtung von Helgi und der Walküre (Zeven, 1959), p. 60, agrees with B. Sijmons and H. Gering *(Kommentar zu den Liedern der Edda,* II [Halle, 1931]) that irony is intended; but he seems to have in mind a sexual context for his translation "keck, wie 'nen jungen Kater" in view of his comment "hier ist an den jungen, werbenden und noch nichts vermögenden Kater gedacht" and the parallel he cites from *Hávamál* 96ff. (the scorn of *Billings mey*). But a sexual sense is quite impossible for the other instances of *neiss* and *óneiss*. Holtsmark has shown that Gering was wrong about the meaning of *óneiss* in his *Wörterbuch* and *Kommentar,* but it is interesting that earlier in his translation (1892) Gering had rendered the phrase ironically while omitting *óneiss:* "... dass er wie kater zum König tauge."

14. "Kattar sonr. Ein merknad til Helgakviða Hundingsbana I, str. 18," *MM*, 1971, pp. 50–51.

15. *Bjarnar saga Hítdœlakappa,* in *Borgfirðinga sǫgur,* ed. by Sigurður Nordal and

about the scornful intention and the ironic discrepancy between the adjective and the term for comparison since at least one well-attested traditional quality of the she-goat was cowardice.[16] The parallel confirms, in essentials at least, results to which Anne Holtsmark seems to have come with a sense of surprise and also Sijmons' much earlier guess that *óneiss* was ironically intended.[17]

Sigrún's scorn, then, is explicit, damaging, and couched in a wittily memorable phrase, and it seems at least possible that it was imagined as having been expressed as verse since there seems to be a special formality and prominence in *qveðinn* here. This is arguable not only from the frequent technically poetic meanings of the verb and its derivatives[18] but also from the structure of the stanza, where the main elements in the first helming answer to elements in the second: *faðir/ek hefir heitit/hefi qveðinn, grimmr/óneiss, Granmars sonr/kattar sonr.* The parallelism is sufficient to establish the expectation that *qveðinn* must answer in precision and weight to *heitit* ("engaged"). The point cannot be proved; but I suspect that if *kveða* here does not mean "I have stated in a *kviðling* (satirical verse)," it must be at least as

---

Guðni Jónsson, *Íslenzk fornrit* 3 (Reykjavík, 1938), pp. 168–69; and cf. R. C. Boer, ed., *Bjarnar saga Hítdœlakappa* (Halle, 1893), pp. 45–46, 99–100). A comparable ironic comparison seems to be present in Hallfreðr's *lausavísa* 1 *(Hallfreðar saga,* ed. by Einar Ól. Sveinsson, *Íslenzk fornrit* 8 [Reykjavík, 1939], pp. 146–47, prose order): "Reiði sannargs allheiðins søkkvis margra troga verðr mér svá nøkkvi œgilig fyr augum, sem ólítill, gamall búrhundr stúri úti fyr búri alls mest við fǫr gesta; stœrik brag." Hallfreðr's verse means: "the wrath of Gríss (his rival) seems to my eyes approximately as fearsome as if a big old housedog should be barking hard at strangers."

16. *HHII* 37: "Svá hafði *Helgi* hrœdda gorva / fiándr sína alla oc frœndr þeira / sem fyr úlfi óðar rynni / geitr af fialli, geisca fullar" ("Such the fear that Helgi's foes / Ever felt, and all their kin, / As makes the goats with terror mad / Run from the wolf among the rocks," Bellows, st. 36.) Cf. *Ǫrvar-Oddr in Biálkaland* (= *Eddica minora...*, ed. by A. Heusler and W. Ranisch [Dortmund, 1903], p. 75): "sem fyr úlfi geitr argar rynni." Other associations with she-goats in poetry are contemptuous in a general way: *HHII* 22, *HH* 43, *Skírnismál* 35, *Hávamál* 36, *Rígsþula* 12 (perhaps also in Finnur Jónsson, ed., *Den norsk-islandske skjaldedigtning* [Copenhagen, 1912], I(B), 167 Anon. (X), IB1 and II(B), 252–53 [Vers af Ragnarssaga, II, 5]); or else insultingly associated with lasciviousness: *Hyndluljóð* 46, 5/8.

17. Holtsmark, p. 150: "No, twist it and turn it as much as we like, a cat never becomes *óneiss*. ... It is not possible to understand Sigrun's words as anything but scorn: Hǫðbrodd is as fearless as a cat!" Cf. Gering-Sijmons, *Kommentar*, II, 82.

18. An example parallel in several respects comes from the saga of Magnús the Good in *Morkinskinna*, ed. by C. R. Unger (Christiania, 1867), p. 28 (my translation): "King Haraldr thought it a dishonor to drink with Þórir and 'spoke' *(qveþr)* the following to him: 'Be silent, Þórir, / you are an unreasonable thane; / I heard that your father / was called Hvinngestr.' Þórir was a proud man and was displeased by the 'squib' *(qviþlingr)*."

formal as "I have pronounced." However, the Vǫlsunga saga, quoted below, supports this deduction only to the extent that its paraphrase presents Sigrún as making a formal vow ("heitit") in contradiction to her father.[19]

Anne Holtsmark established the meaning of óneiss through the formally positive neiss which, however, is shown to have the negative meaning "defenseless," especially in the (proverbial?) phrase neiss ok nøkkviðr, "defenseless and naked." The formally negative (semantically positive), then, would be "not defenseless." The implication of Holtsmark's discussion is that from this point the meanings generalized to "afraid" and "fearless"; but since she also showed that neiss is especially found in contexts of clothing, including particularly war-gear, it seems worthwhile to point out that the cruder "not defenseless" has the advantage of carrying the sense of its opposite "defenseless" close to the surface as óneiss apparently does in its five Eddic occurrences.

This is most obvious in óneiss sem kattar sonr "as 'un-defenseless' as a kitten," which suggests rather "defenseless as a kitten," while "fearless" or other generalized interpretations would mask this reference to the base neiss. After all, a kitten may well be fearless; the point seems to be that, fearless or not, it is weak and helpless. There is a second occurrence of óneiss in HH; when Helgi's forces are gathering for the assault on Hǫðbroddr, Helgi asks his ally Hjǫrleifr: "Hefir þú kannaða koni óneisa?" (23, 7/8) ("Hast thou counted the gallant host?" 24). The konir are Helgi's own men; their numbers and arms make them óneisir "not defenseless," i.e., litotes for "well-defended." But konr is also a "son," and óneiss has just before appeared in a pregnant sense collocated with kattar sonr; it seems almost certain that the reference (with litotes) in stanza 23 to konir óneisir is intended to recall the reference (with irony) in stanza 18 to the enemy who is óneiss sem kattar sonr, i.e. neiss.

In Atlakviða 17 óneiss again has this quality of suggesting its opposite:

langt er at leita   lýða sinnis til,
of rosmofiǫll Rínar,   recca óneissa (17, 3/6).

---

19. The Saga of the Volsungs, ed. by R. Finch (London and Edinburgh, 1965), pp. 14–15; translations from Vǫlsunga saga (= VS) are Finch's.

Ursula Dronke translates: "it is a long way to seek/ for an escort of men/ from the hills of Worms on the Rhine,/ for *valiant* fighters,"[20] but in this interpretation "valiant" becomes otiose since there is no question of Gunnarr and his companions being unvaliant or having left just the valiant men at home. However, if we substitute the ungeneralized, more primary sense of *óneiss* as established from *neiss (ok nǫkkviðr)* the passage gains in precision and depth. Indeed, the meaning "unprotected," specifically by adequate arms, ought to be clear from the preceding stanza where Guðrún says: "Betr hefðir þú, bróðir, at þú í brynio fœrir, / sem hiálmom aringreypom, at siá heim Atla" (16, 1/4) ("You would have done better, brother, if you had come in coat of mail / and hearth-encircling helmets to see Atli's home," Dronke, p. 6). That Gunnarr and his party come relatively unarmed (Hǫgni uses his sword in stanza 19) is further suggested by stanza 14 where the Hunnish guards were "to watch for Gunnarr and his men, lest they should come here seeking with shrill spear to make war against the tyrant" (Dronke's translation); in other words, the guards' task was to determine whether they were coming equipped for peace or for war; and since they are subsequently received with a hypocritical show of friendship (the implicit narrative underlying st. 15), Atli and his guards must have determined that Gunnarr's men came with peaceful intentions and equipage. So by saying in stanza 17 to his sister that "it is a long way to seek ... for warriors who are not defenseless," Gunnarr is implying that he and his followers at Atli's court are *neiss* "defenseless," specifically lacking the arms mentioned in stanza 16. The *Atlakviða* poet, a consummate artist, seems also to be recalling his other, earlier use of *óneiss* in stanza 12 of the poem:

Leiddo landrǫgni	lýðar óneisir,
grátendr, gunnhvata,	ór garði húna (12, 1/4).[21]

---

20. Ursula Dronke, ed., *The Poetic Edda*, vol. 1 (Oxford, 1969), p. 7; Dronke's translation of the adjective is consistent with her assumption that Gunnarr and Hǫgni set out unaccompanied. However, I prefer Detter-Heinzel's notion of this as "Held statt Held und Begleitung" (their commentary to *Atlakviða* 13, 1 [= 12,1], *Vǫluspá* 47, 1 [= 50, 1]; they further point to *Vafðrúðnismál* 17–18 and *Fáfnismál* 14); and Dronke's translation seems to capitulate to the logic of this view when "at varða þeim Gunnari" (14, 13) appears as "to watch for Gunnarr and his men," not "Gunnarr and Hǫgni" as a consistent application of her reading would require.

21. Adopting Dronke's *húna* for Kuhn's *Húna*; Dronke's translation follows.

(They led the prince of the land,   valiant people
weeping led the war-keen men   from their children's courts.)

At home the Burgundians were *óneisir* with reference perhaps to the
storehouses of swords mentioned in stanza 7; the stay-at-homes are,
therefore, "not defenseless," yet weeping, just at this point probably
to imply that the departing party are *neisir*. Certainly that is one's
impression on rereading stanza 12 after careful attention to the
context of the adjective in 16–17.

A fifth occurrence of *óneiss* (as *óneisinn*) in *Guðrúnarkviða in
þriðja*, stanza 4, agrees fairly well with the four usages just examined. Guðrún has been falsely accused of adultery with Þjóðrekr
(Theodorich, Dietrich). Speaking to her husband Atli she offers oaths
and an ordeal and denies the charge "except that I embraced the
governor of hosts (Þjóðrekr), the prince *óneisinn*, a single time."[22]
Even here some version of the primary sense "not defenseless" seems
preferable to Holtsmark's generalized "fearless," for the point in
this passage seems to be that Guðrún admits to having embraced
Þjóðrekr once *in armor* and not in bed. I pointed out the connections of *óneiss* with armor in *Atlakviða*, and Holtsmark's discussion
established a special connection with clothing. Here the specific form
of the accusation is:

> at þit Þjóðrecr   undir þaki svæfit
> oc léttliga   líni verðiz (2, 5/8).
> (... that you and Þjóðrekr   slept under cover
> and tenderly   wrapped yourselves in linen.)

In bed lovers are *neiss ok nøkkviðr* "defenseless and naked"; thus
Guðrún denies the charge of having been in bed with Þjóðrekr by
admitting that she once embraced him *óneisinn*, in a not-defense-
less condition, that is, wearing armor and, of course, not *nøkkviðr*.
Thus all five occurrences of *óneiss* seem to conform to a common
pattern of usage; and this seems to be shared by Bjǫrn's *jafnsnjallr*
since in the collocation with *sem geit* it surely suggests *ósnjallr*, a

---

22. This translation and the next from *Guðrúnarkviða III* are mine; Bellows has the
sense wrong; cf. Kuhn, *Wörterbuch*, s.v. *nema*.

grave insult ranging in meaning from "cowardly" and "inarticulate" to "impotent."

In view of the rather specific associations of *neiss* and *óneiss* it appears that *kattar sonr* should be regarded not as equivalent to "cat" (so Holtsmark[23]) but to "kitten." This interpretation is supported by the paraphrase in *Vǫlsunga saga:* "Hǫgni konungr hefir heitit mik Hoddbroddi, syni Granmars konungs, en ek hefi því heitit, at ek vil eigi eiga hann heldr en einn krákuunga." ("King Hogni … has promised me in marriage to Hoddbrodd, King Granmar's son, but I have vowed to have him no more than I'd have a fledgling crow as a husband.") It seems that the paraphraser found the second helming obscure or too complex; in any case, he substituted a simple promise and a more obvious comparison for the parts of the helming under discussion, *qveðinn* and *óneiss sem kattar sonr*. However, the new comparison makes clear his understanding of the original; a *krákuungi* "fledgling crow" is undesirable as a mate not because it is, for example, ugly but because it is contemptibly weak and defenseless. This is perfectly clear in the only other citation of the word in Fritzner: "siðan tók Erlingr 2 brœðr mína ok festi annan upp sem krákuunga en lét hǫggva annan."[24] ("Then E. took my two brothers and strung the one up like a fledgling crow and had the other killed.")

Bjarne Fidjestøl has, further, suggested that *kattar sonr* is an allusion to Hǫðbroddr's father: *Gran-marr* was interpreted as a kenning "bewhiskered horse," i.e. cat. At first glance this seems unlikely since it would compare Hǫðbroddr with himself ("Hǫðbroddr is as *óneiss* as the son of Granmarr"); but wordplay cannot be reduced to simple paraphrase, and double reference—having one's semantic cake and eating it too—is the essence of paranomasia.[25] The phrase could mean "son of a cat, kitten" and at the same time constitute an allusion to Granmarr; but if so, the only evidence is in the passage itself since

---

23. Perhaps influenced by the only parallel to *sem kattar son* she cites: *sem kǫttr í hreysi.*

24. Johan Fritzner, *Ordbog over det gamle norske sprog*, 3rd ed. rev. by D. A. Seip and Trygve Knudsen (Oslo, 1954–72), s.v. *krákuungi*; my translation.

25. Fidjestøl calls this wordplay a *høveskenning* (occasional kenning); but although it is based on a (perceived) kenning, I cannot see that any established poetic term fully accounts for it. It resembles *ofljóst* and name-kennings in requiring a shift based on homophony but reverses the internal order of stages; cf. generally B. Fidjestøl, "Kenningsystemet. Forsøk på ein lingvistik analyse," *MM*, 1974, pp. 32–34; Roberta Frank,

the *Vǫlsunga saga* paraphraser simplified the wordplay—if he recognized it as such—out of existence, and Fidjestøl has not offered any supporting parallel.[26] A further bit of support for Fidjestøl's proposition can, however, be extracted from the passage itself. I have pointed out above how a certain symmetry informs the stanza; the second helming, linked by the adversative sense of *enn,* partly replicates the first, contrasting the actions of father and daughter in a framework of parallelism. The syntactic symmetry ends with the different types of object after each verb, but in place of a grammatical parallelism we find a combination of lexical repetition and symmetrical placing in the last line of each helming: l. 4 *Granmars syni*: l. 8 *sem kattar son.* Though final proof is impossible, I think Fidjestøl is correct in perceiving wordplay here.

The possibility has been raised by Holtsmark that the Icelandic poet and storyteller Stúfr blindi was alluding to *Helgakviða Hundingsbana I,* 18 when he told King Haraldr harðráði: "Kattar son em ek" (I am [a] *kattar sonr).*[27] Like the paraphraser of *Vǫlsunga saga,* Stúfr could simply have by-passed the putative pun, which would have been irrelevant to his situation. However, the evidence for Stúfr's acquaintance with the poem is not strong, depending entirely on this phrase and

---

"Onomastic Play in Kormakr's Verse: the Name Steingerðr," *MScan,* 3 (1970), 7–34; and "Anatomy of a Skaldic Double-Entendre: Rǫgnvaldr Kali's *lausavísa* 7," pp. 227–35 in *Studies for Einar Haugen Presented by Friends and Colleagues,* ed. by E. S. Firchow et al. (Mouton, 1972).

26. The parallel offered, *nosgás* = duck *(Heiðreks gátur* [st. 27, 2] in *Eddica minora),* seems inadequate. I have not found a fully convincing parallel, but cf. A. Kjærs' idea that *gofugt dýr* is a similar wordplay on *Sig-(f)røþr* ("Zu Fáfnismál str. 2," pp. 54–60 in *Festschrift, Eugen Mogk zum 70. Geburtstag* ... [Halle, 1924]), which Gering-Sijmons reject abruptly. Bugge *(The Home of the Eddic Poems, with Especial Reference to the Helgi-Lays,* rev. ed., tr. by W. H. Schofield [London, 1899], pp. 38–40) also thought *kattar sonr* a kind of surname, but the context (Irish influence) of this agreement with Fidjestøl is generally rejected. Ordinary name-puns (e.g., Skúta = *skuti,* in *Víga-Glúms saga,* Íslenzk fornrit 9: 54) seem distant, and the mysterious insult in *arfr Fiǫrsunga (HHII* 20), though perhaps related to the present passage, explains nothing. The most secure parallel I have found is offered by Gerd Weber's clever interpretation of the Altunastone ("Das Odinsbild des Altuna-steins," *BGDSL,* 97 [1972], 332–33) where a name is interpreted as a kenning to a referent in ordinary life, which is then produced as a symbol for the name: Arn-fastr = an eagle on his *fastr* or prey, so that a picture of an eagle on his prey in turn = Arnfastr; as Gran-marr = (metaphor for) a cat, so that the word *kǫttr* can refer back to Granmarr.

27. Quoting the independent and superior version, Íslenzk fornrit 5: 280–90; the short version in *Morkinskinna* gives "Ek em kattar sun"; basic discussion in Holtsmark, pp. 151–55.

being tempered by the facts that Stúfr's father really was called *kǫttr* "cat," his nickname, and that a sufficient motive for calling himself *kattar sonr* instead of *Þórðar sonr* is supplied, in the context of Stúfr's story, by Stúfr's wish to touch very obliquely on King Haraldr's father's nickname *sýr* ("sow"). It seems unlikely that this part of Holtsmark's discussion can profitably be taken further. Nevertheless, I cannot resist the speculation that *if* Stúfr was playing on the passage from *Helgakviða Hundingsbana I* and the king's knowledge of it, then he may also have been expecting Haraldr to remember the adjective *óneiss* "not defenseless"; for the purpose in Stúfr's story of the witty hero's naming himself *kattar sonr* is to indicate subtly to Haraldr, whom tradition characterized as given to lampooning the people around him, that the Icelander's tongue could be dangerous, that he was not without defenses.[28] Thus this very indirect and finally quite doubtful allusion to *óneiss* would fall in line with that of *Helgakviða Hundingsbana I*, 23, 7/8 where a litotic sense of *óneiss* ("undefenseless" = very well defended) is evoked by reference to an ironic use *(HH* 18: "undefenseless as a kitten" = defenseless).

II. Grámagaflím

The saga about Bjǫrn Champion-of-the-Hítdalers tells how Bjǫrn and his life-long bête noire Þórðr engaged in a series of mutual provocations and attacks that at last culminated in Bjǫrn's death, and many of the hostile acts are satirical sallies, especially in verse, since both men were adept skalds of the "serpent-tongued" variety. In fact the structure of the saga itself resembles an acting out of the alternating dramatic exchanges of a flyting. At one point Bjǫrn had composed a lampoon ...

> And not long before Bjǫrn had composed a lampoon *(flím)* about Þórðr; and it was at that time rather well-known to certain men. But

---

28. This interpretation of dramatic tension between the king and the Icelander is based on the longer, independent version where it is more pronounced than in the condensed king's saga version; for Haraldr's concern with fathers in a context of satire, cf. *Hreiðars þáttr heimska* and Haraldr's encounter with Magnús the Good and his brother Þórir in *Morkinskinna* and *Flateyjarbók* (ref. and discussion in Erik Noreen, "Studier i fornvästnordisk diktning," *Uppsala Universitets Årsskrift*, 1922, Filosophi, språkvetenskap och historiska vetenskaper 4 [Uppsala, 1922], pp. 50–51).

its contents were to the effect that Arnóra, Þórð's mother, had eaten the kind of fish he called a *grámagi*, and he claimed that it had been found on the shore and that from eating it she had become pregnant with Þórð, and so he was not entirely of human origin on both sides of his family. And this is in the lampoon:

1. The flood went up on the sand, and a fish went up on the land. Like to a lump-sucker slime was on its flesh. The wolf-bitch-of-the-gown (= Arnóra, the mother) ate the "gray-belly," carrion blended with poison. There is much that's evil in the sea.[29]

2. The bride's belly rose down from her breast, so that that oak-of-the-scarf (= Arnóra, the mother) would walk bent quite backward and painful in her gut. She became much too fat.[30]

3. A boy came to light. The lady said to her collector-of-wealth (her husband) that she wished to raise it up. As he lay there he seemed to her a dog-biter, just as bold as a she-goat, when she looked in his eyes.[31]

---

29. *einhaga ylgr* is a scornful kenning that suggests the animalistic hunger of Arnóra. Cleasby-Vigfusson treats *grámagi, grámaga* as the female of the lump-sucker, just as *rauðmagi* is the male; but the male gender in the poem argues against this as does the phrasing *hrognkelsi glíkr*. Boer seems to have the right explanation: "hrognkelse: ... das männchen dieses fisches heisst, wie mir Finnur Jónsson mitteilt, rauðmagi, was Bjǫrn durch grámage ersetzt, um eine gewisse ähnlichkeit, doch nicht vollständige identität mit dem rauðmagi anzudeuten" (p. 99). I would add that the replacement of *rauð*-"red" by *grá*- "gray" may be conditioned by the secondary meaning of *grár* as "evil, malicious," a meaning that is conspicuous in the opening lines of *Bjarnar saga* itself: "Ekki var Þórðr mjǫk vinsæll af alþýðu, því at hann þótti vera spottsamr ok grár við alla þá, er honum þótti dælt við" (p. 112); but since the female of the lump-sucker is regularly called *grásleppa*, Bjǫrn may simply have combined the first morpheme of the female with the second of the male—cf. the androgynous Loki myth cited below. The quaint resemblance of this stanza to the verse on the front panel of the Franks Casket is presumably due to the limited language of Old Germanic verse.

30. The lump-sucker is a bloating fish that feeds on the "garbage" of the ocean floor. Is this not a fitting model for Arnóra, who is pictured as feeding off carrion on the beach and then swelling in pregnancy? I understand from Icelandic friends that lump-suckers are actually caught on the beach after a storm (Cleasby-Vigfusson gives *hrognkelsa-fjara* as the name of such a "fishing" expedition) and that the female is actually eaten in a ripe condition (like the delicacy *hákarl*, rotten shark).

31. *auðar gildir* may be no more than a colorless kenning for "man" (so *Lexicon poeticum*); but both editors agree in giving it a primary sense "increaser-of-wealth" (Nordal and Guðni Jónsson: "[sem eykur gildi e-s]: mann-kenning"; Boer: "vermehrer des reichtums, ein mann"), and since we expect the equivalent man-kenning to be constructed on the pattern "destroyer-of-wealth," i.e. "generous man," I think there is reason to believe that Bjǫrn meant to construct a satirical inversion: "increaser-of-(his own)-wealth," i.e. "miser." For the formula *líta í augu* ("look into the eyes") cf. *Vǫluspá* 28.

The *Grámagaflím* is best understood as a parodistic version of the kind of hero-life we find in the Helgi poems or at least in *Helgakviða Hundingsbana I,* for several of the conventions of the life of the hero of tradition are exploited here in satirical form. In stanza 1 there are the topoi of supernatural conception and the riddle of fatherhood. Readers of Rank, Raglan, and de Vries will remember that the paternity of many heroes is ambiguous since there may be a divine father and a human husband; or the god's intervention may be rationalized as an adulterous or incestuous relationship.[32] The "hero" Þórðr, however, is not the putative son of, say, an Óðinn or a Zeus; rather the supernatural conception here takes the comic form of a well-worn motif in which a woman conceives through eating some special food (T511, Conception from eating; cf. J1532.1, The Snow Child). In fact Bjǫrn may well have had in mind a particular version of this motif, the myth of how Loki became pregnant by eating the half-burned heart of an evil woman:

> A heart ate Loki,—   in the embers it lay,
> And half-cooked found he   the woman's heart;—
> With child from the woman   Lopt soon was,
> And thence among men   came the monsters all.[33]

Strengthening this possible allusion to Loki (or Lopt) is the similarity of *meinblandit (hræ),* "poison-mixed (carrion)" to the *lævi blandit,* "poison-mixed (heavens)" of *Vǫluspá* 25, 6, another Loki reference.

Stanza 2 is a comic description of the resulting pregnancy, a phase which is decently passed over in most serious heroic legend. However, heroes occasionally cry out in the womb (cf. T570–579, Pregnancy); Þórðr apparently lay there like a lump. Stanza 3 gives the birth itself. The doting mother's decision to rear the boy ("sagt hafði drós ... at hon ala vildi") must be understood as a decision *not* to expose the infant; but such a decision was properly that of the father. And by specifying the decision at all Bjǫrn manages to imply that Þórðr's was

---

32. Cf. Stith Thompson motifs Z216, Magic conception of hero; A511.1, Birth of culture hero; A112, Birth of gods; A511.1.3.3, Immaculate conception of hero; T500–599, Conception and birth generally.

33. *Hyndluljóð* 41; Bellows, st. 43.

one of those poor families for which the possibility of exposing its infants, a practice frowned on even during the pagan period, was a real alternative; the phrasing further suggests that Þórðr was actually a marginal case—the decision could have gone either way![34] Perhaps these lines also remind us that traditional heroes were often exposed at birth (typically by the father or maternal grandfather, according to Raglan).

The birth of the hero of tradition is often attended by prophecies of future greatness, and our Þórðr is no exception, for his mother could see at once that he would be a *hundbítr*. The editors differ on the exact sense of the word; Nordal and Guðni Jónsson give "someone who kills dogs (and eats them)," while R. C. Boer interpreted "wer, wie ein hund, von hinten angreift und beisst, ein feigling."[35] In any case, "dog-biter" is no flattery, and this prophecy is expanded by the phrase discussed above, "just as brave as a she-goat." This heroic prophecy is based on baby Þórðr's eyes in parody at the convention of "funkelnde augen ... als das kennzeichen edler geburt" which Gering and Sijmons demonstrate from prose and verse.[36]

Beyond these general features of a satirical treatment of the "myth of the birth of the hero," the *Grámagaflím* bears some special resemblances to *Helgakviða Hundingsbana I*. Both are partial hero-lives; *HH* ends with Helgi's youthful deeds while the *Grámagaflím* does not progress beyond Þórðr's birth. Whether the poem is a fragment, as is usually assumed, is unclear; the saga author knew only the preserved three stanzas, but does he imply that there were once more stanzas ("en þetta er í flíminu" ["and this is in the lampoon"])? The simile makes a rather satisfactory conclusion, but one would like to think the poem originally went on to a satirical *Heldenjugend*, perhaps working out the consequences of the piscine paternity.[37] Apart from

---

34. Boer translates *at hon ala vildi* as "dass sie gebähren wollte (d.h. dass ihre stunde gekommen war)," but Icelandic *ala* means both "give birth" and "rear, bring up (literally: nourish)." Here the collocation with *vilja* tells against "give birth," nor would Arnóra need to announce the wish to give birth to her husband after the boy has already been born *(sveinn kom í ljós)*. See the second meaning (II, 1) in Cleasby-Vigfusson.

35. I think the interpretation of Nordal and Guðni Jónsson is preferable, but the parallels cited below from *HH* and *Rígsþula* do not settle the question.

36. *Commentar*, I, 360.

37. Cf. Thompson motifs B635.1.1, Eaten meat of bear-lover causes unborn son to have bear characteristics; and J1532.1, The Snow Child.

the ultimate origin of all the Vǫlsungs, according to *Vǫlsunga saga*, in a fertility-bringing apple, nothing explicitly supernatural is reported about the conception of Helgi Hundingsbani, though Sigrlinn, mother of Helgi Hjǫrvarðzson, appears originally to have been a valkyrie, and the confused paternity of the Hundingsbani is a late development occasioned by his integration into the Vǫlsung line.[38]

However, the other points of a hero-life are present in *HH*. Helgi's birth is accompanied by impressive supernatural attendants, meteorological effects, and prophecies or blessings (2, 5/8; prophecy of the raven in 5–6, including 6, 7/8 "sá er varga vinr, við scolom teitir": "He is friend of the wolves; full glad are we"). The prophecy is partly based on Helgi's heroic eyes (6, 5/6 "hvessir augo sem hildingar": "His eyes flash sharp as the heroes' are"). Both *Grámagaflím* and *HH* focus special attention on the hero's mother *(HH* 5, 1/4, a difficult passage that may refer to a premonition of Helgi's tragic greatness and so resemble, *mutatis mutandis,* the insight of Þórðr's mother); and both associate the birth of the hero with light *(HH* 6, 4). Finally, two rather far-fetched points of comparison: Helgi was given gifts at birth, apparently by his father (7, 5/8–8),[39] while Þórðr's "father" is mentioned as *auðar gildir* ("collector-of-wealth") at the corresponding moment but gives nothing. With Thompson motif T585.7 ("Precocious hero leaves cradle to go to war, etc."), the raven says of Helgi: "*Stendr í* brynio burr Sigmundar / dœgrs eins gamall" ("In mail-coat *stands* the son of Sigmund, / a half-day old"). Can the recumbent and unprecocious Þórðr be compared: "henni þótti sá / hundbítr, þars *lá*" ("he seemed to her a dog-biter there where he *lay*")?

The focus on the mother, the light, and the heroic eyes are impressive similarities, and one might be tempted to see the prophecy *hundbítr* as an ironic inversion of the prophecy *varga vinr.* However, these parallels probably should only be taken as evidence that Bjǫrn's satire is also a parodistic treatment of elements of a certain *kind* of poem, not as a direct dependence on *Helgakviða Hundingsbana I.* Many of the relevant elements are also present in the conception and birth

---

38. It is not even certain that the attenuated form of the motif of supernatural conception found in T682 ("Hero a posthumous son") applies in Helgi's case; for the legendary-historical development, cf. de Vries, "Die Helgilieder."

39. Cf. *ANF,* 41(1925), 277–80, and *MM,* 1966, pp. 1–10.

of Karl and Jarl in *Rígsþula,* including the divine and human father, pregnancy, and the *accouchement* itself. *Rígsþula* also conjoins the topos of heroic eyes in the infant with an animal simile: "ǫtul vóro augu sem yrmlingi" (34, 7/8). ("Grim as a snake's were his glowing eyes.")[40] The parallel here with "jafnsnjallr sem geit,/ es í augu leit" ("as bold as a goat when she looked in his eyes") is striking, and we can add that the list of the young Jarl's boyish skills includes *hundom verpa* (35, 10: probably "to egg on the dogs")[41] while the anti-hero Þórðr will become a *hundbítr.* These almost equally impressive similarities to *Rígsþula* confirm our suspicion against the postulation of a direct dependence or allusion by Bjǫrn to the Helgi poem.

The "heroes" of the two studies presented here have little more than their connection with satire in common. Helgi is a hero of tradition comparable to Sigurðr, Moses, Arthur, and the others; with a little ingenuity he might score fairly high in Raglan's scale. Formal satire and free-form insults echo around him at several points, and in the passage examined here Sigrún's caustic characterization of the rival Hǫðbroddr is also her declaration of alliance with her chosen hero Helgi. Bjǫrn and Þórðr were historical figures, Icelandic farmer-folk who were never far from the nitty-gritty facts of ordinary life. Yet for them poetry is largely a "martial art," and satire plays a part in shaping their life and death. Despite the differences between Helgi and Bjǫrn our two studies present complementary aspects of a single problem. For the Sigrún passage comprises an incursion through satire of the homely detail of daily life into the lofty career of a semi-mythic hero, while in the satire *Grámagaflím* motifs associated with gods and legendary heroes intrude into the prosaic pattern of real life.

---

40. Cf. *Vǫlundarkviða* 17, 5/6.

41. So Kuhn, *Wörterbuch,* s.v. *verpa* (with query); Bellows gives "and hounds unleashed."

Eddic Poetry as Oral Poetry:

The Evidence of Parallel Passages in the Helgi Poems
for Questions of Composition and Performance

It is usual to take the oral nature of Eddic poetry for granted; even those who view the manuscript tradition as extending back to Norway or make a case for runic transmission seem to assume that the life of such verse was ultimately an oral one.[1] But because of this rare consensus, few efforts have been made to place the *Edda* within a broader survey of specifically oral poetry.[2] This undertaking is overdue, and today the work of Parry and Lord seems an inevitable reference point.[3] Initially many accepted the invitation to regard the brilliantly analyzed South

---

1. Sophus Bugge seems a rare exception in statements like, "The old Norse poems which arose in the British Isles were carried ... to Iceland,—and certainly in written form" *(The Home of the Eddic Poems, with Especial Reference to the Helgi-Lays*, rev. ed., tr. W.H. Schofield [London, 1899], p. xviii).

2. Important older work: Andreas Heusler, *Die altgermanische Dichtung*, 2nd ed. rev. (Potsdam, 1945; rpt. Darmstadt, 1957); H.M. and N.K. Chadwick, *The Growth of Literature*, I (Cambridge, 1932); Einar Ólafur Sveinsson, *Íslenzkar bókmenntir í fornöld* (Reykjavík, 1962), pp. 177–99. Stefán Einarsson's theory in "Harp Song, Heroic Poetry (Chadwicks), Greek and Germanic Alternate Singing," *Budkavlen*, 42 (1963), pp. 13–28 and four earlier articles (*Budkavlen* 30 [1951], pp. 12–32; *Arv*, 7 [1951], pp. 59–83; *Skírnir*, 125 [1951], pp. 109–30; *Skírnir*, 136 [1962], pp. 107–29) relates Germanic to other oral poetry but cannot be considered very successful; cf. also Tauno Mustanoja, "The Presentation of Ancient Germanic Poetry—Looking for Parallels," *NM*, 60 (1959), pp. 1–11.

3. Milman Parry's work is now collected in *The Making of Homeric Verse*, ed. Adam Parry (Oxford, 1971); A.B. Lord's *The Singer of Tales* (Cambridge, Mass., 1960) is available in paperback (New York, 1965); and Lord's "Perspectives on Recent Work on Oral Literature," *Forum for Modern Language Studies*, 10 (1974), pp. 187–210 provides an excellent bibliographical survey. Parry's and Lord's work has been used in

Slavic tradition of epic songs as typical of oral poetry *tout court,* but at least equally important for the *Edda* are modifications that the Oral Theory has passed through in application to other literatures, especially the nearly related West Germanic.[4] Unlike Old English, Eddic poetry is everywhere conceded to be 'in some sense' oral, but the assignment now is to discover 'in what sense'—more precisely, to describe it against the background of what is known and theorized about oral poetries in other traditions. The task would be seriously undermined by ignorance of work done in connection with the Oral Theory, to which many of our conceptual tools and, especially, the fresh *Problemstellung* are due. However, in attempting to work out the nature of Eddic poetry as oral poetry two cardinal mistakes are to be avoided: the force of foreign analogies must not be allowed to stand in the way of discovery of the special nature of the Eddic tradition; and, similarly, we should make sufficient allowance for the heterogeneity of the Eddic tradition itself.

The present small contribution to the needed revaluation follows well-beaten methodological paths deriving from the fact that oral traditions, including the Eddic, may generate parallel texts. The discussion arises partly as a series of reactions to theoretical aspects of recent work on non-Eddic oral literature and touches three topics: (1) the question of textual stability and memorization in our own view and also in that of a thirteenth-century Icelander; (2) compositional units in other oral poetry and in the *Poetic Edda;* and (3) tradition and innovation in the creation of an Eddic poem. However, my conclusions are offered as applicable only to the poems actually discussed, chiefly to *Helgakviða Hundingsbana I*, and are meant to be no more than suggestive for Eddic tradition in general.

Eddic studies by Robert Kellogg, "A Concordance of Eddic Poetry" (Harvard Diss., 1958) and (with Robert Scholes), *The Nature of Narrative* (New York, 1966); and Lars Lönnroth, "Hjálmar's Death Song and the Delivery of Eddic Poetry," *Speculum,* 46 (1971), pp. 1–20 and more superficially by W.P. Lehmann, "The Composition of Eddic Verse," *Studies in Germanic Languages and Literatures in Memory of Fred O. Nolte* (St. Louis, 1963), pp. 7–14; P.B. Taylor, "The Structure of Vǫlundarkviða," *Neophil,* 47 (1963), pp. 228–36; cf. Einar Ólafur Sveinsson, *Bókmenntir,* p. 150 and "The Edda and Homer," *Laographia,* 22 (1965), pp. 531–52.

4. The term 'Oral Theory' seems a desirable loosening of 'oral-formulaic theory' and is now ensconced in the most recent publications, including the useful *Bibliography of Studies Relating to Parry's and Lord's Oral Theory,* by Edward R. Haymes

Parallel Passages / Textual Stability / Memorization

Lord's portrait of the Yugoslavian guslar presents one powerful model of the oral poet. His long narrative songs are improvised in performance, and the 'text' is in constant transition; or to put it another way, there is no text in our sense, only the subject of the poem (the story), the singer, and his technique or singing tradition. No rival model of equal force and clarity exists for Eddic or even for West Germanic verse, despite the shadowy figure of the *scop,* so that we are thrown back on inference from the skimpy evidence for textual flux or stability. Free flux should imply improvisation, where creation and transmission merge, while stability suggests memorization for the transmission of poetry but leaves its creation in doubt. For it is hard to see how 'improvisation' and 'memorization' can be construed without qualification as a simple pair of semantic opposites; and although memorization, as generally understood, has no role in the pure improvisational tradition of the South Slavic 'men's songs,' all traditions may not be so pure.[5] In the absence of a recognized term for the opposite of 'improvisation'—that is, for a type of composition which takes place in private before a performance—I suggest 'deliberative composition.' Thus some of the possibilities:

Types:	1	2	3	4	5	6
Creation:	Impr.	Impr.	Impr.	Delib.	Delib	Delib.
Transmission:	Impr.	Mem./Impr.	Mem.	Mem.	Mem./Impr.	Impr.

(Publications of the Milman Parry Collection, Documentation and Planning Series, No. 1 [Cambridge, Mass., 1973]); in connection with West Germanic Larry D. Benson's "The Literary Character of Anglo-Saxon Formulaic Poetry," *PMLA,* 81 (1966), pp. 334–41 should be mentioned as fundamental and thereafter the articles noted below.

5. In *The Singer of Tales,* Lord prefers 'oral (-formulaic) composition' to the more pedestrian 'improvisation'; this is justified for Yugoslavia since unqualified use of the ordinary word could mislead the reader into the assumption that he had a prior understanding of the mechanisms of the singing tradition. But the result of extending Lord's terminology would beg the question of the nature of composition in Eddic poetry by implying that all composition in an oral culture is improvised. Lord's latest statement seems to reject 'improvisation' as a concept by redefining it in a way I cannot accept: "... the poet does not 'improvise,' that is to say, he does not make up consciously entirely new lines or entirely new passages ... [he] is not afraid of using old expressions—a special kind of 'improvisation,' if you will, but not improvising out of whole cloth. In my attempts in the past to combat the idea of a fixed text that was memorized, I have apparently given the impression that not only is the text different at each singing by a given singer (which is true, of course), but that it is radically different, entirely

Examples of Type 1 are the South Slavic men's songs; of Type 3, skaldic short poems like Gísli's fatal *kviðling;*[6] and of Type 4, longer skaldic poems like *Hǫfuðlausn.* Type 5 may be represented in *Hjálmar's Death-Song,* and two interpretations of Old English poetry discussed below hazily imply Type 2, but living traditions offer more certain examples.[7] Finally, Type 6 exists, after a fashion, wherever the guslars have learned from a written source, such as one of the early songbooks, and the re-entry of written material such as fairy tales into an extemporaneous prose tradition is widespread; but for the survival of a tradition of deliberative composition, some transmission would, of course, have to be memorial. However, the mixed transmission of Types 2 and 5, and the possibility that poetic creation too could mingle its two modes, suggest that we should actually imagine a spectrum rather than discrete pigeonholes, even though the use of categories is necessary to discussion. In any case, there appears to be no direct way (failing significant external evidence) to determine where long-dead traditions like the Eddic and West Germanic belong in a range determined by the co-ordinates creation and transmission.

Alison Jones in 1966 seems to have been the first to realize the importance in this context of the famous *Parallelstellen* of Old English poetry.[8] From a comparison of the *Azarias* with the corresponding lines of the *Daniel,* she concluded that they are variants of a common 'original'; and from the fact that where they differ, they differ in formulas, she surmised that the medium involved in their 'transmission' was that of oral-formulaic singers, although she also speaks of

---

improvised. This is not true. South Slavic oral epic is not, nor, to the best of my knowledge is any oral traditional epic, the result of 'free improvisation'" ("Perspectives," pp. 202–03). My disagreement is less with the substance of what is said here than with a definition that forces 'improvisation' to mean totally new, ex nihilo creation rather than extemporaneous, in-performance creation. I intend to use the word (in what is, I think, the ordinary sense) as a synonym of 'extemporaneous,' in semantic opposition to 'premeditated, prepared.' I am certainly not denying that the materials are pre-existing (as in musical improvisation, for which cf. R. Stevick, "The Oral-Formulaic Analyses of Old English Verse," *Speculum,* 37 [1962], pp. 385–86).

6. *Gísli sezk niðr ok gerir at trénu, horfir á hauginn Þorgríms en konur sátu upp í brekkuna, Þordís systir hans ok margar aðrar. Gísli kvað þá vísu, er æva skyldi. . . Þordís nam þegar vísuna, gengr heim ok hefir ráðit vísuna* (Gísla saga in Vestfirðinga sǫgur, ed. Björn K. Þórólfsson and Guðni Jónsson, ÍF, VI [Reykjavík, 1943], pp. 58–59 [ch. 18]).

7. Jeff Opland, "The Xhosa Tribal Poet and the Contemporary Poetic Tradition," *PMLA,* 90 (1975), pp. 185–208, esp. pp. 187–92.

8. "*Daniel* and *Azarias* as Evidence for the Oral-Formulaic Character of Old English Poetry," *MÆ,* 35 (1966), pp. 95–102.

the importance of memory. Jones apparently did not see the contradiction between her results and the classic oral-formulaic theory, and it remained for Alan Jabbour in 1969 to indict the brevity of Lord's treatment of memorization in contrast to its evident importance in the Old English poetic tradition.[9] His method was to compare all the significant parallel passages in Old English poetry on the assumption that the less the variability between parallel passages, the greater the probability of memorization, and the more the variability, the more the proportion of improvisation. The illogicality of the simple opposition between a mode of creation (or transmission) and a mode exclusively of transmission (reflecting the influence of Lord's analysis of the Serbocroatian heroic songs) somewhat muddles Jabbour's results, but his clear statement on the significance of variant texts was an advance.

Lars Lönnroth, in his article "Hjálmar's Death-Song and the Performance of Eddic Poetry" argues, in general, that the Eddic tradition is more memorial than improvisational. (Be it noted that Lönnroth's admirable article deals with many other aspects of oral poetry in the *Edda*—for example, the external evidence touching performance, music, social setting and function—but the principal focus is on the issues discussed here.) Lönnroth cites Heusler on the difference between *yrkja* 'to compose a poem' and *flytja, færa fram* 'to present a poem' and discusses *Egils saga* on the composition and presentation of *Hǫfuðlausn*.[10] Conceding that this evidence for deliberative composition and memorization is skaldic and not Eddic, he concludes that nevertheless "the burden of proof must surely rest with anyone wishing to claim that any longer Norse poem, as we now know it, was based on an improvised performance" (p. 3). The main evidence for memorization is again that of

---

9. "Memorial Transmission in Old English Poetry," *Chaucer Review*, 3 (1969), pp. 174–90; Lord, *Singer of Tales*, pp. 99, 125 (short texts more likely to be memorized than long) and Lord and Béla Bartók, *Serbo-Croatian Folk Songs* (New York, 1951), pp. 248–49, 259, n. 1, and notes to texts. For an exemplary application of this method see W. Holland, "Formulaic Diction and the Descent of a Middle English Romance," *Speculum*, 48 (1973), pp. 89–109.

10. Lönnroth, p. 3; Heusler, *Altger. Dichtung*, pp. 120–21; however, *kveða* is ambiguous (Heusler, *Altger. Dichtung*, pp. 109, 119–20) and can mean improvise. The new dissertation by Gert Kreutzer, *Die Dichtungslehre der Skalden. Poetologische Terminologie und Autorenkommentare als Grundlage einer Gattungspoetik* (Kronberg, 1974) should bring important evidence together for the first time (so *Germanistik*, 17 [1976], p. 167); I have not yet seen the book.

parallel passages; Lönnroth's examination of *Hjálmar's Death-Song* shows that where the two versions disagree they tend to be more conventional and formulaic, and he argues that unusual expressions have to be either remembered "intact, changed considerably, or dropped completely" (p. 17). As I interpret his results, Lönnroth has concluded that the formulas indicate a degree of improvisation within a tradition of memorial transmission, just as Jones apparently regarded formulaic variations between parallel passages as evidence that formulas were used "as a kind of stop-gap to bolster up lapse of memory" (p. 102).

I am largely in agreement with Lönnroth's interpretation of the Old Norse oral-literary milieu in general. However, the reasoning from formulas to improvisation must be recognized as based on the South Slavic analogy and regarded skeptically: formulaic variations between parallel texts do not necessarily point to improvisational patching any more than formulas anywhere infallibly indicate improvisational origin. Jones and Jabbour have also been silently influenced by Lord's practical abolition of the boundary between creation and transmission in the men's songs; this resulted in an uneasy model of Old English poetic tradition in which creation was improvisational but transmission at least partly memorial. But Lönnroth followed the drift of Eddic scholarship in adumbrating a tradition with deliberative composition (which is not especially formulaic) and memorial transmission which is occasionally botched by improvisation (indicated by formulas). Both of these models ease the problem of the 'transitional text,' but both create models of tradition that violate the South Slavic analogy from which they all draw their central premise: formulaic therefore improvised. More-over, all three tend to slight the possibility of variations being those of 'conscious revisers,'[11] albeit impeccably *oral* revisers. Yet the poet of *Azarias,* an independent poem, may have had other intentions than that of *Daniel,* where the *Parallelstelle* is part of a longer whole, and one can at least see certain tendencies which may be intentional, not the accidents of failing memory in a performance

---

11. A.B. Friedman, "The Formulaic Improvisation Theory of Ballad Tradition—A Counterstatement," *JAF*, 74 (1961), pp. 113–15; Jabbour acknowledges Friedman's conscious revisers in a memorial tradition (p. 181), but does not examine the parallel passages of Old English in this light.

situation, in the versions of *Hjálmar's Death-Song*.[12] Certainly the more we build up a case for deliberative composition *(yrkja),* with memorization *(nema, festa)*[13] and public presentation *(flytja),* in Eddic poetry on the skaldic pattern, the more we must reckon with conscious oral revision.

The present discussion, like its predecessors, must operate with the precarious concept of 'memorization' and the even more fundamental 'same and different,' but the cultural relativity of these terms as applied to stories, poetic passages, and wording itself obscures some of the work stimulated by the Oral Theory. Lord's informants often insisted they were singing the 'same' song, but we find each performance 'different.' Even within our own cultural parameters various degrees of identity are meant by users of these words—a textual critic, perhaps at one extreme and a folklorist at the other—and oral societies appear to vary almost as much if there is any force in the contrast of the wide latitude given 'same' in Yugoslavia with the arguments over textual purity by illiterate audiences in Somalia.[14] The structural method of isolating meaningful linguistic units, in which a native speaker renders a decision on 'same' and 'different,' can hardly be imitated for the documents of oral literatures, and yet Lord's

---

12. On these problematical relationships see *The Exeter Book*, ed. G.P. Krapp and E. van Kirk Dobbie (New York, 1936), pp. xxxiii–xxxiv for the older scholarship, and *Daniel and Azarias*, ed. R.T. Farrell (London, 1974), esp. pp. 38–45 for the newer. The version of *Hjálmar's Death-Song* from Qrvar-Odds saga *(OS)* clearly emphasizes Princess Ingibjǫrg, the mutual tragedy of Hjálmarr and Ingibjǫrg, and the royal setting at Uppsala and Sigtúnir, while in the *Hervarar saga (HS)* version Hjálmarr's own loss in the context of his property and family dominates; Ingibjǫrg's grief and the Uppsala setting survive as vestiges but are de-emphasized by their context. A full discussion would have to consider critically the adequacy of Lönnroth's hypothetical process of improvisational change (p. 17) and his assumption that the variants constitute the 'same' poem (p. 10) which shows no progression (p. 12); for the moment I would like simply to test Lönnroth's hypothesis against a single example: *HS* has *Hrafn flýgr austan* (st. 8), while *OS* has *Hrafn flýgr sunnan* (st. 12). These are apparently meaningless formulaic variants, and yet *HS* also has *Hvarf ek ... austr við Sota* (st. 7) just where *OS* has *Hvarf ek ... ut með Sota* (st. 4). Is it not plausible that the emphasis on the east, precisely in *HS*, is intentional? *(Eddica Minora: Dichtungen eddischer Art ...,* ed. A. Heusler and W. Ranisch [Dortmund, 1903], pp. 49–55.)

13. Lönnroth, p. 3, and Heusler, *Altger. Dichtung,* p. 120, on *Egils saga (hafði fest svá at hann mátti kveða um morgininn)*; for *nema,* to 'learn, memorize,' see n. 6 above and *Darraðarljóð (Njáls saga,* ch. 157; Heusler and Ranisch (eds.) *Eddica minora,* p. 60).

14. B.W. Andrzejewski and I.M. Lewis, *Somali Poetry: An Introduction* (Oxford, 1964), pp. 45–46.

informants actually provide plenty of material for understanding the 'ethnic' view in their singing tradition.[15] Such an insider's understanding of degrees of identity in early Germanic oral literature—in what sense the young Alfred the Great was understood to have 'recited' the book of poems, or exactly how much leeway King Haraldr harðráði allowed to the 'saga-wise' Icelander[16]—would be of great interest even if it is unrecoverable in detail. (Though it would not replace our own conceptual tools—the definition of which is luckily a task for psychologists.) Some clues do emerge from the parallel passages of *Helgakviða Hundingsbana I* and *II (HH* and *HHII)*, the surviving instances of parallel transmission most likely to yield information about the oral poetic tradition in Old Norse.

Codex Regius of the *Elder Edda* preserves two poems on the life of Helgi Hundingsbani and one on Helgi Hjǫrvarðsson. The two Helgis share so many biographical features that folkloristically-oriented scholars regard them as ultimately the 'same,' probably variants derived from a common ritual pattern in which a Helgi 'the hallowed one' mated with a goddess, probably of tribal sovereignty, and was ritually slain by a near relative.[17] In addition this pattern was apparently realized in the career of Helgi Haddingjaskati, hero of the lost *Károljóð;* various other Helgis offer resemblance in isolated motifs but probably do not derive from the ritual pattern.[18]

This variation within a single schema, so characteristic of oral literature, is also recognized by the 'Collector' (the man or men responsible for the final form of the Codex Regius). His 'critical

---

15. For the contrast of 'ethnic' or native with 'analytic' or contemporary western (our) perceptions see Dan Ben-Amos, "Analytic Categories and Ethnic Genres," *Genre,* 2 (1969), pp. 275–301.

16. *Asser's Life of King Alfred* ..., ed. W.H. Stevenson, rev. D. Whitelock (Oxford, 1959), ch. 23 (p. 20): "recitavit," (cf. ch. 22 [p. 20]: *Sed Saxonica poemata die noctuque solers auditor, relatu aliorum saepissime audiens, docibilis memoriter retinebat);* also L.C. Jane, tr., *Asser's Life of King Alfred* (London, 1926), p. 117; *Þorsteins þáttr sǫgufróða,* ed. Jón Jóhannesson, ÍF, XI, pp. 335–36.

17. The major work, incorporating the results of earlier insights by Uhland and Much, is Otto Höfler, "Das Opfer im Semnonenhain und die Edda," in *Edda, Skalden, Saga: Festschrift zum 70. Geburtstag von Felix Genzmer,* ed. Hermann Schneider (Heidelberg, 1952), pp. 1–67, but the 'ritual pattern' emerges more simply from Bertha Phillpotts, *The Elder Edda and Ancient Scandinavian Drama* (Cambridge, 1920), pp. 144–75. Further significant developments (especially on the nature of the valkyrie) are to be found in Alfred Ebenbauer, *Helgisage und Helgikult* (Diss. Wien, 1970).

18. *Károljóð* is mentioned at *HHII,* prose after stanza 50 (p. 42), in *Eddadigte III:*

metaphor' is rebirth: Helgi Hjǫrvarðsson and Sváva were reborn as Helgi Hundingsbani and Sigrún and they in turn as Helgi Hadding-jaskati and Kára. However, rebirth is an embarrassing superstition (kerlingavilla) for the Collector and for us proves opaque as an 'ethnic' literary-historical concept: the rebirth of the Helgi and the valkyrie is rightly evidenced to support ritual descent but does not lend much precision to a search for the degrees of literary relatedness perceived by the audience of Eddic poetry.

The situation is different when we come to HH and HHII, patently regarded by the Collector as two 'different' pieces about the same hero. From Jan de Vries' study of the relationships among all the Helgi poems, I wish to adopt the notion that the Collector intended HH and HHII to be complementary: that is his chief reason for including both where in the interests of saving valuable vellum he might have been expected to harmonize them to one poem or saga.[19] As he wrote out HHII, the Collector replaced with prose synopsis passages where the Vorlage duplicated the first Helgi poem. Thus HHII summarizes the hero's birth in prose (from HH) but reports an otherwise unknown incident from the feud with Hundingr in verse; HHII's prose report of the slaying of Hundingr derives from HH's verse, but the following stanzas telling of the first meeting of Helgi and Sigrún are given because they do not correspond with HH; and so on. This explanation by de Vries calls for qualification in several respects,[20] but the principle of complementarity probably did have an effect on the form of HHII: the Collector (here as redactor of HHII) was trying to give the whole story of Helgi but without repeating himself.

Heltedigte, første del, ed. Jón Helgason, Nordisk filologi, series A 8 (Copenhagen, 1968); I will cite this edition where possible. Summarizing the older literature on Helgi Haddingjaskati: H. Gering and B. Sijmons, Kommentar zu den Liedern der Edda, (Halle, 1931), II, pp. 27–32; more recent: Ursula Brown, "The Saga of Hromund Gripsson and Thorgilssaga," SBVS, 13 (1947–48), 52–77 and Ebenbauer; the major 'other Helgis' are Helgi Hálfdanarson in Hrólfs saga kraka and Saxo's confusing Helgo's.

19. "Die Helgilieder," ANF, 72 (1957), pp. 123–54.

20. De Vries' article is unsatisfactory on several particular points (e.g. on rógapaldr in Helgakviða Hjǫrvarðssonar), but one major problem lies in his confused interpretation of the relationship of Vǫlsungakviða in forna, HHII, and HH; he asserts, for example, that the source of HHII was "weitgehend ähnlich" (p. 125) to that of HH before the parallel verses were reduced to prose. But the notion of the present HHII as

As he progressed through the life of Helgi in the *Vorlage* of *HHII*, the Collector came to the flyting corresponding to that of *HH* and suppressed it with a reference, almost a 'see above,' to his copy of *HH* a few leaves back:

Þá kvað Guðmundr, svá sem fyrr er ritat í Helgakviðo:

> "Hverr er fylkir
> sá er flota stýrir
> ok feiknalið
> fœrir at landi?"

Sinfiǫtli Sigmundar son svaraði, ok <er> þat enn ritat (*HHII*, pr. after st. 18).

Here it seems obvious (with de Vries) that the form of *HHII* is determined by *Raumersparnis* vis-à-vis *HH;* yet a little further on, and in a position which is totally out of order, the Collector abruptly inserts the flyting from *HHII*'s *Vorlage*. Jan de Vries explains: "Aber vielleicht hat der Dichter von HHII [i.e. the Collector in this case] das [the flyting] nicht vornehm gefunden und mit Helgis Vorwurf, es sei unziemlich *ónytom orðom at bregða* eingestimmt. Hat er deshalb das ganze Stück erst einfach fortgelassen, später hat er dann doch die Strophen noch einmal durchgenommen und mit denen in HHI verglichen; er mußte dabei einige Abweichungen feststellen ... die ihm zu wichtig dünkten, um sie ganz zu unterdrücken" ("Die Helgilieder," p. 124). Moral aversion on the part of the Collector is very dubious in view of his faithful transcription of the much nastier first flyting in *HH* and made supererogatory by the principle of complementarity; but the words of the Collector clearly indicate that the flyting is not copied at first because of its presence in *HH*, and the impossible placing, when after all it is copied into *HHII*, suggests that de Vries is right in implying that the Collector noticed too late that the flyting was different in the *Vorlage* of *HHII* and recklessly interpolated it where he happened to be at the moment.

---

a saga made up of disparate sources, one of which was *Vǫlsungakviða in forna*, is much more consistent with the textual facts, and de Vries apparently gave up the contradictory arguments of this article when he came to write *Altnordische Literaturgeschichte*, 2nd rev. ed. (Berlin, 1964), I, pp. 309–10.

In other words, we have here the Collector's decision on identity. How exact is the repetition?

The six stanzas of flyting in *HHII* correspond to a passage of 15 stanzas in *HH*, 120 *fornyrðislag* half-lines compared with fifty, plus two prose inquits. The passages are most similar at the beginning *(HHII* 19, 20; *HH* 32, 33, 35) and especially at the end *(HHII* 23, 24; *HH* 45, 46). They share twelve lines, exactly repeated, in common, and eleven of those exactly shared lines occur in the last two stanzas (within 16 lines of *HH*, 18 of *HHII*).

Perhaps the Collector gave a further hint about what he regarded as the 'same' passage by strongly abbreviating the last two stanzas of *HHII's* flyting. Although not all the lines that are exactly alike are abbreviated, the deviations are clearly indicated, and the abbreviated lines seem to increase in frequency as if the Collector progressively realized that the stanzas were identical:[21]

		HH		HHII
45,	1	"Vẹri ycr, Sinfiotli .q.	23	"Þer er, Sinfiotli
	2	sẹmra myclo		sẹmra myclo
	3	gvnni at heýia		gvnni at heyia
	4	*oc* glaþa orno		*oc* glaþa orno,
	5	en se onyto*m*		e*nn* onyto*m*
	6	orþo*m* at bregðaz,		o. a. d.
	7	þot h*r*ingb*r*otar		þot*t* hilldingar
	8	heipt*ir* deili.		heipt*ir* deili.
46,	1	Þicciat m*er* god*ir*	24	Þiccit m*er* goþir
	2	Granmars syn*ir*,		gran. s.
	3	þo dvg*ir* sikli*ngom*		þo d. s.
	4	sat*t* at mẹla		s.a.m.
	5	þ*eir* hafa marcat		þeir mẹrcþ h.
	6	a Mói*n*shei*m*om		a. m. r.
	7	at hvg hafa		at hvg hafa
	8	hioro*m* at bregda."		hior. a. b.
	9			e*r*o. hildi*n*gar
	10			haullzti sniall*ir*."

---

21. Diplomatic text here and below from Sophus Bugge, ed., *Norrœn fornkvæði* ... (Christiania, 1867; rpt. Oslo, 1965), pp. 186–95 and nn. there. My interpretation

Thus the more substantial deviations from the previously copied *HH* (the grammar of 23/1 and 5; word choice of 23/7; word choice and order of 24/5; and the plus lines 24/9–10) are written out, even though some exactly repeated lines are also copied in full. Other significant agreements between the parallel flytings are less easy to judge. One closely similar passage appears in a different location and shows, in addition to one common line, pervasive small variations similar to those in the closing stanzas:

		HH		*HHII*
35,	1	Þar mv*n* Hauðbroddr	20	Her ma Haudbroddr
	2	Helga fi*nn*a		Helga ke*nn*a
	3	flaugtrauþan g*ram*		flotta trauþan
	4	i flota miþio*m*		i flota miþio*m*.

But the shared line is not abbreviated. Two prose inquits in *HHII* correspond to verse in *HH* (*HHII*, prose before st. 19: *Þetta kvað Guðmundr Granmars son*, *HH* 32: *Frá goðborinn / Guðmundr at því*; and *HHII*, prose before st. 20: *Sinfiǫtli kvað*, *HH* 33/1–8: *Sinfiǫtli kvað*, etc.), but here the Collector is not necessarily referring back to *HH*.

The first four lines of the flyting are preserved in three variants which can be explained in terms of the Collector's perception of same and different. First he copied down *HH* 32/3–6:

> Hverr er landreki
> sá er liði stýrir
> ok hann feiknalið
> fœrir at lande?

Later when he came to the opening of the flyting in the *Vorlage* of *HHII* he found:

---

of the abbreviations here is supported by Jón Helgason, who remarks of stanza 23/6 "forkortelsen af linjen må imedlertid opfattes som henvisning til den tidligere skreyne parallelstrofe" and of stanza 24/2–8 "skrives i R forkortet, fordi strofen er skr. før" (p. 37, nn.); such abbreviation is frequent in the Codex Regius where obvious and extensive repetitions occur (e.g., in *Alvíssmál*) and is, of course, to be distinguished from ordinary abbreviation.

Hverr er skjǫldungr
sá er skipom stýrir?
lætr gunnfana
gullinn fyrir stafni (st. 19/1–4)

Apparently, the similarity was sufficient to cause him to hesitate to copy it in; perhaps he skimmed through and noticed the conspicuously similar stanza 20 *(Hér má Hǫðbroddr,* etc.) and the nearly exact two closing stanzas. In any case the similarity, whether of the first two lines only or of the whole passage, was sufficient to dictate his 'see above,' and as de Vries argued it must have been upon a second look that he decided to copy in *HHII* 19–24. The third variant is probably due to the Collector's trying to quote *HH* from memory without turning back a few leaves to check:

Þá kvað Guðmundr, svá sem fyrr er ritat í Helgakviðo:

'Hverr er fylkir
sá er flota stýrir
ok feiknalið
fœrir at landi?'

He forgot *landreki—lið* and substituted *fylkir—floti;* the resulting line is less good (in the sense of less normal) than the original in *HH* because of the run-on alliteration, and it seems possible that his substitution of an A-line with *fylkir* for an original C with *landreki* occurred because he had before him the variant in *HHII* which is also an A *(Hverr er sá skjǫldungr).*

From all this some feeling for the Collector's sense of identity in poetry may emerge. By omitting and then taking up again the flyting he makes it clear that he regards those stanzas as a coherent unit, and despite the difference in wording of the opening lines and the difference in length, his initial (hasty?) reaction was to drop the unit as a repetition, probably under the stimulus of the principle of complementarity; but upon closer examination he must have seen that there were important differences. His treatment of the passage has less in common with the latitude of Lord's singers than with our own view, not least in that he becomes more and more pedantic about textual variation the closer he looks. It is a valid objection that the evidence of the Collector, a man of the pen despite his prob-ably poetic activity in composing the variant with *fylkir—floti,* is of limited value; at least he is a contemporary. To *us,* at any rate, the degree of identity between the comparable stanzas is likely to argue for according a large role to memory in the transmission of this poetry. On the other hand, the differences between the two *sennur* considered as wholes show that mere memorial transmission, even with changes due to forgetting coupled with improvisational supple-ments, cannot explain the relationships.

Compositional Units: The *Senna*

The Collector's treatment of the *senna* in HH and HHII strongly suggests that it was felt to be a semi-independent unit, and this impression is confirmed by the presence of a similar semi-indepen-dent flyting in *Helgakviða Hjǫrvarðssonar* (HHv), the so-called *Hrímgerðarmál,* which also contrasts in meter with the remainder of HHv. Closely comparable passages in Old Norse poetry number at least twelve, suggesting that the battle of words is a stock compo-sitional unit.[22] The two principals are usually prevented by some

---

22. HH; HHII; HHv; *Lokasenna; Hárbarðsljóð;* four poetic episodes from *Ketils saga hœngs* and *Gríms saga loðinkinna (Eddica minora,* XV, "Scheltgespräche" A, B, C, and D); three episodes from Saxo: Gro and Gram (1:IV:3–10), Ericus disertus and Grep (5:III:2–5), and Ericus disertus and Gotwar (5:III:17). (Cf. J. Svennung, "Eriks und Götvaras Wortstreit bei Saxo," *ANF,* 57 [1942] 76–98, general discussion pp. 85–88). The index of O. Elton and F. York Powell's translation of Saxo *(The Nine Books ...)* lists six more passages which all seem to me questionable as flytings; Heusler discusses "Qrvar-Odds Männervergleich" *(Eddica minora,* XII), "Útsteins Kampfstrophen" (XIII), and "Qrvar-Oddr in Biálkaland" (XIV) in this context, but he is not attempting to define a corpus for formal study *(Altger. Dichtung,* pp. 105–07). Alois Wolf (cited below) adds the quarrel of the queens Brynhildr and Guðrún/Kriemhilt in the different versions (not represented in extant Eddic verse); *Bandamanna saga, Qlkofra þáttr,* and *Njáls saga,* ch. 35, presuppose a model like *Lokasenna,* and the quarrel of St. Ólafr and Kálfr Árnason at Stiklastaðr is cited by Anne Holtsmark in *KHL,* s.v. *senna,* the fullest recent discussion. Inger M. Boberg, *Motif-Index of Early Icelandic Literature,* Bibliotheca Arnamagnaeana, XXVII (Copenhagen, 1966) adds *Sigurðar saga þǫgla,* ch. 5, *Ásmundar saga víkings ins írzka,* ch. 7 (under H507.5 Contest in scolding as introduction to battle), and *Magnússona saga* in *Heimskringla,* ch. 21 (under the allied motif H507 Wit Combat). The verbal encounters between Beowulf and Unferth in *Beowulf* (and to some extent the dialogue between Beowulf and the coastguard ll. 229ff.) and between Byrhtnoth and the viking messenger in *Maldon* are perhaps to be considered English analogues along with more full-bodied later pieces like *The Flyting of Dunbar and Kennedy.*

circumstance, at least for the moment, from converting the words to blows, and besides the main opponents, there may be a third who intervenes as in the three Helgi poems. The major insults are cowardice, sexual deviances, and unfree social status. The insults and threats are framed in fairly regularly alternating exchanges, and it would be possible to consider most extant examples of the *senna* in terms of a single dramatic schema or pattern: a preliminary, comprising an Identification (in the form of a question and answer) together with a Characterization (which may be insulting, factual, or even laudatory) and then a central exchange, consisting of either Accusation and Denial, Threat and Counterthreat, or Challenge and Reply or a combination.[23]

The *senna* in *HHv* illustrates all these elements, and lends itself to comparison. The opponents are Atli, the hero's *stafnbúi,* and the giantess Hrímgerðr; Helgi intervenes at the end, and the debate takes place between the protagonists on a ship at anchor and an antagonist on land. The relationships among the dramatis personae and the physical setting are closely paralleled in *HH* and *HHII,* and the unfriendly words between Gro and Bess, the lieutenant of Gram, are similarly ended by Gram himself (Saxo 1:IV 3–10); elsewhere the hero himself chides with a single adversary or a series. The Identification begins with Hrímgerðr's

> Hverir ro hǫldar
> í Hata firði?
> ... kennið mér nafn konungs!

She is answered with *"Helgi hann heitir,"* etc. *(HHv* 12–13), and the whole process is repeated for Atli (stanzas 14–15) and Hrímgerðr (stanzas 16–17). Besides *HH* 32 and 35 and *HHII* 19–20, each of the *Scheltgespräche* in *Ketils saga hœngs* and *Gríms saga loðinkinna* begins with Identification (single or double), as does, in Saxo, the Gro and Gram episode and Ericus disertus' debates with Grepus and

---

23. This informal model could easily be made more precise by, for example, specifying optional and obligatory features, but there is a danger that such a typology, especially one cast in form of generative rules, will beg the literary-historical questions at issue (cf. Pardee Lowe, "Discourse Analysis and the þáttr: Speaker Tagging," in *Studies for Einar Haugen,* ed. E.S. Firchow et al. [The Hague, 1972], pp. 11–23).

with Olmar. The Characterizations are descriptive details attached to either the question or answer of the Identification; the most typical give the father's name and fame as in:

> Hrímgerðr ek heiti,
> Hati hét minn fadir,
> þann vissa ek ámátkastan iǫtun.
> *(HHv 17)*

Hrímgerðr's description of Helgi's ships and men, with its handsome parallels in *HHII* and Saxo,[24] can also be assigned to a Characterization. Passing over more problematic elements in the *Hrímgerðarmál,* we can clearly recognize in *HHv* 20 an Accusation of *ergi* and in stanza 21 a Denial. The central portion of the *senna* in *HH* is a series of such Accusations, but only once does the poet pause to provide a Denial, which, however, immediately passes to a new Accusation:

> "... ek var einn faðir þeira!"
> "Faðir varattu
> ... sízt þik geldo
> fyr Gnipalundi
> þursa meyiar
> á Þórsnesi!" *(HH 39/4–40/8)*

In *Hrímgerðarmál* we can also recognize one or two Challenges with Reply (stanzas 22–23 [an evasion]; stanzas 24–25 [a refusal]) with perhaps another in *HH* 43/8—44/7. Threats and Counterthreats meld into other elements; for example, Atli's Denial in *HHv* 21 contains a threatening element as do some of the Characterizations (e.g., *HHv* 13/2–6). Purer examples are to be found in Heusler's *Scheltgespräche* (e.g., the mutual threats of Gúsir and Ketill). Elsewhere Threats may pass over into straightforward curses (e.g., *HHv* 16/4–6; *HH* 44/8; *Hárbarðsljóð* 60; Saxo 1:IV:3–10) and toward

---

24. Saxo 1:IV:4 (p. 14); *HHII* 19; *HH* 33; cf. Paul Herrmann, *Erläuterungen zu den ersten neun Büchern der dänischen Geschichte des Saxo Grammaticus*, Zweiter Teil: Die Heldensage des Saxo Grammaticus (Leipzig, 1922), p. 83; and S. Bugge, *Helgi-Lays*, ch. 16.

the end of *Hrímgerðarmál* to questions and answers involving lore or news *(HHv* 27–28). No standard pattern emerges for the endings of the extant *sennur:* in *HH* (and in *HHII?*) Guðmundr rides away to prepare the battle that follows; Hrímgerðr is petrified by the rising sun; all of Heusler's *Scheltgespräche* lead directly to a fight; when Grep is worsted in words he rides home to raise the alarm (like Guðmundr), but an open fight is prevented, and he must resort to *níð;* Thórr parts with Hárbarðr with threats; and so on.

From this brief survey it appears that the *sennur* are typologically recognizable compositional units: stereotyped but variable in form, traditional in content, repeated in the poetic corpus, structurally (and contextually?) predictable within limits. Stock compositional units are regarded by Lord and others as integral components of an oral style, and characteristics like those just listed are generally considered essentials of the strict literary 'grammar' that informs and makes possible oral-traditional literature. But how much further do the similarities to the compositional units of the Oral Theory go?

Parry and Lord recognized only one such unit, ranking in the 'grammatical' hierarchy between formula and system on the one hand and story pattern on the other. These 'themes' were the "groups of ideas regularly used in telling a tale in the formulaic style of traditional song," and instances from South Slavic tradition include: a Council, the Gathering of an Army, or a Wedding.[25] Magoun's 'theme' of the Beasts of Battle in Old English verse, however, was something much smaller,[26] while Rychner treated "les thèmes" broadly, like Lord, but as comprising constituent 'motifs';[27] and there have been still other comparable systems independently arrived at and still other derivations from Parry and Lord aiming at the isolation of literary units from the point of view of composition. But it will be sufficient here simply to adopt for comparison the dual

---

25. *Singer of Tales*, ch. 4; Parry, "Studies in the Epic Technique of Oral Verse-Making, I: Homer and Homeric Style," *HSCP*, 41 (1930), 73–147 or *Making of Homeric Verse*, pp. 266–324; cf. also Fry's discussion cited below ("Formulaic Themes").

26. F.P. Magoun, "The Theme of the Beasts of Battle in Anglo-Saxon Poetry," *NM*, 56 (1955), pp. 81–90; cf. A. Bonjour, *"Beowulf* and the Beasts of Battle," *PMLA*, 72 (1957), pp. 563–73, and R.E. Diamond, "Theme as Ornament in Anglo-Saxon Poetry," *PMLA*, 76 (1961), pp. 461–68.

27. Jean Rychner, *La Chanson de Geste* (Geneva, 1955), esp. p. 126; also see Fry's brief but comprehensive discussion ("Formulaic Themes," cited below).

system proposed for Old English by Donald Fry who recognized (1) type-scenes and (2) themes.[28]

The type-scene is the more tangible; in Fry's definition it is "a recurring stereotyped presentation of conventional details used to describe a certain narrative event, requiring neither verbatim repetition nor a specific formula content" (p. 53). For example, Sea Voyages recur in Old English poetry in similar forms comprising conventional details; and Fry and others have devoted especially elaborate analysis to Approach-to-Battle type-scenes in Old English.[29] The technical term itself derives from Homeric studies, where such units as Arming or Sacrifice are obvious to all.

At first glance the *senna* may seem to have much in common with this conception of the type-scene. It recurs fairly frequently, given the small size of the surviving corpus, and is a "stereotyped presentation of conventional details." However, it does not describe a 'narrative event' in the ordinary sense: 'type-*scene*' would have to have an almost theatrical meaning to accord with the more *dramatic* nature of Old Norse poetry by comparison to Old English. (The relationship between drama and narrative in the *sennur* is complex; some insults narrate the past and some threats the future; and in some cases this dramatically enclosed narrative is relevant to the larger narrative context.)[30] However, the most immediately striking difference from the type-scene of Old English verse is that the *senna* enjoys 'ethnic' recognition in the form of a native term. Old English possesses the much-debated 'fit' and some vaguely generic terms for types and subdivisions of poems but hardly a label for something

---

28. Donald K. Fry, "Old English Formulaic Themes and Type-Scenes," *Neophil*, 52 (1968), pp. 48–53.

29. Donald K. Fry, "Themes and Type-Scenes in *Elene* 1–113," *Speculum*, 44 (1969), pp. 35–45, and "Type-Scene Composition in *Judith*," *AnM*, 12 (1972), 100–19; F.J. Heinemann, "*Judith* 236–291a: A Mock-Heroic Approach to Battle Type Scene," *NM*, 71 (1970), pp. 83–96; L.C. Ramsey, "The Theme of Battle in Old English Poetry," Diss. Indiana, 1965 (= *DA* 26 [1965], 2758) and "The Sea Voyage in *Beowulf*," *NM*, 72 (1971), 51–59; George Clark, "The Traveler Recognizes his Goal: A Theme in Anglo-Saxon Poetry," *JEGP*, 64 (1965), pp. 645–59; also Fry, "The Present State of Oral Literary Studies in Old English," unpublished paper.

30. Heusler comments briefly in *Die altgermanische Dichtung*, p. 105; Larry D. Benson mentions that an important function of the *senna* in *Beowulf* is the recognition and reconciliation of different versions of a story ("The Originality of *Beowulf*," in *The Interpretation of Narrative: Theory and Practice*, ed. Morton W. Bloomfield, *HES*, 1 [1970], pp. 1–43, esp. 20–22), and this function is plain in the near *senna* in *Fáfnismál* 7–8.

like the Approach-to-Battle.[31] Not only does the *senna* have a name of its own and corresponding treatment, but it exists in a wide range of sizes. Its generic context also varies: the *senna* in *HH* is part of a *kviða,* in *HHII* and *HHv* of a heavily poetic 'saga,'[32] in Saxo and the instances from the *Eddica minora* it is part of a regular *fornaldarsaga.* In *Lokasenna* and *Hárbarðsljóð,* the *senna* expands to become a genre in its own right rather than a 'building block' (as Lord calls his themes) of a larger composition. Variety of length is characteristic of the type-scene in Old English, Homer, and the South Slavic epic also, but the relatively uniform cast of these epic literatures makes for an inevitable contrast with the greater generic variety of Old Norse; and of course a type-scene in the sense used in studies of Old English, Greek, and Serbo-Croatian epic poetry can almost by definition not become an independent genre: there are no poems which are Approaches-to-Battle or Armings.

'Theme,' as it has recently been used in studies of Old English poetry, is considerably more elusive. Not literary *forms* like the *senna* nor scenes or events of the narrative or dramatic surface, not even discrete units to most eyes, this kind of theme is defined by Fry as a "recurring concatenation of details and ideas, not restricted to a specific event, verbatim repetition, or certain formulas, which forms an underlying structure for an action or description."[33] Themes in this sense are difficult to detect; Greenfield's 'exile' is relatively easy because of the way its expression has become predictable and because we have a common concept for it,[34] but Crowne's 'hero on the beach' is more puzzlingly interesting.[35] This theme, which is

---

31. The recent discussion by David R. Howlett, "Form and Genre in *Beowulf,*" *SN*, 46 (1974), pp. 309–25, attempts more precision than is possible.

32. Lönnroth, pp. 9–10; de Vries, *Literaturgeschichte*, I, p. 310; Gering-Sijmons, *Kommentar*, II, pp. 27–32.

33. Fry, "Formulaic Themes," p. 53; in the unpublished paper referred to in note 29 above, Fry criticizes J. Thormann ("Variation on the Theme of 'The Hero on the Beach' in *The Phoenix*" *NM*, 71 [1970], pp. 187–90) for "seeing the elements of the same theme scattered over 677 lines ... rather than concentrated in a discrete unit" (p. 3). I agree with the criticism, but it is hard to see how recurring concatenations forming underlying (semantic?) structures ever amount to discrete units except of larger underlying (semantic?) structures.

34. Stanley B. Greenfield, "The Formulaic Expression of the Theme of Exile in Anglo-Saxon Poetry," *Speculum*, 30 (1955), pp. 200–06.

35. David K. Crowne, "The Hero on the Beach: An Example of Composition by Theme in Anglo-Saxon Poetry," *NM*, 61 (1960), pp. 362–72; Donald K. Fry, "The Hero

said to occur some twenty times in Old English verse and has been thoroughly studied, is supposed to comprise the following elements: (1) the hero (2) on a beach (3) with his retainers (4) before or after a journey or voyage (5) in the presence of a flashing light. Crowne and Fry quote *Beowulf* (ll. 1963–66) as a concentrated expression of the theme:

Gewat him ða se hearda	mid his hondscole,
sylf æfter sande	saewang tredan,
wide waroðas.	Weorldcandel scan,
sigel suðan fus.	Hi sið drugon . . .[36]

Even here, where the "details are ideas" are "concatenated" in brief space, the result is hardly a scene, and usually these elements are scattered with less obvious surface coherence over a longer stretch of text. Theme in this sense comes close to a semantic 'deep structure'; but it has not been treated as such, and the 'meaning' of the hero on the beach (as opposed to exile) is obscure.

The very recent discussion of themes by Michael Nagler employs different terminology at every point, but his 'motif sequence' in Homer does bear a resemblance to the Old English theme of Fry in being a kind of subsurface semantic structure with a variety of realizations. Nagler discusses the 'convenership sequence' in Homer in terms of three components: "waking, preparing (dressing, arming, or both), and the convening of an assembly of some kind."[37] There is a natural order of elements which, however, can be manipulated; the parts may themselves be type-scenes (clearest for arming), but the sequence is, like the Old English theme, rather to be thought of as the relationships underlying events and even scenes of widely varying verbal form. Unlike both Fry's theme and Nagler's motif sequence, the *senna* is less a subsurface set of coherences than a single stock dramatic unit, potentially complete in itself. Instead of

---

on the Beach in Finnsburg," *NM*, 67 (1966), pp. 27–31 and "The Heroine on the Beach in *Judith*," *NM*, 68 (1967), pp. 168–84.

  36. Ed. F. Klaeber, 3rd ed. rev. (Boston, 1922); Crowne, p. 368.

  37. *Spontaneity and Tradition: A Study in the Oral Art of Homer* (Berkeley, 1974), p. 113; cf. Mark W. Edwards, "Type-Scenes and Homeric Hospitality," *TAPA*, 105 (1975), pp. 51–72, esp. pp. 52–53.

concatenations, the *senna* is based on alternation; instead of narrative, chronological, or mysteriously traditional order its structure is dialectic; the 'details and ideas' of the content are traditional but not necessarily their arrangement.

This is not to say that there are no recognizable themes in Fry's sense in Eddic poetry. In fact the stanzas of *HH* in which the valkyrie, accompanied by lightning, first appears to Helgi, where the theme underlies the transition from a brief voyage and battle to a dialogue, do seem to constitute the elements of the hero on the beach.[38] If the theme is more than an accident at this point and if it is as old as presence in Old English, Old Norse, and perhaps Middle High German[39] indicates, one might be tempted to see here a hint of the original

---

38. The *journey* (st. 13) leads to battle; after which the *hero (vísi*, st. 14/1) and his *retainers (hildingar*, st. 13/1; *hildingom*, st. 16/6) rest in a scene imagined as an island with cliffs, if not precisely a *beach (at Logafiǫllom*, st. 13/4; *um ey*, st. 13/8; *und Arasteini*, st. 14/4 etc.); the *light* is first supernatural *(lióma*, st. 15/1), then meteorological *(en af þeim liómom / leiptrir kvómo*, st. 15/3-4), then, in parallel construction, reflected *(en af geirom / geislar stóðo*, st. 15/9-10). The *battle* is not supposed to form part of the theme, but "the theme ... frequently precedes a description of (or reference to) a scene of carnage in which the theme of the Beasts of Battle is used" (Crowne, p. 373). (Fry mentions that the order of elements, as implied by Crowne's "precedes" here, cannot be maintained ["*Elene*," p. 36] and further associates the beasts with the hero on the beach in his edition cited below.) The beasts of battle are represented in the *HH* passage by "fara Viðris grey / valgiǫrn um ey" (st. 13/7-8) and are also present in the passage from *Finnsburg* mentioned below.

39. Alain Renoir ("Oral-Formulaic Theme Survival—A Possible Instance in the *Nibelungenlied*," *NM*, 65 [1964], pp. 70-75) identifies this theme in *NL* (B) sts. 1837-49; Fry, "Hero on the Beach in *Finnsburg*," approves and adds *Finnsburg* (ll. 2-12) as a further instance in which the hero is not on a beach but in a doorway (a "juncture between two worlds," according to Renoir, p. 73). However, it seems to me that a different and quite unmysterious heroic topos is being employed in *NL* and *Finnsburg:* one retainer holds watch or wakens early and prevents a surprise attack when he notices signs of the enemy and notifies one or more of his companions. This (and not the hero on the beach) is the essence of these two passages and of an episode in *Haralds saga Sigurðarsonar* in Snorri's *Heimskringla* (ch. 35; ÍF, XXVIII p. 116) where it is compounded with a similar 'mythicizing' allusion to the tactics of Fyrisvellir. In what is probably the prose resolution of some verses in *Hálfs saga ok Hálfsrekka* (ed. A. LeRoy Andrews, Altnordische Saga-Bibliothek, XIV [Halle, 1909], p. 107) the first retainer wakens, notices smoke in the hall, and nods off again; the pattern is repeated by a second; finally the king himself notices and *hann stóð upp ok vakti liðit ok bað þá vápnaz.* The best known instance of the topos is associated with the *Bjarkamál:* in the prose resolution of *Hrólfs saga kraka* (ed. D. Slay, Ed. Arn., B, 1 [Copenhagen, 1960], pp. 112-14) Hjalti notices activity in the enemy camp as he goes to the house of his mistress (presumably at night) and takes his time about returning to alert King Hrólfr; in the prose Hjalti's words *(vakid herra kongur þui ofridur er j gardinum*, p. 113) are inappropriate since Hrólfr and the champions are not asleep but sit drinking, careless and ignorant of the danger. This

meaning: the shedding of light as a marking of the hero's special status, like the sign of *charis* that accompanies a hero's preparation in Homer.[40] But however intriguing the speculations raised by the hero on the beach with his flashing (why flashing?) light, I am not entirely convinced that mere chance in Old Norse or direct borrowing from Old English are not to blame for the 'thematic' pattern in *HH*.[41]

These results are mainly negative. Despite shared general characteristics, the *senna* is not closely similar to the type-scene of epic verse and is even less like the subsurface 'themes.' Its dramatic nature and 'ethnic' recognition suggest that it may typologically antedate the 'host' narrative. Heusler maintained that the form was old but derived from everyday life, and an origin in ritualized or socially organized abuse-games seems an attractive hypothesis;[42] in any case, the *senna* will have had a history of its own, separate from both *kviða* and *saga*. This may explain its functional variety (another contrast with type-scene, if not with theme) and the way it mediates between part (as in *HH)* and whole (as in *Lokasenna*). It remains to be seen whether or not it is a mistake to regard the *senna* as representative of the compositional units of Eddic poetry; the *hvǫt*, the *mannjafnaðr*, and the *spá*, at least, share its characteristics. Alois Wolf, of recent Eddic scholars, comes closest to adumbrating a system of such 'middle-level' (above 'language' and below 'poem') units, in his *Gestaltungskerne*, with a method which attempts an illumination of individual works by

---

speech is derived from the old *Bjarkamál* which probably opened *Vaki æ ok vaki, vina hǫfuð* (ÍF, XXVII, pp. 361–62; *Eddica minora*, p. 31); and Saxo makes the night setting explicit *(Noxque haec aut finis erit aut vindicta malorum*, etc., *Eddica minora*, p. 22). The topos seems to be parodied in *Hreiðars þáttr heimska* (ÍF, XX, p. 248: *Ok snimma um morgininn, áðr menn væri vaknaðir, stendr Hreiðarr upp ok kallar: 'Vaki þú, bróðir,'* etc.).

40. Nagler, pp. 117–19, esp. p. 118, n. 11 (references associating *charis* with light).

41. Bugge, *Helgi-Lays*, esp. pp. 11–27, 155–73 *(senna*, pp. 163–64), 196–209; Dietrich Hofmann, *Nordisch-englische Lehnbeziehungen der Wikingerzeit*, Bibliotheca Arnamagnaeana, XIV (Copenhagen, 1955), pp. 114–30; Hofmann summarizes his study of *HH* with the probability that "ein dem *Beowulf* ähnliches Gedicht die Handlungsführung des Helgiliedes beeinflußt und den Dichter ... angeregt hat," and that "die Tendenz zum breiteren epischen Stil ... auf Impulse aus der angelsächsischen Dichtung zurückgeht" (p. 130).

42. Heusler, *Altger. Dichtung*, pp. 105–07; an example of abuse games: the 'dozens,' cf. pp. 39–60 in Roger D. Abrahams, *Deep Down in the Jungle: Negro Narrative Folklore from the Streets of Philadelphia*, rev. ed. (Chicago, 1970). A new Harvard dissertation by Joaquín Martínez Pizarro (1976) can be expected to throw an anthropological light on *senna* origins (private communication from T.M. Andersson).

bringing to bear 'the typical.'[43] But a poetics of Eddic poetry as oral poetry ought first to discover and describe common features—here the middle-level units—and construct a compositional theory stimulated but not prejudiced by the Oral Theory.[44]

Such a theory could not ignore borrowing. The Oral Theory tends to explain repeated features as products of a common style, either filtered by a common poetic grammar or selected from a common pool, and the surviving poetic corpora appear as productions of a single generative device: the tradition. But on close inspection this synchronic view does not do justice to all the problems in Old English and perhaps also in Homeric verse[45] and has never been in vogue for the *Poetic Edda*. There the variety of styles, dates, and provenances is all too obvious, and instead Eddic scholars have usually worked with concepts of borrowing and allusion very similar to those that apply to modern written literature. Eddic scholarship seems to have overestimated the individual borrowings and undervalued the force of collective tradition, especially at the level of lexical choice and phrasing.[46] Yet in our test case it is impossible to overlook some kind of genetic relationship between the poems about Helgi Hundingsbani and particularly their *sennur*.

The Skaldic Revision

Eddic scholarship is rightly still concerned with dating and establishment of a relative chronology based, partly, on borrowings at oral stages. In *HH* and *HHII* the exactness and extent of the parallels

---

43. *Gestaltungskerne und Gestaltungsweisen in der altgermanischen Heldendichtung* (Munich, 1965); Wolf discusses the *hvöt* in connection with *Hamðismál*, pp. 16–37, esp. pp. 22–23, and in sagas, pp. 109–47, the *senna*, pp. 179–96.

44. Before Wolf and Heusler, an important start was made by R.M. Meyer, *Die altgermanische Poesie nach ihren formelhaften Elementen beschrieben* (Berlin, 1889) and R. Heinzel, *Der Stil der altgermanischen Poesie*, Quellen und Forschungen zur Sprach- und Culturgeschichte der germanischen Völker, XX (Strassburg, 1875).

45. At the beginning of the controversy, Claes Schaar, "On a New Theory of Old English Poetic Diction," *Neophil*, 40 (1956), pp. 301–05, pointed out the diachronic/synchronic problem; cf. G.S. Kirk, *The Songs of Homer* (Cambridge, 1962) and several essays, including "The Search for the Real Homer," *Greece and Rome*, 2nd series, 20:No.2 (1972), pp. 124–39.

46. Cf. F.P. Magoun, "Two Verses of the Old-English Waldere Characteristic of Oral Poetry," *Beitr* (Halle), 80 (1958), pp. 214–18.

and their context in versions of the same story forms convincing evidence of a more or less direct historical connection, and the scholarship generally concedes greater age to *HHII,* at least for the relevant portions. Perhaps, then, something can be learned about the composition of at least one Eddic poem by investigating *HH* in terms of transmission and innovations from a known starting point in *HHII?* Such a study is compromised at the outset by an obvious circularity as well as by uncertainties about the form and sources of *HHII.* I cannot argue all the relevant points here but must simply assume that one of the sources of *HHII* was the poem referred to in *HHII* as *Vǫlsungakviða in forna,* which must have included the source of the extant stanzas 14–18 (meeting of Helgi and Sigrún) and stanzas 19–24 (flyting) and probably also stanzas 25, 26 and 28 (interview on the battlefield) of *HHII.* I assume that the obviously parallel parts of *HH* also derive somehow from *Vǫlsungakviða in forna.*[47] If the *senna* in *HHII* is closer to the common original, then one feature of the manner of composition in the *HH* passage is dilation. The basic idea of the *senna* and its narrative context is preserved along with some of the original wording at the beginning and end, but at the beginning this framework is expanded by several minor poetic devices—including versified inquits (sts. 32/1–2, 33/1) and a narrative interruption within an inquit (st. 33/2–8).[48] The sources of inspiration in several of these stanzas are fairly clear even where no wording is borrowed.[49] The framework is just slightly terser (by two

---

47. Accepted common assumptions about *HH* and *HHII* will not be documented individually; see the general treatments of de Vries, "Helgilieder," and *Literaturge-schichte,* S. Bugge, *Helgi Lays,* and the articles by Wessén and A. Bugge cited below.

48. The interrupted inquit is certainly characteristic of Old English (e.g., *Beowulf,* ll. 405–07 "Beowulf maðelode—on him byrne scan, / searonet seowed smiþes orþancum—: / 'Wæs þú, Hróðgár, hál!'") but apparently rarer in Old Norse (e.g., *Atlakviða* has two: sts. 2 and 15; *Vǫlundarkviða, HHII, HHv* none); the three instances in *HH* (sts. 33; 54–55; and less impressively 24–25) may be further evidence for the Bugge-Hofmann thesis of Old English influence. Cf. the 'envelope pattern' in A.C. Bartlett, *The Larger Rhetorical Patterns in Anglo-Saxon Poetry* (New York, 1935), pp. 9–29.

49. For example, *HH* 33/2–4 *slǫng upp við rá / rauðom skildi, / rǫnd var ór gulli* seems to be a modernizing adaptation of *HHII* 19/2–8 *lætr gunnfana / gullinn fyrir stafni; / þikkia mér friðr / í farar broddi, / verpr vígroða / um víkinga.* The *herskjǫldr* is characteristic of the viking period (cf. Wessén, cited below, p. 27) and belongs with realistic viking age vocabulary like *leið* (Wessén, p. 22 and n. 2) while *gunnfani gullinn* seems reminiscent of an earlier time (cf. *Beowulf,* l. 47 *segen geldene;* l. 1021 *segen gyldenne;* l. 2767 *segn eallgylden;* l. 1022 *hroden hildecumbor;* and ll. 1204, 2505, 2776, 2958; elsewhere in Old English *guðfana, fana*).

lines) at the end (despite the internal repetition, sts. 45/5–8, 34/1–4). Most of the dilation in *HH* is accomplished by sandwiching a series of eight or nine stanzas generated by recursive use of the central paradigm of any *senna* (Threat [and Counterthreat], Accusation [and Denial], etc.) between the parts of the inherited (and partly modified) framework. There is no strict overall narrative order in the new exchanges, though some of the stanzas demand a certain sequence (sts. 38–40, 43–44); instead the internal order depends on the logical-dramatic structure of *senna* exchanges and the conceptual structure of the charges and countercharges themselves. The contents of the insults in the central portion suggest that the poet was drawing on a knowledge of law and old lore to expand the original with material partly from the legendary history of Sinfiǫtli, partly from current insult-formulas, and probably partly from lost stories.[50] The South Slavic epic tradition produces similar dilations of themes and whole songs in particularly favorable performance situations, but in *HH* the framework of near and exact repetitions from *Vǫlsungakviða in forna* together with the predictable structure and origins of the new material argue rather that the passage is a conscious revision of a remembered core.

Another distinction from the expansion of a theme by a gifted guslar is the way intentions, *Tendenzen,* in the dilations match with the modified framework and the poem as a whole. By comparison to *HHII,* the poet of *HH* speaks with an extreme voice; the humor is of a drastic kind, the 'colors' strong and simple. A *mountain* of shame is heaped on Guðmundr by Sinfiǫtli, and Guðmundr does not spare to *repeat* Sinfiǫtli's crimes (sts. 36 and 41); both sides are so stained by

---

50. Gering-Sijmons, *Kommentar,* is adequate for most of these points; in addition see Bo Almqvist, *Norrön niddiktning: Traditionshistoriska studier i versmagi.* 1 Nid mot furstar, Nordisker texter och untersökningar, XXI (Stockholm, 1965). Examples of the 'commonplace' nature of these insults: st. 36/3–4 *ok brœðr þinom / at bana orðit: Beowulf,* l. 587 *þeah ðu þinum broðrum to banan wurde* (cf. ll. 1165b-68a); st. 41/9–10 *gøðir þik frœgian / af firinverkom : Beowulf,* l. 2480 *fæhðe ond fyrene, swa hyt gefrœge wæs* (cf. ll. 879, 915); st. 44/8 *deili grǫm við þik : Hárbarðsljóð* 60 *Farðu nú, þars þik hafi allan gramir* (and see Gering-Sijmons); st. 42/1 *brúðr Grana* (see Gering-Sijmons on *Lokasenna* 23); st. 39/1 *Níó átto vit,* etc. (Gering-Sijmons on *HH* 41, *Lokasenna* 23, and Almqvist); st. 38/1–2 *þú vart en skœða, / skass, valkyria* (read: *en skœða skag[s] valkyria):* a poem preserved on one of the Bergen rune-staves *við inni skœðu skag-valkyrja* (Aslak Liestøl in *Viking,* 1963, pp. 41 f. [unavailable to me but reported by Ólafur Briem, ed., *Eddukvæði,* Íslenzk úrvalsrit, V (Reykjavík, 1968), p. 274]).

the mudslinging that Helgi with his welcome intervention shines the more heroically forth. These tendencies are most obvious where *HH* can be closely compared with *HHII*. The flyting in *HHII* is relatively gallant; in stanza 19 Guðmundr positively admires the approaching enemy; in *HH* 32 this initial question has become insulting, and the idea of *HHII* 19/3–8 is taken out of Guðmundr's mouth and put into the narrator's in *HH* 33/2–4. Part of Sinfjǫtli's first answer, *HHII* 20/5–8, seems to include an obscure insult or at least a threat; in *HH* the equivalent stanza (35) escalates to an obvious insult and retains the admirably defiant answer (stanza 35/1–4) in a less emphatic position (after st. 34). The main exchange in *HHII* 21 and 22 is fairly decorous, with both sides sounding a bit like the warriors at the Battle of Maldon;[51] the source of *HHII* 22 seems to be the inspiration for the less sporting gibe in *HH* 34, and Guðmundr's noble defiance in *HHII* 21 is compromised by reference to the gibe *(HH* 44). In short, in *HH* a poet of radical sensibilities reinterprets the older passage predominantly in terms of praise and blame.

One epithet in *HH* apparently does not agree with the tendency to vilify and exalt; but I think a countering trend toward allusion, either mythic allusion or the linguistic allusion summed up as 'wordplay,' explains why *Guðmundr* is called *goðborinn* (st. 32).[52] Mythic allusions are very prominent in the *senna*: Guðmundr is said to have been a *vǫlva* (st. 37) and a *valkyria* of *Alfaðir* (st. 38) and Loki-like to have given birth to wolf-monsters *(fenrisúlfar,* st. 40) on *Sága's* promontory (st. 39); *þursa meyiar* and *Þórsnes* (st. 40), *Grani* and *Brávellir* (st. 42) are invoked. Some other allusions may be to unknown myths

---

51. The resemblances to Byrhtnoth's defiant parley with the *wicinga ár*, lying mainly in the scene itself and a few expressions, probably do not warrant the assumption of any extensive generic influence from the *senna* on *The Battle of Maldon* (ed. E.V. Gordon [London, 1937]); the similarities: (1) *HHII* 20/1–4 *Hér má Hǫðbroddr / Helga kenna, / flótta* trauðan, / *í flota miðiom* : Maldon, l. 51 ... *her stynt unforcuð eorl mid his werode;* (2) *HHII* 20/5–8: *Maldon,* l. 52 (note *eðli: eþel,* but the sense of the passages appears to be very different); (3) *HHII* 21/1–4: *Maldon,* ll. 46–47, 60–61 (the irony and the rhetorical 'before'); (4) *HHII* 21/5–8; *Maldon,* ll. 55b–58 (the general idea); (5) *HHII* 22/7–8 *þat er þér blíðara / en brimis dómar* : *Maldon,* ll. 31b–33 *ond eow betere is / þæt ge þisne garræs mid gafole forgyldon / þonne we swa hearde hilde dælon* (the rhetoric and sense; cf. also *HHII* 23/1–2). Further comparison with *HH* brings out the idea of the return message (*HH* 34–35: *Maldon,* ll. 49–55a), and general resemblances include the attitude *(Maldon,* l. 27 *on beot)* and common expressions (e.g., *orðom skipta: wordum mælan*).

52. Höfler, p. 16, n. 62, and p. 54.

or heroic legends. Wordplay is less obvious: _landreki_ ... _liði_ _stýrir_ ...
feiknalið _foerir at_ _landi_ (st. 32) presents a pattern of chiastic repetition _(ploce)_. (Broken underlining for 'conceptual rhyme.') Stanza 33 is
echoed in the negative by stanza 36: _('Sinfiǫtli_ ... _sá er svara kunni /
ok við ǫðlinga / orðom skipta': 'Fátt mantu, fylkir, fornra spialla,
/ er þú_ ǫðlingom / _ósonno bregðr!')._ Further echoes in stanzas 45
and 46 form parts of a pattern, a theme (in the ordinary sense) of
language, truth, and art.[53]

These features of the _senna_ in _HH_—stylistic extremism in the
service of praise and blame, mythic and verbal allusiveness—agree
with the skaldic affiliations of _HH_ as a whole. Scholars have often
pointed out that like skaldic praise poems, _HH_ has a more developed
vocabulary for 'prince' than any other Eddic poem; and Wessén
adds that the synonyms for 'prince' are an important feature of the
verse itself in this poem.[54] _HH_ has more kennings and _heiti_ than
any Eddic poem except _Hymiskviða,_ regarded as the most skaldic in
language, and _HH's_ language is rich in new compounds which find
their closest parallels in skaldic poetry. The poem seems to borrow
from left and right; but among its skaldic models, _Haraldskvæði_
stands out as sharing (among many other things) the extensive
vocabulary of battle and battle sounds.[55] Wessén explains several
puzzling expressions in _HH_ out of skaldic practices; for example,
skalf mistar marr, / hvar<s> megir fóro (st. 47/7–8) is clarified as
a bold reversal of a traditional skaldic kenning: "Ytterst vanligt
är nu i skaldepoesien, att havet benämnes 'sjö-konungens land
(väg).' Omvänt skull då jorden, med en djärv bild, kunna kallas
för 'valkyrjans hav.'"[56] The spirit of the poem is that of skaldic
panegyric, glorifying the victorious king, portraying the fleets and
armies of the real-life viking prince (and in proper technical terms)

---

53. See further stanzas 37/4; 41/3; 41/9–10; 43/8.

54. Elias Wessén, "Eddadikterna om Helge Hundingsbane, I-II," _Fornvännen_, 22
(1927), pp. 1–30, 65–95, here p. 13, n. 3, and p. 29; cf. Alexander Bugge, "Arnor
jarlaskald og det forste kvad om Helge Hundingsbane," _Edda_, 1 (1914), 350–80, 367;
and S. Bugge, _Helgi-Lays_, p. 27.

55. Wessén, pp. 12–14, 24–25; S. Bugge, _Helgi-Lays_, p. 394; B.M. Ólsen, "Et
Bidrag til spørgsmaalet om Helgedigtenes oprindelse. Efterladt afhandling," _ANF_,
39 (1922–23), pp. 97–130, here p. 119, n.; A. Bugge, pp. 366–67.

56. Wessén, p. 21; for S. Bugge's rival explanation, cf. _Helgi-Lays_, pp. 14–17;
references to other attempts, Wessén, p. 20, n. 1.

rather than the individual acts, personalized history, of the older heroic poetry.[57] There is a scholarly consensus dating the poem to the mid to late eleventh century and placing it at a king's court, and Alexander Bugge's impressive attempt to assign the authorship to the *hǫfuðskáld* Arnórr jarlaskáld at the court of Magnús Óláfsson of Norway (c. 1046) remains the most probable effort of its kind.[58]

HH recasts the Helgi legend in a form suitable for performance before a king and *hirð*. The skaldic revision comprises the diction and rhetoric, the vocabulary and topoi,[59] but extends also to the structure of the legend. The story is arrested with Helgi's greatest victory and ends with a kind of battlefield consecration that might imply a coronation or wedding as the occasion of its composition. The latter, in the primitive form of the king's espousal to the tribal goddess, may inhere in the Helgi material from the beginning, but the poet has clearly *selected* just this segment, the rising action of an ultimately tragic legend, for his fable. Like the typical skaldic *konungs drápa*, *HH* is jubilant in praise of the king; nevertheless, it is not deeply optimistic. However we regard the norns' activity at the opening (sts. 3, 4) and interpret the puzzling introduction to the raven's prophecy (st. 5: *"Eitt var at angri,"* etc.),[60] it is certain that a courtly audience could hardly miss the ironic tension of celebrating a victorious young king through a tragic legend; and the confident concluding words (clearly the original end of the poem) are not vouched for by the narrator but assigned to the fated king's lover: *þá er sókn lokit!* But this irony of mortality is no more foreign to

---

57. Wessén, pp. 21–23.

58. Sophus Bugge, *Helgi-Lays*, offered no name but argued that the author was a Norwegian at the court of the Scandinavian king of Dublin, composing 1020–1035 with Canute in mind; Wessén, like A. Bugge, thought the poet must be an eleventh-century Icelander but did not name him; de Vries *(Literaturgeschichte)*, p. 309, thinks of the court of Sveinn Úlfsson of Denmark about 1070; Asgaut Steinnes, ("Noko um Helge-dikte i Edda," *MM* [1963], pp. 3–25) proposes Vest-Agder about 1050–1150 and three possible poets: Kali Sæbjarnarson (d. 1099), his contemporary Sigurðr sneiss, and Rognvaldr kali (d. 1158).

59. *HH* 35/5–8, *sá er opt hefir / ǫrno sadda, / meðan þú á kvernom / kystir þýiar,* seems to comprise a mainly skaldic topos; cf. Cecil Wood, "Nis þæt seldguma: *Beowulf* 249," *PMLA,* 75 (1960), pp. 481–84 and F. Detter and R. Heinzel, *Sæmundar Edda,* II (Leipzig, 1903), p. 336.

60. Wessén, pp. 2–9 with references to earlier work; A. Bugge, p. 360; Heinz Klingenberg, *Edda—Sammlung und Dichtung,* Beiträge zur nordischen Philologie, III (Basel and Stuttgart, 1974), pp. 58–78.

praise poetry than is the kind of vilification we find in the *senna;* both are present in *Haraldskvæði,* to name one example.

We cannot determine with certainty the whole shape of the *HH* poet's main source, what I am calling *Vǫlsungakviða in forna.* He must have known that Helgi was to be sacrificed by Sigrún's surviving relative, but he may well not have known the Lenore theme (the revenant lover) at the close of *HHII.* If he knew of the first meeting of Helgi and Sigrún and the name-giving by the valkyrie *(HHII* 5–13), he has suppressed it and given us instead an escalating sequence of three fights (Hundingr, st. 10; Hundingr's sons, sts. 11–14; Hǫðbroddr, sts. 21-end), the third and weightiest being prefaced by the valkyrie's mission. Some elements of the passage on Helgi's birth and childhood (sts. 1–9) have obvious models,[61] but as a whole the passage is unparalleled in Old Norse poetry; perhaps the poet altered some form of the childish pranks told in *HHII* to add royal dignity and destiny. The naming of the hero by the valkyrie in *HHII* 10 and 13 (cf. *HHv* 6–7) is probably an ancient religious feature which our poet changed to a sonorous state occasion (st. 8); similarly the valkyrie's gift of a sword in *HHv* 8 may once have been a primitive cultic component but has become royal realism here (sts. 7–8).[62] Such is the direction of the skaldic revision in stanzas 1–9, but we cannot be as sure of the form of the source as when dealing with the *senna.*

After the *Parallelstellen* of the *senna,* only one other passage allows certain conclusions about the process of composition; *HHII* 14–18 (explicitly said to be from *Vǫlsungakviða in forna)* is almost certainly the major source of *HH* 15–20. Although this is the second meeting of Helgi and Sigrún in *HHII,* it must have been the first in *Vǫlsungakviða in forna* as in *HH;* so the situation has been taken over intact. The sequence of ideas is basically the same: Sigrún sought out Helgi *(HHII* 14/1–8: *HH* 15–16) and spoke, first of her own

---

61. S. Bugge, *Helgi-Lays,* pp. 7–11, 386–87; Wessén, pp. 2–10; the recent book of Klingenberg (esp. pp. 37–78) now presents the most important discussion of Helgi's birth and childhood, but the book has come into my hands too late to be useable here.

62. Naming: Höfler, pp. 13–19, 23–25; Sijmons-Gering, *Kommentar,* to *HHv* 7, *HH* 8. The sword: W. Wiget, "Ítrlaukr," *ANF,* 41 (1925), pp. 277–80; Gering-Sijmons, *Kommentar,* to *HHv* 8 and *HH* 7; A. Bugge, p. 353, n.; S. Bugge, *Helgi-Lays,* pp. 11–14; Klingenberg, pp. 65–66. Ebenbauer comments extensively on both.

sexual relationship to Helgi *(HHII* 15/1–4: *HH* 17), and then of her forced engagement to Hǫðbroddr *(HHII* 16/1–2: *HH* 18/1–4), of her aversion to the match *(HHII* 16/3–4: *HH* 18/5–8), and of her need for Helgi's protection *(HHII* 17/3–4: *HH* 19/1–6); Helgi answers that she should not fear *(HHII* 18/1–4; *HH* 20/1–2). However, only a few phrases seem verbal echoes *(HHII* 14/6 *und hiálmi: HH* 15/5 *und hiálmom; HHII* 16/7 *hefi ek míns fǫður / [munráð brotit]: HH* 18/1–6 *Hefir min faðir / ... / ... ek hefi ... [kveðinn]; HHII* 18/1–2, *Hirð eigi þú / Hǫgna reiði: HH* 20/1–2 *Uggi eigi þú / Ísungs bana!),* and the other shared vocabulary items are not necessarily products of textual dependence *(HHII* 17/1 and 18/5 *mær: HH* 19/5 *mey; HHII* 16/5 *fylkir: HH* 19/1 *fylkir).* To these similarities we may add the rhetorical-syntactic similarities in *HHII* 16 and *HH* 18 (compared below) and *HHII* 18/1–2 and *HH* 20/1–2.

It is evident, then, that the *HH* poet has expanded this passage, though less fully than in his treatment of the *senna* (dilation from 32 to 44 lines compared with 50 to 120 in the *senna);* both poems have an even balance of third-person narrative and dialogue at this point (16+16 lines: 22 + 22). Many of the characteristic interests apparent in the *senna* and throughout are also here: 'mythification' through place names and more god-like conception of the valkyrie, who significantly does not ride alone (sts. 15–16); obvious influences on the scene from skaldic poems like *Hákonarmál* and *Haraldskvæði* in stanzas 15–17; and the highly colored, semi-skaldic diction already discussed (e.g., st. 16/2 *ór úlfíði).* The skaldic reviser also made some interesting changes in the relationship between Helgi and Sigrún. In *Vǫlsungakviða in forna* Sigrún loved Helgi before she had ever seen him (st. 15/1–4); she made the first advances (st. 14/5–6, *kysti ok kvaddi konung und hiálmi)* before he warmed to her (st. 14/7–8); she emphasizes her fears (st. 16/5–8) and expresses her dependence on Helgi's favor directly (st. 17/3–4). In *HH* this romantic relationship becomes roughly playful as Sigrún changes from human to divine: not the hero but the valkyries are *und hiálmom* (st. 15/5); here Helgi speaks first, not to offer tender devotion but a straightforward sexual 'proposition' (st. 16); Sigrún's cool reply, far from the maidenly fears of *HHII,* belittles the proposal, brushing it aside for the moment in favor of the more manly war-work ahead (sts. 17, 18); and the earlier heroine's rather vague request for Helgi's *hylli* becomes an unsentimental exposition of consequences and alternatives (st. 19).

Another significant set of changes reduces the importance of the father/ daughter conflict in *Vǫlsungakviða in forna*. The earlier Sigrún was torn between her destined love of Helgi *(HHII 15)*, the 'other hero' whom she 'wished' to possess *(HHII 16/3–4)*, and her family loyalty; she fears her relatives' wrath *(HHII 16/5–6)* and sounds touchingly conscience-stricken at violating her father's will *(HHII 16/7–8)*. The earlier Helgi's reassurance is directed against *Hǫgna reiði* and even generally against *illan hug ættar þinnar* (st. 18/1–4), and his consoling speech climaxes in an affecting and unusual idea: let your lover *become* your family:

> þú skalt, mær ung,
> at mér lifa;
> ætt áttu, in góða,
> er ek siámk *(HHII 18/5–8)*.[63]

This conflict of love and blood must have been a main theme of the old poem but would have detracted from the jubilant effect, the happy ending, and the panegyric concentration on the figure of Helgi as hero and king sought and achieved by the poet of *HH*. De-emphasizing the intra-familial conflict, the skaldic reviser was able in part to substitute more weight on the opponent Hǫðbroddr *(HH* 18–19). For example, when adapting Helgi's speech at the climax of the scene, the *HH* poet omitted references to Sigrún's father and family, and the substitution of *Ísungs bani* for *Hǫgna reiði* is almost certainly meant to shift the reference from Hǫgni to Hǫðbroddr *(HHII* 18/1–4: *HH* 20/1–2); and in the closing lines of the stanza and passage the idea of the woman's dependence on her husband

---

63. The 'standard' interpretation of Gering-Sijmons, *Kommentar*, to *HHII* 16 (p. 115), "you have a family ... which I do not fear," requires an emendation that goes back to Lüning *(es eigi seomk)*; but Neckel seems to have been right *(Edda ...*, ed. G. Neckel [Heidelberg, 1914], I, 149–50, n. to st. 18/8) in not emending and is silently supported by Detter-Heinzel and Jón Helgason. The unemended reading, improved by removal of the comma (*ætt áttu in góða* = your *good*, i.e. real, family), fits the fragment of *Vǫlsungakviða in forna* very well.

as a new family is replaced by the simpler notion of Helgi's warlike defence *(HHII 18/5–8: HH 20/3–4).*

Many of the features of the *HH* poet's method may be viewed in the microcosm of a single stanza:

HHII		HH
st.16/1 "Var ek Hǫðbroddi		st.18 "Hefir minn faðir
í her fǫstnoð,		meyio sinni
en iǫfur annan		grimmom heitit
eiga vildak;		Granmars syni;
þó siámk, fylkir,		en ek hefi, Helgi,
frænda reiði;		Hǫðbrodd kveðinn
hefi ek míns fǫður		konung óneisan
munráð brotit."		sem kattar son."

The sentimental language *(munráð)* and the inappropriate part of the plot, the family theme, in the second helming are eliminated as far as possible, but the plot still required the mention of Hǫgni here and in the final battle (st. 52/1). The substance of the first helming is doubled to fill the whole stanza except that the *romantic* antithesis and shy expression of the original ('engaged to Hǫðbroddr, but I wanted another,' i.e. Helgi) has become a *satirical* antithesis boldly expressed (engaged to Hǫðbroddr, but he is unworthy). The new poet has also adopted the rhetorical structure of antithesis turning on *en* but has taken it much further; his stanza presents a nearly complete set of syntactic and verbal contrasts that can perhaps be schematized thus: subject—*faðir/ek;* verb—*hefir heitit/hefi kveðinn;* object 1— *meyio sinni/Hǫðbrodd;* object 2—*grimmom syni Granmars/óneisan (sem kattar son).* The types of object are grammatically different, but verbal repetition and the parallel positioning of their last lines *(Granmars syni: sem kattar son)* helps make clear the wordplay that is apparently intended here with *kattar son,* for it has been argued that this is a kind of name-kenning alluding to a playful interpretation of *Gran-marr* as 'bewhiskered horse,' that is, 'cat.'[64] The plus passages

---

64. Anne Holtsmark, *"Kattar sonr,"* SBVS, 16 (1962–65), pp. 144–55; Bjarne Fidjestøl, "Kattar sonr. Ein merknad til Helgakvida Hundingsbana I, str. 18," *MM,* 1971, pp. 50–51.

in the *HH* stanza tend to magnify the figure of Hǫðbroddr; the engagement *í her* in the original poem gives way to an attribute, *grimmr;* Hǫðbroddr is first alluded to with a patronymic periphrasis, then by name, and finally the kenning-allusion is added. Here and throughout the poem Hǫðbroddr is elevated to Helgi's worthy enemy; this replacement for the excised family-feud theme helps to lend glory and finality to the poem's conclusion where Helgi can be praised for having slain *inn flugar trauða / iǫfur, þann er olli / ægis dauða* (st. 55/6–8). This heroic development of Helgi's opponent is not diminished by the satire of the comparison to a *kattar sonr* in the mouth of Sigrún (who also praises Hǫðbroddr here and at the end) any more than it is by the long *senna* assigned to Sinfjǫtli: praise and blame are two sides of the same coin in skaldic art.

The skaldic revision was carried out by a poet of brilliant surfaces. Like 'aureate' poets elsewhere his strong points are not psychology and the penetration of human tragic depths. His figures are like icons: one-dimensional, unemotional, brightly colored public symbols. However, icon-like symmetry of parts (like the stanza just discussed) and a firm, almost rigid sense of overall structure[65] combine with an underlying ironic stance toward the plot, the characters, and the exhuberant language itself. The audience for these "enamelled termes," allusions, satirical squibs, and mythification of kingship is best imagined as a Norwegian royal court.

Conclusions

The composition of one Eddic poem seems to be extensively recoverable in *HH*, but 'skaldic revision' of older oral sources was not always so fastidious and probably not so firmly based in a king's court. The parallel transmission of stanza 4 of *Brot* presents a brief and simple example; I assume that *Vǫlsunga saga* here presents a later revision of a stanza which its poet had heard in a form very similar to that of the Codex Regius:

	Codex Regius	*Vǫlsunga saga*
st.4, 1	Sumir úlf sviðo,	Sumir viðfiska tóko,

---

65. Cf. Klingenberg, esp. pp. 78–91.

2   sumir orm sniðo,   sumir vitnishræ skífðo,

3   sumir Gothormi   sumir Guthormi gáfo

4   af gera deildo,   gera hold

5   áðr þeir mætti,   við mungáti

6   meins um lystir,   ok marga hluti

7   á horskom hal   aðra í tyfrom.[66]

8   hendr um leggia.

The traditional rhetorical pattern and the ideas of the first helming are preserved, though lines three and four can aptly be described as corrupt; the poor meter in connection with very similar wording shows that they were probably not purposely recomposed, rather the second poet could not remember exactly and substituted a more prosaic and explicit wording. But in lines one and two the later poet has clearly attempted a 'skaldic revision' by the simple device of substituting alliterating kennings for *úlfr/ormr* of the original. In the event he lost a more subtle 'beauty' that we also associate with skaldic influence, the rhyme *sviðo/sniðo,* replacing it with the very prosy *tóko* and the kitchen-word *skífðo.* In the second helming he totally deserts the tersely narrative original and continues to expand the ideas of the first helming: "What potables were served with the wolf and serpent flesh? Why small beer, of course." And, he adds helplessly, "many more things in magic potions." This stanza presents a simple skaldic revision in the substantive substitutions of lines one and two but also exemplifies the expanding and prosifying tendency and the plebeian taste we find much more fully developed in *Atlamál,* certainly a revision of an older poem.[67]

There is nothing new in the idea that some Eddic composition was in fact revision. *Hymiskviða* is another obvious example of a skaldic reworking of older material, but skaldic 'influence' is often noted in other Eddic poems. A particular skald has been forcefully proposed as "der Dichter der *Atlakviða.*"[68] Apparently the word 'skald' is linked only once to an Eddic poem, fittingly to the variant

---

66. Neckel, *Edda,* p. 318.

67. See T.M. Andersson, "Did the Poet of *Atlamál* Know *Atlaqviða?*" [in *Edda: A Collection of Essays,* ed. by Robert J. Glendinning and Haraldur Bessason (Winnepeg, 1983), pp. 243–57 (Eds.)]; older references there.

68. Felix Genzmer, "Der Dichter der Atlakviða," *ANF,* 42 (1926), pp. 97–134.

stanza cited above from *Vǫlsunga saga;* but the distinction between Eddic anonymity and the named authors of skaldic poetry is further mediated by the authorial names associated with the Eddic verses of *Kálfsvísa (Alsvinnsmál)* and *Þorgrímsþula.*[69] The opposition skaldic: Eddic is indispensable, of course, and does reflect real differences, but it may be appropriate to think of stylistic gradations rather than irreconcilably different types of poetry. Along the spectrum we find *Haraldskvæði,* a praise-poem by a known skald with a strongly 'epic' imagination, *Hákonarmál,* which has even more narrative and invents an end to its hero's life as *HH* does a beginning, and *Eiríksmál,* anonymous, mythic, and narrative/dramatic, like the Eddic poems but still occasional and panegyric like the skaldic. *HH* follows naturally in this series, probably praising a particular king on a particular occasion but extending the fictitious trappings of the "Eddic praise-poems"[70] (talking ravens, Valhǫll in the background) to a traditional story treated perhaps as political allegory; *Hymiskviða* also belongs somewhere in this spectrum, but the occasion for that poem seems to have been a private one.[71]

Snorri's *Háttatal* tells how Þorvaldr veili was shipwrecked on a skerry in cold weather. There he *orti … kvæði, er kallat er: kviðan skjálfhenda eða: drápan steflausa, ok kveðit eptir Sigurðar sǫgu.*[72] Snorri's interest in the matter lies in the invention of the meter *skjálfhenda,* a modification of *dróttkvætt,* but the larger significance of the passage comprises the information that a known skald composed a poem in what is surely a contemplative situation rather than in public performance and that the poem was on the story of Sigurðr;

---

69. B. Sijmons, *Einleitung* (to Gering-Sijmons, *Die Lieder der Edda* [Halle, 1906]), pp. clxii–clxxi, esp. p. clxv, n.; pp. clxv-clxvi; *Vǫlsunga saga* (ch. 30 in the edition of S. Bugge and W. Ranisch [Berlin, 1908]).

70. Felix Genzmer, "Das eddische Preislied," *Beitr,* 44 (1919), pp. 146–68.

71. Konstantin Reichardt, "Hymiskviða. Interpretation. Wortschatz. Alter," *Beitr,* 57 (1933), pp. 130–56; de Vries, *Literaturgeschichte,* II, pp. 113–17 and "Das Wort *goðmálugr* in der Hymiskviða," *GRM,* 35 (1954), pp. 336–37; the occasion suggested by *goðmálugr* (st. 38), an obvious calque on *theo-logus* (or, with de Vries, on *poeta theologus*), might be a disagreement with some other twelfth- or thirteenth-century mythographer even one as late as Snorri Sturluson (so Reichardt, but cf. de Vries in *GRM*).

72. Ch. 36, pp. 211–12 in *Edda Snorra Sturlusonar,* ed. Þorleifr Jónsson (Copenhagen, 1875); ch. 35, p. 16 in *Háttatal Snorra Sturlusonar,* ed. Th. Möbius (Halle, 1881), the only editions available to me here.

perhaps the poem made use of the Sigurðr material for self-consolation or complaint or was being prepared as an epic praise poem against the day Þorvaldr should reappear at court. In any case, it was not a single *lausavísa* like the exercises by Thjóðolfr Arnórsson, for it was known as a *kviða*—or by a name that would also fit our idea of *HH: steflaus drápa*.[73]

For the problem of characterizing Eddic poetry as oral poetry these skaldic connections bear an obvious relevance but one limited to a few of the extant poems. If a poem such as *HH* or *Hymiskviða* or Þorvaldr's lost *steflaus drápa* can be regarded as skaldic revision of more or less remembered older poems or stories, then the model of skaldic composition probably applies to them as well. The sources speak of extemporized skaldic *lausavísur* in a way that makes it clear they were, if not rare, at least regarded as *tours de force,* but the references to *drápur* and *flokkar* suggest deliberative composition, memorization, and later recitation. In fact this skaldic model may well be more appropriate to some Old English poetry than usually thought; in his latest study Fry shows beyond doubt that Caedmon did not extemporize but worked out his compositions in advance.[74] That some improvisation, however, co-existed in England with Caedmonian deliberative composition ("quasi mundum animal ruminando" in Bede's phrase) is still very probable.[75]

Recent work on oral as contrasted with literate cultures is open to charges of exaggeration or oversimplification;[76] the skaldic-Eddic literary milieu before the twelfth or thirteenth century evinces a greater variety than would be suggested by the sharp oppositions sometimes offered. There is evidence for different types of composi-

---

73. The skaldic *stef* itself is very close to the various types of Eddic refrains, esp. in *Vǫluspá*. Thjóðolfr's exploit appears in *Sneglu-Halla þáttr (Eyfirðinga sǫgur,* ed. Jónas Kristjánsson, ÍF, IX [Reykjavík, 1956], pp. 267–69).

74. Donald K. Fry, "Caedmon as a Formulaic Poet," *Forum for Modern Language Studies,* 10 (1974), pp. 227–47.

75. *Beowulf* (ll. 867–915) still seems (with Klaeber, notes, and C.L. Wrenn, ed., *Beowulf with the Finnesburg Fragment,* rev. W.F. Bolton [London, 1973], notes) to presuppose improvisation of sorts, despite Norman Eliason, "The 'Improvised Lay' in *Beowulf,*" *PQ,* 31 (1952), pp. 171–79; cf. Jeff Opland, *"Beowulf* on the Poet," *Mediaeval Studies,* 38 (1976), pp. 442–67, esp. pp. 457–58.

76. For example, Franz H. Bäuml and Edda Spielmann, "From Illiteracy to Literacy: Prolegomena to a Study of the *Nibelungenlied,*" *Forum for Modern Language Studies,* 10 (1974), pp. 248–59.

tion and transmission as well as, obviously, many types of poems and audiences; yet all this poetic activity is, with very few doubtful exceptions,[77] just as 'oral' as that of the Yugoslavian coffee houses. At least one of the traditional compositional units of Eddic poetry, the *senna*, is not easily assimilable to imported categories, but the more general insight—not exclusively one of recent years—that a highly organized and recursive poetic 'grammar' is proper to oral poetry does seem to extend to the Eddic material. But much more work on the structure and significance of this 'grammar' is desirable and further integration with studies of foreign oral poetries and also with the results of the newly revived domestic interest in oral saga.[78]

---

77. From oral poetry preserved in runes (e.g., Egill's *Sonatorrek* according to Thórgerðr's proposal in *Egils saga*, ch. 78) to poetry intended from the beginning for runic writing is a short step; the recently unearthed rune-staves from Bergen mediate further between the two types of composition, as does Magnus Olsen's famous theory about the runic basis of Egill's two *lausavísur* against Eiríkr and Gunnhildr ("Om troldruner," *Edda* [1916], pp. 225–45). Cf. also Jón Steffensen, "Hugleiðingar um Eddukvæði," *Árbók hins íslenzka fornleifafélags*, 1968 (publ. 1969), pp. 26–38.

78. Dietrich Hofmann, "Vers und Prosa in der mündlich gepflegten mittelalterlichen Erzählkunst der germanischen Länder," *FMAS*, 5 (1971), pp. 135–75 and "Die mündliche Vorstufe der altnordischen Prosaerzählkunst," *AUS*, 10 (1961), pp. 163–78; Peter Buchholz, "Fornaldarsaga und mündliches Erzählen zur Wikingerzeit," [in *Les Vikings et leur civilisation. Problèmes actuels*, ed. by Régis Boyer, Ecole des Hautes Etudes en Sciences Sociales: Bibliothèque arctique et antarctique, 5 (The Hague, 1976), pp. 133–78 (Eds.)]; H.M. Heinrichs, "Mündlichkeit und Schriftlichkeit: ein Problem der Sagaforschung," in *Akten des V. internationalen Germanisten-Kongresses: Cambridge 1975* (Bern, 1975), pp. 114–33; T.M. Andersson, *The Problem of Icelandic Saga Origins* (New Haven, 1964) and various articles.

Saga as Historical Novel

My title is "Saga *as* historical novel," not "Saga *is* historical novel." Obvious as it is, the distinction must be made because in the context of a contemporary debate over the poetics of the sagas and especially over genre, several influential scholars have rejected the application of "analytic" or modern generic systems to the saga literature: systems like the standard taxonomy in terms of "sagas of Icelanders," "kings' sagas," and so on.[1] From this position, to apply other modern terms

---

Versions of this paper were read at the Medieval Circle, University of California, Santa Barbara, January 1975; Conference on Medieval Historiography, Stanford University, February 1978; and at Cornell University, November 1980.

1. Lars Lönnroth, "Tesen om de två kulturerna: Kritiska studier i den isländska sagaskrivningens sociala förutsättningar," *Scripta Islandica*, 15 (1964), 1–94; M. I. Steblin-Kamenskij, *The Saga Mind*, tr. Kenneth Ober (Odense, 1973) and Steblin-Kamenskij's articles "An Attempt at a Semantic Approach to the Problem of Authorship in Old Icelandic Literature," *ANF*, 81 (1966), 24–34 and "Zur Bedeutung der altisländischen Literatur," (tr. K. Menger), *Nordeuropa*, 3 (1969), 171–76. Lönnroth's views in "Tesen" are attacked in my "Genre and Narrative Structure in Some *Íslendinga þættir*," *SS*, 44 (1972), 1–27 and "Theme and Genre in Some *Íslendinga þættir*" *SS*, 48 (1976), 1–28, and further debated by Lönnroth, T. M. Andersson, and me in *SS*, 47 (1975). Relevant to the genre discussion in other ways are also Fritz Paul, "Zur Poetik der Isländersagas. Eine Bestandaufnahme," *ZDA*, 100 (1971), 166–78, and "Das Fiktionalitätsproblem in der altnordischen Prosaliteratur," *ANF*, 97 (1982), 52–66; and Gerd Wolfgang Weber, "'Fact' und 'Fiction' als Massstäbe literarischer Wertung in der Saga," *ZDA*, 101 (1972), 188–200, and "Synkretische oder ästhetische Wahrheit? Zur Methodenkritik in der Saga-Forschung (1)," *Skandinavistik*, 11 (1981), 141–48. Further reactions to Steblin-Kamenskij may be found in *Mediæval Scandinavia*, 7 (1974), 102–17, where Peter Hallberg's "The Syncretic Saga Mind: A Discussion of a New Approach to the Icelandic Sagas" makes several of the same objections raised here; Steblin-Kamenskij defended his views in "Some

like "historical novel," "romance," or "novella" to Icelandic sagas must seem not merely rash but perversely anti-historical. The Soviet folklorist and linguist M.I. Steblin-Kamenskij greets such modern terms with sarcasm:

> ... it is sometimes flatly asserted that the family sagas are historical novels by the intent of their authors. It is quite beyond doubt, of course, that the family sagas had certain literary prototypes. But could these prototypes be works that appeared six hundred years later? The historical novel, as is known, appeared as a genre only at the beginning of the nineteenth century ... and was the result of a lengthy process, the stages of which are well known. It may, of course, be assumed ... that the prototype of a given saga was another saga, and this latter saga was actually a historical novel. But what was the prototype of this other saga? *Ivanhoe* or some other novel of Walter Scott?[2]

For a literary audience this view is likely to appear naive and amusing, perhaps even absurd and unworthy of criticism. On the other hand, it is true that comparisons of the kind I am advocating here run the risk of being historically misleading and reductive, and I am prepared to admit that their secret snares can be treacherous and subtle; so can the attempt to avoid such comparisons. But to do Steblin-Kamenskij justice, his glance at the genre question comes in the context of a serious book-length attempt to discover the "saga mind" through a vaguely anthropological method—a method which, at least in Steblin-Kamenskij's hands, creates a gulf unbridgeable by literary criticism between the modern world and that of the sagas.

His book attempts an ethnography but relies solely on the preserved words of the culture, and reading it one is bound to find the "saga mind" peculiarly empty; for Steblin-Kamenskij is continually arguing *e silentio* and further *ad silentium,* from the absence of distinctions in the lexicon to their absence in life. The fallacy in this is that a real ethnographer also observes life and questions informants—a

---

Considerations on Approaches to Medieval Literature," *MScan,* 8 (1975), 198–91. For a more sympathetic review by a Westerner see the appropriate section of Carol J. Clover's survey of recent saga scholarship in *Old Norse-Icelandic Literature: A Critical Guide,* ed. Carol J. Clover and John Lindow (Ithaca, N.Y., 1985).

2. *Saga Mind,* pp. 28–29.

methodology closed to us in dealing with a dead culture. So it is fitting that when in his final chapter Steblin-Kamenskij does produce his "informant," the revenant ghost of a thirteenth-century Icelander, all this "Thorleifr" can do, being equipped with only the "conceptions" the author has given him, outside a social context, and limited entirely to talk, is to shake his head in puzzlement over our distinctions, especially over the notion of literary criticism, or, as he calls it with disgust, that "saga about a saga."[3]

Steblin-Kamenskij's radical methodology has its most basic manifestation in his version of "truth" and hence of history for the saga mind: medieval Icelanders, on the evidence of their lexicon, did not recognize the distinction between our "history" or "real truth" and "fiction" or "artistic truth" but only what Steblin-Kamenskij calls "syncretic truth," a category that contains "latent fiction" and is opposed to "lying." But most of us would deny the simple positivistic notion of a "real truth" in "modern culture" (a concept he also treats as having a unified meaning) and would insist that the positive evidence for medieval Icelandic conceptions in this area is inadequate and the negative evidence inconclusive. Steblin-Kamenskij's focus is entirely on "intention," which he treats as accessible only through the very sparse "meta"-level vocabulary; but whatever the intentions of the authors, there remains the fact of the saga literature itself, offering, from *our* point of view, both history and fiction existing, for them as for us, on a gradient rather than as exclusive categories. To limit oneself to the thirteenth-century point of view as evidenced in vocabulary—a method I, in any case, find inadequate—is to confine oneself to willful silence. Nor are Steblin-Kamenskij and his Thorleifr any more sympathetic to the metaphorical language of criticism than to a modern point of view, but it seems to me that it is the duty of a critic to go beyond the tautology of calling a spade a spade or a saga a saga: we first begin to learn something beyond the obvious when we are forced to metaphorical levels in talking about a text. Despite Steblin-Kamenskij's fears, the danger of someone's rewriting literary history to derive the Icelandic sagas from Walter Scott is slight, and I mean only to try on the sagas—and not for the first time[4]—the

---

3. *Saga Mind*, pp. 141–52.

4. Since Sigurður Nordal, *Hrafnkatla*, Studia Islandica 7 (Reykjavík, 1940); *Hrafnkels saga Freysgoða: A Study*, tr. R. George Thomas (Cardiff: University of Wales Press,

label of "historical novel" for what that critical metaphor can suggest about this body of realistic historical fiction—a heuristic device that assumes more familiarity with the second term than the first, in this case more familiarity with writers like Walter Scott, whose Waverley novels I take to be paradigmatic for the early historical novel, than with the Sagas of Icelanders and related works. Through the third terms of such comparisons the modern reader may find a point of entry into the saga world and even into the real "saga mind."

The most basic similarity, of course, is that both sagas and the early historical novels contain both real and fictional events and persons which are separated from and connected with author and reader by *historical* distance, not merely "set in the past," conveying a sense of the differences between the time of the action and the time of the reading and simultaneously a sense of historical-causal entailment.

This quality—the essential, historical aspect of the historical novel—seems to flow from a simple, basically dualistic vision of historical process in which the past past is replaced by the past future in a dialectic that is causally related to the writer's present. The content and structure of the historical novel in many of the classical practitioners are informed by such a historical vision underlying their private fictions. The lives of the private fictional characters wind in and out among those of historical characters, situations, and events and are made historically meaningful to us or at least to their original audiences by their association with an essentially liminal or transitional moment of historical significance, as if their presence at an important historical rite of passage sanctified them as witnesses.[5] This assumes, of course, a consensus between author and audience about the historical process just described, the mutual understanding that made historical fiction in the two periods under discussion a *popular*

1958), the idea has been implicit in many literary treatments of the sagas. In a recent essay Forrest S. Scott, "The Icelandic Family Saga as Precursor of the Novel, with Special Reference to *Eyrbyggja Saga*," *Parergon*, 6 (1973), 3–13, offers an explicit and theoretical justification for the treatment of saga as novel.

5. If historical fiction does arise in a historically liminal zone, or rather in the contemplation of such a zone, its kinship with Victor Turner's attractive theory of myth becomes striking and the transition to Weber's *Geschichtsmythos* (in the article cited below) is eased; e.g., Victor Turner, "Myth and Symbol," *International Encyclopedia of the Social Sciences*, ed. David L. Sills, vol. 10 ([N.Y.], 1968), 576–77.

art. The morphology of the historical passage itself is essentially stable: a monolithic new order overtakes an individualistic ancient one, empire, for example, succeeding provincialism. The paradigm can be expanded with other opposed qualities. The balance of the two orders is, of course, never static, and a static presentation of the oppositions would in any case be ironically undermined by our knowledge that the new order, though modified in the dialectic of history, represents the way of the future, the writer's present.

This rather abstract model of the view of history in the classical historical novelists is gratefully pilfered from the less general theory argued by George Dekker.[6] He adds many more common features that are not applicable even metaphorically to medieval Icelandic historical fiction, though some are suggestive; for example, the liminal zone is, at least fleetingly, the locus of many of the heroes. Another critic of Scott has said that "in fiction, no principle of organization is superior to a rich and awesome dichotomy,"[7] and I would add that one appeal of this kind of dichotomy, in Scott at least, is its essential ambiguity: it allows author and reader to invest with value either side or both. The general picture, then, derived from the Scottish sequence of Scott's Waverley novels makes national history the story of the replacement of the Stuarts, the feudal order, and the ancient agrarian economy by the Hannoverians and the new men of developing capitalism. Scott's fictional characters and plots in *Waverley, Rob Roy, The Bride of Lammermoor, Heart of Midlothian, Old Mortality,* and *Redgauntlet* are brought in contact with historical characters and situations, but in general he does not try to make great men—Hegel's "world-historical figures"—and the history of nations the *direct* subject of his fiction. (The virtue of this plan was a source of controversy among his imme-

---

6. My introduction to serious work on the historical novel stems from Dekker's teaching at Stanford in 1973. His in-progress book on the American historical "romance" will be important beyond its field [*The American Historical Romance* (Cambridge: Cambridge Univ. Press, 1987), Eds.]; in the meantime one may consult his "Sir Walter Scott, the Angel of Hadley, and American Historical Fiction," *Journal of American Studies*, 17 (1983), 211–27.

7. R. C. Gordon, *Under Which King? A Study of the Scottish Waverley Novels* (New York, 1969), p. 10; Gordon further relates his historical dichotomy by way of "projection" to the division in Scott himself between the claims of passion and necessity. Similar analyses of Scott's divided loyalties are widespread in the literature devoted to him, e.g., in Angus and Jenni Calder, *Scott* (= Arco Literary Critiques, New York, 1969), passim, and in Lukács, cited below.

diate followers).[8] And this relationship between private fiction or fictionalized private history and true though "interpreted" public history is similar to what the sagas offer: *Old Mortality* describes the Battle of Bothwell Brig through the eyes of Henry Morton, a fictional character suggested by actual prototypes; *Egils saga* presents the victory at Brunanburg in 937 as mainly the work of an Icelandic farmer, Egill Skallagrímsson, a real person much influenced by fictional patterns. Dekker emphasizes ethnic aspects of the general picture—the fated highlanders of Scott, doomed Indians of Cooper, and marginal Cossacks of Tolstoi—and adds the striking observation that the two terms of the dialectic—"civilization and barbarism" in one view—the halves of the "rich and awesome dichotomy" and the liminal zone of transition are mirrored geographically in a border setting or a frontier. Here the sagas offer no direct analogy; Iceland and the other new settlements contained no primitive peoples, and no experienced reader of the sagas will look for romantic notions about the Skrælings. However, there is a striking geographical aspect to sagas where the action spreads out over the whole northern world. The authors, their own horizons shrinking throughout the thirteenth and fourteenth centuries, were obviously interested in the expanding world of their forebears in the Viking Age, and geographical scope in the sagas can, to a certain extent, be interpreted as a transformation of historical scope.

So despite great differences, the basic model of historical process derivable from many of the novels is general enough to be very suggestive for many sagas. And in fact, underlying a significant portion of the realistic historical fiction of the sagas we find a similar dialectic, the terms of which are on one side the unity of the Christian new order and its hand-in-glove partner Norwegian imperialism, and on the other, individualistic paganism and Icelandic independence. It is not a question, at this point at least, of the objective truth of this view of Scandinavian history but of the interpretation of the past favored

---

8. On the problem of relating the individual vision of life to the essentially supra-individual vision of history, see Herbert Butterfield, *The Historical Novel* (Cambridge, 1924) and John Maynard, "Broad Canvas, Narrow Perspective: The Problem of the English Historical Novel in the Nineteenth Century," *Harvard English Studies*, 6, 237–66 (= *The Worlds of Victorian Fiction*, ed. Jerome H. Buckley [Cambridge, Mass., and London, 1975]).

by the authors. Nevertheless, I find it an interesting confirmation when an anthropologist studying the transformation of Viking Age worldview due to its encounter with European Christianity independently employs a comparable model derived from the study of modern peasant societies in relation to advanced industrial ones, what she calls the model of the Great and Little Traditions:

> The Little Tradition refers to the little community and to that which is transmitted informally (predominantly orally) from generation to generation; while the Great Tradition refers to the corps of disciples within a civilized society and to special wisdom, preserved in scriptures, which they guard and transmit.[9]

In the saga literature the oppositions associated with religion, rather than politics, will be the most obvious because in a few familiar texts this is treated as an explicit "theme," but the more general fact must not be overlooked that the Saga Age itself, the new heroic age that the Icelandic saga-men of the thirteenth and fourteenth centuries chose to celebrate, was precisely the age of the conversion, 930–1030. Of course this coincided with other important developments in the Icelandic state, but it seems significant that in Iceland it was less the frontier period, the Settlement Age from 870–930, or the more distant or more recent past, than the years surrounding the watershed of the "siðaskipti" or "change of customs," in the suggestive Icelandic term for the conversion in 1000, that attracted the writers of historical fiction.

In the absence of what A. Ya. Gurevich, writing on the historical sense of the sagas, calls "direct general reasoning" in Old Icelandic historiography, we cannot turn, as Dekker and Avrom Fleishman, a recent writer on the English historical novel, have done, to historical theorists contemporary with the authors or even to authorial prefaces like those of Scott for evidence of this "historical conception."[10] Rather

---

9. Rosalie H. Wax, *Magic, Fate and History: The Changing Ethos of the Vikings* (Lawrence, Kansas, 1969), p. 15 (the concepts are borrowed from the work of the anthropologist Robert Redfield).

10. A. Ya. Gurevich, "The 'Historical Conception' of Snorri Sturluson," *MScan*, 4 (1971), 42–54, citation, p. 51; Avrom Fleishman, *The English Historical Novel: Walter Scott to Virginia Woolf* (Baltimore and London, 1971).

main fact—setting, character, and action—becomes a cultural symbol
we must interpret to discover the "certain attitude to the course of
human affairs" that Gurevich affirms but does not describe.[11] Hence
the significance of the enormous interest in the reigns of the two
evangelizing kings of Norway, Óláfr Tryggvason, 995–1000, and
Óláfr Haraldsson, the saint, 1015–1030, and their contemporary
rivals from the house of Hlaðir. Snorri's *Heimskringla,* for example,
devotes about two-thirds of its content to this brief period, making
it the focal point of Norwegian history, and a persistent theory holds
that the genesis of saga writing lies with the first *vita* of St. Óláfr.[12]
It is abundantly clear, too, that the thirteenth-century authors felt a
real historical distance from Saga Times, both before and after the
conversion; the obvious antiquarian interests of a saga like *Eyrbyggja*
are good evidence of this, especially where the author compares or
juxtaposes "our" customs with those of "our ancestors." However, the
new order was not imagined as arriving overnight, and the spookiest
happenings in the sagas seem to occur in the transition period; for
example, the Fróðá wonders in *Eyrbyggja* are ended by a pre-Christian rite and confirmed by a Christian exorcism, and the halloween
atmosphere of *Eiríks saga rauða* is unmistakably associated with this
transition. The unsagalike style of one version of *Fóstbrœðra saga*
is useful here because, in this respect at least, it makes explicit what
is legible only between the lines of sagas in the tight-lipped classical
style: "People said that [Gríma] was skilled in many things, in fact,
was a sorceress. [And because at that time the Christian faith was still
young and weak it seemed to many a matter of importance if a person
was skilled in witchcraft]"; "They guarded the wares which had been
on board the ship until Illugi arrived. [For though Christendom still
was young in Iceland at the time, yet it was not considered right to
appropriate the goods of men who had been slain]"; and much more
to the same effect.[13]

So the saga authors seem to have traced the birth of their own

---

11. Gurevich, p. 53.

12. The classic statement in English is in G. Turville-Petre, *Origins of Icelandic Literature* (Oxford, 1953).

13. *The Sagas of Kormák and The Sworn Brothers,* trans. with introduction and
notes by Lee M. Hollander (Princeton, 1949), p. 111 = *Vestfirðinga sǫgur,* ed. Björn K.
Þórólfsson and Guðni Jónsson, Íslenzk fornrit 6 (Reykjavík, 1953), p. 161; Hollander, p.
139 = ÍF 6:212–13.

world to the transitional period between Haraldr Fairhair and St. Óláfr, and this is clearest in their treatment of the coming of Christianity. This interpretation of their own history is reasonable and perhaps even inevitable, for it is likely that it was in fact the historical moment of the conversion that created the necessary conditions for the birth of the body of historical fiction the saga authors were cultivating, and another analogy lurks in the recognition of this probability. Lukács' famous theory of the rise and early development of the historical novel in the nineteenth century identifies the French Revolution, with its mass movements, national armies, and leaders of heroic proportions, as the "world-historical moment" that generated the historical consciousness out of which Scott wrote.[14] Lukács' perhaps somewhat overstated theory is widely accepted, but an equally persuasive case could probably be made for the Icelandic analogy. Christianity introduced not only the necessary technology for cultivation of a history but, more importantly, history itself. It is probable that before Germanic paganism met Christianity it was what we would call a primitive culture with only an approximation to our linear concept of history. It probably had recurring sacred times and myths that were not chronologically ordered; the tense system, lacking a morphological future, is suggestive in this respect. Actually, however, adequate evidence is lacking for a confident reconstruction of an early Germanic time sense, despite a recent attempt, and there are important counterinstances to even the generalizations I have just ventured.[15] The question is complex, but it does seem clear that Christianity, with its very strong historical basis, its teleological orientation, and its comprehensive system of historical relations, will have introduced a new conception of the past, as it necessarily did of the future. Only a Christian historical conception can explain the main features of periodization in the historical conception of the sagas, especially the selection of the conversion period as the locus for the epoch, for the general nature of early Christian historical conception must have provided the model for the Icelandic view in

---

14. Georg Lukács, *The Historical Novel*, trans. Hannah and Stanley Mitchell with an introduction by Frederic Jameson (Lincoln and London, 1983; original English ed., 1962).

15. Paul C. Bauschatz, *The Well and the Tree: World and Time in Early Germanic Culture* (Amherst, Mass., 1982).

terms of two great epochs separated by the radical intervention of God in history.[16]

Aspects of my theme here have often been touched on in studies of the sagas. After Nordal came, for example, Baetke's demonstration that the portrayal of pagan religion in the sagas is in large part a projection from Christianity, but Baetke's emphasis and the focus of related work in the field of mythography were squarely on the ethnographic value of the thirteenth-century literature for a knowledge of the earlier culture.[17] The strictly *literary* use of the Christian ethic as projected onto the past has only gradually been unfolded; as milestones marking the line of development one might cite much of the work of Hermann Pálsson and Marlene Ciklamini's early essay on *Valla-Ljóts saga*,[18] Theodore M. Andersson on the development of an ethic of *communitas*,[19] and a series of articles by Paul Schach, who shows that the saga writers "were keenly conscious of what is sometimes called the discrepancy between cultural milieu and cultural reference," in other words, of the historical development of their society.[20] One main

---

16. Two recent and richly annotated studies of the Christian sense of time and history are: C. A. Patrides, *The Grand Design of God: The Literary Form of the Christian View of History* (London, Toronto, 1972), published in an earlier form as *The Phoenix and the Ladder: The Rise and Decline of the Christian View of History* (Berkeley, 1964); and Morton W. Bloomfield, "Chaucer's Sense of History," in his *Essays and Explorations: Studies in Ideas, Language, and Literature* (Cambridge, Mass., 1970), pp. 13–26 (originally in *JEGP*, 51 [1952], 301–13).

17. Nordal, cited above; Walter Baetke, "Christliches Lehngut in der Sagareligion," in *Christliches Lehngut in der Sagareligion. Das Svöldr-Problem. Zwei Beiträge zur Sagakritik*, Berichte über die Verhandlungen der sächsischen Akademie der Wissenschaften zu Leipzig, Phil.-hist. Klasse, Bd. 98, Heft 6 (Berlin, 1952); Olaf Olsen, *Hørg, hov og kirke: Historiske og arkaeologiske vikingetidsstudier* (Copenhagen, 1966), esp. pp. 19–34; J. S. Martin, "Some Comments on the Perception of Heathen Religious Customs in the Sagas," *Parergon*, 6 (1973), 45–50. From a large number of studies of this type devoted to the mythography one may instance Anne Holtsmark, *Studier i Snorres mytologi* (Skrifter utgitt av Det Norske Videnskaps-Akademi i Oslo, II. Hist.-Filos. Kl., N. S. 4, Oslo, 1964); Ursula and Peter Dronke, "The Prologue of the Prose Edda: Explorations of a Latin Background," in *Sjötíu ritgerðir helgaðar Jakobi Benediktssyni*, I (Reykjavík, 1977), 153–76; and Anthony Faulkes, "Pagan Sympathy: Attitudes to Heathendom in the Prologue to Snorra Edda," in *Edda: A Collection of Essays*, ed. Haraldur Bessason and Robert Glendinning (= Manitoba Icelandic Series 4, [Winnipeg], 1983), pp. 283–314.

18. For example, Hermann Pálsson, *Art and Ethics in Hrafnkel's Saga* (Copenhagen, 1971); Ciklamini, "The Concept of Honor in *Valla-Ljóts saga;*" *JEGP*, 65 (1966), 303–317.

19. "The Displacement of the Heroic Ideal in the Family Sagas," *Speculum*, 45 (1970), 575–93; cf. Calder on the theme of peace and violence in Scott (e.g., p. 143).

20. Paul Schach, "Antipagan Sentiment in the Sagas of Icelanders," *Gripla*, 1 (1975),

"discrepancy," as he sees it, proceeds from religious development, but Schach also adumbrates a political aspect (though not the one I suggested above): "the sagas reveal that the advent of Christianity in Iceland loomed quite as large and momentous in the minds of thirteenth-century saga writers as did the colonization of their country."[21] In these three articles Schach seems to concentrate on three different artistic ways of recognizing the "discrepancy": Christian writers might condemn pagan practices, revealing their "antipagan sentiment" even while giving the pagan ancestors their moment on stage; or they might simply focus on describing aspects of conversion itself, especially on the kind of *resistance* to conversion that a later good Christian (such as Kjartan Ólafsson) might offer; or again they might see the "discrepancy" chiefly in the contrast of personalities within a family, in a "generation gap." This last is a useful concept for saga criticism and a significant part of the historical conception of the sagas, for if the family is itself a kind of microcosm of historical continuity, such "gaps" will represent in little the major historical disjunctions. In this discussion Schach exemplifies chiefly "the transition from the savage culture of the Viking Age to the farming community of the Icelandic Commonwealth," but also shows "the conversion from paganism to Christianity" reflected in generation gaps.[22]

That the saga authors did employ this personal and dramatic structural formula to convey supra-personal and historical conceptions is absolutely clear, but an example not used by Schach may demonstrate briefly how the gap can be used with artistic indirection. At the end of *Hœnsa-Þóris saga* the feuding parties are represented (mainly) by an older generation, Gunnarr Hlífarson and Tungu-Oddr, and a younger generation, Jófríðr, daughter of Gunnarr, and Þóroddr, son of Tungu-Oddr.[23] The feud is resolved, of course, by marriage, but not before

105–34; "Some Observations on the Generation-Gap Theme in the Icelandic Sagas," in *The Epic in Medieval Society: Aesthetic and Moral Values*, ed. Harald Scholler (Tübingen, 1977), 361–81; and "The Theme of the Reluctant Christian in the Icelandic Sagas," *JEGP*, 81 (1982), 196–203; citation, "Antipagan Sentiment," p. 105.

21. "Reluctant Christian," p. 186. For a comparable view of the role of settlement history, see Kurt Schier, "Iceland and the Rise of Literature in 'Terra Nova': Some Comparative Reflections," *Gripla*, 1 (1975), 168–81.

22. "Generation-Gap," p. 373; cf. Wax, above.

23. *Hœnsa-Þóris saga*, in: *Borgfirðinga sǫgur*, ed. Sigurður Nordal and Guðni Jónsson, Íslenzk fornrit 3 (Reykjavík, 1938), pp. 42–47.

the generations have been contrasted in terms of something like "epic and romance."[24] In the summer Jófríðr spent her time sitting in a tent, "finding this less dull."[25] By accident Þóroddr happened to ride by; he walked into the tent and up to Jófríðr. She greeted him in a friendly fashion, and he sat down beside her to talk. Now, Þóroddr is not a wandering knight, but despite the absence of a silk-clad serving maid, wine, and a harper and granting the perfect plausibility of the scene, it is still clear that the meeting of these young people is flavored by "romance," and their engagement, mooted in this scene, is achieved a few paragraphs later in a broader parody of the arch-heroic (or "epic"): Old Oddr means to attack Gunnarr with an overwhelming force, but young Þóroddr arrives first with a substantial war-party. Gunnarr withdraws to his house, the lone defender of the "narrow place against Odds,"[26] and readies his bow. Gunnarr's laconic reaction to the arrival of his enemies is surely a mild send-up of the old-heroic type: "'Já,' sagði Gunnarr, 'svá er þat,'" ("'Aye,' said Gunnar, 'so there are'"); and at this moment the narrator compares him to his more famous name-sake, the hero of the greatest last stand in the literature: "hann skaut allra manna bezt af honum, ok er þar helzt til jafnat er var Gunnarr at Hlíðarenda" ("he was the best shot of any man, and only Gunnar of Hliðarendi was reckoned his equal").[27] Asked if he is willing to compromise, Gunnarr's laconism is relaxed sufficiently for him to utter the last word in last words: "'Ek veit eigi, at ek eiga nǫkkut at bœta; en hitt væntir mik, áðr þér fáið mitt vald, at griðkonur mínar muni stungit hafa nǫkkura þína félaga svefnþorni, áðr ek hníga í gras'" ("'I don't know ... that I have anything to make an offer for. On the other hand, I believe that before you work your will on me, these arrow-maids of mine will have stung some of your comrades with a sleep-thorn ere I sink on the grass'"). Warned that Tungu-Oddr is determined to kill

---

24. I am referring, of course, to these concepts as set forth in W. P. Ker's classic *Epic and Romance: Essays on Medieval Literature* (New York, 1957; original, 1897).

25. *Hœnsa-Þóris saga*, p. 42: "Jófríðr, dóttir Gunnars, átti sér tjald úti, því at henni þótti þat ódaufligra." Translations from *Eirik the Red and Other Icelandic Sagas*, tr. Gwyn Jones (London, 1961), p. 33.

26. Ker's much-quoted phrase (p. 5) takes on an amusing appropriateness here, but of course he wrote "odds."

27. *Hœnsa-Þóris saga*, p. 44; see also pp. 44–45, n. 4, and *Hœnsa-Þóris saga: Mit Einleitung, Anmerkungen, Glossar und einer Karte*, ed. Walter Baetke (Altnordische Textbibliothek, N. F. 2, Halle, 1953), p. 72, n. 19; Jones, p. 36.

him, Gunnar continues: "'vel er þat; en þat mynda ek vilja, at ek hefða mann fyrir mik áðr ek hníga at velli'" ("'Very well then ... Yet I rather fancied taking a man with me when I fell on the field'").[28] In the end Þóroddr is a "góðr drengr," not a *riddari;* his methods, a combination of the trickster and the *Realpolitiker,* are thoroughly Icelandic, but he is more modern, conciliatory, and romantic than either Gunnarr or Oddr, whose comment, when Þóroddr opposes revenge on the father of his new fiancée, is: "'Heyr hér á endemi ... væri þér þá verra at eiga konuna, þótt Gunnarr væri drepinn áðr ... ?'" ("'Listen to the fool! ... Would you be any worse off marrying the girl if Gunnar was killed first ... ? '").[29]

Hœnsa-Þóris saga shows perhaps even less "direct general reasoning" than most sagas; yet it is not overreading, I hope, to insist that this beautifully told episode is imbued with a sense of history as "discrepancy" in which generations embody the historical trends. In this passage, too, though not necessarily everywhere, "discrepancy" is isomorphic with "comedy" in its large meaning: history is progress and amelioration and comic integration in its classic form, marriage.

The principal "milestones" in the interpretative developments I am tracing, however, are Lars Lönnroth's article "The Noble Heathen: A Theme in the Sagas" and Gerd Wolfgang Weber's "Irreligiosität und Heldenzeitalter. Zum Mythencharakter der altisländischen Literatur."[30] One manifestation of the thirteenth-century authors' attempt to come to terms with the otherness of their ancestors, as Lönnroth shows masterfully, was through imputing to the best of their pre-Christian ancestors intimations of the new religion: the saga writers made such "Virtuous Pagans" spokesmen and "signposts" (a trick of Scott's too) of the new historical order that was looming on the horizon. The theological (hence also historiographic) problems involved in the fate of their pagan ancestors had already been faced by the Irish and the Anglo-Saxons, and the appeal to a Natural Law,

---

28. p. 45; cf. n. 3 and Baetke's edition, p. 72, n. 20; Jones, p. 36.
29. p. 46; Jones, p. 37.
30. "The Noble Heathen," *SS,* 41 (1969), 1–29; "Irreligiosität," in *Specvlvm Norroenvm: Norse Studies in Memory of Gabriel Turville-Petre,* ed. Ursula Dronke, et al. (Odense, 1981), pp. 474–505. Note that my account of the relevant scholarship is not chronological.

beside the Old Law and the New Law, established a solution that allowed for the existence of good men before Christianity,[31] and Lönnroth shows how this historical theory is worked out in the family sagas.

Weber's article brilliantly draws the logical consequences of many strands in the sequence of studies I have been alluding to and surely represents the "state of the art" on this general subject. For example, where Lönnroth had shown us how the saga authors *used* the figure of the man who "believes in his own might and main," Weber demonstrates that this formula is part of a more complex topos which also includes refusal to worship the pagan gods and a faith in fate or fortune, and with great learning establishes that the entire complex has origins in Christian thought (pp. 477–94). Another example of drawing full consequences: Schach discusses Kjartan Óláfsson's conversion to show how different versions handled the scene, including especially the swimming contest, but Weber shows that the scene, with its gift of a mantel, *prefigures* Kjartan's later baptism, with its baptismal robe.[32] Among the valuable contributions of Weber's article, then, is a further device of the thirteenth-century writers for relating events of the more remote to the less remote past or to the present: the device of typology.

Weber, too, recognizes that in the center of the "historical perspective" of thirteenth- and fourteenth-century Scandinavia stands "die heilsgeschichtliche Peripetie des Übertritts zum Christentum" (p. 474). But his larger historiographical point concerns (in part) the applicability of typological thinking, derived of course from biblical exegesis and ultimately from Jewish historical-religious thought,[33] to the "certain attitude to the course of human affairs" in Norse

---

31. Put thus briefly it may seem as if the pagan ancestors were rather cheaply redeemed, but the more uncompromising Augustinian tradition is represented by major thinkers such as Alcuin, who was certain that the pagan ancestral hero Ingeld was lost and lamenting in hell. By contrast a Norse analogue in *Þorsteins þáttr skelks* treats the damned heroes jokingly. Beyond Lönnroth, "Noble Heathen," see Charles Donahue, "*Beowulf* and Christian Tradition: A Reconsideration from a Celtic Stance," *Traditio*, 21 (1965), 55–116, and W. F. Bolton, *Alcuin and Beowulf: An Eighth-Century View* (New Brunswick, N. J., 1978).

32. Weber, p. 502; Schach, "Reluctant Christian," pp. 192–95.

33. For general treatments of these concepts, Erich Auerbach, "Figura," in his *Gesammelte Aufsätze zur romanischen Philologie* (Bern and Munich, 1967), pp. 55–92 (originally, 1939); Friedrich Ohly, "Halbbiblische und ausserbiblische Typologie," in his *Schriften zur mittelalterlichen Bedeutungsforschung* (Darmstadt, 1977), pp. 361–400

historiography. In the case of the "irreligiosity topos" Weber has not only established the Christian origins of the elements of the topos and demonstrated their development—how "signals" from older heroic tradition were reinterpreted in the course of reception—but, more important in the present argument, convincingly located the topos in a context of "secular" typology and related both to "secular" political history as a "Geschichtsmythos" or "historical myth" of Icelandic freedom (especially, pp. 497–505). (The categories of secular and sacred turn out to be at very least intricately interwoven, and my perhaps artificial distinction at this point is merely convenient.)

When we consider Icelandic medieval historiography in this light, we notice an interesting twist: Biblical typology ultimately meant interpreting the present to conform with the sacred past (the "Geschichtsmythos" of the Jewish past). But in twelfth- and thirteenth-century Scandinavia it meant re-"writing" (revising) the past to create antecedent types for the Christian present. Thus Lönnroth has shown how the story of the first Óláfr was shaped by the second,[34] and he and others have shown how "present," twelfth- and thirteenth-century, Christian-medieval concepts are projected into the past.[35] Such projection, however, (and this is implicit in Weber's argument) is not random but patterns roughly according to typological principles to constitute a "historical myth." But if the process of making the historical myth is *regressive*, the force of typological history in the final product is just as *progressive* as in standard Judeo-Christian salvation history.

(originally biblische, 1976); Jean Danielou, *From Shadows to Reality: Studies in the Biblical Typology of the Fathers*, tr. W. Hibberd (London, 1960); Charles Donohue, "Patristic Exegesis in the Criticism of Medieval Literature: Summation," in *Critical Approaches to Medieval Literature*, ed. Dorothy Bethurum (New York, 1960), pp. 61–82 (and cf. Patrides, above). It is interesting that typological thought was the dominant strain in the historiography of the early North American colonies, more recent "types" of *terra nova*; cf. Sacvan Bercovitch, *The Puritan Origins of the American Self* (New Haven and London, 1975), especially ch. 2 "The Vision of History."

34. "Studier i Olaf Tryggvasons saga," *Samlaren*, 84 (1963), 54–94.

35. Not always meeting sweet accord; e.g., Lars Lönnroth, "Kroppen som själens spegel—ett motiv i de isländska sagorna," *Lychnos*, 1963–64, pp. 24–61; Peter Hallberg, "The Concept of *gipta-gœfa-hamingja* in Old Norse Literature," in *Proceedings of the First International Saga Conference, University of Edinburgh, 1971*, ed. Peter Foote, Hermann Pálsson, and Desmond Slay (London: Viking Society for Northern Research, University College London, 1973), pp. 143–83; Lönnroth, *Njáls saga: A Critical Introduction* (Berkeley, Los Angeles, London, 1976), pp. 123–28.

Such *interpretatio Christiana* was sometimes quite conscious, more frequently probably only half-conscious. We have to recognize creative erudition when Oddr Snorrason, a monk, opens his biography of Óláfr Tryggvason by showing that the same typological relationship that held between John the Baptist and Christ also described the two Norwegian conversion kings:

> Ok á inu fimmta ári hans ríkis helt Óláfr konungr nafna sínum undir skírn ok tók hann af þeim helga brunni í þá líking sem Jóan baptisti gerði við dróttin, ok svá sem hann var hans fyrirrennari, svá var ok Óláfr konungr Tryggvason fyrirrennari ins helga Óláfs konungs.[36]

> And in the fifth year of his reign King Óláfr Tryggvason held his name-sake Óláfr Haraldsson in baptism as godfather at his christening and received him from the holy baptismal font in the same way as John the Baptist did for the Lord. And just as John was his forerunner, so was King Óláfr Tryggvason the forerunner of the king, Saint Óláfr.

The more interesting challenge to the literary critic comprises all those less explicit cases in which aspects or transformations of the historical myth seem to inform literary works.[37] It is the essence of the sagas that fictional motifs like the Noble Heathen and fictionally developed traditional reports—the love stories, biographies, family chronicles, and above all accounts of famous feuds and cases at law—acquire a historical context by reference to Icelandic and Norwegian history and often by reference to events and lands further abroad, but the sense of epoch, of history with a goal and form other than mere sequence, would be missing if the private plots were not placed in or selected from the crucial transitional period, and it should be of

---

36. *Óláfs saga Tryggvasonar eftir Odd Munk* in *Konunga sögur*, ed. Guðni Jónsson, I (Reykjavík: Íslendingasagnaútgáfan, 1957), p. 3; *Saga Óláfs Tryggvasonar af Oddr Snorrason munk*, ed. Finnur Jónsson (Copenhagen, 1932), p. 1.

37. My "Christian Form and Christian Meaning in *Halldórs þáttr I*," *Harvard English Studies*, 5 (1974), 249–64, takes up a similar challenge and pushes to such detailed results that not every reader will agree. Other "milestones" that should be noted here are: Marlene Ciklamini's "Divine Will and the Guises of Truth in *Geirmundar þáttr heljarskinns*," *skandinavistik*, 11 (1981), 81–88; Lise Præstgaard Andersen, "Nogle kompositionselementer i islændingesagaen," *APS*, 31 (1976), 176–87; and Thomas D. Hill, "The Evisceration of Bróðir in 'Brennu-Njáls saga'," *Traditio*, 37 (1981), 437–44.

further specifically literary interest to see how the plots are related to the sense of history implicit in the works as a group. I propose to do this by surveying a group of stories in which the plot of history, as the authors interpreted it, coincides closely with the content and structure of the private fictions.

This correlation is probably most obvious in the þættir or novellas that make the contrast of paganism and Christianity their explicit central theme and the conversion of individuals their common structural element.[38] *Rǫgnvalds þáttr ok Rauðs, Þáttr Eindriða Ilbreiðs*, and *Vǫlsa þáttr* all climax in a confrontation of the evangelizing king with non-Christians, who soon see the error of their ways and are baptized. The wonderful satire of *Vǫlsa þáttr*, where the heathens are depicted worshipping as their fetish a pickled horse's penis, is the exception rather than the rule, though in general the treatment of heathenism is humorous.[39] Two other þættir, *Sveins þáttr ok Finns* and *Helga þáttr ok Úlfs*, as well as *Rǫgnvalds þáttr* and *Vǫlsa þáttr*, combine an element of generational conflict within a family with the conversion theme, and the familial reunion or reconciliation is made to coincide structurally with the conversion. The old order here is perverse and ridiculous, but it did give rise to strong and idiosyncratic individuals; the new order, interpreted here mainly in religious terms, does not tolerate pluralism, and the historical figure of the king dominates the forces that are shaping the future.

Besides these realistic short stories there is a group of þættir that use nonrealistic and nonchronological means to bring the early

---

38. For a fuller treatment see my "Folktale and Thattr: the Case of Rognvald and Raud," in *Folklore and Medieval Studies*, ed. Carl Lindahl and Erika Brady (= *Folklore Forum*, 13 [1980]), pp. 158–98, esp. pp. 162–67. Most of the short stories mentioned (and some other relevant ones) can be consulted most conveniently in *Fornar smásögur úr Noregskonunga sögum*, ed. Edwin Gardiner, with an introduction by Sir William A. Craigie (Reykjavík, 1949) or in the editions of *Flateyjarbók. Norna-Gests þáttr* is separately edited in *Die prosaische Edda im Auszuge nebst Völsunga-saga und Nornagests-tháttr*, ed. Ernst Wilken, 1 (Paderborn, 1877; rev. 1912) and in editions of the *fornaldarsǫgur*.

39. Most of the scholarship on *Vǫlsa þáttr* is understandably concerned with distinguishing and evaluating the ancient, heathen elements of the tale; see, for example, Gro Steinsland and Kari Vogt, "'Aukinn ertu Uolse ok vpp vm tekinn': En religionshistorisk analyse av *Vǫlsaþáttr* i *Flateyjarbók*," *ANF*, 96 (1981), 87–106. Without specifically taking issue with this point of view I will argue in a future paper that the final literary form and temper of the story are a product of Christian satire.

Christian reigns of the two Óláfs in contact with the distant pagan and heroic past. *Tóka þáttr* and *Norna-Gests þáttr* both tell how a mysterious old man arrives at court; it develops that the old man is cursed with a supernaturally long life and remembers the heroes of ancient times—Sigurðr Fáfnisbani, Starkaðr the Old, Hálfr and his Hálfsrekkar, Bǫðvarr-Bjarki, and so on. Like the Old English scop Widsith, the old men of these two þættir recount stories based on their own wanderings among the vanished heroes. At the end Tóki and Gestr ask for baptism and die. *Sǫrla þáttr* is comparable but lacks the framework provided by the old saga-teller: at the end of a series of loosely concatenated myths concluding in the eternal battle of Hǫgni and Heðinn, the *Hjaðningavíg*, King Óláfr Tryggvason lands on the island where the battle is still going on after some five centuries, and one of the king's champions—Ívar "Beam-of-light," appropriately enough—ends the conflict by giving the heathen warriors the permanent death that only a Christian could effect; however, Heðinn did not die before explaining the curse. A fourth tale, *Albani þáttr ok Sunnifu,* is somewhat similar. Like such an unrealistic historical sketch as Hawthorne's "Main Street" they present history in a foreshortened form with supernatural machinery and (in part) with a commentator. However, the mainstream of saga literature, in so far as it can be approached "as historical novel," is firmly realistic.

I have argued elsewhere that the common structural idea of all nine of these "conversion þættir" must be derived from Christian history since they are all constructed on the principle of the contrast of an Old Dispensation with a New and motivated by divine intervention in history. The principle does not seem to be very far removed from that described by Friedrich Ohly:

Typologisches Geschichtsdenken gewahrt einen Umsprung der Geschichte am Ort des Einbruchs göttlicher Offenbarung in die Welt mit Christus. Im umwertenden Licht der Epiphanie des Heiles—*ecce facta sunt omnia nova*—nunmehr als dunkler andeutende Prophetie erscheinend, geht das Alte als *figura* "Vor-Bild" nicht verloren, wird es im Zeitgedächtnis als im Neuen Erfülltes aufgehoben. Man schämt sich, wo die Voroffenbarung im Licht der Offenbarung aufging, des Vergangenen, der unauslöschlichen Spur zum Heute, nicht, verklärt es aber auch—im Gegensatz zu jedem Erneuerungsverlangen aus

Ungenügen an der Gegenwart—nicht, es sei denn als die Zeit der Sterne, die vor Tagesaufgang leuchten.[40]

The "conversion þættir" realize their underlying three-part structure in a variety of ways, but seem, as a generic group, to derive from the general European-Christian type of conversion story (St. Martin, Paul).[41]

Saga-length works as well as þættir may closely correlate Salvation History in the conversion period with the private tale of a family feud. The best and earliest example is the *Saga of the Faroe Islanders*, a fictionalized family history of the Faroes during the period 970–1040.[42] The main action is a tightly articulated cause and effect sequence; nevertheless it comprises two parts, the first involving three generations and a time span of about forty-five years. The family history also contrives to be convincingly coordinated with that of the whole northern world, for the hero Sigmundr's exile and coming of age take him to Norway and on far-flung viking expeditions. When Sigmundr returns to the Faroes for his revenge, it is with the backing of the Norwegian ruler Earl Hákon; Earl Hákon is to judge the case between Sigmundr and Þrándr, and throughout Sigmundr is in close contact with the Norwegian rulers, acting as their representative and tax-gatherer in the islands.

The saga's implicit comparison between Sigmundr and the other main character Þrándr is a good example of old and new interwoven in

---

40. "Ausserbiblisch Typologisches zwischen Cicero, Ambrosius und Aelred von Rievaulx," in his *Schriften*, p. 360 (originally, 1976). Northrop Frye states the connection between typology and historiography in characteristically strong form: "Typology is a figure of speech that moves in time.... What typology really is is a mode of thought, what it both assumes and leads to is a theory of history, or more accurately of historical process.... Our modern confidence in historical process ... is probably a legacy of Biblical typology: at least I can think of no other source for its tradition" *(The Great Code: The Bible and Literature* [San Diego, New York, London, 1983], pp. 80–81).

41. Harris, "Folktale and Thattr," pp. 165–67—After completion of the present essay, Bernadine McCreesh, "Structural Patterns in *Eyrbyggja Saga* and Other Sagas of the Conversion," *MScan*, 11 (1978–79 [published 1982]), 271–80, came to my attention, an interesting article with obvious complementary relevance for my argument here.

42. The translations given are from *The Faroe Islanders' Saga*, tr. George Johnston ([n.p.], 1975); standard edition: *Færeyingasaga: Den islandske Saga om Færingerne*, ed. Finnur Jónsson for "Det kongelige nordiske Oldskriftselskab" (Copenhagen, 1927); I have also consulted the important recent edition in modern orthography: *Færeyinga saga*, ed. Ólafur Halldórsson, Íslenzk úrvalsrit 13 (Reykjavík, 1978 [1st ed. 1967]).

a feud plot. Þrándr is underhanded, treacherous (not least to his own kin), secretive, a great manipulator, a magician. An Odinic figure, he himself never fights but uses his three nephews and others in his feuds. Instead of youthful viking adventures, *de rigeur* for characterizing heroic heroes like Sigmundr, Þrándr went on a single *trading* expedition where he amassed his fortune through several unethical but highly amusing dodges; early in the saga he is directly described: "Thrand was red-haired, freckle-faced, handsome in looks."[43] A little later the saga offers another portrait of Þrándr, which (despite some conflict with the earlier passage) gives a fuller picture: "Thrand was a big man, red-haired and red-bearded, freckled, hard-faced, dark in his ways, sly and shrewd enough for any trickery, high-handed and ill-natured with common people, soft-spoken with the more important men, and always two-faced."[44] Whichever description is original, Þrándr was clearly conceived as the shifty red-headed man of the medieval proverbs.

Sigmundr is a generation younger, handsome, popular, frank and open, generous, honest, brave and strong, but not very careful. Above all, it is Sigmundr who is commissioned by King Óláfr Tryggvason to bring Christianity to the Faroes, and that confrontation with Þrándr, falling just in the middle of the saga, forms a stage in their long conflict.[45] In his first effort to convert the islanders, Sigmundr was thwarted by a trick of Þrándr's. Later he was successful in converting Þrándr only by using force; even so his behavior was unwisely charitable; as his cousin truly predicted: "Your death and your friends' death, says Thorir, if Thrand is let off now."[46]

In preparation for his great evangelical effort King Óláfr Tryggvason had recalled Sigmundr, then still unbaptized, to Norway, and in an extraordinary speech, he establishes a parallelism, a sort of secular typology, between himself and Sigmundr:

---

43. Johnston, p. 19; Finnur Jónsson, p. 1, n. 14: "Þrándr var rauðr á hár ok freknóttr í andliti, fríðr sýnum." Ólafur Halldórsson, p. 56.

44. Johnston, pp. 124–25; Finnur Jónsson, p. 4: "Þrándr var mikill maðr vexti, raudr á hár ok freknóttr, greppligr í ásjónu, myrkr í skapi, slægr ok ráðugr til allra véla, ódæll ok illgjarn við alþýðu, blíðmæltr við hina meiri menn, en hugði jafnan flátt." For the textual problems here, see Finnur Jónsson, p. 1, n. 14, Ólafur Halldórsson, pp. 60–61, n. 3, and Johnston, pp. 124–25.

45. Johnston, chapters 29–30; Finnur Jónsson, chapters 30–31; Ólafur Halldórsson, chapters 30–31.

46. Johnston, p. 68; Finnur Jónsson, p. 49: "Þórir mælti: 'þat er þinn bani ok þinna vina, ef Þrándr gengr nú undan." Ólafur Halldórsson, p. 118.

Some men, moreover, consider that fellowship between us two would be not unbecoming because we are both considered not unvaliant, and we both suffered teen and trouble for a long while before we achieved the honour that was owing to us, for some things have happened to us two not unlike in exile and oppression: You were a child and looked on when your father was killed without cause, and I was in my mother's womb when my father was treacherously killed, without cause....[47]

Óláfr continues with a version of Sigmundr's life-story, emphasizing that his luck is the gift of God, and then with his own parallel auto-biography or *ævisaga*, concluding:

Now it has come round at last that we two have each come back into our patrimony and to our parent soil instead of long lacking of happiness and honour. And so mostly because of what I have heard, that you have never worshipped a carved god as other heathen men do, I have good hope that the high King of Heaven, maker of all things, may bring you to the knowledge of His heavenly name and holy faith through my persuasion, and make you partaker with me in the true belief just as you are in might and manly skills and other of His manifold gifts of grace, which He has bestowed on you as He did on me long before I had any knowledge of His glory.[48]

Finally Óláfr urges that Sigmundr follow his example as missionary: "Now may the same Almighty God grant that I may bring you to

---

47. Johnston, p. 63; Finnur Jónsson, pp. 45–46: "Er þat ok mál sumra manna, at okkarr félagskapr sé eigi óviðkœmiligr sakir þess, at vit erum nú báðir kallaðir eigi óhreystiligir, en þolat lengi áðr vás ok vandræði en vit fengim okrar eiginligar sœmðir, þvíat okkr hafa sumir hlutir eigi ólíkt at boriz í útlegð ok ánauð. Þú vart barn ok sátt upp á, er faðir þinn var drepinn saklauss, en ek var í móðurkviði, er minn faðir var sviksamliga drepinn útan alla sǫk." Ólafur Halldórsson, pp. 112–13.

48. Johnston, p. 64; Finnur Jónsson, pp. 46–47: "Nú er svá komit um síðir, at hvárr-tveggi okkar hefir ǫðlaz sína fǫðurleifð ok fóstrland eptir langan missi sælu ok sœmðar. Nú allra helzt fyrir þá skyld, er ek hefi spurt, at þú hafir aldri blótat skurðgoð eptir hætti annarra heiðinna manna, þá hefi ek góða ván á, at hinn háleiti himna-konungr, skapari allra hluta, muni þik leiða til kynningar síns helga nafns ok heilagrar trúar af mínum fortǫlum ok gera þik mér samfélaga í réttum átrúnaði svá sem jafnat at afli ok allri atgǫrvi ok ǫðrum sínum margfǫldum miskunnargjǫfum, er hann hefir þér veitt sem mér lǫngum tíma fyrr en ek hafða nǫkkura vissu af dýrð hans." Ólafur Halldórsson, pp. 113–14.

the true faith and the yoke of His service, so that you may by His grace and my example and urging bring unto His glory all your subjects...."[49]

In answer Sigmundr refers respectfully to his former lord, the dead pagan Earl Hákon, but continues: "But since I can perceive by the fairness of your entreaty that this belief which you proffer is in all respects brighter and more blessed than that which heathen men hold, then I am eager to follow your counsels and win your friendship; but I did not sacrifice to carved gods because long ago I saw that that religion was worthless, though I did not know a better."[50] Sigmundr is a Noble Heathen converted, and at least one of the components of Weber's "irreligiosity topos" clearly appears in his characterization.[51] But the further import of these remarkable speeches is to establish not only a direct connection but a kind of typological relation between the hero of the private fiction and the "world-historical character" of King Óláfr, and Óláfr's speech seems thoroughly imbued with the spirit of history as progressive repetition: Sigmundr's life has recapitulated his own and will continue "by my example."[52]

---

49. Johnston, p. 64; Finnur Jónsson, p. 47: "Nú veiti þat sá hinn sami alsvaldi guð, at ek gæta þik leitt til sannrar trúar ok undir hans þjónostu, svá at þaðan af megir þú með hans miskunn ok mínu eptirdœmi ok áeggjan leiða til hans dýrðar alla þína undirmenn." Ólafur Halldórsson, p. 114.

50. Johnston, p. 65; Finnur Jónsson, p. 47: "En svá sem ek skil af yðrum fagrligum fortǫlum, at þessi átrúnaðr, er þér hafið, er í alla staði fegri ok fagrligri en hinn, er heiðnir menn hafa, þá er ek fúss at fylgja yðrum ráðum ok eignaz yðra vináttu; ok fyrir því vilda ek eigi blóta skurgoð, at ek sá lǫngu, at sá siðr var ǫngu nýtr, þó at ek kynna ǫngvan betra." Ólafur Halldórsson, pp. 114–15.

51. In addition to Sigmundr's preconversion rejection of heathen gods, we can perhaps recognize a reflection of faith in one's own might and main in Óláfr's pious hope that God will "gera þik mér samfélaga í réttum átrúnaði svá sem jafnan *at afli ok allri atgørvi* ok ǫðrum sínum margfǫldum miskunnargjǫfum, er hann hefir þér veitt sem mér lǫngum tíma fyrr en ek hafða nǫkkura vissu af dýrð hans" (Finnur Jónsson; pp. 46–47).

52. Does the biblical Joseph cast his shadow on Sigmundr's youth ("your kinsmen cast to kill you ... and you were sold into slavery, or rather money was paid over to have you borne away and bound thrall and in this wise banished and bereft of your birthright and birth land, and you had no help in a strange country for a long while except what alms were offered you by unkindred men through His power and providence to whom all things are possible" [Johnston, p. 63]), the slaughter of the innocents and its Mosaic precursor loom behind Óláfr's own youth ("No sooner was I born than I was beset and ill treated ...," [Johnston, pp. 63–64])? Ólafur Halldórsson, "Nokkur sagnaminni í Færeyinga sögu," *Einarsbók: Afmæliskveðja til Einars Ól. Sveinssonar 12 desember 1969*, ed. Bjarni Guðnason, Halldór Halldórsson, and Jónas Kristjánsson ([Reykjavík]: Útgefendur nokkrir vinir, 1969), pp. 260–66, parallels the exile of Sigmundr and Þórir and the later

The parallels continue through Sigmundr's evangelical mission and his death a few years after Óláfr's; of the interregnum between the two Óláfrs, the saga reports:

> Now Christianity went on in the Faroes as elsewhere in the lands of the Earls, everyone lived as he liked, but the Earls themselves kept their faith well.
>
> Sigmund kept his faith well, and all his household, and he had a church built at his steading.
>
> They say that Thrand pretty well throws off his faith, and so do all his companions.[53]

But Sigmundr is neither a cardboard figure nor a mere calque of Óláfr. From the beginning his association with Óláfr is shaded by Sigmundr's reluctance to renounce his former lord, Óláfr's predecessor the pagan Earl Hákon: "It is known to you, my lord, for you touched on it in your talk, that I was bound in service to Earl Hakon; he showed me great favour, and I was well satisfied with my service, for he was gracious and good in counsel, generous and glad-hearted with his friends, however fierce and treacherous he may have been toward his enemies, though there is a long way between your faith and his."[54] Later the king asked Sigmundr to give him a certain bulky arm-ring: "I shall not part with this, says Sigmundr, because when Earl Hakon gave me the ring, with much feeling, I promised that I would not part with it, and I shall keep my word, because the giver, as the Earl was, seemed good to me then, and he did well for me in many ways."[55] Óláfr did not take this reply well and predicted that

---

revenge for their father with various similar tales, for example from the cycle of Hrólfr kraki.

53. Johnston, p. 72; Finnur Jónsson, pp. 52–53: "Nú fór um kristni í Færeyjum sem víðara annarstaðar í ríka jarla, at hverr lifði sem vildi, en þeir sjálfir heldu vel sína trú. Sigmundr helt vel trú sína ok alt lið hans ok lét kirkju gera á bœ sínum. Þat er sagt frá Þrándi, at hann kastar raunmjǫk trú sinni ok allir hans kumpánar." Ólafur Halldórsson, p. 123.

54. Johnston, p. 65; Finnur Jónsson, p. 47: "þat er yðr kunnigt herra, sem þér kómuð við áðan í yðru máli, at ek var þjónostubundinn Hákoni jarli, veitti hann mér gott yfirlæti, ok unða ek þá allvel mínu ráði, þvíat hann var hollr ok heilráðr, ǫrlyndr ok ástúðligr vinum sínum, þó at hann væri grimmr ok svikall óvinum sínum; en langt er á milli ykkars átrúnaðar." Ólafur Halldórsson, p. 114.

55. Johnston, p. 70; Finnur Jónsson, p. 51: "Eigi mun ek þessum lóga, segir Sigmundr, því hét ek Hákoni jarli, þá er hann gaf mér hringinn með mikilli ǫlúð, at ek munda honum

the pagan earl's gift would cause Sigmundr's death: "And never again afterward did the King become as free-hearted with Sigmundr as before," although they parted in friendship.[56] In this theme we may recognize the kind of "resistance" that Schach discussed, whether it is taken as signifying a flaw or integrity of character, but the effect of combining the type "noble heathen converted" with the "reluctant Christian" is to give Sigmundr some complexity and depth of character. Óláfr was killed in battle against Earls Sveinn and Eiríkr, leaders of a partly pagan reaction in the year 1000; Sigmundr reached an accommodation with the Earls, who were not themselves pagans, but by about 1005 Sigmundr had been brutally murdered—for the fatal arm-ring.[57]

So even though Sigmundr is slain three-fourths of the way through the saga and Þrándr lives on, it is clear that, like King Óláfr Tryggvason, the future belongs to Sigmundr and his ways; and this is worked out in the narrative of the second part of the saga where, during the reign of St. Óláfr, when Christianity was restored permanently in Norway, and during that of Magnús Óláfsson, the heirs of Sigmundr stamp out the faction of Þrándr, and the old trickster dies, the saga says, of

---

eigi lóga, ok þat skal ek ok efna, þvíat góðr þótti mér nautrinn er jarl var ok vel gerði hann við mik marga hluti." Ólafur Halldórsson, p. 121.

56. Johnston, p. 70; Finnur Jónsson, p. 52: "en þetta tal fell niðr, ok var konungr aldri jafnblíðr sem áðr til Sigmundar." Ólafur Halldórsson, p. 121.

57. Ólafur Halldórsson, "Sagnaminni," pp. 272–73, addresses two close parallels to Sigmundr's death; there are also general ones (e.g., *Ragnars saga loðbrókar*, ch. 1); but one other particularly close parallel lends force to the notion that Sigmundr's resistance to Óláfr was the ultimate cause of his death, for one version of *Steins þáttr Skaptasonar* ends as follows: "En þau urðu ævilok hans, at hann braut skip sitt við Jótlandssíðu ok komsk einn á land. Han var þá enn skrautliga búinn ok hafði mikit fé á sér ok var dasaðr mjǫk. Kona nǫkkur fann hann, er fór með klæði til þváttar. Hon hafði vífl í hendi. Hann var máttlítill ok lá í brúki. Hon sá, at hann hafði mikit fé á sér. Síðan fór hon til ok barði hann í hel með víflinni ok myrti hann til fjár, at því er menn segja eða hyggja um. Gafsk honum svá af ofmetnaði ok óhlýðni við Óláf konung." *(Íslendinga þættir*, ed. Guðni Jónsson [Reykjavík, 1945], p. 266; "But the end of his life was that his ship was wrecked on the west coast of Jutland, and he alone reached land. At that time he was still dressed in a showy fashion and had a lot of valuables on him, and he was very exhausted. A certain woman found him when she was going to wash clothes; in her hand she had a club for beating the washing. He was faint and lay among clumps of seaweed. She saw that he had a lot of valuables on his person. Then she walked up and beat him to death with the club and hid the body to get the valuables, according to what is said and conjectured about it. That's how it turned out for him because of his presumption and disobedience to King Óláfr." Cf. Johnston, pp. 78–79; Finnur Jónsson, p. 57; Ólafur Halldórsson, pp. 131–32).

grief. Sigmundr is one of the sterling heroes of the saga literature, but I do not mean to imply that the stiff-necked old wizard Þrándr is not much the more interesting character; and the author does treat Þrándr with affectionate humor despite his treachery. The famous episode of Þrándr's credo is the best brief demonstration of that.[58]

Of more symmetrically bipartite construction is the *Qgmundar þáttr dytts ok Gunnars helmings*, a short story that radically breaches the primitive biographical unity usually (and wrongly) expected of the saga literature.[59] The first half concerns Qgmundr and the second Gunnarr; originally the parts will have been drawn from separate bodies of story material, but we find them brilliantly fused by a central scene in which the heroes of the two parts meet as strangers and exchange cloaks, literally passing the "mantle of hero" from Qgmundr to Gunnarr. The first part takes place mostly in the last years of Earl Hákon, the last pagan ruler, the second part, in the first years of King Óláfr Tryggvason; the exchange of cloaks took place just after the conversion of Norway or about 996. A single theme is common to both parts of the þáttr: the testing, apparent failure, and ultimate success of a young man; but in the first part Qgmundr is tested against a set of social expectations that may be abbreviated as "the heroic ethic," while in the second part Gunnarr appears at first to be a renegade Christian but at last proves true to Christianity and to its representative King Óláfr—in other words, he is tested against a "Christian ethic."

The comic pattern of this short story is mirrored in tragedy on a grand scale in the equally bipartite *Njáls saga*, probably the supreme artistic realization of the idea of Northern history as turning on the conversion and of the implications of this idea in the lives of individuals.[60] The

---

58. Johnston, ch. 54; Finnur Jónsson, ch. 56; Ólafur Halldórsson, ch. 57. Cf. Peter Foote, "Þrándr and the Apostles," and "A Note on Þránd's *kredda*," in his *Aurvandilstá: Norse Studies*, ed. Michael Barnes, Hans Bekker-Nielsen, and Gerd Wolfgang Weber (Odense, 1984), pp. 188–208 (with postscript; original publication 1969). Other important critical literature on the saga includes Foote, "On the Saga of the Faroe Islanders," in *Aurvandilstá*, pp. 165–88 and Ólafur Halldórsson, pp. 32–45. My interpretation is at variance with Erik Skyum-Nielsen, "Færeyingasaga—Ideology Transformed into Epic," in the papers of the International Saga Conference, Reykjavík 2–8 August 1973. Not accessible to me here at Cornell is Klaus Guldager, *Færinge saga som eksempel på ideologi i det islandske Middelaldersamfund* (Odense: Centerboghandelen, 1975).

59. See my "*Qgmundar þáttr dytts ok Gunnars helmings*: Unity and Literary Relations," *ANF*, 90 (1975), 156–82 [Reprinted in this volume, Eds.].

60. Harris, "*Qgmundar þáttr*," pp. 179–80.

saga comprises five major narrative blocks, Unnr's dowry, the quarrel of the wives Hallgerðr and Bergþóra, the feud leading to Gunnarr's death, the feud leading to Njáll's death, and finally the revenge on the burners leading to the reconciliation of Flosi and Kári. Early scholarship recognized the slight narrative connection between the first three blocks and the last two by speaking of an original "Gunnars saga" having been joined to an original "Njáls saga." It is no libel on the well-established artistic unity of the whole work to recognize the two analogous feud structures separated (very approximately) by the great digression on the Icelandic conversion;[61] and (as in the bipartite story of Ǫgmundr and Gunnarr helmingr) this structural symmetry in *Njáls saga* inevitably throws into contrast a pre-Christian "heroic" culture and the earliest phase of a Christian ethic, though its portrayal of the period before the conversion is of course more complex and sympathetic than that of the þáttr. Gunnarr's life, set in pre-Christian times, is worked out in terms of a heroic ethic: a martial man of honor, he loses his life fighting against odds through the operation of fate, the envy of lesser men, and a certain strain of hubris. He lives on after death, happy enough in his funeral mound.

To some extent the structure of Njáll's story, the second half of the saga, replicates that of Gunnarr in the first, but the parallelism highlights the differences: Njáll's fall takes place in Christian times with the attendant deeper meaning of action expressed in Flosi's moving words about Christian responsibility just before the burning and in Njáll's pregnant words about a future life. In terms of Northrop Frye's still satisfying categories, we may contrast *Njála* and *Ǫgmundar þáttr* as tragedy and comedy: as the stories of Ǫgmundr and Gunnarr helmingr confirm the heroic and Christian codes through comedy, the integration of the hero into society, so *Njála* ratifies them through tragedy, the isolation of the heroes, Gunnarr of Hlíðarendi and Njáll of Bergþórs-hváll, in death.[62]

---

61. As in T. M. Andersson, *The Icelandic Family Saga: An Analytic Reading* (Harvard Studies in Comparative Literature, 28, Cambridge, Mass., 1967). On the details of the integration of the Conversion see Ian Maxwell, "Pattern in *Njáls saga*," *SBVS*, 15 (1957–61), 17–47, especially pp. 37–44. My interpretation is in close agreement with Lönnroth, *Njáls saga*, especially Chapter IV "The Clerical Mind."

62. For an extension of this argument to the bipartite þættir *Svaða þáttr ok Arnórs kerlinganefs* and *Þórhalls þáttr knapps*, see Harris "*Ǫgmundar þáttr*," pp. 177–79.

However, the two parallel parts of *Njála* do not, in my opinion, exist in a static balance, such as Tolkien attributed to the bipartite structure of *Beowulf,* because they are caught up in a genuine historical sequence. Instead it seems that in the basic plan of the saga the familiar *topos* of *fortitudo et sapientia,* a formula balanced and static by nature, has been interpreted in a dynamic sense as terms of a historical dialectic. The extensive description of the conversion, really the center and hinge of the saga, ends the glorious pagan past in which Gunnarr, *exemplum fortitudinis,* embraced his fate, and introduces the era of Christian *sapientia,* exemplified in the parallel tragedy of Njáll the Wise.[63] The saga's second great digression, the Battle of Clontarf in 1014, marks with drama and supernatural portents the end of the heroic period in the death-throes of paganism.

The world of Gunnarr and Njáll presents a "rich and awesome dichotomy" in motion, calquing (I would suggest) in imitative form the "thesis" and "antithesis" of historical dialectic, conceived of course according to *Heilsgeschichte* rather than Hegel. The saga's concluding "synthesis," then, is peopled by figures still heroic but of lesser proportions. The revenge on the burners leads the opponents Kári and Flosi on parallel paths to Rome and back; and with their sudden reconciliation at the end, the private action completes a descent to the flatlands of social community. With this long coda and the concluding reconciliation the author has managed to suggest the outcome of the dialectic of history and with Flosi and Kári, the survivors, admirable but more nearly ordinary men, to indicate a convergence of the two virtues of the topos in the middle way of the future.

It is significant that almost all the feud sagas conclude with a decline from socially disruptive action to community and from heroic to lay figures.[64] The inevitable comparison with Scott's famous middling protagonist—Waverley and Morton are the best examples—suggests

---

63. This point is anticipated by at least two scholars, Michael Chesnutt, "Popular and Learned Elements in the Icelandic Saga-Tradition," *Proceedings of the First International Saga Conference,* University of Edinburgh 1971, ed. Peter Foote, Hermann Pálsson, and Desmond Slay (London: Viking Society for Northern Research, University College London, 1973), pp. 53–54 and Carol J. Clover, *"Njáls saga,"* forthcoming in *Dictionary of the Middle Ages,* but is also in my *The King and the Icelander: A Study in the Short Narrative Forms of Old Icelandic Prose,* Diss. Harvard (1969), pp. 111–14.

64. The first statement of this idea is probably in Andersson, "Displacement."

that an audience could identify with these men closer to themselves in time and stature and through figures like Kári and Flosi and Þorsteinn Egilsson could imagine the world of Njáll and Gunnarr and Egill Skallagrímsson. In any case, even Scott did not surpass the *Njála* author in realizing and almost symbolizing his vision of the plot of history in his private fictions and in harmonizing private with public history.

I suggested earlier a political aspect of the paradigm of old and new in the sagas.[65] The period of settlement, 870–930 in the traditional chronology, was frequently portrayed in terms of heroic defiance of the tyranny of King Haraldr Fairhair. Haraldr fulfilled his vow to become the first *einvaldskonungr,* sole king over a united Norway, and this brought him into conflict with the older independent aristocracy and free farmers as well as with the petty kings and their clans. Icelandic historians presented this as the clash of a relatively modern idea of the state with ancient liberties; many families were forced to save their dignity by emigration, itself a defiance of Haraldr. The emigrants transferred the ancient system to Iceland where, despite sporadic attempts of the Norwegian kings to establish sovereignty, it survived well into the thirteenth century.

Egils saga Skallagrímssonar is, of course, the greatest and most direct expression of this—call it "imperial"—aspect of the view of history in the family sagas. The main plot is, as in most of the family sagas, a feud, not however a feud between private persons or families but between Egill's family and that of King Haraldr. The private plot is here part and parcel of the plot of history: the ancient way of life represented by Egill, his father Skallagrímr, and his grandfather Kveldúlfr is strange and powerful but fated to make way before Haraldr's sole sovereignty, his taxes, and his new men; the saga clearly treats Egill as the last of an epoch. With his old age, the theme of opposition to the Norwegian throne is allowed to lapse, but in the purely Icelandic setting of the close of the saga it remains clear that the old man is the last of his kind. His son and son-in-law were baptized when Christianity came to the country; and the pastness of Egill's age is suggested when much later his outsized bones are exhumed

---

65 Cf. Schach and Weber, cited above.

and a trial axe-blow proves ineffectual on the great skull: "... from that anybody could guess that the skull wouldn't be easily cracked by small fry while it still had skin and flesh on it. Egill's bones were re-interred on the edge of the graveyard at Mosfell."[66] The author might almost have added that there were giants on the earth in those days, for his treatment of the troll-like Egill humorously melds admiration and abhorrence: his stand against the king is heroic but extreme, his defense of his rights grades into fanaticism, at the end in Iceland he is at once a great patriarch and an *ójafnaðarmaðr* or tyrant.[67] Like Scott's extreme characters—Fergus MacIvor, Redgauntlet, Burley, Cedric the Saxon—Egill offers much to admire and much to blame or ridicule, but again as with the comparable figures from Scott, our ultimate point of view and that of the thirteenth-century audience is conditioned by the irony of history.

An important question would be to what extent the political theme in *Egils saga* and elsewhere is a conscious transposition into the past of a thirteenth-century issue, the Norwegian imperialism that increasingly encroached on the Iceland of the saga-writing period and at last led to the recognition of Norwegian sovereignty in the years 1262–64. Did the author of *Egils saga,* for example, have the specific contemporary situation of the decade 1220–30 in mind, or is the political theme of the saga simply an expression of the general historical conception underlying this and other sagas? The Swedish critic Hans O. Granlid calls a similar question as applied to the classical and modern historical novel the "analogy problem"; he finds there a spectrum from lack of concern with an "analogy" in most of Scott to high consciousness of "analogy" in many serious modern works, and this feature usually coincides with a gradation of historical

---

66. *Egil's Saga,* tr. Hermann Pálsson and Paul Edwards (Harmondsworth, 1976), p. 238; *Egils saga Skalla-Grímssonar,* ed. Sigurður Nordal, Íslenzk fornrit 2 (Reykjavík, 1933), p. 299: "ok má af slíku marka, at hauss sá mundi ekki auðskaddr fyrir hǫggum smámennis, meðan svǫrðr ok hold fylgði. Bein Egils váru lǫgð niðr í útanverðum kirkju-garði at Mosfelli." Cf. Maxwell's eloquent commentary: "That terrible relic, coming up out of the earth in a Christian and comparatively civilized countryside, gathered into itself all that the saga had been saying about the grim world before the change of faith, and its power was in proportion to its commonplaceness" ("Pattern," p. 21).

67. Cf. Kaaren Grimstad, "The Giant as a Heroic Model: The Case of Egill and Starkaðr," *SS,* 48 (1976), 284–98; Preben Meulengracht Sørensen, "Starkaðr, Loki og Egill Skallagrímsson," in *Sjötíu ritgerðir helgaðar Jakobi Benediktssyni 20 júlí 1977,* ed. Einar G. Pétursson and Jónas Kristjánsson (Reykjavík, 1977), II, 759–68.

accuracy.[68] Some Icelandic scholars have, in fact, interpreted *Njáls saga* and *Hrafnkels saga* as virtually *romans à clef* that refer to similar private events in the thirteenth century,[69] and there are a number of well-known and noncontroversial examples of intrusion of thirteenth-century events, more or less veiled, into the accounts of life in the Saga Age.[70] When the intrusions are matters of law, we seem to be dealing with simple anachronism;[71] but when social ideology, from revulsion with the violence of the Sturlung Age to class struggle, colors the interpretation of the past, the result is of more literary interest and not far from "analogy" in the historical novel. In fact, the projection of a current social problem onto the past could itself amount to a historical theory, but the younger generation of Marxist-influenced critics in Iceland, besides being divided among themselves, have not taken this general view of the class conflicts and social analyses they are persuasively arguing for the family sagas.[72]

In my opinion Granlid's formulation with the phrase "analogy problem" is not the happiest one either for the classical historical novel or for the sagas. The concept suggests a *merely* analogical relationship and almost denies the consecutive causal connection between present and past that is the particular strength of the best historical fiction. Scott avoided merely tricking out a contemporary problem in antique dress, and despite some anachronisms, I am not convinced that construction of socio-political analogies is a major mode in the sagas. Instead the sagas, at their best, organically connect

---

68. Hans O. Granlid, "Das Analogieproblem im historischen Roman," *Nordeuropa*, 1 (1966), 49–62, and *Då som nu. Historiska romaner i översikt och analys* (Stockholm, 1964), especially pp. 304–06. Cf. Fleishman, passim, especially pp. xii, xv, 13–14.

69. Barði Guðmundsson, *Höfundur Njálu* (Reykjavík, 1958); Hermann Pálsson, *Hrafnkels saga og Freysgyðlingar* (Reykjavík, 1962). See Carol Clover's survey of saga scholarship for a full account of these trends (note 1 above).

70. For example, the incident in *Laxdœla saga* in which a killer dries blood from the murder weapon with a widow's apron (chapter 55) seems to be based on an actual event of 1244; Andreas Heusler, review of Johannes van Ham, *Beschouwingen over de Literaire Betekenis der Laxdoela Saga*, in his *Kleine Schriften*, ed. Helga Reuschel, I (Berlin, 1969), 364 (original review 1932). Cf. Clover's survey (n. 1).

71. E.g., Alan Berger, "Old Law, New Law, and *Hœnsa-Þóris saga*," *Scripta Islandica*, 27 (1976), 3–12. Cf. Clover's survey (n. 1).

72. E.g., Njörður P. Njarðvík, "Laxdæla saga en tidskritik?," *ANF*, 86 (1971), 72–81; Vésteinn Ólason, "Concentration of Power in Thirteenth-Century Iceland and Its Reflection in Some Íslendingasögur," in the papers of the International Saga Conference, Reykjavík, 2–8 August 1973. Cf. Clover's survey (n. 1).

their audience with the past by stories involved with historical forces that shaped the present—forces interpreted according to a thirteenth-century analysis, of course.

If a thirteenth-century Icelander had expressed himself about his relationship to the past of the Saga Age, it could not have been in a formulation such as "analogy problem" or the "necessary anachronism" of Hegel and Lukács (and Goethe):[73] he would have spoken of stories of his ancestors, and it is clear that the role played for, say, Scott's audience by national consciousness in connecting the past and the present is in thirteenth-century Iceland played, *in the first instance,* by genealogy. Thus, while Egill is the last of a heroic age, he is not the last of his family. A recent article on "Beginnings and Endings in the Icelandic Family Sagas" emphasizes the function of genealogical framing as anchoring the stories in Icelandic history: "Saga narrative technique suggests that writers worked by looking at the span of Icelandic history from settlement to their own times, and composed by running an eye along the whole length, usually along one blood line ... Reaching the main action chronologically, the writer deals with it, trying (in so far as possible) to trace the action to the return of social equilibrium ... and thus works outward from the plot back into the historical continuum which, by common knowledge, comes down genetically to his own audience."[74] Explicit historical analysis in terms of institutions extended at least to "Christendom" and "kingship," but for the medieval Icelandic everyman historical forces were probably felt as operating through his direct tie with the past, the blood lines. Thus, at the end of *Egils saga* the two strands, dark and light, ugly and handsome, of Egill's family—earlier established as different types with different relations to the kingship, though both fated—are alluded to and the distinction extended toward the present, with the significant qualification: "but most of the men of Myrar were outstandingly ugly."[75]

Instead of an "analogy," then, in the sense of a contemporary problem transposed arbitrarily to a previous period, the best sagas

---

73. Lukács, especially pp. 60–63.

74. Kathryn Hume, *MLR*, 68 (1973), 594–606, citation p. 605.

75. Pálsson and Edwards, p. 239; Nordal, p. 300: "en fleiri váru Myramenn manna ljótastir."

seem to present a situation in the past which contains the *seeds* of the saga-writer's present. However, a better case for a specific "analogy," which is nevertheless of a historical rather than local-social sort, could probably be made in connection with the thirty-odd short stories that trace the dealings of an Icelander abroad with a Norwegian king. Despite a shared narrative pattern, in which a visiting Icelander is estranged from and then reconciled with the Norwegian king, there is a great deal of variety in these stories. Two of them contain, within the common, genre-bound narrative framework, enclosed conversion tales, like those we have already glanced at, quite skillfully coordinated with the main plot.[76] As a group these stories have a more religious complexion than the subject matter and generic form would suggest;[77] the "analogy problem," however, emerges most clearly as proud and humorous Icelandic self-portraits in a series of underdog heroes who assert themselves against Norwegian court prejudice and hold up their heads in the royal presence. In many of this group it seems reasonable to see projection of contemporary wishes onto stories set in the past, in, for example, *Gull-Ásu-Þórðar þáttr, Halldórs þáttr II,* and *Sneglu-Halla þáttr,* but aspects of Icelandic self-assertion can be seen in almost all.[78]

I have tried to give some instances of the stories that treat Saga Age history in terms of conversion in isolation from those that emphasize the spread of royal power, but the distinction cannot often be maintained.[79] These two aspects of the new order are closely related throughout the literature, but are especially close in a saga like *Færeyinga saga,* where Þrándr is identified with provincial resistence to the crown and Sigmundr's mission of conversion is closely bound up with the payment of tribute to Norway. The close relation of these two "themes" suggests that a possible contemporary historiographical source for the view of the Saga Age I have been describing, a source beyond the general ones already offered, would be the standard European ideas of history as *translatio studii* and *translatio imperii.*[80]

---

76. *Egils þáttr Síðu-Hallssonar* and *Þorvalds þáttr tasalda* in *Íslendinga þættir.*

77. Cf. my "Theme and Genre" (n. 1 above).

78. "Theme and Genre," especially n. 40.

79. Weber shows how the political ideal of freedom has deep roots in Christianity (especially pp. 497–505).

80. A standard treatment is E. R. Curtius, *European Literature and the Latin Middle Ages,* trans. W. R. Trask (New York and Evanston, 1953; original 1948), pp. 28–30.

Snorri Sturluson gives a classic Icelandic instance of the *topos* of transmission of civilization or learning in his Preface to the *Prose Edda,* but in general, I think, the Icelanders differed from the Latin Middle Ages in harboring ambiguous feelings about the advance of *studium* and surely about the advance of *imperium,* feelings, I have to point out, like those that divided Walter Scott.

Nor did the saga authors have equally clear, compelling, and weighty analyses for the ideas of empire and conversion: Egill's scorn-pole stands more isolated as a symbol of the political theme than the all-pervasive, if habitually unstated, contrast of hammer and cross. This is not to say that even the recent trend in criticism toward ever greater recognition of Christian thought in the sagas could read them as glosses on the Beatitudes; yet the *historical* aspect of the Sermon on the Mount might not be so inappropriate a point of comparison: "You have heard that it was said by the men of old, 'You shall not kill ...' But I say that everyone who is angry with his brother shall be liable to judgment" (Mt. 5.17–48); "'... we must either abandon the attack, which would cost us our own lives, or we must set fire to the house and burn them to death, which is a grave responsibility before God, since we are Christian men ourselves'" *(Njáls saga).* The significance of such a comparison, however, would lie not in content (as suggested by particular textual juxtapositions) but in the broad structure of a historical vision that presented Christ and, perforce, the Church as fulfilment of what was good and correction of what was bad under the Old Law. This is not to deny that we read the sagas rather for their "dramas of the will" than for Christian instruction, but the historical-Christian vision makes the choice unnecessary: "'Think not that I have come to abolish the law and the prophets; I have not come to abolish them but to fulfill them.'" The function of the palinode in mainstream European literature seems to be to facilitate the mystery of having cake and eating too, allowing the enjoyment of pagan values while "correcting" them just in time. In this light the pilgrimages that participate in the close of so many feuds serve as the sagas' palinodes.

Applied to our meditation on the metaphor of saga as historical novel the palinode principle dictates that we close by recognizing the analogy as no more than an analogy. Sagas are not historical novels, but it is remarkable that six centuries before Walter Scott a species of historical fiction grew up in Iceland that anticipates the historical novel in its ambiguous retrospective view of the passing of heroic ages, and the comparison at least throws into relief the knotty genre problems of the saga literature. But recent renewals of interest in the reception of the literature of the past might lead to the question whether the reversal of our analogy, "historical novel as saga," has more to offer than entertaining pastiche (Rider Haggard's *Saga of Eric Brighteyes)* or rousing adventure (John Buchan's *The Isle of Sheep)*. Both these examples lack a significant historical dimension, but among the possible lessons the historical novel might learn from the saga we might note: how to correlate a private plot with history, how to invest private individuals with historical significance, how to effect mimesis of history in genealogy and events of a plot, and how to cultivate objectivity and a claim to some kind of truth in the face of history. Luckily the question is one for other critics, but (to allay Steblin-Kamenskij's pretended anxiety that elementary literary history would be reversed) it appears that there is at least some possibility that Scott's reading of *Eyrbyggja saga* stimulated or crystallized his ideas for *Waverley* and that the saga thus stood godfather to the modern historical novel.[81]

---

81. John M. Simpson, "Scott and Old Norse Literature," in *Scott Bicentenary Essays: Selected Papers read at the Sir Walter Scott Bicentenary Conference,* ed. Alan Bell (Edinburgh and London, 1973), pp. 300–13, especially pp. 312–13; Edith C. Batho, "Sir Walter Scott and the Sagas: Some Notes," *MLR,* 24 (1929), 409–15.

Gender and Genre:

Short and Long Forms in the Saga Literature

Maðr er manns gaman.
Hávamál

The male world of the *þættir* (singular: *þáttr*) or short stories of the
Old Norse-Icelandic saga literature can be exemplified in a telling
form by the thirteenth- or fourteenth-century tale about Gestr of the
Norns, *Norna-Gests þáttr*.[1] The guest, a visitor from the distant pagan
and heroic past, finds his way to the court of the first Christian king
of Norway, Óláfr Tryggvason (the year would have been 998). An
atmosphere of tension accompanies the stranger, who is not Christian
but has been primesigned; and the mystery peaks when Gestr, challenged by a wager, produces a fragment of a golden saddle buckle
that had belonged to the ancient hero Sigurðr Fáfnisbani. Pressed for
an explanation, the old man begins his reminiscences of the heroic
age with the story of Sigurd's youth, including a minor incident in

---

1. Critical text in Ernst Wilken, ed., *Die prosaische Edda im Auszuge nebst Volsunga-saga und Nornagests-tháttr*, Theil I: Text (Paderborn, 1877), pp. 235–261. (Wilken's 2nd ed. rev. of 1912 omits the introductory discussions; cf. there pp. vi–vii.) There are two versions: *Flateyjarbok: En samling af norske konge-sagaer mid indskudte mindre fortæl-linger*, [ed. C. R. Unger and G. Vigfússon] 3 vols. (Christiania, 1860–68), I, 346–359; and *Norrøne skrifter af sagnhistorisk indhold*, ed. Sophus Bugge, I [=Det norske oldskriftselskabs samlinger, VI] (Christiania, 1864), 47–80 [from "S" (= MS. AM 62) with readings from *Flateyjarbók*]. See further Nora Kershaw (Chadwick), ed. and tr., *Stories and Ballads of the Far Past* (Cambridge, 1921), pp. 11–12 (pp. 14–37 translate "A", a text close to Wilken and *Flateyjarbók*); Friedrich H. von der Hagen, *Volsunga- und Ragnars-Saga nebst der Geschichte von Nornagest*, Altdeutsche und altnordische Helden-Sagen, vol. 3, 2nd ed. rev. Anton Edzardi (Stuttgart, 1880), pp. lxii–lxiv (pp. 345–397 translate Bugge's edition of S). The literature on the story is cited in Joseph Harris and Thomas D. Hill, "Gestr's 'Prime Sign': Source and Signification in Norna-Gests þáttr," *Arkiv för nordisk filologi* 104 (1989), 103–122.

which Gestr, then Sigurd's servant, acquired the buckle, and goes on to the story of Sigurd's death at the hands of his brothers-in-law. The next day Gestr's saga-telling continues with an account of Brynhildr's death and Gestr's experience with the sons of Ragnarr Loðbrók. The reminiscences conclude with the virtues of a series of six kings ranging from the fifth to the ninth centuries, all from Gestr's direct experience. Now Gestr volunteers the explanation of his destiny: when he was an infant, spae-wives *(nornir)* came to his home; the first two prophesied good, but the third said he should live no longer than the candle beside him would burn. He now carries the candle with him. Having lived three hundred years, he had come to Olaf to be baptized; and after a short period as one of the king's retainers, he quietly lighted his candle and expired in Olaf s presence.

Here Olaf s all-male court frames narratives from the pre-Christian past; the retainers and, especially, the king himself evaluate Gestr and his old stories against an implicitly masculine, Christian, and courtly standard, and the consummation of Gestr's life is acceptance into the retinue, baptism, and death in the very presence of the king as his candle burns out. The only "couple" here is obviously the lord and his loving warrior, but the story is not totally without women, for most of Gestr's old lore paraphrases Vǫlsung and Nibelung material which, of course, prominently concerns women—Sigrdrífa/Brynhildr, Guðrún, Grímhildr, Oddrún, Svanhildr—and could be described as a series of misalliances. Gestr's mysterious harping included a lay, "the ancient Wiles of Guðrún," but the centerpiece of his saga-telling was his account of Brynhild after Sigurd's murder, including a text of "Brynhild's Hell-ride" that deviates interestingly from that of Codex Regius of the Elder Edda. As Gestr concluded his account of Brynhild's pagan funeral, her flyting with a troll-woman, and this ogress's final shriek and leap from a cliff, the audience of retainers shouted "That's fine! Go on and tell us some more!"[2] But the king, mindful of their spiritual welfare, intervened: "You need not tell us any more about things of that kind," and continued: "Were you ever with the sons of Lothbrok?"[3] The only other women in *Norna-Gests þáttr* are the norns, the prophetic, semi-divine vagabonds, who determined Gestr's

---

2. Translations from Kershaw (Chadwick), here p. 33.
3. Kershaw (Chadwick), pp. 33–34.

fate ages ago, and Gestr's own mother who, like Meleager's, preserved her son's life-token, the candle.

In literature a long life, especially a supernaturally long life—we find the device from the early Old English *Widsith* to the Čapek-Janaček *Makropoulos Case*—is an opportunity to display a slice of history or history *tout court*,[4] and *Norna-Gests þáttr* presents its audience with a version of history in which different eras are corollated with different conceptions of "the couple." The most ancient pre-Christian stage begins with a family, but Gestr's father presides over a household which is the scene of a rite performed entirely by women; the religious atmosphere is primitive, pre-heroic, inhabited by nameless collective female powers to which the individual male is subject. The second stage features heroic individuals of both sexes, together with the tragic couples and triangles of the Vǫlsung-Nibelung stories; woman does not control fate, but in the person of Brynhild she participates fully in the heroic struggle against it. The gods are individual and male, disposal of the dead is by fire; in short, it is the pre-Christian heroic age. Olaf, however, puts an end to tales of cremation and proud, violent suicides and adultresses like Brynhild and pointedly turns the saga-telling to an all-male, military milieu verging on the Christian period: "Were you ever with the *sons* of Lothbrok?" And the remainder of Gestr's account of "history as I witnessed it" is a survey of kings and courts ending with the most Christian, Louis the Pious. The final stage, the framing setting in Olaf's court, implicitly stretches on to the writer's present.

Norna-Gests þáttr is not isolated in the saga literature; its analogues include a group of brief anecdotes in which Óðinn or some other representative of the pagan past entertains a Christian king and his men,[5] but it has a close twin in the *Tale of Tóki Tókason*.[6] Tóki was

---

4. For *Norna-Gests þáttr* in this connection see Friedrich Panzer, "Zur Erzählung von Nornagest," in *Vom Werden des deutschen Geistes: Festgabe Gustav Ehrismann...*, ed. Paul Merker and Wolfgang Stammler (Berlin and Leipzig, 1925), pp. 27–34, and Margaret Schlauch, "*Widsith*, *Víthförull*, and Some Other Analogues," *PMLA* 46 (1931), 969–987.

5. Discussed in Harris and Hill; an analogue omitted there is to be found in *Flateyjarbók*, II, 397–398: before vanishing into the sea Þórr tells tales of the past which include his slaying demonic women.

6. *Tóka þáttr Tókasonar* is found in *Flateyjarbók*, II, 135–138 and in *Fornar smásögur úr Noregs konunga sögum*, ed. Edwin Gardiner, with a foreword by Sir William A. Craigie (Reykjavík, 1949). Translations mine.

fated to live through two life-times and sought out St. Olaf to complete his primesigning with baptism, "and he wore his white baptismal clothing until his dying day." Tóki's saga-telling mentions no women and reflects only military *Männerbünde* comparable to Norna-Gestr's service with the sons of Lothbrok; though the setting is pre-Christian, the purpose in *Tóka þáttr* is less a contrast with the Christian present than a comparison of Hrólfr kraki, the great Danish hero-king, and his warriors, with the similar figure from Norway, Hálfr, and his comitatus, the Hálfsrekkar.

Further, we may be justified in seeing in a third story, *Þorsteins þáttr skelks*,[7] a less obvious analogue of this group of tales: The Icelander Þorsteinn is among Olaf Tryggvason's retinue on a progress; in the middle of a spooky winter night Þorsteinn went alone to the privy, an outhouse fitted with two rows of eleven seats. A devil popped up out of the innermost seat, identifying himself as a figure from the heroic age, Þorkell hinn þunni (Thorkel the Thin) who fell in the battle of Brávellir with King Haraldr Wartooth. Þorsteinn began asking him about the torments of Hell: no hero bears them better than Sigurd Fáfnisbani and none worse than Starkaðr the Old, who screams in pain. Now Þorsteinn begs the fiend to "Howl like Starkad, just for a little,"[8] and an escalating series of three mighty howls follows as the goblin moves several seats nearer with each howl. The last scream knocked Þorsteinn into a coma, but just then King Olaf had the church bell rung, and the devil fled groaning back down the privy. Þorsteinn had, of course, been playing for time and banking on the screeches waking King Olaf, who would know what to do. The folktale motif of the boy who does not know what fear is emerges in a concluding dialogue with the king in which Þorsteinn receives the new nickname of *skelkr* "shudder." Basically, however, this þáttr is a polished Christian satire on the old pagan heroes, conceived with real humor and realized in snappy dialogue that I have not tried to paraphrase. But the story is also, arguably, a parody of the type of story represented by *Norna-Gests þáttr* and *Tóka þáttr*.

---

7. Found in *Flateyjarbók* and *Fornar smásögur*; the literature on the story is cited in John Lindow, "*Þorsteins þáttr skelks* and the Verisimilitude of Supernatural Experience in Saga Literature," in *Structure and Meaning in Old Norse Literature: New Approaches to Textual Analysis and Literary Criticism,* ed. John Lindow, Lars Lönnroth, and Gerd Wolfgang Weber (Odense, 1986), pp. 264–280.

8. Translation by Jacqueline Simpson, *The Northmen Talk: A Choice of Tales from Iceland* (London and Madison, 1965), pp. 152–155, here p. 154.

Here the wanderer through time is not primesigned but a pagan hero; he does not enter the hall to stand before the king on his high seat but sidles up to a retainer on the toilet seat; his encounter with the Christian does not end with baptism, acceptance by the Männerbund, and death near the king, but with the plunge back into the privy (a kind of baptism!), rejection, and eternal life in suffering. In the architecture of the privy, travestying that of a noble hall, and in the devil's moving from seat to seat we might see parody of a motif like that of *Tóka þáttr* where the hero goes along the benches trying the strength of each retainer in order to find his level and his seat; the comparison of ancient heroes—a historical *mannjafnaðr* or comparison of men—reminds again of *Tóka þáttr*, while the vilification of Starkaðr in comparison with Sigurd is reminiscent of *Norna-Gests þáttr*. In any case, whether or not the parodistic reading is justified, it is certain that women are completely absent and the value structure of the story is based entirely on king, court, and muscular Christianity.

A cruder analogue, but a richer subject for gender analysis, is called *Sǫrla þáttr*.[9] We can recognize, as in *Norna-Gests þáttr*, three or four narrative segments that represent stages of history. The first is a mythic prelude in which the actors are the old gods, here distorted in another Christian satire, but this time a humorless one. Freyja is Odin's mistress; one day she sees where four dwarves are forging a magnificent necklace (elsewhere called the Brísingamen); they refuse to sell it but agree to give it to her in return for four nights of sex. Odin heard how Freyja had acquired the jewelry and determined to punish her by sending Loki to steal it; Loki managed this by turning into a fly, then a flea. Freyja begged Odin to return the necklace and he relented on condition that Freyja agree to cause a quarrel between certain kings who would live in the distant future; the fight was to be eternal unless "there be some Christian man so brave and so much favoured by the great good fortune of his liege lord that he shall dare to take arms and enter among the combatants and slay them."[10] Odin's conditions, of

---

9. *Flateyjarbók; Fornar smásögur;* and editions of the *fornaldarsögur.*

10. Translation by Kershaw (Chadwick). On connections between *Srlaþáttr* and *Þorsteins þáttr uxafóts (Flateyjarbók; Íslendinga þœttir,* ed. Guðni Jónsson [Reykjavík, 1945]) see Alan L. Binns, "The Story of Þorsteinn Uxafót," *Saga-Book of the Viking Society* 14 (1953-55), 36-60, esp. 38-42: Þorsteinn is the son of Ívarr ljómi and in one episode ends a feud between "dead" pagans by administering a lasting death; like the episode of Ívarr's intervention, Þorsteinn's is put into a Christian perspective.

course, predict the course of the rest of the story, a narrative trajectory ultimately modeled on salvation history. In this first, mythic stage of history, then, "the couple" is illegitimate, and woman is presented in her lowest form as bitch-goddess; foreknowledge and design of the future stem from the weak and immoral Odin but are carried out by the evil goddess. As in *Norna-Gests þáttr,* fate is female and can be broken only by a Christian man, a member of the king's Männerbund.

The second narrative stage is the pre-Christian heroic age which culminates in a version of the *Hjaðninga víg,* the widely-known story of Heðinn's elopement with Hildr, daughter of Hǫgni. Prefixed to this is the short but complicated *fornaldarsaga* of Sǫrli, a Norwegian viking, who slew King Hálfdan of Denmark to acquire his precious warship; later Sǫrli, accompanied by his own father, encountered the sons of Hálfdan, Hákon and Hǫgni, in battle. The only survivors of the two families were Sǫrli and Hǫgni; having orphaned each other, they became blood brothers, "and both remained true to their oaths as long as they lived."[11] When Sǫrli finally fell in one of his viking raids, Hǫgni avenged him. Sǫrli's story has a chaste all-male cast; the precious object is not acquired by Freyja's unpleasant means, and good clean violence leads to that most masculine of fantasies, the *Waffen-bruderschaft.* (More precisely, the fantasy is of a man's meeting his match in battle and, after fighting to a draw, creating a brotherhood of arms: this fantasy is found most famously, perhaps, in Gilgamesh's wrestling with Enkidu, but the violent inception of the friendship of Robin Hood and Little John also comes to mind.) The "couple" in this phase is not the king and his retainer but its more primitive prototype, the "warrior male" and his double—if I may borrow for a moment from the language of Klaus Theweleit in his *Männerphantasien.*[12] This stage of Hǫgni's life is free of women and woman-borne fate, but in the next phase of the story female elements re-enter.

Heðinn is a pirate-king of Serkland, imagined perhaps as the Barbary Coast. Alone in a forest he meets a goddess, whom we deduce to be Freyja though she calls herself by the valkyrie name Gǫndul. This scene and Heðinn's subsequent meetings with Gǫndul have a strongly

---

11. Kershaw (Chadwick), p. 48.

12. *Male Fantasies,* tr. Stephen Conway, Erica Carter, and Chris Turner, 2 vols. (Minneapolis, 1987–89; originally Verlag Roter Stern, 1977–78).

erotic aspect, but her charms are used with a purpose, to infect Heðinn with the desire to surpass King Hǫgni. When he arrives in Denmark, Heðinn is made welcome, and the two heroes compete to a draw in all manner of sporting tests; finally they swear blood-brotherhood and promise to share everything equally. But Sǫrli's model cannot be recreated with women on the scene to spoil the warrior idyll; we now learn that Hǫgni has a wife and as only child a daughter whom he loves exceedingly. And now Heðinn again encounters Gǫndul who gives him a drink of forgetfulness and reawakens his sense of emulation: for his honor's sake, she persuades him, he must do away with Hǫgni's wife and abduct the daughter Hildr by force. The author explains: "The wickedness and forgetfulness contained in the ale which Hethin had drunk had so got the better of him that there seemed to him to be no alternative, and he had not the slightest recollection that he and Högni were 'foster-brothers.'"[13] Meanwhile Hildr has seen the future in dreams and tries to reason with Heðinn but realizes that "in this case you are not your own master." The murder of the queen in a sort of sacrifice may pattern with the acquisition of a valued object in the first two parts of the þáttr; afterward Heðinn again meets Gǫndul, again drinks, falling asleep in her lap; Gǫndul devotes them all to Odin, and Heðinn awakens to catch a glimpse of her disappearing, "big and black." He now understands the evil he has done, but the murder has barred any retreat; the abduction and pursuit must proceed as in the traditional versions of the story.

Heðinn finally makes a stand on the island Hoy; when the two men meet, both seem to understand the agency behind the murder and abduction, but they embrace their doom with tragic nobility. Because of Freyja's evil magic any man slain in the battle would have to start up and fight again and again, and the torture of this battle lasted, not until Ragnark as in more traditional versions, but 143 years until the first year of King Olaf Tryggvason's reign in 995. Meanwhile Hildr, whose name means "battle" and who bears the blame for the *Hjaðninga víg* in more traditional versions—Hildr sat in a grove and watched. This third section of *Sǫrla þáttr*, then, is heroic in a full-blooded sense that makes it comparable to the Vǫlsung story in *Norna-Gests þáttr*: the setting is pre-Christian, men and women both have an opportunity to

---

13. Kershaw (Chadwick), pp. 51–52.

feel and to struggle gallantly. But the era is cursed and the "couple" is ill-fated; a wife and mother must be crushed beneath a viking ship, while an abducted bride must spend an immensely long wedding night watching her father and her husband, the would-be blood brothers, kill each other: male *Waffenbruderschaft* is wrecked by devilish pagan interference, an interference gendered female. These fundamentally noble heathens never have a chance against the corrupting sex and magic of the goddess.

The fourth and last section of the þáttr takes place in the early days of the Christian present and is briefly told: Olaf and his warrior retinue land on Hoy, and Ívarr ljómi, a good Christian strengthened by the luck of his king, has the honor of giving the *coup de grace* to Hǫgni, Heðinn, and all their good men. The theology of this conclusion is not learned, but death is presented as a release from torment, and the basic pattern of salvation history—divine intervention in the history of calamities that was the pagan world—is not hard to see. Interestingly enough no disposition of Hildr is mentioned; we are left with the image of her seated in a grove and watching the battle, and there she seems to belong. In the Christian present "the couple" is constituted by the king and his warrior Ívarr in the company of their comrades-at-arms.

The four stories mentioned so far show a common attitude toward history, religion, and gender, inclusion and exclusion, in short a common value structure. With this pattern established, let me pause briefly to place these short narratives in the context of the saga literature generally. The literary study of þættir might be said to begin with Wolfgang Lange's 1957 article "Einige Bemerkungen zur altnordischen Novelle."[14] Before Lange excellent historical and editorial work was done on individual stories, but glimpses of the place of short narratives in what Northrop Frye called "an order of texts" are few and far between.[15] The importance of Lange's modest article is that it brought precisely this sense of a literary-historical order to bear and first mooted questions of genre that continue to be fruitful. I had not discovered Lange, however, when I began working on the þáttr in 1967; my inspiration came instead from T. M. Andersson's newly published *The*

---

14. *Zeitschrift für deutsches Altertum* 88 (1957), 150–159.

15. Discussed or registered in Joseph Harris, "Genre and Narrative Structure in Some *Íslendinga þœttir*," *Scandinavian Studies* 44 (1972), 1–27, and in "Þættir," in *Dictionary of the Middle Ages*, ed. J. R. Strayer, vol. 12 (New York, 1989), pp. 1–6.

Icelandic Family Saga: An Analytic Reading.[16] Analysis of narrative structure gave me a key, I thought, to justifying some order among the hundreds of unordered short stories I had been reading in textual conglomerates such as *Morkinskinna* and *Flateyjarbók*; at the same time Andersson's method seemed to ignore or suppress all the fascinating problems of narratological theory and genre and so to be in need of supplementation. The subject of the short narrative forms blossomed from the end of the 1960s through the '80s, closely linked to the development of literary-theoretical interest in the saga literature generally.[17] Anyone who writes about short forms must have in mind some kind of contrast with long forms,[18] but beyond that general contrast any characterization of the þættir very quickly becomes characterization of one group of their texts. The same could be said of "saga"—how many brief references to "the saga" or "sagas" really refer only or principally to the family sagas? Despite theoretical gaps, however, the short narrative forms are now established as a particular set of themes within discourse on the saga literature. In evidence I would cite the most recent comprehensive history of Old Norse-Icelandic literature; Jónas Kristjánsson's *Eddas and Sagas: Iceland's Medieval Literature* from 1988 is a conservative work but the first to offer a separate chapter on þættir on the same level of organization as that of major genres such as the sagas of the Icelanders.[19] That is canonization!

The boundaries of the field, however, remain extremely vague. Most of the hundreds of short narratives in Old Norse-Icelandic are included within larger collections with a narrative arrangement; *Norna-Gests þáttr,* for example, is preserved as an episode in the longest of the biographies of Olaf Tryggvason *(Óláfs saga Tryggvasonar in mesta).* How can we tell what was an independent literary work, and wouldn't the very notion of independence—so central to our conception of literature—be a historically relative one?[20] Lange estimated the total corpus of þættir at over one hundred, but this

---

16. (Cambridge, Mass, 1967); the first result was a dissertation, "The King and the Icelander: A Study in the Short Narrative Forms of Old Icelandic Prose," Harvard 1969.

17. Bibliographical survey in Harris, "Þættir."

18. For interesting thoughts along these lines, see Mary Louise Pratt, "The Short Story: The Long and the Short of It," *Poetics* 10 (1981), 175–194.

19. Tr. Peter Foote (Reykjavík).

20. The problem is discussed but not solved in Joseph Harris, "Theme and Genre in Some *Íslendinga þættir*," *Scandinavian Studies* 48 (1976), 1–28 [reprinted in this volume, Eds.], and in "Þættir."

guess shows more courage than clarity of generic conception. The "ethnic" or native terminology does not offer a safe guide,[21] but some regions of the hazy terrain of the short narrative have been convincingly mapped. In my last taxonomical effort of this kind I recognized seven fairly well-defined groups of þættir that account for at least sixty stories.[22]

The kind of cultural-historical question raised by the present conference has scarcely been posed of this corpus of tales. There have been literary interpretations of individual þættir, of course, and I did discuss what Wellek and Warren called "inner form" in the best-known subgroup, thirty-one texts that chart the changing relationship of an Icelander with a Norwegian king: twenty-six seemed to have certain common denominators of "theme," seventeen having "humanistic" and nine "religious" themes; and by a still more general measure, that of Weltanschauung, these short forms seemed to embody a high-medieval "comic" ethos by comparison to the heroic and tragic ethos of the longer sagas.[23] Very recently Vésteinn Ólason has interrogated a small subset of þættir for "the self-image of the free man"; he finds that the "essence of these tales seems to be a solution to the contradiction that a 'free' man increases his honour and his worth by subordinating himself to another man, the king."[24] This analysis is fully convincing, but to the extent that Vésteinn Ólason has rightly captured the "essence" of the þættir, their promise as a mirror of "the making of the couple" seems slight. Here the saga literature once again seems to stand distinctly outside the mainstream of European literature, to be in respect to the "couple" quite unlike *fabliaux, Märchen, novelle,* or *Schwänke.* This conclusion runs counter to the Europeanizing trend in saga studies[25] and to the tendency of good essays by Walther Heinrich Vogt and Wolfgang Mohr on the "Wandel des Menschenbildes" from tragic to comic,

---

21. Ethnic and analytic genre terms were especially debated in three articles on "Genre in the Saga Literature" by T. M. Andersson, Lars Lönnroth, and Joseph Harris in *Scandinavian Studies* 47 (1975).

22. "Þættir."

23. "Theme and Genre."

24. "Den frie mannens selvforståelse i islandske sagaer og dikt," in *Medeltidens födelse,* Symposier på Krapperups Borg, 1, ed. Anders Andrén (Nyhamnsläge, 1989), pp. 277-286, here p. 285.

25. The trend is defined and reviewed by Carol J. Clover, "Icelandic Family Sagas (*Íslendingasögur*)," in *Old Norse-Icelandic Literature: A Critical Guide,* ed. Carol J. Clover and John Lindow, Islandica 45 (Ithaca, N. Y., 1985), esp. p. 251.

as attested, in part, by such stories as our þættir.[26] It even runs counter to my own just paraphrased generalizations on the medieval, rather than heroic ethos of þættir! But the contradiction is more apparent than real.—Let us return to the stories in search of "the couple" or its absence.

One recognizable generic nucleus[27] comprises tales that focus on the clash of pagan and Christian cultures in the conversion period. In some of the group this generic idea is realized in a precise and personal form: one of the evangelizing kings is brought into contact with heathens; after a conflict, the pagans are converted and integrated into Christian society[28]—unless the conversion element is negated and, like Rauðr inn rammi, the resistant pagan is martyred.[29] One instance of the standard pattern would be *Þáttr Eindriða ilbreiðs* where a Noble Heathen undergoes testing in sports in direct competition with the king; the result is not quite brotherhood, as in the comparable struggle of Heðinn and Hǫgni, for Olaf's superiority is divinely sponsored.[30] But the young man is baptized and received into the retinue: "and the king took him into his own company with the greatest affection. And Eindriði never parted with the king again as long as they both lived, and he was always thought the most splendid of men." The young hero is unmarried and never brought into contact with a woman, though he does honor the pleas of his mother and sister in the archery contest—a version of the international William Tell motif. Continental influence is patent in this tale,[31] but just as obviously the basic value system we have already explored is at play here: what counts is male, Christian,

---

26. Vogt, "Wandel im altnordischen Menschentum," *Preussisches Jahrbuch*, Sept. 1923, pp. 315–322; Mohr, "Wandel des Menschenbildes in der mittelalterlichen Dichtung," *Wirkendes Wort*, 1. Sonderheft (1952), pp. 37–48; rpt. *Wirkendes Wort: Sammelband II* (Düsseldorf, 1963).

27. Some discussion of the idea of genre implied in this phrase is to be found in "Genre and Narrative Structure," pp. 22–23.

28. This group of þættir is further discussed in Joseph Harris, "Folktale and Thattr: The Cas of *Rognvald and Raud*," in *Folklore and Medieval Studies*, ed. Carl Lindahl and Erika Brady (= *Folklore Forum* 13 [1980], 158–198), and in "Saga as Historical Novel," in *Structure and Meaning in Old Norse Literature*, pp. 187–219 [Reprinted in this volume, Eds.].

29. *Flateyjarbók* and *Fornar smásögur*.

30. *Flateyjarbók* and *Fornar smásögur*.

31. Perhaps Irish influence is ultimately behind the "feat" in which the king juggles knives while running around his moving ship on the oars.

and courtly; the highest good is to live and die with your king. The conversion group comprises at least twelve þættir; but not all stress the courtly Männerbund quite as much as our example. In one a mother urges compassion;[32] in another the only female character, a wife and mother, is instrumental in bringing the heathen father and son to God and to the king, and thus also in ending their estrangement from each other.[33] But in another story from this group, *Sveins þáttr ok Finns,* a divided family, apparently made up only of men, is restored to unity through conversion, but this time *without* female agency—clearly a story with the same value system we have been encountering.[34] The generational conflict that is often a concomitant of the conversion theme in the saga literature appears also in *Helga þáttr ok Úlfs,* which at least allows its single female a role in the family.[35] The three stories we have already examined, *Norna-Gests þáttr, Sǫrla þáttr,* and *Tóka þáttr,* are the best representatives of what in my taxonomy is a subgroup of conversion þættir in which the king is brought into contact with the heathen-heroic past; in a broader sense, however, any tale about conversion told from the vantage point of the securely Christian Middle Ages is an encounter between a doomed old order and a historically inevitable new order.

Finally, one tale from the conversion group constitutes an interesting exception to the absence of the "couple" as family; this is *Vǫlsa þáttr,* a spritely Christian satire with something of the air of Continental short-story forms.[36] It is easy for a modern audience to appreciate

---

32. *Svaða þáttr ok Arnórs kerlingarnefs* in *Flateyjarbók* and *Íslendinga þættir.*

33. *Rǫgnvalds þáttr ok Rauðs* in *Flateyjarbók* and *Fornar smásögur;* for literature on the story see Harris, "Folktale and Thattr."

34. In *Flateyjarbók* and *Fornar smásögur;* for literature see Elizabeth A. Rowe, "Searching for the Highest King: St. Christopher and *Þáttr Sveins ok Finns,*" forthcoming in *Arkiv för nordisk filologi* [105 (1990), 131–39. Eds.].

35. *Flateyjarbók* and *Fornar smásögur;* on generational conflict see Paul Schach, "Some Observations on the Generation-Gap Theme in the Icelandic Saga," *JEGP* 81 (1982), 196–203, and Harris, "Saga as Historical Novel."

36. *Flateyjarbók* and *Fornar smásögur;* cf. Harris, "Historical Novel"; for significant recent work on the þáttr see Gro Steinsland and Kari Vogt, "'Aukinn ertu Uolse ok vpp vm tekinn': En religionshistorisk analyse av *Vǫlsa þáttr* i *Flateyjarbók,*" *Arkiv för nordisk filologi* 96 (1981), 87–106; they understandably omit mention of the misleading Herbert S. Joseph, "Völsa Þattr: A Literary Remnant of a Phallic Cult," *Folklore* 83 (1972), 245–252. The classic analysis is still Andreas Heusler, "Die Geschichte von Völsi, eine altnordische Bekehrungsanekdote," *Zeitschrift des Vereins für Volkskunde,* 1903, pp. 24–39 (rpt. in *Kleine Schriften,* II, 372–387). Translations mine.

because its skillful construction, satirical tone, and humorous sense of the absurd readily appeal to our skeptical tastes. The simplicity of the central narrative, told in short simple sentences, as well as the domestic setting and cast of characters, are reminiscent of fairytales; the unsaga-like characters are anonymous types—except for the comic touch of a named dog of unnamed masters. A long tradition lies behind the extant text, but in the form left by the final author the story assaults pagan superstition from a position of Christian rationalism with little overt moralizing. The message is principally embodied in the parody of paganism in which cult members worship an object called the *vǫlsi*—a pickled horse penis! This perversion of religion is related to the family's isolation and to the personal propensities of individual family members, and the Christian satirist implies a relationship between *social* inversion within the household dominated by the wife and this "unnatural" cult, instigated and perpetuated by the "proud" old woman. The party of the vǫlsi—the wife, the libidinous servant girl, and the rowdy son—are effectively contrasted with the anti-vǫlsi group: intelligent but passive father, virginally squeamish daughter, and plain, honest manservant, who would rather have a nice loaf of bread than the sacred fetish. The logic of Christian myth may lie behind the fact that the household's "fall" is blamed on the wife while the maiden daughter is first to note the "advent" of the saint King Olaf, who will convert the family to the True Faith; the author adds that "the old woman was slow taking to the Faith, but the farmer rather readier"; and "After they had been instructed in Whom they ought to believe and had come to recognize their Creator, they saw what a foul and unmanly way of life they had had and how deviant from all other good men." A "manly" standard within the family seems to depend on restoration of the traditional hierarchy as much as on religious orthodoxy.

The best-known group of þættir comprises thirty-one stories which concern, almost by definition, exclusively male relationships; their focus is principally on vertical relationships between the king and the Icelander (the relationships studied by Vésteinn Ólason under the aspect of "freedom"), but the stories also concern horizontal male relationships, mostly within the *Gefolgschaft*. Very few women or male-female couples play a role. At the end of his story Auðun does return to Iceland to care for his mother, but she is the only woman mentioned in this most celebrated of þættir.[37] The much admired and much translated *Story of Brandr the Generous* mentions no women at all,[38] and ten others of the group, including some of the best, have no use at all for women.[39] These thirty-one stories are based on a male dyad, a pair of roles usually filled by an Icelander and a king; the difference in power between the two roles is crucial, and the plots can be understood as variations on an alienation phase followed by a reconciliation phase.[40] This core plot structure is often framed by a journey from and return to Iceland, and a number of specific variations on the generic plot structure have been described. Essential in the present context, however, is that the only "couple" consistently in sight is male, and the generic plot normally ends in re-establishment of solidarity between them, though it is not strictly a solidarity of equals. There are some incidental women: Gísl Illugason is guarded in the king's jail by an old woman, probably only because the verse attributed to him in this situation addresses a woman.[41] Egill Síðu-Hallsson brought his wife and daughter to Norway, first leaving them in a rented house but later moving them right into the court, but the purpose of this brief episode is made clear when the king prophesies that the girl will be lucky: "and it turned out that way ... for she is the mother of the holy bishop Jón."[42] This little passage may be an interpolation introduced as an oral variant ("Svá segir sumir menn...›"); in any case it is a narrative excrescence. A protagonist's wife back in

---

37. Íslenzk fornrit 6; among the more recent literature on the þáttr is Edward G. Fichtner, "Gift Exchange and Initiation in the *Auðunar þáttr vestfirzka*" *Scandinavian Studies* 51 (1979), 249–272; but see especially the review of folk narrative connections in John Lindow, "Hreiðars þáttr heimska and AT 326: An Old Icelandic Novella and an International Folktale," *Arv* 34 (1978), 152–179, supplemented by Harris, "Folktale and Thattr."

38. *Brands þáttr ǫrva* in Íslenzk fornrit 4; recent literature: *Stories from the Sagas of the Kings*, ed. Anthony Faulkes (London, 1980), and Hermann Pálsson, "Brands þáttur örva," *Gripla* 7 (1990), 117–130; also cf. Sverrir Tómasson, "Vinveitt skemmtan og óvinveitt," in *Maukastella: fœrð Jónasi Kristjássyni fimmtugum* (Reykjavík 10. April, 1974), pp. 65–68 (mimeographed).

39. *Hreiðars þáttr heimska, Odds þáttr Ófeigssonar, Stúfs þáttr blinda, Þorsteins þáttr austfirðings, Þorsteins þáttr sǫgufróði, Þorvarðar þáttr krákunefs, Þáttr Þormóðar, Þorsteins þáttr skelks,* and *Þorsteins þáttr Síðu-Hallssonar.*

40. The structural analysis is elaborated in Harris, "Genre and Narrative Structure."

41. *Gísls þáttr Illugasonar* in Íslenzk fornrit 3; cf. Roberta Frank, "Why Skalds Address Women," in *Poetry in the Scandinavian Middle Ages*, ed. Teresa Pàroli (Spoleto, 1990), pp. 67–83.

42. *Egils þáttr Síðu-Hallssonar* in *Íslendinga þættir*, ed. Guðni Jónsson; translation mine.

Iceland may be alluded to *(Þorgríms þáttr Hallasonar)*,[43] or she may have a minor part to play in introductory events in Iceland before the journey to Norway *(Þórarins þáttr Nefjólfssonar)*.[44] Since several of these stories relate the youthful adventures of a man who returns and settles in Iceland, we might expect to find the "couple" established at the end of the tale, but this is not the case. When it is told of an Icelander such as Hreiðarr heimski that "many men are descended from him," we must assume that mention of his marriage is simply elided.[45] Þorsteinn austfirðingr declines King Magnús's invitation to marry and settle in Norway; and though he settled in Iceland and was thought a *gœfumaðr* or man of good luck, the story does not say that he had descendants—probably because he is purely fictional.[46] Only *Ísleifs þáttr byskups,* which does deal with historical material, actually makes the establishment of a family part of the story's conclusion.[47]

In the dozen or so stories of this group in which a woman does play a more than nominal role, she is usually an agent (or merely an incident) in the alienation or reconciliation of the men. Bergljót, wife of Einarr Þambarskelfir, is prepared to intervene with arms against her husband to save Halldórr Snorrason,[48] and another great lady acts in a similar manner in *Steins þáttr Skaptasonar.*[49] There is nothing distinctively female about this role of helper and mediator, which is played much more often by men in the stories generally; there is, however, a passing interest in the dynamics of the royal or nearly royal couple in four or five stories. Take *Sturlu þáttr* for example: Sturla Þórðarson finds himself seriously on the outs with King Magnús Hákonarson; the intervention of a friend has not healed the breach, and now Sturla

---

43. *Íslenzk fornrit* 9.

44. *Íslendinga þœttir* (chapters 8–11 only; cf. Harris, "Genre and Narrative Structure," p. 3, n.).

45. So also for Auðunn vestfirzki of *Auðunar þáttr.*

46. Cf. Joseph Harris, "The King in Disguise: An International Popular Tale in Two Old Icelandic Adaptations," *Arkiv för nordisk filologi* 94 (1979), 37–81 [reprinted in this volume, Eds.]; Hermann Pálsson, "Early Icelandic Imaginative Literature," in *Medieval Narrative: A Symposium,* ed. Hans Bekker-Nielsen, et al. (Odense, 1979), pp. 20–30.

47. Ed. B. Kahle in *Kristni saga ...* (Halle, 1905); the wooing and other incidents in the life of Ísleifr are treated as separate episodes in "Genre and Narrative Structure," p. 15; in retrospect I would treat them as episodes within the structural segment Conclusion.

48. *Halldórs þáttr Snorrasonar I* in *Íslenzk fornrit* 5; cf. Joseph Harris, "Christian Form and Christian Meaning in *Halldórs þáttr I,*" *Harvard English Studies* 5 (1974), 249–264 [reprinted in this volume, Eds.], and Faulkes, *Stories from the Sagas of the Kings.*

49. *Íslendinga þœttir.*

must spend some time in close quarters on shipboard with the King and Queen.[50] His reception among the crew and retainers is cool until he entertains them with a saga-recital; the queen sees the crowd and conceives an interest in hearing the story. The next day, in a passage famous for its implications about saga-entertainment or *sagnaskemmtun*,[51] the queen's mediation prevails to the extent of sending for Sturla to come to the poop-deck to entertain the royal couple. The saga-telling leads to permission to perform a praise poem before the king; and so, little by little and with much applause from the queen, Sturla is led into full favor and earns the king's accolade: "It's my opinion that you recite better than the Pope himself." Eventually Sturla achieves membership in the retinue and the title of *skutilsveinn*. Notice, incidentally, that the subject matter of Sturla's saga-telling is a *Huldar saga*, "about a huge she-troll"; here Christianity presumably plays no role, but the presentation of the demonized, primitive, female *Stoff* to an enthusiastic male audience is similar to the situation in *Norna-Gests þáttr*.[52]

In *Sturlu þáttr* and generally in these stories the female member of a couple shows more conciliatory good sense and goodwill than the male and is shown getting round him, getting her way by diplomacy or power or both. An amusing variation on the same idea occurs in the second of the þættir about Halldórr Snorrason where the generic apparatus of reconciliation comes to nothing, and the final interview of those old comrades Halldórr and King Haraldr parodically inverts a reconciliation scene: instead of appearing hat in hand before a king sitting in state in his beer hall, the Icelander breaks into the king's

---

50. Edited separately in Guðni Jónsson, ed., *Sturlunga saga*, III (Íslendingasagnaútgáfan, 1954), 367–383; see discussion of manuscripts and semi-independent status of text, p. xi. Translations used here are from Simpson, *Northmen Talk*, but this is an incomplete rendering; see Julia McGrew and R. George Thomas, tr., *Sturlunga saga*, II (New York, 1974), pp. 489–499, for a complete translation. Úlfar Bragason, "Sturlunga saga: Atburðir og frásögn," *Skáldskaparmál: Tímarit um íslenskar bókmenntir fyrri alda*, 1 (Reykjavík, 1990), 73–88, demonstrates the influence of literary patterns on the supposedly raw historical *Stoff* of the *Sturlunga saga* complex partly in a detailed discussion of this story.

51. Cf. Hermann Pálsson, *Sagnaskemmtun Íslendinga* (Reykjavík, 1962), esp. pp. 52, 116, 168–169.

52. Huld may be the troll-witch of that name who took on the form of a mare to trample King Vanlandi to death in *Ynglinga saga*; however, the name is generic for "witch"; cf. Preben Meulengracht Sørensen, *Saga og samfund: En indføring i oldislandsk litteratur* (Copenhagen, 1977), pp. 162–163.

bedroom and stands towering, fully armed, over Haraldr and the queen as they lie in bed; and instead of presenting a gift or a poem or a task accomplished, Halldórr demands the queen's ring in payment for money owed him. Haraldr tries to temporize, but the queen intervenes:" 'Give him the ring,' said the queen. 'Can't you see the way he's standing over you, the killer?'"[53]

In two stories, *Qgmundar þáttr dytts ok Gunnars helmings* and *Þorvalds þáttr tasalda,* an adventure among pagans is part of the story's generic reconciliation section and includes a conversion and marriage to a formerly heathen woman.[54] But the inclusion of a little conversion story as part of the reconciliation of king and Icelander is found most brilliantly realized in *Þórarins þáttr Nefjólfssonar,* where the retrospectively told conversion episode involves the mother of one of the protagonists. This generic juxtaposition resembles that found in the tale of the encounter of Þorsteinn skelkr with the devil, where the incident we examined in connection with narratives of the *Norna-Gests þáttr* type is set within an alienation-and-reconciliation framework concerning an Icelander and his king.

The well-made story of Hrafn Hrútfirðingr, also known by his mother's name as Guðrúnarson, probably gives more space to woman and family couples than any other of the group of thirty-one.[55] The long prelude in Iceland is a typical feud saga in little; Guðrún is the main figure (with a role a bit like that of the mother of Víga-Glúmr): she endures after the killing of her husband until her son will be old enough to take revenge, and she uses all her wiles to get him safely out of the country when he does. The second part in Norway is a quite regular alienation-reconciliation story, except for the prominence given women. Hrafn's offences begin with his attentions to his host's daughter, but she and her mother attempt to intercede for Hrafn. When the offences escalate and Hrafn is outlawed, the women drop out of the story, but when King Magnús Óláfsson is finally reconciled with Hrafn,

53. *Halldórs þáttr Snorrasonar II* in Íslenzk fornrit 5; translation from *Hrafnkel's Saga and Other Stories,* tr. Hermann Pálsson (Harmondsworth, 1971); cf. Harris, "Genre and Narrative Structure," p. 19.

54. A couple is encountered in the adventures in *Þórodds þáttr Snorrasonar* and in *Þorvalds þáttr;* Íslenzk fornrit 27: 255–261 (and pp. l-li); Íslenzk fornrit 9: 119–126.

55. Íslenzk fornrit 8, and W. H. Wolf-Rottkay, ed., *Altnordisch-isländisches Lesebuch* (Munich, 1967); translations mine.

the denouement includes marriage to the girl and fetching his mother from Iceland to join the newly established—mostly female—family in Norway. But this probably fictional tying-up of loose ends does not prevent the more genre-specific concluding formula: "Hrafn was ever after with King Magnús, as long as the king lived."

The wealthy widow Ása figures importantly in the story of a certain Þórðr, sans patronymic, who was satirically nicknamed for his association with her, Gull-Ásu-Þórðr, Rich-Ása's Thord.[56] The relationship, partly business, partly pleasure, is the cause of trouble, as the poor but energetic Icelander is seen in Norway as a social climber. The main interest of the story, however, lies not in Ása and Þórðr as a couple, but in the clever way the underdog Icelander overcomes hostility and prejudice, and, like several others of the group, the story especially thematizes friendship. The relationships in question are among men, but the real point is an unsentimental conception of friendship as reciprocity for favors given. The story ends with marriage, social approval, and wealth.

A relationship to a woman is also the cause of trouble in a third story, *Óttars þáttr svarta*: the famous Icelandic poet had composed love verses about Olaf Haraldsson's queen. The reconciliation also comes, as so often, through poetry, but the queen too is active in the reconciliation.[57] The author of this anecdote—almost too brief to analyze—is interested in the ambiguous relationships within the royal couple and among the three characters. The situation is charged but inexplicit, perhaps not yet "triangular desire," but pointing in that direction.

Perhaps the funniest story of the group is one of the least unified, *Sneglu-Halla þáttr.*[58] Here Haraldr harðráði's rough and often bawdy sense of humor is on display from the very first episode, which involves clever repartee around the consummate male insult, passive sodomy. In the fuller and more original version, King Haraldr's queen, who did not like Halli, is mentioned near the beginning and reenters near the end of the þáttr where she criticizes the king for associating with the foul-mouthed poet; the incident goes like this:

---

56. *Gull-Ásu-Þórðar þáttr* in Íslenzk fornrit 11; my translations.

57. *Óttars þáttr svarta* is ch. 4 of "Sighvats þáttr" in *Íslendinga þœttir*; cf. the explanation in Harris, "Genre and Narrative Structure," p. 3 n., and Simpson's treatment in *Northmen Talk*.

58. Íslenzk fornrit 9; my translations.

[Halli was staring admiringly at a valuable silver-chased axe in the king's hand:] The king noticed that right away and asked whether the axe pleased Halli. He answered that he liked it very much. "Have you ever seen a better axe?" Halli answered, "I don't believe so." The king asked, "Would you let yourself be buggered for the axe?" "No," said Halli, "but it seems to me excusable that you would want to give the axe away the same way you acquired it." "And so it shall be, Halli," said the king, "you take it and make the best use of it: for it was freely given to me, and so I shall give it to you." Halli thanked the king. In the evening, when the company had sat down to their drinking, the queen told the king clearly that it was bizarre and not at all appropriate to give that treasure of an axe to Halli—"something which is hardly property for men of non-noble rank, bestowing it in return for his filthy language. Meanwhile, some men get little for their good service." The king answered that he himself would decide to whom he gave his treasures: "I do not want to turn Halli's words—those which are ambiguous—to the worse interpretation."[59]

King Haraldr goes on to offer the queen a further demonstration of linguistic ambiguity and how interpretation is a two-edged sword. He calls on Halli to compose an ambiguous verse about her—"'and let's see how she takes it.'" The verse is racy and philologically difficult, but the gist is that she, Queen Þóra, is the person most suitable to perform certain sexual services for Haraldr. "'Take him out and kill him,' said the queen, 'I will not put up with his slander.' The king commanded that no one be so bold as to lay a finger on Halli for this—'but something can be done about it if you think some other woman is more suitable to lie beside me and be queen. And you don't know praise of yourself when you hear it.'" This is a triangular situation we know from modern life: the wife and the free-living friend as rivals for the established and powerful figure, the husband.

Another form of the triangle appears in the last of this group of

---

59. ÍF 9: 293–294; on the versions of the þáttr, cf. pp. cix–cxiv. The passage I have translated here is briefly discussed by Preben Meulengracht Sørensen, *The Unmanly Man: Concepts of Sexual Defamation in Early Northern Society*, tr. Joan Turville-Petre (Odense, 1983), p. 27, in the general context of defining *níð*, and compare Michael Minkov, "Sneglu Halli, 2: 11: *Dróttinserðr*" *Saga-Book of the Viking Society*, 22, pt. 5 (1988), pp. 285–286.

stories I mean to mention, *Ívars þáttr Ingimundarsonar*.[60] Ívarr was
at the court of King Eysteinn Magnússon and sent a message home
to Iceland to a woman there, declaring his love and asking her not
to marry anyone else. The messenger was Ívarr's own brother, but
the brother betrayed Ívarr and married the woman himself. Ívarr
had already arrived in Iceland when he learned of this situation, but
he immediately returned to Norway and the king's court. Most of
this very short story is occupied with King Eysteinn's attempts to
discover the cause of Ívarr's resulting depression and then to cure it.
The king's suggestions of the other-fish-in-the-sea cure and his offer
of money are greeted glumly, but his third suggestion does work:
"We'll talk about this woman to your heart's content for as long as
you wish, and I'll devote my time to it. Sometimes a man's grief is
soothed when he can talk about his sorrows." This idea has echoes
not only in the *Roman de la Rose* but in the Norse *Hávamál*,[61] and the
talking cure, as psychotherapy is sometimes called, must be universal.
The original triangle situation obviously relates this story to a whole
series of Icelandic sagas, *Bjarnar saga Hítdœlakappa*, *Kormaks saga*,
Gunnlaugs saga ormstungu, *Hallfreðar saga vandrœðaskálds*, and
Laxdœla saga, and beyond them to a worldwide narrative structure
of triangular desire.[62] In all these sagas the couple that should have
come into being but did not, the absent couple, haunts long texts that
deal with the rivalry of two men. The desire they feel toward the same
woman feeds on imitation, is the "imitative desire" of René Girard's
triangle, and the jealousy between them is a bond to which we could
assign different names. But what is interesting in the present context
is the *contrast* with *Ívars þáttr*. In the full-length sagas the triangle is
sustained to the death, and this is presumably what originally made
the material *sǫguligt*, worth telling in a saga. But in the short story
the spell of the triangle is broken, and the narrative retreats to the
male dyad, the warrior and his loving lord. (In Germanic imagina-

---

60. *Íslendinga þœttir*; for manuscripts and editions see Ulset p. vii; translation from
Hermann Pálsson, *Hrafnkels saga and Other Stories*.

61. *Roman de la Rose*, ll. 3099–3110; *Hávamál*, 121, 8–10; 124, 1–3; cf. Harris,
"Theme and Genre," p. 26, n. 29.

62. The Baldr-Hǫðr-Nanna story as told by Saxo (book three) may be cut from the same
cloth, and the tale of Helgi Hjǫrvarðsson, his brother Heðinn, and the valkyrie Sváva may
have been more comparable in a more original form *(Helgakviða Hjǫrvarðzsonar*, prose
after st. 30 to end).

tive life, insofar as it is documented in literature, *this* "couple" is the older; one thinks, for example, of the OE Wanderer searching far and near for a lord who will not only cheer and support him but who would "know my loving thoughts" ["(minne) myne wisse"].) In the thirteenth-century saga literature the exploration of the erotic triangle belongs to Icelandic settings and to the longer genre, the sagas, but the þáttr-hero Ívarr returned to the court and the king. In terms of genre, one might say, exaggerating a bit, that Ívarr's story begins as a saga but reverts to þáttr status. In fact, the treatment is that of the short story throughout, and it is only through the comparanda that we know the initial situation was treated by preference in saga-length works. Within the story, however, the king replaces the woman and the rival; and while the triangular stories of the sagas end tragically, the þáttr takes leave of its hero, his cheerfulness restored, on what Northrop Frye might have called a comic note of incorporation or reincorporation into the courtly Männerbund. The closing benediction on Ívarr is "And he remained with King Eystein."

Our conclusions about the couple in þættir—at least about the couple in the sense of our conference theme—must be moderately negative. In the medieval North short narrative forms were *not* found notably suitable for exploring domestic problems, but *Ívars þáttr* does point the way to anyone who would wish to pursue the problem of the couple in early Icelandic literature. The *skáldasǫgur,* the group of sagas chiefly about the lives of poets and constructed on an enduring love triangle, would be a beginning.[63] After that almost all the great family sagas would offer rich materials, and the student of the couple in these longer forms could build on the relatively rich secondary literature on aspects of gender already in place.[64] *Njáls saga* shows that the domestic couple could have a narrative significance even in the absence of a love triangle, but an irritant, a third factor, is necessary to the generation of a narrative, for the marriage portraits in the sagas contain few cries or whispers of post-Romantic inwardness. In the family sagas that

---

63. Cf. Bjarni Einarsson, *Skáldasögur: Um uppruna og eðli ástaskáldasagnanna fornu* (Reykjavík, 1961), and the contextualization by Clover, "Icelandic Family Sagas," esp. pp. 249–251.

64. Especially conspicuous is Thomas Bredsdorff, *Kaos og kærlighed: En studie i islæn-dingesagaens livsbillede* (Copenhagen, 1971); and cf. Clover's survey in "Icelandic Family Sagas," pp. 256–259.

irritant is usually competition, outward conflict, or some stage of a feud: for instance, the couple comes memorably to the fore in *Hávarðar saga Ísfirðings* in the context of delayed revenge. Two sagas would stand out, however, as especially important for the treatment of the couple: *Gísla saga Súrssonar* and *Laxdœla saga*. *Gísla saga* is the more intense and narrower of the two, showing the failure of most human institutions—oath brotherhood, servant-master loyalty, female same-sex friendship, blood kinship, kinship overvalued in incestuous desire, perhaps also religion—but it is the bond of the married couple that emerges from the story as the least weak.[65] A reading of *Laxdœla saga* from the point of view of the couple would have to be, I would argue, considerably more complicated. Admittedly the saga appears simple in the central constellation of Kjartan, Bolli, and Guðrún where it draws on the classic structures of triangular desire in the sense of René Girard.[66] The solution of the tension here is neither the institutionalization of the triangle as in the *skáldasǫgur* nor Ívarr's retreat to the male bond; instead *Laxdœla saga* revives the pattern of the Vǫlsung-Nibelung story with two couples superseding but never quite dissolving the triangle and of course leading to a re-enactment of the tragic paradigm of the ancient heroic story. For its part *Gísla saga*, also famously haunted by the Vǫlsung material,[67] deploys its quadrangles and triangles in interlacements that are less predictable but no less tragic. But when we go beyond the core narrative to consider the sweep of *Laxdœla saga* from Unnr in djúpúðga through the unforgettable last words of Guðrún Ósvífsdóttir, it is clear that permutations of the triangle would not be adequate to the saga's discussion of sexual politics.

Our survey of þættir has delved into only two groups, totaling some forty-five short stories. Outside these groups a few texts may be more

---

65. One of the most recent contributions to the study of gender-related themes in *Gísla saga* is Preben Meulengracht Sørensen, "Murder in Marital Bed: An Attempt at Understanding a Crucial Scene in *Gísla Saga*," in *Structure and Meaning in Old Norse Literature*, pp. 235–263.

66. *Deceit, Desire, and the Novel: Self and Other in Literary Structure*, tr. Yvonne Freccero (Baltimore and London, 1966 [French original 1961]); cf. Eve Kosofsky Sedgwick, *Between Men: English Literature and Male Homosocial Desire* (New York, 1985).

67. See, for example, Heinrich Matthias Heinrichs, "Nibelungensage und Gísla saga," in *Beiträge zur deutschen und nordischen Literatur: Festgabe für Leopold Magon zum 70. Geburtstag, 3. April 1957*, ed. H. W. Seiffert, Veröffentlichungen des Instituts für deutsche Sprache und Literatur, 11 (Berlin, 1958), pp. 22–29, and Meulengracht Sørensen, "Marital Bed."

directly relevant to the thematics of the couple.[68] The jolly *Hróa þáttr heimska* comes to mind: there the socially modest Danish hero moves from the patronage of the king, Sven Forkbeard, to a wealthy marriage to the clever daughter of a famous Swedish lawman; the male world of the first part of the þáttr thus stands in contrast to Hrói's dependence on the wisdom of his wife (and her father) in the second part, and Hrói's trials eventuate in a good marriage, literally "the making of a couple." The author was, however, probably most interested in his nordicization of the central motifs of the story from the *senex cœcus* tale of the *Seven Sages*; moreover, *Hróa þáttr* is an isolated case.[69] My impression is that also *outside* the two main groups of þættir surveyed here, the short forms were not an important instrument for thinking through problems of the couple. Of the long forms, the saga genres, I have glanced only at the family sagas, but there, it seems to me, we do find a fairly extensive problematization of marriage, jealousy, and the politics of the couple. How can we explain this literary-historical pattern where long and short forms roughly reverse expectations formed from continental literature?

A hint may be given by the echoes of the mythic and heroic stories in the sagas, what has been called their heroic legacy, eddic perspective, or *eddischer Blick*.[70] Problematic love relationships in the Nordic mythic material, where they are common enough, tend to be seen from

---

68. Conspicuously absent from our survey is the small group of þættir that deal with Icelandic feuds, texts such as *Gunnars þáttr Þiðrandabana* (Íslensk fornrit 11) and the first part of the *Hrafns þáttr* discussed above. These operate with the same narrative structure as the family sagas; in fact, the justly well-known *Þorsteins þáttr stangarhǫggs* served Andersson's *Family Saga* as a structural model for the feud saga, and the dearth of such feud þættir in the corpus has been thought due to their having been early absorbed into or expanded as feud sagas (Herbert S. Joseph, "The Þáttr and the Theory of Saga Origins," *Arkiv för nordisk filologi* 87 [1972], 95; cf. Clover, "Icelandic Family Sagas," pp. 291-294). Domestic relations probably come in for about the same amount of attention there as in the family sagas. *Gunnars þáttr*, for example, repeats an incident of *Laxdœla saga* in which Guðrún Ósvífsdóttir rides roughshod over her fourth husband at their wedding feast—an anecdote significant for cultural history but probably not part of a gender/genre pattern.

69. Dag Strömbäck, "En orientalisk saga i fornnordisk dräkt," in *Donum Grapeanum: Festskrift tillägnad överbibliotekarien Anders Grape på sextiofemårsdagen, den 7 mars 1945* (Uppsala, 1945), pp. 408–444; rpt. in *Folklore och filologi*, Skrifter utg. av Gustav Adolfs Akademien för Folklivsforskningen 48 (Uppsala, 1970), 238–254.

70. Andersson, "The Heroic Legacy," in *Family Saga*, ch. 3; Roberta Frank, "Onomastic Play in Kormakr's Verse: The Name Steingerðr," *Mediaeval Scandinavia* 3 (1970), 7–34, esp. 27–34; Ulrike Sprenger, *Praesens historicum und praeteritum in der altisländischen Saga* (Basel, 1951), esp. p. 17.

the male perspective;[71] but in the heroic poetry this problematics of the couple is registered to a great extent in women's voices or from a female point of view—so much so that a term like "heroine-ic poetry" would not be out of the question if it were not so unwieldy. It may be that the family sagas inherited not only the specific motifs and story-patterns noted by earlier scholars such as Guðbrandur Vigfússon and Magnus Olsen and not only their spirit and rhetorical structure as argued by the likes of W.P. Ker and T.M. Andersson, but also this aspect of their thematics.[72]

Against the eddic legacy of the family sagas we might set the *skaldic legacy* of the major groups of þættir. Of course our conventional term "skaldic poetry" covers a great variety of poetic phenomena over time and space, but one can recognize more or less central and more or less marginal areas, and praise of the ruler, especially in "court-meter" *(dróttkvætt)*, is agreed to lie at the heart. Skaldic praise-poetry was, according to the stereotypes, presented by the poet before his lord in the presence of the warriors of the court; the dramatis personae and scene are, therefore, also typical for the þættir we have surveyed, and a great many of the short stories are, like *Ívars þáttr* and *Sturlu þáttr*, stories of poets or saga-tellers. In an inventive article John Lindow suggested that the inherent ideology of such poetry correlated with its notoriously difficult, riddle-like style; it functioned as a kind of test or sign of initiation into the *drótt* or court: "Early skaldic poetry might, therefore, be regarded as a device for isolating non-members, i.e. the lower classes and women, from the *drótt*. It functioned, in effect, as a kind of secret language in which the members of the *drótt* could maintain their collective traditions in a special way and also communicate without being wholly understood by others, indeed to the exclusion of others."[73] Similarly the þáttr-hero wants to be included in his lord's

---

71. Pointed out by Bjarni Einarsson, *Skáldasögur*, pp. 11–14, and Roberta Frank, "Onomastic Play," p. 27.

72. See Andersson, *Family Saga*, for the earlier references; some later studies in this kind are: Anne Heinrichs, "Beziehungen zwischen Edda und Saga: Zur Interpretation zweier Szenen aus der Heiðarvíga saga," *Zeitschrift für deutsches Altertum und deutsche Literatur*, 99 (1970), 17–26; Oskar Bandle, "Isländersaga und Heldendichtung," in *Afmælisrit Jóns Helgasonar, 30. júní 1969*, ed. Jakob Benediktsson, et al. (Reykjavík, 1969), pp. 1–26; Haraldur Bessason, "Mythological Overlays," in *Sjötíu ritgerðir helgaðar Jakobi Benediktssyni 20. júlí 1977* (Reykjavík, 1977), I, pp. 273–292.

73. "Riddles, Kennings, and the Complexity of Skaldic Poetry," *Scandinavian Studies* 47 (1975), 311–327, quotation: pp. 322–323.

favor and ranked among the retainers; it is, as we have seen, a value system based on the male dyad in the context of the Männerbund. Implicitly it excludes women, family, and the heterosexual couple.[74] Unlike the sagas, where the heroic legacy is woven into warp and woof, the þættir seem, as we have already seen, to fence off eddic influences with a distancing frame or to exclude them altogether; but the "skaldic legacy" is part and parcel of their stories.[75]

One is reminded of the comparison of the two verse forms by Haraldr harðráði, about whom so many þættir tell: he improvised a stanza in the easy eddic meter *fornyrðislag,* but immediately corrected himself: "That is badly composed, and I must make a second stanza and make it better."[76] The content of the better poem is quite similar, but the form is that of the elaborate court meter. (Presumably any women who happened to be marching along toward destiny at Stamford Bridge would have understood the first stanza but not the second! Obviously any theory can be pushed to absurdity.)[77] Like eddic verse the sagas were a relatively open form, expansive enough to accommodate several kinds of materials and influences and to develop several themes; open too in the sense of being self-explanatory and accessible to mixed audiences which would have shaped the treatment and thematic repertoire.

By comparison skaldic court verse and the central groups of þættir are closed forms, with a smaller range of themes and values implying, probably, a narrower audience. Consider again the example of Sturla Þórðarson: he told a saga with what we might call "late eddic" content and featuring a demonized female; the audience ranged from the crew to the king, but especially appreciative was the queen. When Sturla recited a skaldic poem, however, it was explicitly for the king, though the queen listened in. Her approving comment was greeted by the king with irony: "Are you able to follow it quite clearly?" She extracts

---

74. Sedgwick, *Between Men,* argues that even relationships that seem to exclude women are inscribed with the whole question of gender arrangements; p. 25 and passim.

75. The chief instance of other eddic manifestations in þættir would perhaps be the incident in *Sneglu-Halla þáttr* in which Þjóðólfr Arnórsson is directed to compose verses portraying quarreling commoners, a smith and a tanner, first as Þórr and Geirrøðr, then as Sigurd and Fáfnir (Íslenzk fornrit 9: 267–269).

76. So in *Heimskringla;* for the other sources, see Íslenzk fornrit 28: 187–188.

77. On women skalds see Guðrún P. Helgadóttir, *Skáldkonur fyrri alda,* I (Akureyri, 1961).

herself with a tactful ambiguity, but as a woman and a Dane she may have had two strikes against her as a critic of skaldic verse.[78] (Some comments in the sources suggest, though, that not every male ruler who was willing to pay for a poem could actually understand it.) Internally, then, we see two different audiences correlated with gender and genre, but who formed the audience of *Sturlu þáttr* itself, or of *Gísls þáttr* or *Stúfs þáttr* or any of them? There is no reason external to the texts to suppose the audiences actually restricted to any sort of Männerbund; yet in a vague way this narrower ancestry seems inscribed in the stories. Like courtly eulogy, stories of the kind we have been discussing had a limited future, but the structural limits of the genres or subgenres probably are an essential part of the high level of literary achievement we find among the þættir.

Our conference topic comprises two themes, the couple and short narrative forms, and invites the consideration of short forms as a favored instrument of medieval literature for consideration of the problems—copious in all ages—of the core of every family. For the continental mainstream this is undoubtably one of the roles of *fabliaux, Mären, novelle,* and the like, while the contemporary West Scandinavian literature of the thirteenth and fourteenth centuries seems to offer a contrast and counterinstance. The thesis of a favored nexus between short forms and the domestic theme of the couple should be viewed, however, as a special case of a more general hypothesis connecting gender and genre. At this deeper level the þættir constitute strong confirmatory evidence.

---

78. Cf. Simpson, *Northmen Talk,* p. 4, n.

Love and Death in the *Männerbund*:

An Essay with Special Reference to the *Bjarkamál* and *The Battle of Maldon*

Erum Magnús vér vægnir,
vildak með þér mildum
(Haralds varðar þú hjǫrvi
haukey) lifa ok deyja!

Sighvatr Þórðarson (c. 995–1045) concludes his *Bersǫglisvísur*, "straight talk" of admonition to the young King Magnús, with what appears to be a reference to the power and dignity of the relationship between the leader and his man and poet: *meðal okkar alt's háligt* (all is holy between us two).[1] The relationship, while it cannot be equal, is reciprocal, and, in the last words of the poem, Sighvatr "relents" from his threat to transfer his allegiance to another king: "I give way, Magnús—you who guard with sword Norway, the hawk-isle of Haraldr—with you, generous one, it is my wish to live and die."[2] Sighvatr's jealousy, his emotional giving in, and his devotion to the death, despite his famous criticism of his lord, is presented in biographical terms in *Heimskringla* where we get to know both parties as individuals, but a larger understanding would proceed from the context of their institutional setting: Emile Benveniste comments that "it is society and social institutions which furnish concepts which are

1. *Den norsk-islandske skjaldedigtning*, ed. Finnur Jónsson, BI (Copenhagen: Gyldendal; Kristiania: Nordisk forlag, 1912), pp. 238–39. The phrase might refer to Sighvatr's baptismal relationship as godfather to Magnús (so Samuel Laing, trans., Snorri Sturluson, *Heimskringla*, Part Two: *Sagas of the Norse Kings*, rev. by Peter Foote [London: Everyman, 1961], p. 140 n.), but Lee M. Hollander seems to be right in seeing the more general reference as primary in the context *(The Skalds: A Selection of their Poems* [Princeton: American-Scandinavian Foundation, 1945], p. 174, n. 65).

2. Alfred Vestlund, "Om strofernas ursprungliga ordning i Sigvat Tordarsons 'Bersǫglis-vísur'," *Arkiv för nordisk filologi*, tilläggsband till band XL ny följd (XLIV) (1929): 281–93, esp. 292.

apparently the most personal."[3] The ideal of men dying with their lord in the nearly contemporary poems *Bjarkamál* and *The Battle of Maldon* has for some time constituted a scholarly problem, though it is not thoughts of death among warriors that seem to need an explanation; rather it is the special form those thoughts take and the historical relationships implied. The interpretive hurdle seems less formidable, however, when this "ideal" is not isolated, for the institutional context links death with other expressions of love and solidarity.

The institution in question is traditionally identified as the *comitatus*, whether in first-century Germania or thirteenth-century Norway, but the continuity and distinctiveness of the institution are now in serious doubt. Yet all that was formerly identified as belonging to the *comitatus* can still be ascribed with confidence to all-male groups with aggression as one major function, and these, in turn, can be located under the umbrella of the concept *Männerbund* in the extended sense in which the word is currently used. There is no doubt that the problematic ideas about warrior self-sacrifice were in the air in the hypertrophy of heroic ethos of the late Viking Age,[4] but this essay, casting its net very broadly, will propose the importance of a timeless psychological context in terms of male associations.

*   *   *

As a concept for analysis of Old Germanic social groupings, the *Männerbund* fell into an undeserved disrepute as a result of reaction against the excesses of Otto Höfler's famous book *Kultische Geheimbünde der Germanen* and of the generally positive reception of its theories and its author by the National Socialists.[5] Höfler combed Germanic sources, early and late, for traces of secret cultic societies, often associated with

---

3. Emile Benveniste, *Indo-European Language and Society*, trans. Elizabeth Palmer (Coral Gables, Fla.: Univ. of Miami Press, 1973; French orig. 1969), p. 271.

4. Hans Kuhn, "Uns ist Fahrwind gegeben wider den Tod: Aus einer großen Zeit des Nordens," *Zeitschrift für deutsches Altertum und deutsche Literatur* 106 (1977): 147–63.

5. Otto Höfler, *Kultische Geheimbünde der Germanen* (Frankfurt am Main: Dieterweg, 1934). The book is volume 1 of a planned three volumes (see p. xi, n. 1); the later volumes were never published, but Höfler's *Verwandlungskulte, Volkssagen und Mythen*, Österreichische Akademie der Wissenschaften, philosophisch-historische Klasse, Sitzungsberichte, 279, No. 2 (Vienna, 1973) is in some sort a continuation.

masks and animal affinities and based on an ecstatic union of the living member with the ancestors. He had a great deal of success with Tacitus's Harii and Chatti, with the Old Norse *einherjar,* the berserks, and the werewolf life of Sigmund and Sinfjötli in *Vǫlsunga saga*—to name just a few high points. For Höfler the confraternities formed part of the Odinic religion, and he argued strenuously for a cultural continuity that directly entailed modern customs and beliefs, such as the Wild Hunt. It is a great and frustrating book, exemplifying too much of the kind of afflatus it celebrates, but for that very reason obviously valuable to the fascist movement in the year of its publication, 1934. Yet even within the movement there were readers who gagged. A review by Harald Spehr in the 1936 issue, the third year of *Rasse: Monatsschrift der Nordischen Bewegung,* opens with the skeptical question *Waren die Germanen 'Ekstatiker'?*[6] Not everyone who wished to make the Germanic past useful and relevant in the Third Reich welcomed Höfler's irrationalism and ecstatic religion; apparently Albert Rosenberg preferred the very different myth of the past in Bernard Kummer's *Mitgards Untergang* (1927).[7] Certainly the one time I personally met Otto Höfler, he took the occasion to regale me with a Hitler anecdote to Rosenberg's discredit, but it is to the contemporary secondary accounts by Klaus von See and especially to the splendid obituary of Höfler by Helmut Birkhan that I owe any real understanding of Höfler's coy relationship to the Party itself, to the SS's cultural foundation, *Ahnenerbe,* and to the rival intellectual faction.[8] After the war few German scholars were willing to touch Höfler's subjects unless, like von See, with condemnation; but to accuse Höfler of making Germanic heroic legend serviceable for Stalingrad,

6. Pp. 394–400.

7. Höfler's own critique of Kummer is contained in one huge footnote, number 169, pp. 335–39.

8. The most relevant of von See's many works in this area: *Kontinuitätstheorie und Sakraltheorie in der Germanenforschung: Antwort an Otto Höfler* (Frankfurt am Main: Athenäum, 1972); "Der Germane als Barbar," *Jahrbuch für Internationale Germanistik* 13, No. 1 (1981): 42–72; "Die Altnordistik im Dritten Reich," in Bernd Henningsen and Rainer Pelka, eds., *Die Skandinavistik zwischen gestern und morgen: Bestandsaufnahme ... eines "kleinen Faches,"* Schriftenreihe der Akademie Sankelmark, n.s. 59 (Sankelmark, 1984), pp. 39–51; "Das 'Nordische' in der deutschen Wissenschaft des 20. Jahrhunderts," *Jahrbuch für Internationale Germanistik* 15, No. 2 (1984): 8–38; "Kulturkritik und Germanenforschung zwischen den Weltkriegen," *Historische Zeitschrift* 245 (1987): 343–62; "Politische Männerbund-Ideologie von der wilhelminischen Zeit bis zum Nationalsozialismus," in *Männerbünde—Männerbande: Zur Rolle des Mannes im Kulturvergleich,* ed. Gisela Völger

as von See does, does not refute but only contextualizes Höfler's arguments. Von See has successfully attacked many parts of Höfler's total oeuvre, but I agree with a recent comment on the *Männerbünde* book that no objective evaluation has yet been attempted.[9]

It is interesting that the central term and most of the main concepts of Höfler's famous book were introduced by a woman, Lily Weiser, in a much more modest work inspired within the same Vienna School by Rudolf Much's teaching. Höfler copiously acknowledged Weiser's *Altgermanische Jünglingsweihen und Männerbünde,*[10] but he differs, apart from tonally, in making large claims for the *Männerbünde* as vehicles of historical power and state formation, in emphasizing ecstatic religion, and in his outcroppings, rather mild and traditional, of hostility toward women. The word *Männerbund* was apparently the construction of the anthropologist Heinrich Schurtz, making its first appearance in 1902 in his book *Altersklassen und Männerbünde: Eine Darstellung der Grundformen der Gesellschaft,* where it was intended to provide a concept for a widespread social form in primitive societies.[11] The typical *Männerbund* in the stricter sense is a secret organization in a tribal society to which only men, but not automatically all men, may belong; it will be highly organized under

---

and Karin v. Welck, 2 vols. (Cologne: Rautenstrauch-Joest-Museum Köln, 1990), 1:93–102. See also Helmut Birkhan, "[Nachruf auf] Otto Höfler," *Almanach der österreichischen Akademie der Wissenschaften* 138 (1987/88; Vienna, 1988): 385–406. On Lily Weiser's politics and further to Höfler, see Olaf Bockhorn, "Wiener Volkskunde 1938–1945," in *Volkskunde und Nationalsozialismus: Referate und Diskussionen einer Tagung ...,* ed. Helge Gerndt (Munich: Münchner Vereinigung für Volkskunde, 1987), pp. 235–36, n. 25.

9. Stefanie v. Schnurbein, "Geheime kultische Männerbünde bei den Germanen—Eine Theorie im Spannungsfeld zwischen Wissenschaft und Ideologie," in *Männerbünde—Männerbande* (n. 8 above), 2:97–102; cf. p. 102: "Eine fundierte feministische Kritik an Höflers die Männerbünde und männliche Tugenden verherrlichenden, häufig direkt frauenfeindlichen Schilderungen der kultischen Geheimbünde wäre der kritiklosen Übernahme der Höflerschen Ergebnisse und ihrer Umdeutung in feministische Richtung sicher vorzuziehen." Even the very critical review of Höfler by Friedrich von der Leyen (*Anzeiger für deutsches Altertum* 54 [1935]: 153–65) sees value in testing Höfler's inventive hypotheses.

10. Lily Weiser(-Aall), *Altgermanische Jünglingsweihen und Männerbünde: Ein Beitrag zur deutschen und nordischen Altertums- und Volkskunde,* Bausteine zur Volkskunde und Religionswissenschaft I (Bühl, Baden: Konkordia, 1927).

11. Heinrich Schurtz, *Altersklassen und Männerbünde: Eine Darstellung der Grundformen der Gesellschaft* (Berlin: Reimer, 1902).

the mantle of religious mystery and symbolically opposed to everything female in the tribe; explicit goals of such groups differ greatly, but the preservation of male power is everywhere implicit.[12] The evolutionary and psychosexual theories with which Schurtz overlaid his ethnographic descriptions would seem extremely dated nowadays; however, the basic concept not only captured a cross-cultural generality of importance for ethnography, but also filled a need in the German cultural debate, especially in the twenties and thirties—hence the "ideologische Belastung" of the word in present-day German and its virtual disappearance, even, from the German lexicon of sociology.[13] But as a writer for *Die Zeit* tartly reported: "The thing itself ... flourishes and prospers just as before in every conceivable shape and form, be it as officers' club, professional association, ... or secret society."[14]

In the teens and twenties, before male associations became part of Nazi ideology properly speaking, Schurtz's work was developed in an important direction by a literary depth-psychologist named Hans Blüher whose loosely Freudian cultural criticism focused on what he called "the role of love in male society," to translate his most famous title, the 1917 book *Die Rolle der Erotik in der männlichen Gesellschaft*. Blüher was a brilliant writer and potentially more accessible today when we are used to thinking in terms of "desire" and "gender" and are equipped with a word like "homosocial" for an all-encompassing concept of male associations.[15] But in his time Blüher was extremely

12. Paraphrased from Georg Höltker, *"Männerbünde,"* in *Handwörterbuch der Soziologie,* ed. Alfred Vierkant (Stuttgart: Enke, 1931), pp. 348–53, at p. 348.

13. Gisela Völger and Karin v. Welck, "Zur Ausstellung und zur Materialiensammlung," p. xix; René König, "Blickwandel in der Problematik der Männerbünde," pp. xxvii-xxxii; Jürgen Reulecke, "Das Jahr 1902 und die Ursprünge der Männerbund-Ideologie in Deutschland," pp. 3–10; all in *Männerbünde—Männerbande* (n. 8 above), vol. 1.

14. Sigrid Löffler, "Das herrliche Geschlecht," *Die Zeit,* 27 April 1990 (No. 17), p. 24, col. 3: "Die Sache selbst ... blüht und gedeiht nach wie vor in allen möglichen Ausprägungen und Gestaltungsformen, sei's als Offiziersverein, Berufs- oder Karriereklub, sei's als ... oder Geheimgesellschaft."

15. Hans Blüher, *Die Rolle der Erotik in der männlichen Gesellschaft: Eine Theorie der menschlichen Staatsbildung nach Wesen und Wert,* new ed. by Hans Joachim Schoeps (Stuttgart: Klett, 1962). For a discussion of the "homosocial" see Eve Kosofsky Sedgwick, *Between Men: English Literature and Male Homosocial Desire* (New York: Columbia Univ. Press, 1985), esp. Introduction and chap. 1.

controversial, and Höfler does not allude to him or deal significantly with the emotional life of his *Männerbünde.*[16]

In contemporary Germany, since, say, 1968, the women's movement and other influences too familiar to mention have revived interest in what bonds men, even though contemporary scholars will obviously evaluate their material very differently. The most relevant of the newer studies known to me are two: a two-volume compendium deriving from a 1989 museum exhibition in Cologne under the title "Männerbünde—Mannerbande: Zur Rolle des Mannes im Kulturvergleich" and Klaus Theweleit's vast literary meditation *Männerphantasien,* its two volumes published in Germany (1977–78) and in America (1987–89).[17] The museum exhibition and accompanying volumes took their point of departure from Schurtz and anthropology; but the book includes ninety-eight substantial essays covering not only the psychological and sociological theory, the anthropological instances, and the German heritage, as one might expect, but many chapters I would not have predicted—for example, on the Dervishes, the Assassins, the monastic community of Mt. Athos, Freemasonry, Oxbridge colleges, Rotary Clubs and the like, Turkish cafés in Cologne, and Eskimo whaling communities. Schurtz had already impressed his readers in 1902 with the suggestion that the social structures he had investigated were based in a psychosocial binarism—sexual difference—that persisted through evolution and that, therefore, modern European mens' clubs and the like were not only "survivals" like other folk remnants but still vital responses to human essentials. In the book from the Cologne exhibition, we see not only the predictable feminist values and cultural relativism but a readiness to generalize the definition of the phenomenon further and to investigate its margins. Theweleit's study is equally imbued with contemporary liberal and radical values but is based chiefly on the autobiographies and novels of Freikorps-men, members of the private armies that were part of

16. Höfler was well aware of the contemporary sociological debates, as his language and specific indebtedness to Alfred Baeumler (on whom see Reulecke, "Das Jahr 1902," n. 13 above, p. 10) make clear. Weiser (*Jünglingsweihen,* n. 10 above, p. 42 n.) notices and rejects Blüher.

17. *Männerphantasien,* trans. as *Male Fantasies,* 2 vols., by Stephen Conway, Erica Carter, and Chris Turner (Minneapolis: Univ. of Minnesota Press, 1987–89) and n. 8 above. See also Bernd Widdig, *Männerbünde und Massen: Zur Krise männlicher Identität in der Literatur der Moderne* (Wiesbaden: Westdeutscher Verlag, 1991).

the chaotic German scene after the First World War. In this corpus Theweleit seeks common psychological features of what he calls the "Warrior-Male," and any student of Old Germanic literature wading through Theweleit's thousand pages will hear many familiar echoes despite the author's hostile relation to his subject.

Outside Germany at least one important modern work should be mentioned: Lionel Tiger's *Men in Groups*.[18] Tiger had obviously not read Schurtz, to whom he barely alludes under a garbled title, and he does not know Blüher's work at all. Yet he recapitulates Schurtz's general argument that the gendered difference in bonding in historical cultures is a product of adaptive evolution (and therefore innate) and a precondition for aggression and other cultural advances. This socio-biological theme is, however, only half the book; and the descriptive parts seem to me a useful background, full of echoes for the student of Old Germanic male groups.

Classical *Altgermanistik* was somewhat tentative about appreciating the relevance of Schurtz's *Männerbund* concept, apart from the narrow application beginning with Weiser in 1927. This is peculiar because Schurtz himself attempts a discussion of the initiation of young men in Old Germanic times and makes connections with post-medieval German folk customs (pp. 110–24). The great *Reallexikon* of 1907, compiled by Hoops, has no entry for *Männerbund,* but by 1913 Friedrich Kauffmann was citing Schurtz's analogous materials copiously in footnotes to his *Deutsche Altertumskunde,* and was probably generally influenced by Schurtz in his presentation of early Germanic social group-ings.[19] One reason for the tardy welcome may have been reticence to put the ancestors, already "barbarians," on a level with primitive peoples;[20] another may be positivistic reluctance to extend Schurtz's narrower concept, despite his own example. The *Männerbünde* of Weiser and Höfler are not to be understood in any metaphorical sense; their rituals are not somehow immanent in the *disjecta membra* of the evidence. Instead, their claim, imbued with the ritual theory in its most literal form, is for the real historical existence of cultic societies

---

18. Lionel Tiger, *Men in Groups,* 2nd ed. (New York: Boyars, 1984); Tiger's Preface to the second edition gives some idea of the stormy reception of this book.

19. Friedrich Kauffman, *Deutsche Altertumskunde,* 2 vols. (Munich: Beck, 1913–23), chiefly 1:436–49; 2:385–414.

20. Cf. Birkhan, "[Nachruf auf] Otto Höfler" (n. 8 above), p. 403.

such as those that actually exist or existed in Africa and elsewhere in the realms of ethnography. But the more obvious male institution, the *Gefolgschaft* or *comitatus*, plays relatively little role in Höfler's conception; Weiser, on the other hand, several times notices the transition and overlap from age classes and secret societies to the retinue (e.g., p. 25).

That the *comitatus* was a *Männerbund* has already been recognized explicitly by some commentators. For example, Jan de Vries assigns it qualities of *Männerbünde* in other early Indo-European and primitive peoples, including even a religious dimension.[21] An influential essay by Felix Genzmer discussed cultic *Männerbünde*, with their death-and-rebirth initiations, then passed to the *comitatus*: "Auch die Gefolgschaft ist ein *Männerbund*," even though it *lacks* features such as religious sanction.[22] In a soberer postwar vein, Reinhard Wenskus seems to look favorably on such an understanding of the retinue in early Germanic times.[23] One value of this identification is that it allows the sparse data for the *comitatus* to be filled out by references to the normal morphology of the *Männerbund* cross-culturally understood; the tentativeness of this exercise is already evident in the disagreement just alluded to over putative cultic correlatives.

Kauffmann's presentation of 1913 already shows this kind of analogical filling out of the paradigm: At puberty the boy was separated from women, passing into the care of his father or a male substitute; the initiation includes tests and ends in the bestowal of weapons. But the boy passes from his father's protection into the household of a *princeps*, where he will serve and learn; the inner structure of the closed group is imitated from the family. Ultimately, however, the retinue is a free association around a leader. The companion is free to leave and usually exits the retinue when it is

---

21. Jan de Vries, *Die geistige Welt der Germanen*, 2nd ed. (Halle/Saale: Niemeyer, 1945), pp. 156–65; *Altgermanische Religionsgeschichte*, 2 vols., 3rd ed. (Berlin: de Gruyter, 1970), 1:492–99.

22. Felix Genzmer, "Staat und Gesellschaft," in *Germanische Altertumskunde*, ed. Hermann Schneider (Munich: Beck, 1938), pp. 123–70, at p. 142; Cf. Weiser (*Jünglingsweihen*, n. 10 above, p. 32): "Auch die Gefolgschaft ist im Grunde eine Kampfgenossenschaft. Das Gefolge besteht der Hauptsache nach aus Unverheirateten und diese werden auch im Heer die Kerntruppen gebildet haben," etc.

23. Reinhard Wenskus, *Stammesbildung und Verfassung: Das Werden der frühmittelalterlichen gentes* (Cologne and Graz: Böhlau, 1961), esp. pp. 361–63.

time to marry. As initiation begins the age-cohort of the "youth," so marriage begins that of the middle-aged men. *Heirat* and one Old English word for the *comitatus, hīred,* are cognates, but notice that actual marriage stands in complementary distribution to *comitatus* service. Yet the retinue contained some older men also, and recognition of age stratifications survives, for example, in the OE *duguð ond geoguð.* One word for the older bachelors is OE *hægsteald,* German *Hagestolz,* and traditional pictures of the retinue in the literature often cite an oldest companion, a *Waffenmeister* like Dietrich's Hildebrand, Gizurr of *Hlǫðskviða,* or the *eald geneat* of *Maldon* and the *eald æscwiga* of *Beowulf's* Ingeld episode. In the context of reciprocal loyalty that constitutes the inner bonds of the group, Tacitus mentions a *sacramentum* or oath that many connect with the *bēot* or *heitstrenging* of later texts, and it is, of course, in this context that we hear the famous sentiments about shame and the ideal of men dying with their lord. Tacitus commentators have supplied early parallels as well as later ones.

So far some traditional features of the picture of the *comitatus.* I am aware that this trips lightly over many vexed questions and that the whole subject has become more complicated in postwar scholarship. The two major problems, especially since Hans Kuhn's "Die Grenzen der germanischen Gefolgschaft," would seem to be the continuity of the institution and the distinction between this institution and similar ones. The gist of Kuhn's formidable study is that more discriminations erase the appearance of continuity.[24] Kuhn's narrow definition of the *comitatus* allowed him to recognize it in only two periods, that of Tacitus and that of the late Viking Age, where it was a new growth responding to the same social circumstances. There must be an ideological context to Kuhn's shift from a traditional treatment in 1938 to the new and fragmentary view of 1956,[25] but it is enough to cite Wenskus's balanced assessment of Kuhn: Kuhn is often hypercritical in this monograph, and the hypothesis of continuity sometimes seems

---

24. Hans Kuhn, "Die Grenzen der germanischen Gefolgschaft," *Zeitschrift der Savigny-Stiftung für Rechtsgeschichte* 73, Germanistische Abteilung (1956): 1–83; repr. in his *Kleine Schriften,* vol. 2 (Berlin: de Gruyter, 1971), pp. 420–83.

25. Hans Kuhn, "Kriegswesen und Seefahrt," in *Germanische Altertumskunde* (1938): 98–122, esp. p. 101 (n. 22 above).

to make better sense of the evidence.[26] Kuhn's essay was impressively answered by the historian Walter Schlesinger and by the philologist D. H. Green.[27] Helmut Gneuss remained ambivalent; he adopted much of Kuhn's theory of non-continuity, yet he showed conclusively that the English evidence through the eighth century can hardly do without the concept of the *comitatus*.[28] There would be, of course, a great deal to be said about the historical questions.

If, however, in this post-feminist age, our interest is in the *comitatus* as a *Männerbund* and in the psychosocial explanatory power of the realization that the members of these groups were not just men in the sense of persons but male men (cf. OE *wæpnedmen)*, it is not necessary to take a position on these questions of continuity and discrimination: virtually all the social forms bordering the *comitatus* would also qualify as male associations in the current loose understanding, though internal organization and the intensity of feelings will have varied. This emotional life can be understood, if at all, through the literature; but in view of the questionable continuity of the *comitatus*, we need to replace pre-war formulations with something like this: *comitatus*-like all-male groups with aggression as one major function continued through the entire Old Germanic period as important sponsors of poetry in which their ethos can (fragmentarily) be read.[29] Most of these emotional constants are already well known.

In contrast to the family, the *comitatus* and other *Männerbünde* were voluntary associations and therefore "social." The young man is

---

26. Chiefly pp. 346–61 (see n. 23 above).

27. Schlesinger, "Randbemerkungen zu drei Aufsätzen über Sippe, Gefolgschaft und Treue," in *Alteuropa und die moderne Gesellschqft: Festschrift für Otto Brunner* (Göttingen: Vandenhoeck & Ruprecht, 1963), pp. 11–59; repr. in his *Beiträge zur deutschen Verfassungsgeschichte des Mittelalters*, vol. 1 (Göttingen: Vandenhoeck & Ruprecht, 1963), pp. 286–334; Green, *The Carolingian Lord: Semantic Studies on Four Old High German Words: Balder, Frô, Truhtin, Hêrro* (Cambridge: Cambridge Univ. Press, 1965), passim. There are also some qualifications in the generally relevant John Lindow, *Comitatus, Individual and Honor: Studies in North Germanic Institutional Vocabulary*, University of California Publications in Linguistics 83 (Berkeley, Los Angeles, London: University of California Press, 1976).

28. Helmut Gneuss, *Die Battle of Maldon als historisches und literarisches Zeugnis*, Bayerische Akademie der Wissenschaften, philosophisch-historische Klasse, 1976, Heft 5 (Munich), esp. pp. 15–45.

29. The *comitatus* as sponsor of poetry is a widespread idea; e.g., Helmut de Boor, "Dichtung," in *Germanische Altertumskunde* (n. 22 above), pp. 387–88; Andreas Heusler, *Die altgermanische Dichtung*, 2nd ed. (Potsdam: Athenaion, 1941), p. 15. Heusler's book constitutes a definition of "Old Germanic" as used here.

attracted to his leader and could change lords; Caesar and Tacitus comment on what in modern times came to be called the charisma of the leader. There clearly were practical aspects to the relationship of lord and retainer, but it is the passionate and less rational ones that seem most important in literature. Beside *Treue*, there is betrayal, and in Norwegian law and in literature a large body of material reflects the tension of that primary relationship; commentators also note generational conflict.[30] Though the vocabulary for leader, retainer, and *Männerbund* itself has been thoroughly sifted, its evidence for relationships would warrant study. Some vocabulary belongs to an intense emotional sphere: Arminius had his *dilectis*, Chnodomarius, his *tres amici iunctissimi*. The *duguð* or the *dryht* may be *dīere*, the *gesīðas (comites)* may be *swǣse* (dear); the major word for loyalty, *hold*, suggests etymologically two men "inclined" together in conversation. The lord is *lēof* (beloved), from the root of *lufu, lof, lufian*; both lord and retainer are called *wine* (friend) alone and in many compounds, and like *lēof*, this word serves for both male-male and male-female relationships. (OHG *winileodas*, for example, are lovesongs.) The etymology of *wine* includes Latin *venus*, and the same semantic development from love to friendship and kinship took place in this root in Irish. The lord may be a *frēowine* or *frēodryhten* with the IE root **prī-* "love." When Hrothgar adopts Beowulf we are told he will "love him as a son" with the verb *freogan*, and, of course, *frēond* (friend) and its derivatives are from the same root. Frederick Klaeber comments on the phrase *ne his myne wisse* that "desire" for *myne* would be rather out of place; but elsewhere the word does mean "love, desire," and it is Hrothgar's "love" that Grendel, in his role as monstrous hall-thane, cannot know. For the analogue of this line in *The Wanderer* I think the more intimate formulation with "love" is satisfactory, despite some philological difficulties.[31]

The Wanderer's passionate picture of the displaced retainer dwells on language: he has no "dear confidant"; he lacks a "friend" or a

---

30. E.g., Weiser (*Jünglingsweihen*, n. 10 above), p. 23. I would substitute "loyalty problematic" for the "germanische Treue" debunked by František Graus, "Über die soge-nannte germanische Treue," *Historica* (Prague) 1 (1959): 71–121.

31. T. P. Dunning and A. J. Bliss, eds., *The Wanderer* (London: Methuen, 1969), pp. 61–65; Fr. Klaeber, ed., *Beowulf and The Fight at Finnsburg*, 3rd ed. rev. (Lexington, Mass.: Heath, 1950), line 1696 and note, pp. 134–35.

"gold-friend" who will *wēman mid wynnum.* Famous difficulties here, but I would look to Norwegian *ōma,* Icelandic *œmta* (whisper).[32] In his dream it seems as if the Wanderer embraces and kisses his lord and lays hand and head on his knee. These are institutional, not purely personal, gestures, of course; but if they are a part of a ceremony of admittance to the *comitatus*[33] they are here dreamed of as a part of the Wanderer's happy youth in the *Männerbund* (taken together with lines 35–36). The deprivation of the *swǣsne* (dear man), is a wound in the heart (lines 49–50). It is interesting that, to a large extent, the same language, that of retainership, does duty for male-male and male-female attachment. In *The Wife's Lament* only three inflections prove that the speaker is a woman, while everything else could be and has been interpreted as the language of a retainer separated from his lord. In *The Husband's Message* only a single half-line, *þēodnes dohtor* (prince's daughter), assures a female internal audience; but the situation is different with *Wulf and Eadwacer,* and the corpus of old poetry is too small for confidence.

Comradeship among retainers seems less prominent as an emotional value than might be predicted. The Wanderer and *Beowulf*'s Last Survivor grieve for lost mates, and one may find a developed comradely vocabulary, such as *eaxlgestellan* (shoulder companion), and some Norse anecdotes of retainerly solidarity. The more prominent emotion, however, is rivalry; in Tacitus it is *aemulatio,* competition for the place closest to the leader, and Icelandic stories of court life are full of more or less petty envy, emulation, and jealous slander.[34] It appears that *Männerbünde* are rarely egalitarian, and ranking relative to the leader is part of the bonding.[35] A particular variety of the comradeship of arms, of *Waffenbruderschaft,* begins with a direct test of strength. (A timeless motif told of Gilgamesh and Enkidu as well as of Robin Hood

---

32. Ibid., pp. 70, 110 n. to line 29.
33. Ibid., p. 112.
34. In Old English, cf. Deor and Heorrenda.
35. Eric John, "War and Society in the Tenth Century: The Maldon Campaign," *Transactions of the Royal Historical Society,* 5th ser., vol. 27 (1977): 176, commenting on the laws of the *Jómsvíkingar,* alludes to the question of the continuity of the *comitatus:* "What we have here is the ancient *comitatus* made into a new institution by the intensity and permanence of the military life prescribed and what we might call the hardware that enshrined this life." By Kuhn's definition the leaderless viking groups could not have been called *comitatus.*

and Little John, it continues into what Tiger calls "buddy movies.") The motif is applied both to retainer-retainer and to lord-retainer relations. For example, in *Þiðreks saga* heroes are drawn as if magnetically to Þiðrekr, and, as Hans Naumann says, "sometimes the youthful warriors sue for an initial duel with the new foreign lord in ways that otherwise only a lover sues for the first favors of the beloved."[36] The new leader must be the stronger, as in the Icelandic story of Eindriði ilbreiðr. The Icelandic *Sǫrla þáttr* contains two instances of the formula in which two heroes fight to a draw, then swear blood-brotherhood, the first being especially interesting in that obliteration of family ties leads to the warrior idyll.[37]

In the time of Tacitus and later, the *comitatus* seems to have had an educational function, and in a broad sense development of the man is a purpose of *Männerbünde* in general. Naumann emphasizes this function of the *comitatus* in one of the most readable books on the subject, despite its sentimental fascist politics.[38] Weiser regards the period of foreign adventures so common in Norse stories in this light (pp. 72, 81), and the existence of age classes (OE *hyse, geogoð, dugoð*, etc.) in conjunction with a rite of passage is necessarily education in some sense. Traditional German accounts of the *Gefolgschaft*, such as Naumann's, are confident that the *Gefolgschaftsälteste* corresponded to a real-life ceremonial and pedagogical mentor. Tacitus contrasts such *comites* with the adolescents as "the others, men of maturer strength and tested by long years."[39] Naumann discusses,

---

36. Hans Naumann, *Germanisches Gefolgschaftswesen* (Leipzig: Bibliographisches Institut, 1939), p. 15: "manchmal werben die jungen Recken dabei um einen Erstlingszweikampf mit dem fremden neuen Herrn, wie sonst nur ein Liebender um die erste Huld der Geliebten wirbt."

37. On these Icelandic stories see J. Harris, "Gender and Genre: Short and Long Forms in the Saga Literature," in *The Making of the Couple: The Social Function of Short-Form Medieval Narrative*, ed. Flemming G. Andersen and Morten Nøjgaard (Odense: Odense Univ. Press, 1991), pp. 43–66 [reprinted in this volume, Eds.].

38. Weiser (*Jünglingsweihen*, n. 10 above), pp. 28, 29, 42, 43; Naumann (*Germanisches Gefolgschaftswesen*, n. 36 above) points out that Lat. *sc(h)ola*, as well as *magister*, was borrowed into the terminology of the comitatus (p. 49), but note that the relevant Late Latin sense was not transmitted in the educational sphere but already referred to a group of soldiers (see OE *scolu, handscolu, genēatscolu*, OS *skola*, etc.).

39. *Tacitus in Five Volumes*, I: *Germania* [etc.], trans. M. Hutton, rev. by E. H. Warmington, Loeb Classical Library 35 (Cambridge, Mass.: Harvard Univ. Press; London: Heinemann, 1970), pp. 150–51: "[young men] ceteris robustioribus ac iam pridem probatis adgregantur."

among others, Hildebrand, Starkaðr, Innsteinn, Hagen, Thomas in the *Heliand,* Wiglaf, Iring, and Heime. This may be the traditional context in which to understand the moment in the *Finnsburg Fragment* when one warrior attempts to dissuade a young man from risking his life against the proven warrior who holds the door.

Every exclusive group, such as *Männerbünde,* practices some kind of initiation, even if it is only (as our *Zeit* reporter wrote) "saftige Aufnahmegebühren," and, of course, Höfler and Weiser deal in detail with *Jünglingsweihen,* the morphology of rites of passage and their social and religious context. The older sources seem to take little notice of rites of admission to the group—Unferth's challenge may be one example—but Norse sources are full of tests and initiations. The "initiation ceremonials" from the sagas discussed by Mary Danielli in 1945 show the neophyte passing tests for admission into a group of warriors and/or establishing his rank relative to them;[40] but a wider selection and more precise social context had already been brought to bear by Weiser and Höfler. An interesting example of a condition of admission to the select warrior group is reported by Saxo: taking a sword blow on the brow without flinching.[41] Various rules about wounds remind one of the importance of scars in such modern *Männerbünde* as dueling fraternities, but such semiotic aspects—hair is the most obvious—would lead too far afield. To the initiatory patterns in *Hálfs saga* and *Vǫlsunga saga* Weiser adds (without benefit of Propp) that of the *Märchen;* it is, however, worth distinguishing between individual hero initiations in a broad sense and entry into the male warrior band specifically.

Much of the contemporary work on the larger subject of *Männerbünde* dwells on the exclusion and repression of women, but Lily Weiser was already quite clear about this: "Behind the tribal initiations is concealed the battle of two generations ... and

---

40. Mary Danielli, "Initiation Ceremonial from Norse Literature," *Folk-Lore* 56 (1945): 229–45; Danielli makes the suggestion about Unferth's challenge on pp. 241–42.

41. Saxo 7.10.11 (*Saxonis Gesta Danorum,* ed. J. Olrik and H. Ræder, vol. 1 [Copenhagen: Levin & Munksgaard, 1931], p. 209; Saxo Grammaticus, *History of the Danes,* vol. 1: Text, trans. Peter Fisher, ed. Hilda Ellis Davidson, 2 vols. [Cambridge and Totowa, N.J.: D. S. Brewer and Rowman and Littlefield, 1979], p. 228; Weiser, *Jünglingsweihen,* n. 10 above, p. 68).

also the struggle for male authority over against women."[42] With the maleness of the Germanic *Männerbünde* in mind, we may notice a misogynistic strain in the literary tradition. In his chapters on public life and the *comitatus,* Tacitus implies only that the boy becomes a man by moving from the *domus* to the company of men in the public sphere (13), but, in his chapter on the Chatti (31), we encounter a celibate warrior elite without "house or land or any business."[43] A standard comparison to the celibate berserks is augmented in Weiser by reference to the *Hansa* (p. 38). One scholar compared the Chatti to monastic begging orders, and from our quasi-sociological point of view it is indeed a "'convergent' phenomenon."[44] The Chatti were apparently not a tribe or caste, but an order or *Männerbund* composed chiefly of warriors lingering in the state between boy and married man, *Junggesellen,* until they grew old. Whether berserks continue or revive this order is debatable, but they are usually presented as unmarried, dangerous gangs, groups often conceived as brothers.[45] The rules or laws of

---

42. Weiser *(Jünglingsweihen,* n. 10 above), p. 23: "Hinter den Stammesweihen verbirgt sich auch der Kampf zweier Generationen ... und der Kampf um die Herrschaft der Männer den Frauen gegenüber." John Lindow, "Riddles, Kennings, and the Complexity of Skaldic Poetry," *Scandinavian Studies* 47 (1975): 311–27, has suggested that the inherent ideology of Norse *dróttkvætt,* which was named for and flourished in the *drótt* or *comitatus,* correlated with its notoriously difficult, riddle-like style so that it functioned as a kind of test or sign of initiation into the warrior group: "Early skaldic poetry might, therefore, be regarded as a device for isolating non-members, i.e. the lower classes and women, from the *drótt.* It functioned, in effect, as a kind of secret language in which the members of the *drótt* could maintain their collective traditions in a special way and also communicate without being wholly understood by others, indeed to the exclusion of others" (pp. 322–23). For another explanation of *drótt(kvætt),* see Kuhn, "Gefolgschaft" (n. 24 above), pp. 437–40. The anti-feminist trends discussed here need not be considered as contradictory to significant actual power invested in the women on the margins of *Männerbünde;* see Michael J. Enright, "Lady With a Mead-Cup: Ritual, Group Cohesion and Hierarchy in the Germanic Warband," *Frühmittelalterliche Studien* 22 (1988): 170–203, an impressive study discovered too late to influence the present paper.

43. Trans. Hutton, pp. 180–81 (see n. 39 above): "nulli domus aut ager aut aliqua cura."

44. *Die Germania des Tacitus,* erläutert von Rudolf Much, 3rd ed., rev. by Herbert Jankuhn, ed. Wolfgang Lange (Heidelberg: Winter, 1967); reference and quotation, p. 389. Much's famous compendium is relevant at many points of the present essay but for reasons of space cannot be cited each time.

45. Ibid., esp. pp. 389–92; Weiser *(Jünglingsweihen,* n. 10 above), esp. pp. 44, 58, 66.

the viking groups provide for explicit rejection or regulation of dealings with women. The most famous are the laws of the *Jóms-víkingar* that prohibit any member from bringing a woman into the fort or from being away—presumably visiting a woman—for more than three days.[46] The laws of King Frodi in Saxo and the similar rules in *Hálfs saga, Hrólfs saga,* and *Qrvar-Odds saga* give special attention to problems such as rape and marriage. This may be a distant echo of the orgiastic sexual freedom that Schurtz found frequently associated with the liminal period, the Irish *fianna* preserving still more traces.[47]

Rejection of women can be related to success of the male group as warriors: Waltharius is lying to Attila when he voices the following sentiments, but the sentiments must have been plausible in the warrior context:

> If, following my lord's command, I take a wife,
> I will be bound first by my love and care for the girl
> And often kept away from service to the king.
> The need to build a house and supervise my farmland
> Will hinder me from being present in your sight
> And giving to the Huns' realm my accustomed care.
> Whoever once has tasted pleasure then becomes
> Accustomed to find hardships unendurable.
> For nothing is so sweet to me as always being
> In faithful obedience to my lord. I ask you, therefore,
> To let me lead my life free of the yoke of marriage.[48]

---

46. Discussed by Naumann, Kuhn, and Weiser, among many others; see B. R. Berg, *Sodomy and the Perception of Evil: English Sea Rovers in the Seventeenth-Century Caribbean* (New York and London: New York Univ. Press, 1983), for the customary absence of women on pirate ships.

47. See Kim R. McCone, "Werewolves, Cyclopes, Díberga, and Fíanna: Juvenile Delinquency in Early Ireland," *Cambridge Medieval Celtic Studies* 12 (1986): 1–22, esp. pp. 13–15; see also McCone, "Hund, Wolf und Krieger bei den Indogermanen," in *Studien zum indogermanischen Wortschatz,* ed. Wolfgang Meid, Innsbrucker Beiträge zur Sprachwissenschaft 52 (Innsbruck: Institut für Sprachwissenschaft, 1987), pp. 101–54, esp. p. 104.

48. *Waltharius and Ruodlieb,* ed. and trans. Dennis M. Kratz (New York: Garland, 1984), lines 150–60, pp. 10–11; cf. Naumann, *Germanisches Gefolgschaftswesen* (n. 36 above), p. 14.

Saxo tells how two brothers make parallel and comparable viking expeditions: one took married men and met disaster, the other took bachelors and succeeded.[49] Saxo's antifeminism in speeches such as that of Starcatherus in the Ingellus episode is probably rightly related to his monastic position (another *Männerbund*), but he did not entirely misread the Ingeld tradition, for in *Beowulf* the opposition of honor and marriage is already clear so that after incitement and revenge, Ingeld's "woman-loves ... grew colder" *(wīflufan ... cōlran weorðað)*. A symbolic rejection is probably to be read in the Norse *Hrímgerðarmál* where the demonized female is sexually threatening but finally unable to break up the male group.[50]

Hrímgerðr's insults to the retainer Atli are partly sexual, typical concepts from the realm of *níð*.[51] While *níð* abounds in Norse sources, I do not find much correlation with male-group contexts even though the cross-cultural literature on *Männerbünde* would lead one to expect male joking behavior like the Black American insult game of "sounding." One suggestive example, though, is Sneglu-Halli's bawdy joking about how the king acquired a coveted axe.[52] Symbolism of male-male sexual dominance and submission, especially upturned buttocks, has been brilliantly exposed by Preben Meulengracht Sørensen in *Gísla saga*,[53] and it seems to me that literature of the

---

49. Saxo, 7.1.1–2 (Olrik and Ræder, p. 181; Fisher, p. 201; see n. 41 above); Weiser *(Jünglingsweihen*, n. 10 above), p. 67, adds King Hálfr's men among the unmarried.

50. *Beowulf*, lines 2065b-66; *Hrímgerðarmál* in *Helgakviða Hjǫrvarðzsonar*, st. 12–30, in *Edda: Die Lieder des Codex Regius nebst verwandten Denkmälern*, ed. G. Neckel, 4th ed. rev. by H. Kuhn, vol. 1 (Heidelberg: Winter, 1962). Perhaps the original spirit behind the story of Cynewulf and Cyneheard condemned the "woman-visit" *(wīf-cyððu)*; in any case, she is a *meretrix* in one version.

51. For the concept and a recent fundamental discussion, see Preben Meulengracht Sørensen, *The Unmanly Man: Concepts of sexual defamation in early Northern society*, trans. Joan Turville-Petre, The Viking Collection I (Odense: Odense Univ. Press, 1983).

52. *Sneglu-Halla þáttr* in *Eyfirðinga sǫgur*, ed. Jónas Kristjánsson, Íslensk fornrit 9 (Reykjavík: Hið íslenzka fornritafélag, 1956), pp. 293–94; discussed in Harris, "Gender and Genre" (n. 37 above), and by Meulengracht Sørensen, p. 27 (n. 51 above); see also Michael Minkov, "Sneglu Halli, 2: 11: *Dróttinserðr*," *Saga-Book of the Viking Society*, 22, Pt. 5 (1988): 285–86.

53. *Unmanly Man* (n. 51 above), ch. 4, and "Murder in marital bed: An attempt at understanding a crucial scene in *Gísla saga*," in *Structure and Meaning in Old Norse Literature: New Approaches to Textual Analysis and Literary Criticism*, ed. John Lindow et al., The Viking Collection III (Odense: Odense Univ. Press, 1986), pp. 235–63; see also Tiger, *Men In Groups* (n. 18 above), pp. 27, 147.

Männerbund offers two further unnoticed examples: in *Hrólfs saga* when Aðils is *svínbeygðr* (caused to bend over in a swinish fashion) on Fyrisvellir and struck on the rump; and in the *Haraldskvœði* of Þorbjǫrn hornklofi, where wounded enemies tried to hide under rowing benches, "let their rumps stick up, thrust their heads toward the keel" (st. 10 in Finnur Jónsson, BI: 23).

Initiations are often modeled on the two more primary passages of life, birth and death, and it is well known that the symbolic male rebirths of *Männerbünde* are often explicitly births without female agency: the boy was born of the mother, the man of the father or of his own power. A possible example, unrecognized in Tacitus, is the Chatti custom that the young warrior might only cut his beard and hair when he stood over a slain enemy: at that moment, and not before would he cry that he had paid the price of his birth-pangs and was worthy of country and kin.[54] Rudolf Much explains the symbolism "as if nature demanded one life as a sacrifice for another coming into being," but a more precise understanding would result if the enemy, lying in his own blood, were symbolically the male mother.[55] In any case, the initiatory pattern of death and rebirth, *stirb und werde,* is common and documented for Germanic in Weiser and Höfler; I will mention only Sigmund's slaying and revival of his son Sinfjǫtli in a context that, except for the concentration to two characters, is almost paradigmatic for *Männerbünde.* The symbolism of non-female birth can be present in the institution of blood-brotherhood where, as in the familiar instance in *Gísla saga,* previously unrelated males die and are reborn without female agency as "brothers."

In the ideology of the *Männerbund,* candidates for initiation and brothers often stand in a closer relation to death and the dead than do excluded males, children, and women; often they *are* the dead, ritually speaking. Again Weiser and Höfler have thoroughly explored this point, but the transition from, say, the Harii-Einherjar to literary *comitatus*-like groups is a gradual one. I would underscore that the imagination of

---

54. Trans. Hutton, pp. 178–79 (see n. 39 above): "super sanguinem et spolia revelant frontem, seque tum demum pretia nascendi rettulisse dignosque patria ac parentibus ferunt."

55. Much, *Germania* (n. 44 above), p. 387: *"pretia nascendi:* 'den Entgelt für das Geborensein.' Dieser besteht aber nicht in dem Haaropfer, sonder in der Tötung des Feindes, als ob die Natur für ein werdendes Leben ein anderes als Opfer verlangte."

death, not solely from an individual point of view but in a social context, is a frequent feature. For example, Hálfr's warriors must not avoid death or speak fearful words; bloodbrothers and *Jómsvíkingar* must avenge each other. This would seem to be part of the wider institutional framework for Tacitus' sentence: "But to have left the field and survived one's chief, this means lifelong infamy and shame" (ch. 14; Hutton, p. 153 [note 39 below]). Much and other annotators cite as parallels *Beowulf*, the *Heliand*, the capture of Chnodomarius and his retainers as told by Ammianus Marcellinus, the death of the Herulian Fulkaris and his men as told by Agathias, Caesar on Germanic *soldurii*, Tacitus on Chariovalda in the *Annales*, and a certain King Herlaugr in the time of Haraldr hárfagri. The notices of suicide pacts of the Celtiberians are not Germanic; but I cannot agree when Kuhn dismisses the whole phenomenon as rather Celtic than Germanic: "Mir kommt die erörterte Forderung ungermanisch vor, den heißeren Kelten trau ich sie eher zu" ("The requirement under discussion seems to me un-Germanic; I would sooner trust it to the more hot-blooded Celts")—so much for the objectivity of the postwar correction. Other comparable passages would include the famous decisions of the retainers of Cynewulf and Cyneheard; Kuhn objects to the self-sacrifice of a *minister* or *miles* in Bede (in the year 626) that both words indicate vassals rather than retainers.[56] A larger collection of sentiments that in a general way connect death with the bonds of the *Männerbund* could probably be made.[57]

*   *   *

The *Bjarkamál* has been called "das Hohelied der Gefolgschaftstreue." Taken together with its wider narrative context, it is a condensed mythos of the *Männerbund*. Hrólfr kraki's retainers are berserks in

---

56. Much's list of parallels (*Germania*, n. 44 above), pp. 227–30; Kuhn on the hot-blooded Celts, "Gefolgschaft" (n. 24 above), p. 425, and on English instances, esp. p. 447. There are many other discussions of these passages in the literature.

57. For example, *Hrólfs saga Gautrekssonar*, ch. 19: "The crew were delighted to see their King in good shape, because they'd made up their minds, if necessary, to go against the giant and avenge their lord, for they'd no wish to live if their King had been killed" (Hermann Pálsson and Paul Edwards, trans., *Hrolf Gautreksson: A Viking Romance* [Toronto: Univ. of Toronto Press, 1972], p. 89); ch. 29: Hrólfr's men are all killed: "They'd wanted nothing but to do their best to help their King like good retainers" (p. 129).

Snorri's version, and Kuhn produces convincing reasons for believing they were berserks or "champions" in the original tradition.[58] With Kuhn's narrow definition this is grounds for denying the term *comitatus,* but Hrólfr's men certainly qualify as a warlike *Männerbund.* Moreover, Hjalti's initiation shows typical features of Höfler's narrower cultic sense of *Männerbund:* animal affinities, a ritual slaying, a monster, traces of masking. Hjalti's passage into the valued status of man involves change of name, gift of a weapon, membership and ranking; there is rivalry and competition; Bjarki is Hjalti's initiatory guide, perhaps also the *Gefolgschaftsälteste.* In the fourteenth-century saga Bjarki is married to Hrólfr's daughter as a sign of esteem, but more characteristic of the Warrior-Male's attitude to women is Hjalti's visit to his mistress as the final battle looms: he picks a quarrel, and: "'You whore, you shall pay for those words,' cried Hjalti, and going up to her he bit off her nose.... 'You used me ill,' said she.... 'One cannot keep track of everything,'" said Hjalti, whereupon he grabbed his weapons and returned to his comrades, faced with a treacherous attack inspired by Hrólfr's own sister.[59] The nose-biting episode seems a little less arbitrary when we realize that the purpose of the preceding dialogue was to test the woman's loyalty, a test she fails in contrast to the retainers who will never serve another lord after Hrólfr. Saxo tells this segment similarly; when Hialti chooses "bravery before lust," Saxo asks: "Can we guess what affection for his monarch burned in this soldier, who reckoned it better to risk his safety in obvious danger rather than save himself for pleasure?"[60] But the rejection of "woman-loves" was already present in the oldest reconstructable *Bjarkamál* as we can conclude from the agreement of Saxo and the fragments on the following segment of the waking topos: "I do not ask you to learn to sport with young girls," etc.; "I do not wake you to wine, nor to the whispers of a woman, rather I wake you to the hard game of Hildr."[61] The only women proper to these

---

58. Kuhn, "Gefolgschaft" (n. 24 above), pp. 471–76, esp. p. 475; for the characterization with "Hohelied," see p. 458.

59. *Eirik the Red and Other Icelandic Sagas,* trans. Gwyn Jones (London: Oxford Univ. Press, 1961), p. 309; *Hrólfs saga kraka,* ed. D. Slay, Editiones Arnamagnaeanae, B, 1 (Copenhagen: Munksgaard, 1960), p. 113.

60. Saxo 2.7.3 (Olrik and Ræder, p. 53; Fisher, p. 56; see n. 41 above).

61. Saxo 2.7.4 (Fisher, pp. 56–57; see n. 41 above). *Vekka ek yðr at víni / né at vífs rúnum, / heldr vek ek yðr at hǫrðum / Hildar leiki (Eddica minora: Dichtungen eddischer Art ...* , ed. Andreas Heusler and Wilhelm Ranisch [Dortmund: Ruhfus, 1903], p. 31).

bonded men are Hildr or Skuld, valkyrie or death goddess. The contrast of warrior life in the company of comrades with the stay-at-home who spends his time kissing slave girls behind the quern is something of a topos in Old Norse,[62] and it seems to be present in the *Bjarkamál* in a form that would seem familiar to Theweleit's Freikorps-men.

So the *Bjarkamál* and its saga were understandably associated with the last rite of passage. A famous anecdote tells how, on the morning of the battle of Stiklastaðr in 1030, the fatal last stand of St. Olaf, the king asked his poet Þormóðr to perform a poem; Þormóðr's choice, the *Bjarkamál*, moved the hearers, who knew it under the name "Húskarlakvǫt" ("Retainers' Incitement"). According to Snorri, the king rewarded Þormóðr, but the poet replied: "We have a good king, but it is difficult to see how long-lived a king he will be. It is my request [i.e., as reward for the poem], king, that you let the two of us be parted neither by life nor death." The king answered: "As long as I control things, we will all go together if you do not wish to part with me."[63] Þormóðr continues with the topic of loyalty unto death but cannot resist a dig at his rival poet, Sighvatr: "I hope, my king, that whether there is safety or danger, I shall be positioned near you as long as I have any choice—whatever we may hear about where Sighvatr is travelling with his golden-hilted sword." Þormóðr's poem, quoted at this point, repeats these thoughts: "I shall still hover before your knees, bold king, until other skalds draw near [i.e., Sighvatr]; when do you expect them? We shall escape alive, though we feed carrion to the greedy raven, or else we shall lie here. That is certain, o seafarer."[64]

---

62. See Cecil Wood, "*Nis þæt seldguma: Beowulf* 249," *Publications of the Modern Language Association* 75 (1960): 481–84. See *ne to wife wynn* in the OE *Seafarer*, line 45, where *peregrinatio* has perhaps replaced war as the hard life. Perhaps a very old trace of the "not for love, but for war" idea is to be seen in *Germania*, ch. 38, where the Suebi pay attention to grooming, "not for making love or being made love to" but to terrify the enemy (trans. Hutton, pp. 192–95 [see n. 39 above]: "neque enim ut ament amenturve").

63. Snorri Sturluson, *Óláfs saga helga*, ch. 208: *Heimskringla*, II, ed. Bjarni Aðalbjarnarson, Íslenzk fornrit 27 (Reykjavík: Hið íslenzka fornritafélag, 1945), p. 362. The King's phrase *meðan ek rœð fyrir*, and Þormóðr's echo *meðan ek á þess kost*, could be regarded as prose reflection of the heroic "as long as" topos, e.g., *Sár fló égi at Uppsalum / en wá, með hann wápn hafði; Þa hwile ðe he wæpna wealdan moste* (examples from Bertha S. Phillpotts, "'The Battle of Maldon': Some Danish Affinities," *Modern Language Review* 24 [1929]: 172–90).

64. Bjarni Aðalbjarnarson, p. 363 (see previous note); Finnur Jónsson *(Skjaldedigtning*, n. 1 above), BI, p. 265.

Rosemary Woolf's brilliant article on the ideal of men dying with
their lord in *The Battle of Maldon* poses something of an obstacle to
the proposed institutional context of these ideas of death.[65] Here is a
summary of her arguments: (1) the "ideal" is found in precisely three
texts only, *Germania*, *Bjarkamál*, and *Maldon*, and since the "ideal"
was not current in Anglo-Saxon life or elsewhere in Anglo-Saxon
literature, a huge gap must be recognized between the first-century
and tenth-century instances; (2) she considers it possible that the
Maldon author drew the "ideal" directly from Tacitus but silently
rejects (or brackets) this possibility; and (3) she concludes instead that
it was introduced as a "foreign ideal" from the *Bjarkamál* but that the
author of *Maldon* contrived to blend it convincingly into the fabric
of his poem. The case for influence from the *Bjarkamál* to *Maldon*
is based on Bertha Phillpotts's classic article, and I agree that some
form of the *Bjarkamál* was known to the *Maldon* poet. But Woolf
leaves unasked the question of the origin of the "ideal" in *Bjarkamál*.
Since this late tenth-century oral poem can hardly be expected to have
borrowed from Tacitus (and the resemblances to Tacitus are stronger in
Maldon), Woolf's solution for *Maldon* merely transfers the problem
of the gap to the *Bjarkamál*.[66] But her solution for *Maldon* is based
on several errors (as I see it) in her point (1). To arrive at the isolation
of the three texts she is forced to almost theological sophistications
to refine "the ideal" out of its contexts; the resulting separation from
passages such as the Cynewulf and Cyneheard story seems unnatural.
And why should the author adopt a totally foreign ideal at all? This
is not the way ideas are transmitted. The argument that the *Maldon*
author intertwined the "ideal" with other features of a heroic ethos
in order to naturalize it is overingenious: in fact it is so intertwined
because it exists only as part of a larger traditional package. This
package is also to be found in the *Bjarkamál*, which, contrary to
what Woolf's argument would lead us to expect, also presents the
"ideal" only in close context with revenge and other relevant features.
Woolf's treatment of the *Bjarkamál* is cursory; in fact she seems to

---

65. Rosemary Woolf, "The Ideal of Men Dying with their Lord in the *Germania*
and in *The Battle of Maldon*," *Anglo-Saxon England* 5 (1976): 63–81.

66. The date of the *Bjarkamál* is not undisputed; for discussion and references,
see J. Harris, "Eddic Poetry," in *Old Norse-Icelandic Literature: A Critical Guide*, ed.
Carol J. Clover and John Lindow, Islandica 45 (Ithaca: Cornell Univ. Press, 1985), pp.
118–19.

have forgotten about the Icelandic fragments.[67] She finds the "ideal" expressed purely only once in Saxo's prose commentary and goes on to admit that it is "not stated so roundly in Saxo's actual version of the poem" but is merely implicit in tone and structure, its only explicit statement in the poem being intertwined with the physical disposition of the corpses, a motif to be studied below.

Finally, the "ideal" in relatively pure form is expressed in other texts of the period of the *Bjarkamál* and *Maldon*. Woolf seems to have relied here on Phillpotts, who exaggerated the specifically Danish qualities she found in *Maldon*, especially in her claim that certain motifs are shunned in Norwegian and Icelandic verse. Jess Bessinger and other scholars have noticed parallels with Hallfreðr vandræðaskáld's *Óláfs Erfidrápa (Tryggvasonar)*, but a closer parallel with *Maldon* occurs in our Sighvatr's *Erfidrápa* for St. Olaf (c. 1040). Speaking of one of the king's major retainers, Sighvatr's st. 18 says:

> I have also heard that Bjǫrn long ago instructed the retainers with great courage how to keep faith with one's lord. He advanced in battle. He fell there in the host along with the loyal men of the king's bodyguard at the head of his famous lord. That death is praised.[68]

Here in the midst of a disastrous battle we find a vignette similar to those of the second part of *Maldon*; a retainer steps into the spotlight and urges his comrades, now that the lord is dead, to keep faith with him; then the retainer himself advances and falls beside his lord. A few years later Arnórr jarlaskáld composed a funeral poem for the Norwegian king Haraldr harðráði describing his famous ill-fated attack on England in 1066, a poem with several parallels to *Maldon* and including this stanza:

---

67. Woolf ("The Ideal," n. 65 above), pp. 79–80, esp. p. 79: "No close comparison between *Maldon* and the *Bjarkamál* is possible, since the latter is known only from Saxo's translation of it into Latin hexameters."

68. Bjarni Aðalbjarnarson (*Heimskringla*, n. 63 above), p. 386; Finnur Jónsson (*Skjaldedigtning*, n. 1 above), BI, p. 243. Axel Olrik, *The Heroic Legends of Denmark*, trans. Lee M. Hollander (New York: American-Scandinavian Foundation, 1919), p. 170, took the stanza to be an allusion to the *Bjarkamál*; Roberta Frank, *Old Norse Court Poetry: The* Dróttkvætt *Stanza*, Islandica 42 (Ithaca: Cornell Univ. Press, 1978), pp. 129–31, agrees and adds an independent reason for believing in the allusion, the "bear" names Bjarki and Bjorn; Frank also compares this stanza to *Maldon*, p. 123.

The death of the fear-inspiring king was not easy. Points red with treasure did not spare the foe of robbers. All the retainers of the generous
prince chose rather to fall around the war-quick king than that they
would wish peace.[69]

Such literary parallels do not prove that the "ideal" was truly followed
in daily life, but Woolf s apparent belief that the "ideal" was quite
limited in Old Norse seems mistaken; she herself cited several prose
parallels. An implicit argument seems to be that because an idea may
be borrowed from another literary utterance, it is somehow cultur-
ally void. (The "semi-suicidal resolve not to outlive [one's] lord is
peculiar to the *Bjarkamál* and later poems closely influenced by it"
[p. 80].) This assumption seems wrong, for traditional ideas live in
the "texts" of discourse.

Maldon, then, seems to be a poem in touch with traditional oral
literature. It probably draws on an oral *Bjarkamál* but also shares
various features with contemporary Northern European praise verse.
Its articulation of the mythos of the *Männerbund* is realistic and intense
but much narrower than that of the *Bjarkamál* taken together with its
saga. There are no traces of initiation or hostility to women, but
age classes and warrior education are obvious in the poem whether
or not any of the groups mentioned constituted a continuation of
the Tacitan *comitatus*.[70] The features of the mythos dwelled upon in
Maldon are, of course, loyalty and betrayal, oaths, reputation, and
revenge, all in the imminence of death.

---

69. Finnur Jónsson *(Skjaldedigtning,* n. 1 above), BI, p. 325. The other major *Maldon*
parallels in the poem include *uppganga* (which perhaps explains the exceptional weak form
of the same technical term in *Maldon,* line 87, as a further example of "literary dialect"
in the poem [see Scragg, pp. 73–74, n. 71 below, and Dietrich Hofmann, *Nordisch-englische Lehnbeziehungen der Wikingerzeit,* Bibliotheca Arnamagnaeana 14 (Copenhagen:
Munksgaard, 1955), pp. 194–95]) and *ofrausn* (cf. the vexed *ofermōd).* Diana Edwards,
"Christian and Pagan References in Eleventh-Century Norse Poetry: The Case of Arnórr
Jarlaskáld," *Saga-Book* 21 (1982–83): 44, has previously made the latter comparison. I have
not been able to take account of a very relevant article that arrived when the present essay
was substantially complete: Roberta Frank, "The Ideal of Men Dying with their Lord in
The Battle of Maldon: Anachronism or *nouvelle vague,"* in *People and Places in Northern
Europe 500–1600: Essays in Honour of Peter Hayes Sawyer,* ed. Ian Wood and Niels Lund
(Woodbridge: Boydell Press, 1990), pp. 95–106; but Frank also compares the cited stanza
from Arnórr's poem and the two technical words as parallels to *Maldon* (p. 102).

70. Cf. J. Harris, *"Stemnettan: Battle of Maldon,* l. 22," *Philological Quarterly* 55
(1976): 113–15.

Two forms of death are shown. Byrhtnoð's death takes place in the midst of a throng, and the devils *(helsceaðan,* line 180) he imagines threatening his soul in his lorica-like last words mirror the earthly enemies around him *(hæðene scealcas,* line 181). But there is no spiritual analogue of his *heorðwerod* (line 21), and the drama of his death is enacted in Christian isolation between the individual and God: his soul will escape the world and be judged alone. His body, however, remains with the male group as a sign that elicits loyalty or betrayal, and the following deaths in the poem (as well as the desertions) are played out both physically and spiritually in the social context. The deaths of the retainers are individualized only within that context, seen only in relation to each other and the earthly lord, not under the aspect of eternity. Social context is realized as spectacle, addresses to the other retainers, or memory of former addresses. Allusions to dying with the lord seem to escalate in intensity.[71] References to the spectacle of the dead lord, the good man in the dirt, extend through the entire passage, each time conjoined with the idea of self-sacrifice, and every explicit reference to the "ideal" also refers to the visible body of the fallen lord.[72] But the last two major death vignettes in the fragment, those of Offa and Byrhtwold, add a new theme, the "profound fittingness of the body of a thegn lying beside that of his dead lord" (Woolf, "The Ideal," p. 80); of Offa: "He lay in a thanely manner beside his lord" (line 294); of Byrhtwold: "I will not turn away, but rather I think to lie by the side of my lord, beside the man so beloved" (lines 317a-319).[73]

Woolf and Phillpotts take this topos in *Maldon* as a borrowing from the *Bjarkamál,* where Bjarki's last words to Hjalti culminate in:

> Struck down I shall die at the head of my slain leader,
> and you will drop face-foremost at his feet,
> so that one who views body on body may see
> how we make return for the gold received from our master....

---

71. *The Battle of Maldon,* ed. D. G. Scragg (Manchester: Manchester Univ. Press, 1981), lines 206–07; 220–23a; 232–37a (implied in the "as long as" topos); 246–54; 275–76, 279; 289–94; 312–19. In addition the idea seems implicit in lines 258–60; 272; 306–08.

72. *Maldon,* lines 203–04; 222b; 232b–33a; 250b; 276b; 292b–94; 314–15a, 317–19. The three "implicit passages" (see previous note) lack the visual reference.

73. "He læg ðegenlice ðeodne gehende"; "fram ic ne wille, / ac ic me be healfe minum hlaforde, / be swa leofan men, licgan þence."

> Though fearless in war it is proper that earls should fall,
> and embrace their illustrious king in a common death.[74]

Independently of both, Einar Ól. Sveinsson had put together a collection of instances of this topos within the larger self-sacrificial ideal, and we have already encountered one specimen in Bjǫrn digri's death *at hilmis hǫfði* (at the prince's head). The *Innsteinslied* has the retainers Hrókr and Innsteinn falling at foot and head of King Hálfr, obviously influenced by the *Bjarkamál*.[75] And Olrik had pointed out an exact echo of the Danish poem in a Faroese ballad with the arrangement: at the head, at the feet, and finally, "I will rest on my lord's breast."[76] The ordered pile of corpses had been mentioned already in the sixth-century work of Agathias, and Einar Ól. Sveinsson's collection, with a Roman example of death *ante regis pedes* (pp. 51–52), suggests that the idea is either ancient and Indo-European or that it can recur independently. The point of his collection, however, is to provide a context for some historical thirteenth-century Icelandic instances of self-sacrifice, especially two in which followers drop upon the fallen body of their leader who, however, escapes alive from the heap of corpses.

This form of dying seems to be a traditional image, especially at home in the military *Männerbund*. Perhaps it is related to the *aemulatio* or competition to be nearest the leader and generally to ranking, but the physical images—a warrior at the foot of the lord, another at the head, an old retainer lying down beside his lord or embracing *(complexos)* his body—associates the scene in my mind with suttee, especially as reported for the Germanic world by Ibn Fadlán and in *Sigurðarkviða in*

---

74. Saxo 2.7.28 (Fisher, p. 63; see n. 41 above):

> "Ad caput extincti moriar ducis obrutus, at tu
> eiusdem pedibus moriendo allabere pronus,
> ut videat, quisquis congesta cadavera lustrat,
> qualiter acceptum domino pensarimus aurum....
> Sic belli intrepidos proceres occumbere par est,
> illustrem socio complexos funere regem."

75. Einar Ól. Sveinsson, "'Ek ætla mér ekki á braut'," in *Afmælisrit Jóns Helgasonar 30. júní 1969*, ed. Jakob Benediktsson et al. (Reykjavík: Heimskringla, 1969), pp. 48–58; Sveinsson, "Drottinhollusta," *Gripla* 2 (1977): 188–90.

76. Olrik, *Heroic Legends*, pp. 172–73 ("Ulf fan Jærn"; see n. 68 above). Further examples of apparently symbolically ordered corpses are found in the Iring story (murdered lord laid atop murdered enemy), in *Beowulf* (Hildeburh's son laid shoulder to shoulder with his uncle), and in the stanza quoted from Arnórr jarlaskáld.

skamma.[77] There among slain slave women Brynhild has herself laid on one side *(á hlið aðra,* st. 66) of Sigurd, on the other side, "my serving men, and [though here the text becomes tricky] two men at his head *(at hǫfðom),*[78] two at his feet, two hounds and two hawks—then is everything properly arranged" (st. 67). Compare the sense of propriety here with *ðegenlice* in *Maldon* and *par est* in Saxo. The model for the thanely death beside the lord cannot derive from the portion of these ancient funeral customs that applies to hawk and hounds or even to slaves, but it is worth considering the analogy of the widow, who, according to the mythology of suttee, freely chooses death.

If the family is the primary human group, then all-male groups are secondary, and theorists such as Schurtz believe that their organization is ultimately modeled, to some extent, on the family, despite rejection of women. Wenskus and Schlesinger, for example, offer the opinion that the *comitatus* was modeled after the *domus.*[79] Among the very limited number of gender roles and relationships in the primary model, father-son and brother-brother relations seem plausible enough because sex

---

77. For a general account of the Germanic survivals of suttee, see Hilda Roderick Ellis (Davidson), *The Road to Hel: A Study of the Conception of the Dead in Old Norse Literature* (Cambridge: Cambridge Univ. Press, 1943), pp. 14–15, 46–48.

78. The plural could refer to the pair Brynhild and Sigurd, but most translators seem to take her directions here as referring to Sigurd's head alone. Cf. *Dream of the Rood,* ed. Michael Swanton (Manchester: Univ. Press; New York: Barnes & Noble, 1970), line 63: "gestodon him æt his lices heafdum"; Swanton's note (in part): "The form here must probably be understood as a locative singular (cf. Campbell, § 574.4) conventionally applied to the head of a corpse or one similarly recumbent," together with a suggestive parallel. St. 67 is paraphrased and translated here from the reconstruction by Hugo Gering and B. Sijmons, *Kommentar zu den Liedern der Edda,* vol. 2 (Halle/Saale: Waisenhaus, 1931), pp. 275–76. This reconstruction seems to me fully justified.

79. Walter Schlesinger, "Herrschaft und Gefolgschaft in der germanisch-deutschen Verfassungsgeschichte," *Historische Zeitschift* 176 [1953]: 225–75; repr. in *Herrschaft und Staat im Mittelalter,* ed. Hellmut Kämpf, Wege der Forschung 2 (Darmstadt: Wissenschaftliche Buchgesellschaft, 1984), pp. 135–90; p. 149: "Sie heißen wie die Sippegenossen Freunde; hierher gehört das Wort *nôtfriunt,* Kampffreund. Wiederum das Beowulflied überliefert Bezeichnungen wie *maguthegnas* und sogar *magas* für die Gefolgsleute (v. 1015), für die Gefolgschaft das Wort *sibbegedryht* (vv. 3, 87, 729). Die Bindung der Gefolgsleute untereinander scheint also der sippschaftlichen Bindung nachgebildet zu sein. Dem entspricht, daß Tötung eines Mitgliedes die Rache der Gefolgschaft hervorruft. Auch eine Fehde zwischen Angehörigen derselben Gefolgschaft ist wie zwischen Sippegenossen ausgeschlossen, Streitigkeiten schlichtet der Herr." Wenskus *(Stammesbildung und Verfassung,* n. 23 above), p. 363: "Diese Züge künstlicher Verwandtschaft im Gefolgschaftswesen unterstreichen die Beobachtung Schlesingers, der aus sprachlichen Zeugnissen vermutete, daß die Bindung der Gefolgsleute untereinander der sippschaftlichen Bindung nachgebildet sei." This is implicit also in Kauffmann *(Altertumskunde,* n. 19 above).

here coincides with gender, and sometimes such modeling is explicit. But it seems possible, in view of male birth rituals and the like, that gender lines can be crossed in such role-modeling. One impressive example is the archaic metaphor of the poet as the "wife" of the king in Ireland; Proinsias Mac Cana has recently brought forward convincing evidence to argue that this metaphor was Common Celtic and probably even Indo-European.[80] I do not know of similar gender analyses of primitive groups that could be called on for analogical support here, but I cannot repress the speculation that the *Liebestod* which we see fairly clearly in our Germanic materials is ultimately a male suttee. I will not follow this speculation into the suggestive literature on suttee itself, except to notice that in its promise of being together in the afterlife, suttee provides an archaic reason for self-sacrifice lacking in the ethnographic literature but not out of harmony with the connections expected between the *Männerbund* and the dead.

* * *

Many speculations ago, at the beginning of this essay, we left Sighvatr Þórðarson vowing to live and die with King Magnús Óláfsson. We now recognize that his relationship to Magnús is at least partly shaped by his position as *Gefolgschaftsälteste* and by the love and *aemulatio* inherent in the *hirð*. But the leader who molded Sighvatr's life was Magnús's father, St. Olaf. Sighvatr survived Stiklastaðr because he was not there for Olaf's last battle—a fact he had to deal with in his verse. His journey to Rome saved him but exposed him to the jealous criticisms of his comrades. According to Snorri, Sighvatr learned of the fall of Olaf on his return journey:

> One day Sighvatr was going through a village and heard some husband weeping aloud because he had lost his wife; he beat his breast and tore his clothing off, wept a great deal, saying that he would gladly die.

---

80. Proinsias Mac Cana, "The Poet as Spouse of his Patron," *Ériu* 39 (1988): 79–85, and references there, esp. James Carney, *The Irish Bardic Poet: A Study in the Relationship of Poet and Patron* ... (Dublin: Institute for Advanced Studies, 1958; repr. n.p.: Dolmen, 1967), esp. pp. 11–13, 37–40. A milder cross-gender metaphor is implicit in Hjalti's nose-biting episode (woman:retainer :: retainer:king).

Sighvatr spoke this poem: "The man says he is eager to die if he loses the embrace of the woman. Love is dearly bought if (even) a proud man must weep after (the dead). But the unretreating hero who has lost his lord sheds tears of war-fury; our unavengeable loss seems worse to the men of the king."[81]

This husband's voluntary death takes place only in his mind, and it is not the bright mead that must be paid for but love itself; moreover, the gender roles here reverse those of real suttee with the dead king likened to the wife, the retainer to the bereaved husband.[82] Sighvatr expressed his grief in other more or less elegiac poems for Olaf, but, despite the imperfection of its analogy between domestic love-and-death and love-and-death within the *Männerbund,* this *lausavísa* may capture something of the archaic force of the feelings that, at least in imagination, account for the ideal of men dying with their lord.

Postscriptum

Most of the above was written in 1990; its first airings were at oral presentations in the fall of 1990 (Harvard) and spring of 1991 (Princeton, Kalamazoo). I view the piece as an "essay" in the original sense; the evidence and research presented were perforce partial from

---

81. *Magnúss saga ins góða,* ch. 7; *Heimskringla,* III, ed., Bjarni Aðalbjarnarson, p. 15; Finnur Jónsson *(Skjaldedigtning,* n. 1 above), BI, p. 251 (with different interpretation of *oflátinn).*

82. Mac Cana's Indic evidence shows reversals in such gender metaphors. Carney quotes a traditional fifteenth-century bard who goes to visit the grave of his lord: "As he looks at the grave he wishes to die too, and he recalls how things used to be: 'Let us be in the bed as we were before, O prince of Bóroimhe; we did not think a narrow bed too narrow for us two, O Féilim'" (p. 37; *Bardic Poet,* n. 80 above); the allusion here is to the poet as *fear éinleabtha* or "man of the same bed" with the king. A puzzling passage in *Þorleifs þáttr jarlaskálds* may be mentioned here: "I have composed certain verses during the winter which I call *konuvísir* [woman-verses], which I made about Earl Hákon because an earl is metaphorically a *kona* [woman] in poetry" (Íslenzk fornrit 9: 219; n. 3: "Senni-lega hefur verið til einhver kveðskapur, þótt nú sé glataður, þar sem Hákon jarl hefur verið 'kona kenndr'; mun það hafa verið dregið af því, að síðari hlut nafns hans minnir á orðið *konu.*" (Presumably there was some verse, now lost, in which Earl Hákon was likened to a woman; this must have derived from the fact that the latter part of his name recalls the word *kona* [woman]). In support of this explanation, see *Rígsþula's* pun on *kon-ungr.)*

the beginning. Nevertheless, the intervening years have brought to my attention several secondary works that should be mentioned. Margaret Clunies Ross, "Hildr's Ring," *Mediaeval Scandinavia 6* (1973):75–92, had already brilliantly examined some of the same instances of sexual defamation discussed in my essay, together with some glimpses of anthropological background. Especially important is her extensive discussion of *svínbeygja,* which I wrongly thought had been "unnoticed," and the more complex light her discussion throws upon the *jarðarmen* ceremony of blood-brotherhood in Icelandic sources. The Celtic parallel offered in my closing paragraphs can be supported by Katharine Simms, "The Poet as Chieftain's Widow: Bardic Elegies," in *Sages, Saints and Storytellers: Celtic Studies in Honour of Professor James Carney,* ed. D. O. Corráin, L. Breatnach, and K. McCone (Maynooth: An Sagart, 1989), pp. 400–11. Simms offers more examples of the metaphor from late medieval and renaissance Ireland and an arresting analysis that includes recourse to the analogy of suttee: "So regularly and insistently is this theme [of the poets' 'duty to die with their master and share the one grave'] harped on, it is almost as if [the poet] had a duty to committ *suttee*" (p. 404). An important article by Heinz Klingenberg must now color the way we understand the historiographical context of Þormóðr's *Bjarkamál*: "Altnordisch *húskarl,* *Bjarkamál=Húskarlahvǫt* und Stiklastad," in *Festschrift til Ottar Grønvik på 75-års-dagen de 21. oktober 1991,* ed. John Ole Askedal, Harald Bjorvand, and Eyvind Fjeld Halvorsen (Oslo: Universitetsforlaget, 1991), pp. 183–211. A recent publication is Christine Eike [erroneously Eicke on the title page], *Sozialformen der männlichen Jugend Altnorwegens,* Wiener Arbeiten zur germanischen Altertumskunde und Philologie 5 (Vienna: Karl M. Halosar, 1978); this massively documented study should be taken into account when a future evaluation of the Vienna *Männerbund* theory is attempted. I thank Prof. Helmut Birkhan and Dr. Christine Eike for personal communications about the teaching of Höfler and the later career of Weiser-Aall in Norway and for bibliographical help; Birkhan's informative and tasteful "Vorwort" to a selection of Höfler's *kleine Schriften* (to be published by Verlag Helmut Buske, Hamburg) will be of great value to this chapter in the history of the discipline [Otto Höfler, *Kleine Schriften: ausgewählte Arbeiten zur germanischen Altertumskunde und Religionsgeschichte, zur Literatur des Mittelalters, zur germanischen Sprachwissenschaft sowie zur Kulturphilosophie und –morphologie,* ed. by Helmut Birkhan and Heinrich Beck (Hamburg: Helmut Buske, 1992). Eds.]. I wish also to thank Prof. Susan E. Deskis for a helpful critical reading at an early stage.

J. H. 2.14.93

Romancing the Rune:

Aspects of Literacy in Early Scandinavian Orality*

To a graduate student at Harvard in the 1960s oral literature was an exciting topic, but with thirty years' hindsight we seem to have had a narrow grasp of the potential issues. I was a student of Albert Bates Lord and indirectly of Francis Peabody Magoun, but more directly I was the student of Larry Dean Benson, who, in the mid-'60s, so memorably demonstrated the logical gap in the most provocative part of the oral-formulaic theory, the part that encouraged the transference of conclusions from the South Slavic model to all other oral poetry.[1] When I was writing my article "Eddic Poetry as Oral Poetry" in 1974 and '75 (it appeared only in 1983), the problems for the segment of Scandinavian literature I had been studying seemed to be limited to (1) the applicability of Lord's model, especially with respect to memorization and improvisation, (2) Lord's rhetorical appropriation of the term "oral," and (3) problems specific to the eddic tradition, especially the relationship of larger compositional units to an oral poetics.[2] The more exact conclusions of that article

---

*For the original stimulation to write I thank Prof. Patricia Conroy of the University of Washington, Seattle, where the earliest version was presented in April 1993.

    1. Larry D. Benson, "The Literary Character of Anglo-Saxon Formulaic Poetry," *PMLA* 81 (1966): 334–41.

    2. Joseph Harris, "Eddic Poetry as Oral Poetry: The Evidence of Parallel Passages in the Helgi Poems for Questions of Composition and Performance," in *Edda: A Collection of Essays*, ed. Robert J. Glendinning and Haraldur Bessason ([Winnipeg]: University of Manitoba Press, 1983), pp. 210–42. [Reprinted in this volume, Eds.]

are limited to a small group of eddic poems, but at a more general level I came to the conclusion, not predictable from a starting point in the oral-formulaic theory, that there was no need entirely to throw out older eddic scholarship that was mainly concerned with what we would now call intertextuality, especially literary history established through evidence of borrowing. Though I was not especially concerned with formulas, I did and still do agree with the broader implications of Lars Lönnroth's study of eddic poetry in concluding that formulas are used in a variety of ways and do not guarantee the oral-formulaic model for Old Norse.[3]

Outside of Harvard, where spirits were less constrained to assassinate or venerate the fathers, scholarship had already spiraled out into vastly different realms of thought on orality and literacy, taking one of the *other* paths suggested by that seminal quartet of works of the early '60' s—Lord's *Singer of Tales,* McLuhan's *Gutenberg Galaxy,* Goody and Watt's "Consequences of Literacy," and Havelock's *Preface to Plato*—or else non-Harvard scholars were *combining* Parry and Lord's philological way with these approaches from communications, sociology, and anthropology.[4] In the mid-'70s Ruth Finnegan was also busy showing the enormous variety of oral literatures and deconstructing the inherited categories.[5] Researchers unburdened by the Harvard past had discovered that in order to understand orality, they had to study the literacy and literate practices through which it was almost always perceived. In the last decade or so, writers on oral literature have somewhat muted their differences of opinion (at least by comparison to the stridency of the '60s) and quietly subsume contradictions, dipping eclectically into any reservoir of theory that can be harmonized with the general direction of their own thoughts. In America Walter Ong's book *Orality and Literacy* of 1982 has come to be widely regarded as a summa on which to build—if one

---

3. Lars Lönnroth, "Hjálmar's Death-Song and the Delivery of Eddic Poetry," *Speculum* 46 (1971): 1–20.

4. Albert Bates Lord, *The Singer of Tales* (Cambridge, Mass.: Harvard University Press, 1960); Marshall McLuhan, *The Gutenberg Galaxy* (Toronto: University of Toronto Press, 1962); Jack Goody and Ian Watt, "The Consequences of Literacy," in *Contemporary Studies in Society and History* 5 (1963), pp. 304–45 (often reprinted); Eric Havelock, *Preface to Plato* (Cambridge, Mass.: Harvard University Press, 1963).

5. Ruth Finnegan, *Oral Poetry: Its Nature, Significance, and Social Context* (Cambridge: Cambridge University Press, 1977; 2nd ed. rev., 1992).

ignores a few blind spots.[6] And today, as I struggle to keep up with the exploding universe of scholarship in the areas that interest me, Ong's interpretation of the oral/literate opposition appears to have spread almost everywhere as an internalized assumption too basic to be questioned. That this "Great Divide" theory *is* vigorously opposed by Ruth Finnegan and some social scientists qualifies the relative harmony of recent years but has hardly slowed the positive response in humanistic scholarship.[7]

Old Norse has not played much of a role in the burgeoning thought on oral literature. An internal discussion has simmered for decades on oral and written antecedents to the extant thirteenth-century sagas.[8] This debate between *Freiprosa* and *Buchprosa,* the terms of which were set in the time of Andreas Heusler, continues with little influence from the intellectual heirs of Lord, McLuhan, and Goody until the important recent theoretical contribution—Carol Clover's "immanent saga"—an elegant solution, which, however, will probably satisfy neither side.[9] Eddic poetry continues to be the focal point for the more general interest in orality and literacy and, of

---

6. Walter J. Ong, *Orality and Literacy: The Technologizing of the Word* (London: Methuen, 1982). One of the blind spots is Ong's aversion to the term "oral literature"; see my discussion in "Introduction," in *The Ballad and Oral Literature,* ed. Joseph Harris, Harvard English Studies 17 (Cambridge, Mass., and London: Harvard University Press, 1991), pp. 1–17, esp. 9–12.

7. Ruth Finnegan, *Literacy and Orality: Studies in the Technology of Communication* (Oxford: Blackwell, 1988); eadem, "Tradition, But What Tradition and for Whom?" *Oral Tradition* 6 (1991): 104–24; Brian V. Street, *Literacy in Theory and Practice,* Cambridge Studies in Oral and Literate Culture (Cambridge: Cambridge University Press, 1984); *Literacy and Orality,* ed. David R. Olson and Nancy Torrance (Cambridge: Cambridge University Press, 1991). Two examples of humanistic scholars who seem unimpressed with challenges to the "Great Divide" theory: Ursula Schaefer, "Alterities: On Methodology in Medieval Literary Studies," *Oral Tradition* 8 (1993): 187–214, declares the discovery of "the Orality/Literacy Question" to be a paradigmatic change in the sense of Thomas Kuhn's *Structure of Scientific Revolutions;* and John D. Smith, "Worlds Apart: Orality, Literacy, and the Rajasthani Folk-*Mahābhārata,*" *Oral Tradition* 5 (1990): 3–19, illustrates the gap.

8. For a recent survey see Carol J. Clover, "Icelandic Family Sagas (Íslendingasögur)," in *Old Norse-Icelandic Literature: A Critical Guide,* ed. Carol J. Clover and John Lindow, Islandica 45 (Ithaca, etc.: Cornell University Press, 1985); "The Long Prose Form," *Arkiv för nordisk filologi* 101 (1986): 10–39; Else Mundal, "Den norrøne episke tradisjonen," in *Hellas og Norge: Kontakt, komparasjon, kontrast: En artikkelsamling,* ed. Øivind Andersen and Tomas Hägg, Skrifter utgitt av det norske institutt i Athen 2 (Bergen 1990), pp. 65–80.

9. Clover, "Long Prose Form," (n. 8 above).

course, for further study of oral poetry in Parry's philological vein.[10] A recent dissertation by Judy Quinn of the University of Sydney prefaces the fullest available study of the passage of eddic tradition from oral to written by a comprehensive discussion of early Icelandic orality and literacy historically considered.[11] Harry Roe has reviewed the origins and spread of literacy in early Scandinavia in order to argue that the extraordinarily high literacy rate of Iceland through the centuries is not, as he puts it, "a recent response of the human spirit to excessively dreary winters, but the vestige of an ancient tradition of literacy which Iceland held in common with the rest of early Scandinavian society."[12] Roe is speaking here of runic literacy, to which I will return, but Old Norse scholarship has as yet little to compare with the sophistication of recent work in Old English by Seth Lerer, Katherine O'Brien O'Keeffe, and Michael Near.[13] These all deal to some extent with the relationship between written and oral discourse, with transitional literacy, residual orality, the social meaning of the oral and the written, and, my particular interest in this talk, with the hypothesis of distinguishable oral and literate mentalities. The Icelandic First Grammarian, that amazing linguist of the mid-twelfth century, was explicit in his acknowledgment of influence from England, which, he claimed, spoke essentially the same language as his audience. Perhaps Old English scholarship can again suggest a way for Old Norse.

* * *

Latin writing must have come to Iceland with Christianity at the end of the tenth century, more than a hundred years after the settlement of the island by Norwegians and their Irish slaves. However, the first

---

10. Progress to 1983 reviewed in Joseph Harris, "Eddic Poetry," in *Old Norse-Icelandic Literature* (n. 8 above), pp. 68–156.

11. Judy Quinn, "The Eddic Tradition: A Study of the Mode of Transmission of Eddic Mythological Poetry in the Middle Ages," diss. University of Sydney, 1990.

12. H. Roe, "The Origins and Spread of Literacy in Early Scandinavia," *Scandinavian-Canadian Studies* 1 (1983): 49–54 (here p. 53).

13. Seth Lerer, *Literacy and Power in Anglo-Saxon Literature* (Lincoln: University of Nebraska Press, 1991); Katherine O'Brien O'Keeffe, *Visible Song: Transitional Literacy in Old English Verse*, Cambridge Studies in Anglo-Saxon England 4 (Cambridge, etc.: Cambridge University Press, 1990); Michael R. Near, "Anticipating Alienation: *Beowulf* and the Intrusion of Literacy," *PMLA* 108 (1993): 320–32.

vernacular writing we know of in Iceland was the writing down of the traditional laws in the winter of 1117-18: before that the oral preservation and transmission of the laws was part of the elected office of "lawspeaker," a man charged with reciting the whole body of laws in the course of three summer parliaments. Ari Þorgilsson, the historian whose "Book of the Icelanders" (Íslendingabók) of about 1130 gives us the date of codification of the oral laws, also conveys briefly a sense of the burden of reciting the laws: "Grímr Svertingsson of Mosfell took over the office of lawspeaker after Þorgeirr and held it for two summers, but then he got permission for Skapti Þóroddsson, his sister's son, to hold the office, because he himself had grown hoarse."[14] Only about twenty-four manuscripts survive from the twelfth century, compared with some 700 surviving vernacular manuscripts from the entire medieval period, twelfth through fifteenth centuries; and according to Harry Roe there would have been three Latin manuscripts for every one in Icelandic.[15] In saga scholarship the two-hundred-year gap between the writers and the events narrated, mostly from the end of the settlement period about 930 to the end of the conversion period about 1030, is recognized in the expressions "saga-age" and "writing-age," for most of the sagas were written only in the thirteenth century. Genealogies, as well as laws, were written down much earlier.

Nothing comparable to the reliable references to oral laws and genealogies and to their early codification can be cited to clarify the history of the major oral-literary genres: sagas, eddic, and skaldic poetry. For the saga literature the evidence is notoriously slippery. One example: a famous anecdote set about 1050 tells how a young Icelandic sagaman managed to stretch out the tale of the youthful wanderings of King Haraldr Sigurðarson over the thirteen evenings of Yule at the court of and under the eyes of that same crusty king. The anecdote provides a fairly full picture of sagatelling as entertainment and oral history. But scholarship has not noticed that the best, but least familiar, manuscript has the storytelling carried on under the

---

14. *Íslendingabók [,] Landnámabók*, ed. Jakob Benediktsson, I, Íslenzk fornrit 1, pt. 1 (Reykjavík: Hið íslenzka fornritafélag, 1968), p. 19 (ch. 8): Grímr at Mosfelli Svertingssonr tók lǫgsǫgu eptir Þorgeir ok hafði tvau sumur, en þá fekk hann lof til þess, at Skapti Þóroddssonr hefði, systurson hans, af því at hann vas hásmæltr sjalfr."

15. Roe, p. 49.

king's threat: "You won't know, while you are narrating, whether the story pleases me or not, but it's certain that after Yule you will be telling very few sagas if this one is told badly and untruthfully."[16] I think we may have here an echo of Motif J1185 Execution escaped by storytelling;[17] but even without the influence of an international narrative pattern, there are reasons to be skeptical about what the episode, reported in manuscripts of the mid-thirteenth century, can tell about oral sagas two hundred years earlier.[18] How long were they, how fixed was their wording, did they contain verse, were they the "same" sagas as were committed to writing so much later? The richest piece of evidence for oral sagas is the much-discussed description of an Icelandic wedding and the saga-tellings that entertained the guests in the year 1119. The historical saga that contains the report may have been written as early as 1160 or as late as 1237.[19] In any case, the gap between event and written saga is much smaller here, and the incidents mentioned have the confusing particularity of real events. The saga's reason for describing the wedding entertainment was the controversial nature of the reception of the stories told, some hearers insisting that they were true and tracing their ancestry to the heroes mentioned, others scoffing.[20] For us the passage is important as a hint of performance context, in among rejoicing, dancing, and wrestling, and as proof that the genre of mythic-heroic sagas, *fornaldarsögur,* was orally performed long before it is so richly attested in the Danish history of Saxo Grammaticus about 1200. The first performer noted

---

16. *Austfirðinga sǫgur,* ed. Jón Jóhannesson, Íslenzk fornrit 11 (Reykjavík, 1950), pp. 333–36: "En ekki muntu vita, meðan þú segir, hvárt mér þykkir vel eða illa, en vís ván eptir jólin, at fár sǫgur muntu segja, ef mér þykkir þessi illa sǫgð ok ósannliga" (336). The shorter version in the earlier manuscript Morkinskinna, which lacks this idea as well as the Icelander's name, is the one usually translated and commented on, as in Knut Liestøl, *The Origin of the Icelandic Family Sagas* (Oslo, etc.: Instituttet for sammenlignende kulturforskning, 1930), p 57.

17. Stith Thompson, *Motif-Index of Folk Literature,* rev. ed. (Bloomington: Indiana University Press, 1955).

18. Cf. Hermann Pálsson, *Sagnaskemmtun Íslendinga* (Reykjavík: Mál og menning, 1962), esp. pp. 40–42.

19. *Þorgils saga ok Hafliða,* ed. Ursula Brown [Dronke], (London: Oxford University Press, 1952), pp. 17–18 (ch. 10); dating, pp. ix–xxix.

20. An indispensable interpretation of the passage is Peter Foote, "*Sagnaskemtan:* Reykjahólar 1119," in his *Aurvandilstá: Norse Studies,* ed. Michael Barnes, et. al., The Viking Collection 2 (Odense: Odense University Press, 1984), pp. 65–83 (with Postscript); original publication, *Saga-Book of the Viking Society* 14 (1955–56): 226–39.

was Hrólfr of Skálmarnes, who told an adventure story, and the twelfth- or thirteenth-century sagaman or local historian insists that this "Hrólfr had himself composed [*samansetta*] this saga." The second entertainer mentioned was Ingimundr the priest, who "told the saga of Ormr, skald of Barrey, including many verses and with a good lay [*flokkr*], which Ingimundr had composed [*ortan*], at the end of the saga." The saga performed by Ingimundr may have occupied a generic middle ground between the more realistic "sagas of the poets" and the mythic-heroic genre, and the passage suggests that a recurrent formal arrangement in which longer poems, like those of Egill Skalla-Grímsson, cluster at the end of a saga may be very old.[21] It definitely teaches that the prosimetrum or mixed form of prose and verse is much older than the period of saga writing and that the shifting reciprocal relationship between saga prose and verses is likely to stretch back as far as we can reconstruct the tradition.[22] To the literate mind of the "writing-age" historian the entertainers were also "authors," and the controversy over the "truth" of the material can perhaps be understood as the dissonance between a literate and an oral mindset in the reception of tradition.

The genre designation of Ingimundr's *flokkr* suggests that it would have been in skaldic verse; but the nature and age of the oral saga supporting it might argue for eddic verse or a mixed type.[23] The antiquity and orality of the "eddic" poetic tradition is, of course,

---

21. Two further examples: *Qrvar-Odds saga* and *Hákonar saga góða* in *Heims-kringla*.

22. On the prosimetrum of the sagas see, for example, Mundal; Clover, "Long Prose Form," (cited n. 8 above): Dietrich Hofmann, "Vers und Prosa in der mündlich gepflegten mittelalterlichen Erzählkunst der germanischen Länder," *Frühmittelalterliche Studien* 5 (1971): 135–75; Karsten Friis-Jensen, *Saxo Grammaticus as Latin Poet: Studies in the Verse Passages of the Gesta Danorum*, Analecta Romana Instituti Danici, Supplementum XIV, (Rome: L'Erma di Bretschneider, 1987), pp. 39–52 ("The Old Norse prosimetrum").

23. *Flokkr* is only attested as a skaldic term (Gert Kreutzer, *Die Dichtungslehre der Skalden: Poetologische Terminologie und Autorenkommentare als Grundlagen einer Gattungspoetik*, 2nd ed. rev. [Meisenhausen am Glan: Hain, 1977], p. 88), but most recent scholars diminish the eddic: skaldic distinction; and since very little metalevel vocabulary for eddic verse survives, it is likely that when necessary originally skaldic terms were used for eddic verse: for example, "skald" is once used for the poet of an eddic poem. I have a fuller study of Ingimundr's *Orms saga* in the context of saga prosimetrum forthcoming ["The Prosimetrum of Icelandic Saga and Some Relatives," in *Prosimetrum: Crosscultural Perspectives on Narrative in Prose and Verse*, ed. by Joseph Harris and Karl Reichl (Cambridge: D. S. Brewer, 1997), pp. 131–63. Eds.]

strongly argued by agreement of meter, diction, and genre system with the other surviving fragments of Old Germanic poetry. This oral poetics was probably never at the service of a purely fluid epic tradition like the South Slavic, though it would be an understatement to say that opinions can differ on this.[24] The persistence in a certain verse context of an epithet like OHG *suasat*/ON *svási* "dear" from the eighth-century Longobardic *Hildebrandslied* through to the fourteenth-century eddic *Death Song of Hildibrandr* seems to speak for a poetic tradition where composition and performance are different kinds of speech events and where poetics relies on memory.[25] Direct references to eddic performance are few, however.[26] The story of Norna-Gestr offers a representation of a master of prose tales, who also performs eddic poetry.[27] A tradition of *applied* heroic verse, where the performance bore a special relevance to the setting and audience, can be grasped in an allusion to events in Denmark in 1131, but the idea of applied performance is also close to Lars Lönnroth's concept of the "double scene," in which the oral eddic poem is a kind of *mise en abŷme* or intensifying mirror image of its performance setting.[28]

Another reason for insisting on a relatively fixed tradition, with conscious innovators like Ingimundr, might be self-interest, for the literary history of this oral literature depends upon it. Here is an

---

24. Cf. Bjarne Fidjestøl, "Islendingesaga og fyrstedikting: Dikting og samfunn i arkaisk norrøn kultur," in *Hellas og Norge* (cited n. 8 above), 21–44.

25. The Norse reflex of the *Hildebrandslied* is preserved in the fourteenth-century *Ásmundar saga kappabana* and the equivalent narrative material in Saxo; the text is edited as "Hildibrands Sterbelied" in *Edda: Die Lieder des Codex Regius nebst verwandten Denkmälern*, ed. Gustav Neckel, 5th ed. rev. Hans Kuhn (Heidelberg: C. Winter, 1983). Another verbal or formulaic continuity between the old and younger Hildebrand poems is found in the epithet "hoary" of st. IX of the saga (not adopted by Neckel/Kuhn): *inn hári Hildibrandr: Hiltibrant ... her uuas hērōro man* (1.7). Cf. *Zwei Fornaldarsögur (Hrólfssaga Gautrekssonar und Ásmundarsaga kappabana) nach Cod. Holm. 7, 4to*, ed. Dr. Ferdinand Detter (Halle: Niemeyer, 1891), p. 100.

26. Reviewed in Lönnroth, "Hjálmar's Death-Song" (n. 3 above) and in Harris, "Eddic Poetry as Oral Poetry" (above n. 2), with references to the older literature; see also Harris, "Eddic Poetry" (n. 10 above).

27. Commentary and sources in Joseph Harris and Thomas D. Hill, "Gestr's 'Prime Sign': Source and Signification in *Norna-Gests Þáttr*," ANF 104 (1989): 103–22.

28. Harris, "Eddic Poetry" (n. 10 above); Lönnroth, *Den dubbla scenen: Muntling diktning fran Eddan till ABBA* (Stockholm: Prisma, 1978); "The Double Scene of Arrow-Odd's Drinking Contest," in *Medieval Narrative: A Symposium*, ed. Hans Bekker-Nielsen, et al. (Odense: University Press, 1979), pp. 94–119.

example: scholars of the nineteenth and early twentieth century, and most recently Theodore M. Andersson, had already attempted various reconstructions of the lost lays of the Nibelungs.[29] One poem in the repertoire of the wandering entertainer Norna-Gestr seems to belong to this thread of preliterary literary history, for the "title" of this *Guðrúnarbrǫgð in fornu* seems to be equatable with that of the applied heroic poem attested for 1131, "Grimildae perfidia notissima."[30] The saga describes the "Ancient Wiles of Gudrun" as new and unsettling to the men of the Norwegian court; its newness must have resided in the fact that it presents the story in the German, rather than in the Scandinavian version—that is, revenge *on* the brothers, rather than revenge *for* the brothers. If what Andersson and I have written, building on the older scholarship, holds, then we can grasp in a literary historical sense: an oral Saxon lay of the twelfth century; thirteenth-century North Germanic and Middle High German versions of it; and a lost ballad of the fourteenth century, all traceable by their title and by perturbations of their environment.

The core of eddic poetry is constituted by the poems of two anthologies, the final copies of which were written in Iceland in the mid- to late-thirteenth century. The codicological prehistory of these manuscripts, especially of the less fragmentary Codex Regius 2365 4to, has been elaborately studied. The paleographers differ on the age and composition of the written sources, but I tend to believe in indications of fairly early dates around 1200 for the pamphlets that immediately preceded the Codex Regius and in the possibility that some of the poems were written down in Norway.[31] Why and how any of the poems were written down at all has, I think, eluded all scholars, but I think a plausible hypothesis for the construction of the final collection in Codex Regius could begin with the influence of a *book,* Snorri Sturluson's *Prose Edda,* which is, of course, a learned and literate work of c. 1223. One aspect of Snorri's learning is its Christian and European basis; to a certain extent Snorri is making the

29. Theodore M. Andersson, *A Preface to the Nibelungenlied* (Stanford, Cal.: Stanford University Press, 1987) and references there.

30. Joseph Harris, "*Guðrúnarbrögð* and the Saxon Lay of Grimhild's Perfidy," *Medieval Scandinavia* 9 (1976): 173–80; and references there [reprinted in this volume, Eds.].

31. Discussed in Harris, "Eddic Poetry" (n. 10 above).

native cultural past available to the Christian present by negotiating its relationship to European and universal history. His historical ideology emerges from the intense study of the last decade as quite complex; but framed within his ambiguous form of euhemerism, we can recognize a movement from ultimate beginnings and endings in myth descending toward heroic story and history.

When the Codex Regius compiler went to work, perhaps a quarter of a century later, Snorri had cleared the way by making an anthology of pagan mythological poetry followed by heroic poetry imaginable. But by omitting anything like Snorri's euhemeristic framework, the Codex Regius compiler gave his book a more historical thrust in the sense of medieval typological history. For "prefigurations, shadows, and realizations in the fullness of time" have been convincingly found in the Codex Regius by Heinz Klingenberg.[32] Klingenberg, however, grounds its historical sense in the social dissolution of the Icelandic present about the middle of the thirteenth century and stops short of a hypothesis I think is needed to capture the organizing "idea" of the Codex Regius as a book,[33] an hypothesis I've ventured so far only in lectures. How did the Codex Regius of the Elder Edda come to be arranged precisely as a two-part book deeply imbued with a sense of history as a succession of ages? It may be that another book, in fact *the* book of the Middle Ages, suggested the pattern. Perhaps biblical influence, if it is allowed at all, goes no farther than the bipartite succession a New Law upon an Old. "The Sibyl's Prophecy" *(Vǫluspá)* is clearly placed first because it tells the genesis of the world, but that is not an obvious or necessary arrangement.[34] "The Sibyl's Prophecy" opens with a capital five lines high; this is balanced by the only other initial of this size in the manuscript, the first letter of the heroic section that begins with the first Helgi poem.[35] Thus the heroic age, like the New Testament, is emphatically a new beginning, and

---

32. Heinz Klingenberg, *Edda—Sammlung und Dichtung,* Beiträge zur nordischen Philologie 3 (Basel, etc.: Helbing & Lichtenhahn, 1974).

33. Cf. Donald R. Howard, *The Idea of the Canterbury Tales* (Berkeley, etc.: University of California Press, 1976) and Jesse Gellrich, *The Idea of the Book in the Middle Ages: Language Theory, Mythology, and Fiction* (Ithaca, N.Y.: Cornell University Press, 1985).

34. For the literature on the arrangement of the Codex Regius see Harris, "Eddic Poetry" (n. 10 above).

35. As pointed out by Klingenberg.

the first Helgi poem opens with the phrase *Ár vas alda* ("it was early in the ages"), this opening line echoing one of the first lines of "The Sibyl's Prophecy." The biblical analogue in Genesis is "in the beginning," structurally echoed in the Gospel of John, "in the beginning was the word." This line of thought could be carried further,[36] but let me turn from the obvious literacy of the collection back to questions of orality and literacy in the eddic poems themselves.

The oral eddic tradition continued rather strongly in the thirteenth century, as attested for example in dream verses collected in the sagas of contemporary events, especially *Sturlunga saga*.[37] "The Sibyl's Prophecy" survives in three versions, apparently showing some oral variation, as if its poetic tradition were still evolving when written down. In other words, written intervention in the tradition by Snorri, his predecessors, and the compiler of the Codex Regius seems not to have terminated the whole oral eddic tradition, but did it create conditions for a parallel *written* eddic tradition? The compiler has made a real *book* out of oral poems arrested in writing, but I see no compelling reason to believe that any of the poems is itself a written composition. Siegfried Gutenbrunner declared three to be "eddic poems from the scriptorium," but in the case of "Brynhild's Hell Ride" *(Helreið Brynhildar)* he is probably positively wrong because, in addition to a possible echo of the Norse poem's poetic tradition in Old English, there is a second recording that looks very much like an oral variant.[38] For another poem, "The Third Lay of Gudrun" *(Guðrúnarkviða in þriðja)*, there is no significant evidence. What

36. Lars Lönnroth, "The Old Norse Analogue: Eddic Poetry and Fornaldarsaga," in *Religion, Myth, and Folklore in the World's Epics: The Kalevala and its Predecessors*, ed. Lauri Honko (Berlin and New York: Mouton/de Gruyter, 1990), pp. 73–93, interestingly explores the possibility that Elias Lönnrot's study of the *Poetic Edda*, and his explicit desire to emulate it, influenced his arrangement of *runot* in the 1849 *Kalevala*. But, I would argue, by ending his newly minted epic with the flight of the old gods represented by Väinämöinen, the birth of a new hero (cf. Helgi), and the beginning of a new age, Lönnrot would seem to have in mind only the mythological first half of the *Poetic Edda*. The *Shāh-Nāma* and the *Watunna* are two more epics that end with the beginning of the era of a new world religion (Islam, Christianity).

37. For a study see Preben Meulengracht Sørensen, "Guðrún Gjúkadóttir in Miðjumdalr. Zur Aktualität nordischer Heldensage im Island des 13. Jahrhunderts," in *Heldensage und Heldendichtung im Germanischen*, ed. Heinrich Beck (Berlin and New York: de Gruyter, 1988), pp. 183–96; cf. Quinn (n. 11 above), pp. 32–42.

38. Gutenbrunner, "Eddalieder aus der Scheibstube," *ZDP* 74 (1955): 250–63. Cf. the OE *Wife's Lament* and the variant text of *Helreið Brynhildar* in *Norna-Gests Þáttr*.

would be significant evidence? If style cannot prove a poem oral, it also cannot prove it literary; late content is of no significance in view of the flourishing oral dream verses in eddic meters set securely within the mid-thirteenth century; the fact that words, formulas, or lines can be translated into Latin proves only that Gutenbrunner was a fine Latinist.[39] Significant forms of evidence would, I think, be two: (1) intertextual relations with learned writings which are unlikely to have been heard rather than read; or (2) a strong argument that a poem was written for its place in the manuscript. Applied to the poem "Grípir's Prophecy" *(Grípisspá)* these two criteria do at least awaken suspicions, for this insipid preview of Sigurd's life might well have been written to introduce a Sigurd pamphlet, as other scholars have proposed. However, the overall case for a written *Grípisspá* advanced by Gutenbrunner and, indirectly, by Theodore M. Andersson is not compelling. A more throrough attempt to apply the two criteria was made by Klingenberg in his argument that the first Helgi poem was written for its place in the codex. I tried to isolate and disarm some of Klingenberg's arguments, but it remains the best of its kind.[40]

It might be of interest to introduce a new concept into these controversies, Susan Stewart's notion of "distressed genres."[41] "To distress" something, for example a piece of furniture, is approximately "to antique" it, but Stewart is discussing the literary nostalgia of an eighteenth century that produced the ballad revival and figures like Ossian and Chatterton. Distressed genres, then, are made to look old or folkloric or ethnic for complex literary and cultural reasons. This way of looking at the eddic context perhaps contributes an interesting aspect to the Icelandic renaissance of the eleventh- and twelfth centu-

---

39. The presuppositions of this last "test" are that if parts of a text can be easily translated "back" into a language and poetic tradition from which it is hypothesized to have been borrowed, the translation constitutes an evidence of the borrowing. The obvious circularity here is not as illogical as it seems at first glance, however, since "re"-translation is only a special case of explaining linguistic anomalies in the putative borrowing poem by reference to the language, especially poetic language, of the putative lending tradition; see Harris, "Eddic Poetry" (n. 10 above): 102–06.

40. References and arguments given in Harris, "Eddic Poetry" (n. 10 above): 122–25.

41. Susan Stewart, *Crimes of Writing: Problems in the Containment of Representation* (New York: Oxford University Press, 1991), pp. 66–101.

ries,[42] and perhaps it helps to answer the question why an Icelandic litteratus might have wished to write a *Grípisspá*. It cannot help to date the composition, however, or—despite my use of the word litteratus—distinguish it categorically as oral or written in origin. And it cannot help us directly in attempting to name the poet.

I do believe, however, that the eddic tradition, despite its anonymity, was one in which it makes sense to think—alongside tradition itself—of individual tradition-bearers, poets in a variety of senses. Ingimundr prestr was the poet of the *flokkr* that ended his *Orms saga* and probably of the scattered verses of the saga, but some skaldic stanzas attributed to Ormr by Snorri make it likely that Ormr's story had some traditional basis, perhaps with an historical kernel. Sigurður Nordal nominated the Icelandic skald Völu-Steinn as possible poet of *Völuspá:* the time, the nickname, the skill are right, and Nordal made the connection very plausible with evidence of thematic connections.[43] Felix Genzmer, seconded by Konstantin Reichardt, assigned "The Old Lay of Atli" to the Norwegian skald Þorbjrn hornklofi, poet of the semiskaldic praise poem *Haraldskvœði*.[44] Theodore Andersson did not *name* the Greenlandic poet of the later Atli poem but did derive his poem directly from *Atlakviða*.[45] Alexander Bugge nominated as poet of the first Helgi poem the "chief-poet" of King Magnús Óláfsson of Norway, Arnórr jarlaskáld.[46] In my own study of that poem I agreed at least to the extent that I felt the nature of the poetic composition in the first Helgi poem could be partly captured under the concept "skaldic revision" of an older, more eddic poem; this poet would have worked somewhat like Þorvaldr veili, who Snorri says

---

42. The chief study is probably still Andreas Heusler, "Heimat und Alter der eddischen Gedichte. Das isländische Sondergut," *Archiv für das Studium der neueren Sprachen und Literaturen* 116 (1906): 249–281; rpt. in *Kleine Schriften* 2 (Berlin: de Gruyter, 1969), 483–494.

43. Nordal, "Völusteinn," *Iðunn* 8 (1923–24): 161–78; rpt. and translated several times, esp. "The Author of *Vǫluspá*," tr. B.S. Benedikz, *Saga-Book of the Viking Society* 20 (1978–79): 114–30.

44. Genzmer, "Der Dichter der *Atlakviða*," *Arkiv för nordisk filologi* 42 (1926): 97–134; Reichardt, "Der Dichter der *Atlakviða*," *Arkiv för nordisk filologi* 42 (1926): 323–26.

45. Theodore M. Andersson, "Did the Poet of *Atlamál* Know *Atlaqviða?*" in *Edda: A Collection of Essays,* ed. Robert J. Glendinning and Haraldur Bessason ([Winnipeg]: University of Manitoba Press, 1983), pp. 243–57.

46. Alexander Bugge, "Arnor jarlaskald og det forste kvad om Helge Hundingsbane," *Edda* 1 (1914): 350–80.

composed a poem *(kvœði),* which is placed by its metrical names, *kviða skjálfhenda* or refrainless *drápa,* midway between eddic and skaldic.[47] The subject of this lost poem, Snorri tells us, was the story of Sigurd. The situation of composition is not in oral performance, and not in a scriptorium, a perfect situation for what I've called contemplative composition, for the poet was shipwrecked on a skerry and composed the poem apparently to pass the time. If this lost poem had survived, we would have a semi-skaldic poem by a named poet, composed on an eddic subject in a form that could also describe the first Helgi poem.

*   *   *

To affirm a continuum (as I have implicitly been doing) between eddic and skaldic traditions is not to deny that at its most characteristic skaldic verse is drastically different, especially in its linguistic obscurity, and the difficulty of its textual history. One established fact about skaldic poetry, however, is that it was for centuries an oral art. And so it is peculiar that, to my knowledge, no one has attempted to assess skaldic poetry by the fitful light of modern work on orality and literacy and especially of the oral-formulaic theory. Even if it is not the "living laboratory" Lord and Parry found in Yugoslavia, skaldic poetry could be another kind of "laboratory," a test case for the study of the transition of a genre of oral poetry, not only onto vellum, but into a family of genres that arise in close proximity to writing. For skaldic poetry was cultivated to a high art from long before the introduction of writing, and its evolving tradition continued down to the late Middle Ages when literacy is thought to have been fairly widespread in Iceland, making the transition from arch-pagan to fully Christian also.[48] Over 100 poets are named in the thirteenth-century antiquarian work "List of the Poets" *(Skáldatal).*[49] Some skaldic poetry is simply quoted to illustrate diction or meter in Snorri's poetic handbook, giving little or no

---

47. Snorri Sturluson, *Edda: Háttatal,* ed. Anthony Faulkes (Oxford: Clarendon Press, 1991), p. 18 (ch. 35).

48. Several introductions to skaldic poetry are available; see Roberta Frank, "Skaldic Poetry," in *Old Norse-Icelandic Literature* (n. 8 above).

49. *Edda Snorronis Sturlœi,* tomi tertii pars prior (Copenhagen, 1880).

context; but a great deal is preserved in saga narratives that purport to tell the circumstances of composition or transmission. Of course skepticism, even extreme skepticism, about details is in order where it is a matter of specific actions in specific times and places as reported two hundred years later, but the saga literature can be trusted to give typical pictures that were plausible to their hearers or readers in the high and later medieval centuries. Such sagas convey a good deal of information about poets, performances, function, and even the appreciation of skaldic poetry, and one genre of sagas focuses centrally on the life of its subject poet.

So how, on a preliminary assessment, *would* early skaldic poetry measure up as oral poetry? Well, but tautologically well, if we mean, with Ruth Finnegan, simply poetry which is not composed in writing, but badly if our definition is shaped by the South Slavic-Homeric model. First of all skaldic poetry seems not to be in any sense formulaic. At least, I cannot point to a demonstration that it is formulaic; it remains possible that a formulaic structure unlike what we know elsewhere is waiting to be discovered. Bjarne Fidjestøl, whose book on West Norse royal eulogy is the most important publication on skaldic poetry in some years, is quite conscious of the anomaly of a poetry that is "oral but at the same time unchanging";[50] Fidjestøl speaks of a system and a technique "answering to oral-formulaic technique in another type of traditional poetry," but he adds, "Oral formulas are few in skaldic poetry."[51] Russell Poole describes one repeated collocation as "verg[ing] upon the formulaic in battle poetry";[52] but the more general results of his studies suggest that "we cannot distinguish in any general way between improvised, occasional verses on the one hand and the constituent stanzas of longer, more formal poems on the other hand by using ... technical criteria" (p. 6). Kennings, the condensed two-part metaphors that stand in for nouns, are constructed to a set pattern, which can be

---

50. *Det norrøne fyrstediktet* (Øvre Ervik: Alvheim & Eide, 1982); quotation ("munnleg, men likevel varig") from Fidjestøl, "Islendingesaga og fyrstedikting: Dikting og samfunn i arkaisk norrøn kultur," in *Hellas og Norge* (cited n. 8 above), 23.

51. Fidjestøl, *Fyrstediktet* (n. 50 above): 204 ("Oral formulas er det lite av i skalde-diktinga").

52. R. G. Poole, *Viking Poems on War and Peace: A Study in Skaldic Narrative* (Toronto, etc.: University of Toronto Press, 1991), p. 89.

captured as generative rules,[53] but the elements are not distributed formulaicly. In fact, their distribution seems to be fairly unpredictable.[54] Diana Whaley's studies of clause arrangement constitute a step toward predictability within the helming or half-stanza,[55] but, more generally, diction at the skaldic end of the eddic-skaldic spectrum still seems unnatural, artificially fragmented, puzzle-like, a consciously made thing, and—choosing a purposely pregnant adjective—lapidary. The few modern connoisseurs can recognize personal styles, and there is every possibility of borrowing and imitation. Skalds could be influenced by their predecessors and contemporary rivals—Harold Bloom's strong poet in agon with the burdening past can be seen already in 961 in the *Hákonarmál* of the Norwegian Eyvindr Finnsson. In fact, it seems to be Eyvindr's propensity to seek inspiration in others' verse that earned him the sobriquet *skáldaspillir,* "despoiler of skalds," or more tendentiously Eyvind the Plagiarist. Skaldic poetry evinces manuscript variations and corruptions but fewer instances of certain evidence of oral variants than one would expect of such an emphatically oral art, and the nature of oral variation in skaldic textual history does not appear to resemble closely the free variation of a living tradition of oral composition on Parry's model.[56] Fidjestøl's complex discussion of this matter yields only few extended parallel texts in purely oral variation, but it is important to add that he has not parsed the material with exactly the same question in mind as I am proposing.[57] Moreover, the question should be reconsidered in view of Katherine O'Brien O'Keeffe's concept of orally competent scribes. In any case, most skaldic poetry is associated with named skalds; even when there is confusion in

---

53. Bjarne Fidjestøl, "Kenningsystemet: Forsøk på ein lingvistisk analyse," *Maal og minne,* 1974, pp. 5–50; John Lindow, "Riddles, Kennings, and the Complexity of Skaldic Poetry," *Scandinavian Studies* 47 (1975): 311–27.

54. Two schools of skaldic interpretation differ especially in the degree of "naturalness" ascribed to the syntax; see Frank, "Skaldic Poetry," in *Old Norse-Icelandic Literature* (n. 8 above), pp. 165–166.

55. Diana C. Edwards [Whaley], "Clause Arrangement in Skaldic Poetry," *Arkiv för nordisk filologi* 98 (1983): 123–75; 99 (1984): 131–38.

56. Lönnroth (note 3 above) and Harris (note 2 above) discuss the role of parallel texts in an oral poetry.

57. *Fyrstediktet* (n. 50 above) pp. 45–60 (Skriftleg eller munnleg tradering), pp. 61–70 (Overleveringsdublettar eller parallellstrofer?), pp. 71–80 (Parallelar som grunnlag for teksttolking), pp. 199–209 (Handverket).

the sources about who the author is, it is always clear that there is *supposed to be* an author. It is also intensely occasional, praising a patron, describing a shield or house decorations or a vignette from life. There is a strict traditional poetics, but the content is usually not a traditional story like the Sigurd saga, although such material is used in refrains and kennings.

What of the representations of composition and performance in the sagas, and, a related question, what of the intelligibility of skaldic poetry? Frequently the sagas represent such poetry as instantly composed, necessarily in some sense composed in performance, but on closer analysis this seems to be purely conventional. In contrast to West Germanic verse, skaldic poetry is thought not to have been accompanied by music,[58] and real dependence on the stimulation of the moment would usually preclude accompaniment. There is a need for a careful historical evaluation of the contexts described for skaldic performances, and such a study also needs to consider coherence and structure in the poems themselves. If poetry is instantly composed, it is likely to be consumed effortlessly.[59] The audience of Demodocus or Avdo Međedović will not have scratched their heads in puzzlement, at least not for long. Medieval Icelanders did cultivate the art of improvised couplets; and one can read an extensive depiction of a verse-capping session in Þorgils saga ok Hafliða.[60] On the other hand, flowing oral-composition was at least imaginable to the makers of the mythology since Odin was said to speak in verse, and Starkaðr was given the gift as well.[61] Snorri says of the eleventh-century skald Sigvatr Þorðarson that he "did not speak fast in prose, but poetic utterance was

---

58. Cf. Kari Ellen Gade, "On the Recitation of Old Norse Skaldic Poetry," in *Studien zum Altgermanischen: Festschrift für Heinrich Beck*, ed. Heiko Uecker (Berlin and New York: de Gruyter, 1994), pp. 126–56.

59. Cf. Michael Cherniss, "*Beowulf:* Oral Presentation and the Criterion of Immediate Rhetorical Effect," *Genre* 3 (1970): 214–28.

60. Ed. Ursula Brown (Dronke) (Oxford: Oxford University Press, 1952), pp. 13–18.

61. "Qnnur [íþrótt] var sú, at hann [Óðinn] talaði svá sniallt ok slétt, at qllum, er á heyrðu, þótti þat eina satt. Mælti hann allt hendingum, svá sem nú er þat kveðit, er skáldskapr heitir. Hann ok hofgoðar hans heita lióðasmiðir, því at sú íþrótt hófsk af þeim í Norðrlqndum" (Snorri Sturluson, *Ynglingasaga,* ed. Elias Wessén, Nordisk filologi, A 6 [Oslo, etc.: Dreyers, etc., 1964], p. 9 [ch. 6]); "Óðinn mælti: 'Ek gef honum [Starkaði] skáldskap, svá at hann skal eigi senna yrkja en mæla" (*Gautreks saga* in *Fornaldar sögur Norðurlanda,* ed. Guðni Jónsson [Reykjavík: Íslendingasagnaútgáfan, 1950], p. 30 [ch. 7]).

so ready to hand for him that it rolled right off his tongue, just as if he were speaking other [that is, normal] language."[62] This has the ring of exaggeration, but Heather O'Donoghue comments that non-Icelanders may have overestimated the difficulty of improvisation.[63] I am not yet sure whether it is possible to come to a general conclusion about the improvisation of single stanzas in the more complex verse forms, but many stanzas presented by their prose matrix as improvisations in specific situations are suspicious because of their retrospective point of view or because they do not fit the situation of the saga. In these cases one can only say that the circumstances of composition are unknown. One of the difficulties is that when we say "skaldic poetry" we say too much. It sounds as if a single, tightly defined genre were at stake, but the one term covers over many internal differences. Let us look at two prominent representations of composition and performance, resisting the temptation to generalize too glibly to all of so-called skaldic poetry.

In the most famous such scene, the composition of "Head-Ransom" in *Egils saga Skalla-Grímssonar,*[64] an intricate, extended composition requires quiet and solitude. The saga conveys the impression that it is amazing that Egill could have accomplished the feat in a single night, let alone, as the dramatic story has it, in half a night. Yet poetic composition as night work is mentioned at least once in a tenth-century poem, as well as a second time in *Egils saga.*[65] In the saga it is these unusual factors that make the "Head-Ransom" anecdote worth telling, but many appearances of skalds before kings imply that composition of the longer eulogies took place well in advance and was carefully calculated.

---

62. "Sigvatr var ekki hraðmæltr maðr í sundrlausum orðum, en skáldskapr var honum svá tiltœkr, at hann kvað af tungu fram, svá sem hann mælti annat mál" (Snorri Sturluson, *Óláfs saga helga* in *Heimskringla*, vol. 3, ed. Bjarni Aðalbjarnarson, Íslenzk fornrit 27 [Reykjavík: Hið íslenzka fornritafélag, 1945], 292).

63. Heather O'Donoghue, *The Genesis of a Saga Narrative: Verse and Prose in Kormaks Saga* (Oxford: Clarendon, 1991), p. 11, n.; also citing the example of Sigvatr, she reflects briefly on the likelihood of improvisation of individual verses in court meter generally and considers in detail the cases in her saga (passim).

64. *Egils saga Skalla-Grímssonar*, ed. Sigurður Nordal, Íslenzk fornrit 2 (Reykjavík: Hið íslenzka fornritafélag, 1933), pp. 175–95 (ch. 59–61).

65. Einarr skálaglamm, *lausavísa* 1, transmitted in *Egils saga*, *Jómsvíkinga saga*, and *Flateyjarbók (Den norsk-islandske Skjaldedigtning*, ed. Finnur Jónsson, AI (Copenhagen and Kristiania: Gyldendal and Nordisk forlag, 1912), p. 131; *Egils saga*, ed. Nordal (cited n. 64 above), pp. 270–71; prose attributed to Egill in *Egils saga*, ed. Nordal, p. 272.

A short story or *þáttr* set in the twelfth-century gives a very realistic picture of the improvisations of the court poet Einarr Skúlason.[66] (A translation is attached here as an appendix). Each vignette stresses the court's admiration for Einarr's ability to compose an eight-line poem on short notice, but he does not automatically spout verse. In the last of the story's anecdotes, Einarr is challenged to compose a stanza before a certain ship passes a certain headland, and he matches this with a challenge to the audience: the eight of them are each to remember one line, and the skald is to be paid for each line forgotten. The retainers retain none of the lines, but the king is very pleased with himself for having caught not only his assigned line, the first, but also the last of the poem. Understanding skaldic poetry might not have been any easier than remembering it.[67] There are a handful of saga passages which refer to restricted comprehension, and John Lindow's paper on kennings as riddles and court poetry as the secret language of the all-male warrior group is persuasive as far as it goes.[68]

The picture of skaldic composition is, then, not a unified one. But let us after all return to the risky matter of a general assessment of the central traditions called skaldic in the context of other oral poetry. If the standard of oral poetry is to be the South Slavic—and in view of all the factors that make oral skaldic poetry peculiar as measured by the South Slavic standard—it would be tempting to think of skaldic verse as literary *avant la lettre*. For even when obviously pre-literary in any usual sense, it has many features of literary verse. Perhaps it would be better to avoid the Gallic trendiness of calling an oral poetry literary, and I would not want to invoke Derrida's reversal of priority of writing and speech.[69] It would be possible to propose to

---

66. *Morkinskinna: Pergamentsbog fra første halvdel af det trettende aarhundred,* ed. C.R. Unger (Christiania: Bentzen, 1867), pp. 226–28.

67. The specific connection of remembering with understanding (as if the hermeneutics of skaldic poetry required the text to be held in mind and slowly deciphered) has its locus classicus in Gísli Súrsson's verse "Teina sá ek í túni" and its accompanying prose; see my discussion in "The Enigma of *Gísla saga,*" in *The Audience of the Sagas* [Preprints of The Eighth International Saga Conference, August 11–17, 1991, Gothenburg University], vol. 1, pp. 181–192.

68. John Lindow, "Riddles, Kennings, and the Complexity of Skaldic Poetry," *Scandinavian Studies* 47 (1975): 311–27; saga passages on restricted comprehension are cited here and in Harris, "Enigma" (cited n. 67).

69. For Derrida's position see Jonathan Culler, *On Deconstruction: Theory and Criticism after Structuralism* (Ithaca: Cornell Univ. Press, 1982), esp. pp. 98–110; for Walter Ong's response, *Orality and Literacy* (n. 6 above), pp. 75–77, 166–70.

recognize a spectrum of oral poetic traditions from hard (skaldic) to soft (South Slavic). But we already have one such continuum, that of orality and literacy, with the associated notions of oral and literate mentalities, and for the remainder of this essay I would like to entertain the idea that an element of literate mentality might lie at the core of skaldi poetry and constitute the explanation for its peculiarities when viewed through the South Slavic lens. This element, if it existed, would be recognizable not just (circularly) in the mirror of the literary features of skaldic poetry—authorship, possession of the text, relative invariance, etc.—but (non-circularly) in a conceptualization of poetic discourse as something material, language made visible, in O'Keeffe's terms. And this element, if it existed, would derive from the skald's exposure, not so much to Latin manuscripts, as to inscriptions, especially inscriptions in runes—"the letters of the unlettered down to the Reformation," as Einar Haugen has called them.[70]

Runic writing probably developed in a contact area between Germanic and Mediterranean peoples at least by the first century A.D., and seems to have spread rather rapidly to the hinterlands of Scandinavia where finds in the older runic alphabet or futhark begin with the third century.[71] Apparently the level of production in the older or 24 character futhark declined in the seventh century, but in the early ninth century there was a major revision into what is known as the younger or 16 letter futhark and simultaneously a new wave of runic inscriptions. This younger wave coincides with the early development of skaldic poetry, and the Harvard undergraduate whose senior thesis stimulated some of these speculations also aligns the new runic impetus with reinvigoration in a variety of economic and social spheres.[72] The earliest attested skaldic stanza appears inscribed on the Karlevi rune stone on Öland. Its date of about 1000 does not, of course, make this an early skaldic poem, but as Jansson writes, it

---

70. Einar Haugen, *The Scandinavian Languages: An Introduction to Their History* (Cambridge, Mass.: Harvard University Press, 1976), p. 118.

71. Every runologist has his own opinion about these matters, but the recent synthesis (with full references) by Claiborne W. Thompson is convincing to this non-runologist: "Runes," in *Dictionary of the Middle Ages*, ed. Joseph Strayer, vol. 10 (New York: American Council of Learned Societies and Scribner's, 1988), pp. 557–68.

72. Carl Edlund Anderson, "Let us tell a folk memory: The Rök Runestone in the Scandinavian Wisdom Tradition," Senior Honors Thesis (for B.A.) in Program on Folklore and Mythology, Harvard Archives.

is "the only skaldic stanza of which we possess the original text."[73] This poem certainly makes use of established poetic traditions, but it is just as clearly composed for this monumental site and for incision in runes; it is "written" in every sense but stems directly from an oral poetic tradition.

A good deal of verse is preserved in runes, most in simpler eddic meters rather than in skaldic,[74] but our interest lies in the runic monuments' public performance of material language. Many inscribed stones were intended to be seen and admired, to stand "near to the road," as two Swedish stones say,[75] echoing a proverb or sententia preserved in the eddic *Hávamál* ("Words of the High One"): "Seldom do stone monuments stand near to the road, if kinsman does not raise them after kinsman."[76] One Swedish stone leaves no doubt that three things form a single whole in the mind of the rune-master: language made material in letters, stone in which it is ingraved, and a man's reputation; he writes in verse: "Hróðsteinn and Eilífr, Áki and Hákon, those lads raised this eye-catching monumental stone after their father, after Kali dead. Thus must the noble man be mentioned as long as the stone lasts/lives and the letters of the runes."[77] Such uses of runes bring up also the matter of authorship. Here four brothers name themselves; they must count collectively as the authors, runemasters, and construction engineers

---

73. Sven B.F. Jansson, *Runes in Sweden*, tr. Peter Foote (n.p.: Gidlungs [Royal Academy and Central Board of National Antiquities], 1987; Swedish original 1963), pp. 134–36.

74. See Erik Brate and Sophus Bugge, *Runverser: Undersökning af Sveriges metriska runinskrifter* (Stockholm: Hæggström, 1891) and Hans-Peter Naumann, "*Hann var manna mestr óníðingr*: Zur Poetizität metrischer Runeninschriften," in *Studien zum Altgermanischen: Festschrift für Heinrich Beck*, ed. Heiko Uecker (Berlin and New York: de Gruyter, 1994), pp. 490–502; Jansson (cited n. 73 above), pp. 131–43.

75. Tjuvstigen stones in Södermanland and Ryda stone in Uppland in Jansson (cited n. 73 above), pp. 139–40; cf. Brate/Bugge (cited n. 74 above), pp. 155–57 and 142–43. A third instance was on the lost stone from Kungs-Husby kyrkas vapenhus, Brate/Bugge, pp. 135–36 (by the carver of Ryda?); a variant is *brautar kuml* at Sälna, Skånela socken, Säminghundra härad, Upland, Brate/Bugge, pp. 102–05.

76. St. 72: "sialdan bautarsteinar/ standa brauto nær,/ nema reisi niðr at nið" *(Edda: Die Lieder des Codex Regius nebst verwandten Denkmälern*, ed. Gustav Neckel, I: Text, 4th ed. rev. Hans Kuhn [Heidelberg: Winter, 1962]); Jansson (cited n. 73 above), pp. 139–40.

77. Nöbbele stone, Småland; cf. the translation of Jansson (cited n. 73 above), pp. 137–38; cf. Brate/Bugge (cited n. 74 above), pp. 248–49.

of this monument at Nöbbele. Public performance of language here, the compulsion to record name for fame, and the element of authorial ego—all agree with features specific to skaldic tradition though the verse form is eddic. Several times the pride of a runemaster expresses itself in verse, as when in an eddic stanza on the Swedish Fyrby stone Hásteinn and Holmsteinn refer to themselves as "the most rune-skilled men on Middle Earth," and refer like the Nöbbele brothers to setting up "the stone and many rune-staves after their father"—a comment that joins the same three elements—permanence of stone, visible language, and the fame of their father—with a more explicit realization of the fourth. For they have secured their own fame in the same moment and with the same elements.[78]

However peculiar the treatment of language in skaldic poetry, I would, of course, not suggest that the typical preliterary skald actually thought of his spoken words as physical things like the "many runes" of the Fyrby stone, but he was an author, often an author of poems that ensured the fame of his patron, dead or alive, and of himself. *Hávamál* refers to the "word-glory" that "never dies," a social idea of fame that depends not on any *thing* but on human communication.[79] But I doubt we can tell conclusively when this kind of *oral* conception of language passes over into one influenced or tainted by having *seen* word-glory as inscription. (Even a tactile sense of language could result from a monument "near to the road"; the Vietnam War memorial wall perhaps brings home the point). In any case, the connection between the two skills we are considering, poetic composition and runic writing, is fairly widespread. A Swedish inscription (in prose) was signed by Thorbjǫrn Skald, and at least two other Swedish runemasters bear that nickname;[80] many exhortations or challenges to "read these runes" are delivered in verse.[81] A poet of the mid-twelfth century listed runic literacy along with books and

---

78. Jansson (cited n. 73 above), pp. 137–38; cf. Brate/Bugge (cited n. 74 above), pp. 323–26.

79. *Hávamál* 76: "enn orðztírr / deyr aldregi / hveim er sér góðan getr."

80. Jansson (cited n. 73 above), pp. 132–33; and one Swedish inscription may honor a skald, though the reading is very uncertain (Brate/Bugge [cited n. 74 above], p. 287).

81. Jansson (cited n. 73 above), p. 97; Brate/Bugge (cited n. 74 above), pp. 32–34, 143–47; 252–60; 303–04; 201–03; 332–33, etc.

poetry among his nine accomplishments.[82] There are poetic embellishments of the futhark, rune poems,[83] and the association in the realm of magic is very close, as in certain parts of the eddic wisdom poems. There is no question that early skaldic poetry is oral, but does it perhaps betray a touch of runically literate mentality?

Rune-finds are rare in Iceland (about fifty) and, of course, relatively late. His saga does not record how Egill Skalla-Grímsson became a great runemaster, but every reader will remember how Egill erected the scorn-pole against King Eiríkr and Queen Gunnhildr, pronounced a magical curse, and, the saga says, "cut runes on the pole declaiming the words of his formal speech,"[84] and some may know of Magnus Olsen's experiment with runic transcription of Egill's two stanzas cursing King Eiríkr: Olsen hypothesized that it was precisely these stanzas, verses 28 and 29 of the saga, that Egill had inscribed on the scorn-pole, and Olsen's transcription confirmed the hypothesis, at least to his own satisfaction, because the number of runes necessary came out exactly as one of the magic futhark numbers.[85] If Olsen is right, then Egill did have a literate mentality—literally with a vengeance! Later in the saga Egill encounters a host whose sick daughter he is able to cure by shaving off and destroying the runes that caused her illness and substituting healing runes.[86] This treat-

---

82. Rǫgnvaldr kali in *Skjaldedigtning* (cited n. 65 above), BI, p. 478 *(lausavísa* 1). It seems that Rǫgnvaldr is executing "one-ups-manship" on his predecessor Haraldr harðráði (poem c. 1040), for Haraldr's fragmentarily transmitted poem listed the king's *eight* accomplishments (*Skjaldedigtning*, BI, p. 320). Latin writing (the apparent meaning of *bók* in Rǫgnvaldr's verse) may be the added skill; though the later poem is not so close a parody as to permit reconstruction of the eleventh-century poem with confidence, it does appear that runes were one of Haraldr's skills, and poetry is on the surviving list.

83. Maureen Halsall, *The Old English Rune Poem: A Critical Edition* (Toronto, etc.: Univ. of Toronto Press, 1981); the Norse rune poems are printed as an appendix.

84. *Egils saga,* ed. Nordal (cited n. 64 above), p. 171; *Egil's Saga,* tr. Hermann Pálsson and Paul Edwards (Harmondsworth: Penguin, 1976), p. 148.

85. Magnus Olsen, "Om troldruner," *Edda* 5 (1916): 225–45; rpt. in his *Norrøne studier* (Oslo, 1938), pp. 1–23. For doubts about Olsen's case, and further references, see James E. Knirk, "Runes from Trondheim and a Stanza by Egill Skalla-Grimsson," in *Studien zum Altgermanischen: Festschrift für Heinrich Beck,* ed. Heiko Uecker (Berlin and New York: de Gruyter, 1994), pp. 411–20.

86. *Egils saga,* ed. Nordal (cited n. 64 above), pp. 229–30 (ch. 72); Knirk's brilliant article (n. 85 above) is skeptical about the authenticity of the episode and the verse, but the parallel Knirk establishes from a rune stick can be explained as Egill's use of a traditional *sententia* already established in verse form.

ment of runic grooves not as patterned absences of wood but as material signifiers that draw their signifieds, efficacious language, with them is paralleled in several places.[87] A more interesting allusion to runes in Egill's preserved verse occurs in the saga's verse 9, where Egill carves runes on a drinking horn to disable the poison in it; the stanza is semiotically fascinating since it juxtaposes Egill's sign system to the harmful one of the host who poisoned the brew, his runes against the "sign" of his host *(ǫl, þats Bárøðr signdi).*[88] But more pertinent to us is the exact wording of the first two verse lines: "I cut runes on the horn, I redden speech in blood...."[89] The word for "speech" here is *spjǫll,* cognate with English *spell,* but to redden speech you must have a very physical conception of it. Nordal's modern Icelandic translation substitutes "words" *(orðin),* which from our literate point of view is unexceptionable, but in an oral culture the expression "rjóðum spjǫll" must have had a force like "paint a song red." Here a word for speech stands for material signifiers; so there must be a sense of the interchangeability of speech and its signs. However, evidence of a significant "literate residue" in Egill's oral poetry is difficult to establish. In "Head Ransom" *(Hǫfuðlausn)* praise-words constitute a physical thing, Odin's mead, a liquid cargo first to be loaded (st. 1), then stirred by mouth (19) and unloaded (20); on the other hand, battle is a prophecy to be heard (4).[90] In Egill's "Lament for my Sons" *(Sonatorrek)* a physical sense of language gives songs weight (1, 2); the substance of a song is timber to be carried out of a holy place of words, and language itself is the leaves on the timber (5); on the other hand, language is

---

87. For example, in the curse in the eddic poem *Skírnismál.*

88. This verse and its immediate context are under suspicion of being based on an episode of attempted poisoning in a glass that breaks when "signed" with the cross, an episode in a seminal early medieval text, Gregory's *Dialogues;* see Bjarni Einarsson, *Litterære forudsætninger for Egils saga* (Reykjavík: Stofnun Árna Magnússonar, 1975), p. 176 n. The correspondences are interesting, but a common source is real life customs; cf. a famous incident in the saga of Hákon the Good, *Heimskringla* I, 171–72 [ch. 17–18; Íslenzk fornrit 26] where a drinking horn is "signed" *(signaði)* to Odin and the Christian king's cross-gesture over the horn has to be explained to the pagan court as the sign of Thor's hammer. For Egil's verse 9 (of the saga) the question is complicated by a very close relationship between the larger episode surrounding the poisoned and burst cup with a tale in *Orkneyinga saga.*

89. Ristum rún á horni, / rjóðum spjǫll í dreyra" (Nordal's text); my translation; Pálsson and Edwards are too free to use here.

90. Cited by stanza from *Egils saga,* ed. Nordal (n. 64 above), pp. 185–92.

also social action (20–21), and poetry is a skill (24).[91] In his "Lay of Arinbjǫrn" *(Arinbjarnarkviða)* the oral image of language as action with ethical meaning dominates the beginning (1-2), but with the idea of the permanence of poetic fame the image shifts to something like a verbal rune stone: "Now is easily *seen* where, *before a host* of men, in the *view* of many, I shall set up the praise of the mighty kin of noblemen, steeply-climbed with feet of verse."[92] In st. 15 this praise-monument is wood to be carved by the voice-plane, but in the concluding stanza Egill returns to the idea of language as a signal tower, a beacon on a high sea-cliff like Beowulf's barrow: "I was awake early, I carried words together. With the morning works of the slave of language (the tongue) I heaped up a cairn of praise which will long stand unbreakable in the enclosure of poetry."[93] Now Egill had not read Horace's "monumentum aere perennius";[94] in fact there is no reason to believe that Egill had read anyone who did not write in runes, but the fame of Arinbjǫrn is here made equivalent to a monument of stone. And it is hard not to think of the conjunction of stone monument, written language, and fame that we know from some of the Swedish runestones.

*   *   *

I conclude by returning to an earlier hint about opposition to what Ruth Finnegan calls the "Great Divide" theory of orality and literacy. Such opponents might adapt a current phrase and describe the arguments advanced here as "romancing the rune"—slim evidence for

---

91. Cited by stanza from *Egils saga*, ed. Nordal (n. 64 above), pp. 246–56.

92. Cited by stanza from *Egils saga*, ed. Nordal (n. 64 above), pp. 258–67: "Nú's þat sét, / hvars setja skal / bratt stiginn / bragar fótum / fyr mannfjǫlð, / margra sjónir, / hróðr máttigs / hersa kundar." An alternative interpretation of the syntax of "bratt stiginn bragar fótum" is less visual: "I, having climbed steeply with the feet of poetry, shall set up the praise of the mighty kin of noblemen."

93. St. 25: "Vask árvakr, / bark orð saman / með málþjóns / morginverkum, / hlóðk lofkǫst / þanns lengi stendr / óbrotgjarn / í bragar túni."

94. The comparison to Horace's famous phrase is inevitable and probably often indulged in; two instances that have come to my attention are Bjarne Fidjestøl, "Islendingesaga og fyrstedikting" (cited n. 50 above), p. 23, and Carolyne Larrington, "Egill's longer poems: *Arinbjarnarkviða* and *Sonatorrek*," in *Introductory Essays on Egils saga and Njáls saga*, ed. John Hines and Desmond Slay (London: Viking Society for Northern Research, 1992), p. 53.

anything as grand sounding as a literary mentality *avant la lettre*. The physical conception of song as drink comes from ancient mythology. A "staff" is etymologically a physical thing that comes to be used for letters, then words and verbal constructs; in "rune," on the other hand, semantic development apparently moves from an oral act (as in German *raunen)* to the non-literate idea "secret" and on to physical letters, but the further development from "letter" to "(magical) utterance" parallels that of "staff." In both cases a speech act is conceived in terms of chirographic things, letters, but whatever the semantic evidence might mean, it is not limited to skaldic poetry; and no skaldic passages known to me give such an effective picture of the treachery of writing as do the contrasting eddic message scenes in *Atlakviða* (the wolf's hair: an index) and *Atlamál* (the runes: a sign system).[95] It is intriguing, nevertheless, to consider that Ong's dictum "writing restructures consciousness," taken seriously, ought have some consequences for early Norse culture which was, though predominantly oral, for many centuries also runically literate. If so, the utterances of the skalds might well be the place to look for traces that would match Ong's notion of "oral residue" in literacy with a "literary residue" within the most incontestably oral of all early Scandinavian oral literature.

---

95. *Atlakviða*, st. 8, *Atlamál*, st. 4–12, in *Edda*, ed. Neckel (cited n. 76 above).

Appendix
The Story of Einarr Skúlason
[from *Morkinskinna*: See N. 66]

1. Einarr Skúlason was at the court of the brothers Sigurd and Eysteinn, and Eysteinn was a great friend to Einarr. And King Eysteinn asked him to compose an "Ode of Olaf" *[Óláfsdrápa],* and he composed it and recited it up north in Thrandheim in Christ's Church itself. And that was accompanied by many signs, and there came a precious odor into the church. And people say that they were tokens from the [deceased] king himself giving notice that the poem was highly valued.

Einarr stood in high esteem with King Eysteinn, and it is said that once King Eysteinn had taken his seat [for dinner], but Einarr had not arrived.—King Eysteinn had at that time made him his marshal, and this was up north in Thrandheim.—Einarr had been to the nuns' cloister at Bakki. Then the king said, "You are at fault, skald, that you don't come to table, and yet you have the rank of king's skald. Now, we two won't be friends again, unless you compose a stanza right now, before I drink off this flagon."

Then Einarr spoke a poem:

> Abbess distant from all distress
> Made me hungry na'theless,
> Hallowed women did not suffice
> To gird me up gainst that vice.
> But at Bakki with nuns to eat
> Was deemed for Marshal most unmeet.
> The Lady gladdened not within
> Bold audacious ruler's friend.

Now the king was thoroughly pleased.

2. The story is also told that when King Sigurd was residing in Bergen, this incident happened: in the town there were entertainers, and the one was named Jarlmaðr. And this Jarlmaðr commandeered a young goat and ate it on a Friday, and the king intended to punish him for that and gave orders for him to be taken and flogged. And when

Einarr walked up, he said, "Lord, you are now about to deal harshly with our colleague Jarlmaðr."

The king said, "You shall now govern the outcome. You shall compose a verse; and for as long as you are doing the composing, he shall be flogged."

Einarr said, "It will be his wish, this Jarlmaðr, that I don't prove to be one who has much difficulty in composing." But they struck him five blows. Then Einarr said, "Now the verse is done:

> Stole a kid that Christian vile,
> That Jarlmaðr who plays upon the viol—
> Famished for flesh the rude scapegrace—
> Eastward rapt it from the farmer's place.
> The Rod did strike!—wise, well-spoken,
> The Cudgel sang to that 'artiste'
> A harsher laudes, no saint's feast.

3. It happened one summer that a woman came to Bergen who was named Ragnhildr, a splendid woman. She was the wife of Páll Skoptason. She kept a long-ship and sailed as proudly as barons of the realm. She had stopped off there in the town; and when she had begun sailing away, the king caught sight of her passage and spoke. "Which of my skalds is with me now?" said the king. Snorri Bárðarson was in attendance. He was not one who composed fluently, and he didn't get engaged as quickly as the king wished. Then the king said, "Things wouldn't be going this way if Einarr were here in attendance."

He had fallen somewhat into disfavor with the king because of inattentiveness, and the king asked if he were in the town and said that somebody should go to fetch him. And when he stepped onto the quay [*bryggjurnar*, the Bruggen in Bergen], the king said, "Welcome, skald. See now how stately the journey of this woman is begun. Compose a verse now and have it finished before the ship sails out past the island of Hólm."

Einarr answered, "That won't come free." The King asked, "What will it cost?" Einarr answered, "You must promise, for yourself and seven of your retainers in addition, that each of you will remember his line in the poem. And if that fails, then you give me as many kegs of honey as lines which you don't remember."

The King agreed to that. Then Einarr spoke a poem:

> The valiant dame with prows divides
> The hollow waves through Útsteinn's tides,
> The Wind, that Driver-of-fine-rains,
> The swollen sheets on boom it strains.
> No steed-of-the-Sea upon this earth
> Runs homeward hence in greater mirth—
> The broad-planked bottom batters the flood—
> Upon its poop a stately load.

Then the King said, "I believe that I remember:

> 'The valiant dame with prows divides'

—yes, by God:

> 'Upon its poop a stately load.'"

They didn't remember at all what had been in the middle. Einarr then remained with the king's retinue and was in every way in harmony with the king's men.

Ingram Content Group UK Ltd.
Milton Keynes UK
UKHW012145160623
423577UK00002B/171